Alone Together

# Alone Together
## Law and the Meanings of Marriage

MILTON C. REGAN, JR.

New York     Oxford

Oxford University Press

1999

Oxford University Press

Oxford   New York
Athens   Auckland   Bangkok   Bogotá   Buenos Aires   Calcutta
Cape Town   Chennai   Dar es Salaam   Delhi   Florence   Hong Kong   Istanbul
Karachi   Kuala Lumpur   Madrid   Melbourne   Mexico City   Mumbai
Nairobi   Paris   São Paulo   Singapore   Taipei   Tokyo   Toronto   Warsaw

and associated companies in
Berlin   Ibadan

Published by Oxford University Press, Inc.
198 Madison Avenue, New York, New York 10016

Oxford is a registered trademark of Oxford University Press

Library of Congress Cataloging-in-Publication Data
Regan, Milton C.
Alone together : law and the meanings of marriage / Milton C.
Regan, Jr.
p.   cm.
Includes bibliographical references and index.
ISBN 0–19–511003–X
1. Husband and wife—United States   2. Husband and wife—
Psychological aspects.   3. Husband and wife—Social aspects.
I. Title.
KF509.R44   1999
346.7301'63—dc21        97-51283

9 8 7 6 5 4 3 2 1

Printed in the United States of America
on acid-free paper

TO NANCY

*And did you get what
you wanted from this life, even so?
I did.
And what did you want?
To call myself beloved, to feel myself
beloved on the earth.*

Raymond Carver
"Late Fragment"

# Preface

In Richard Ford's novel *Independence Day*, the protagonist muses about his ex-wife, Ann, and his current companion, Sally. "In marriage," he observes, "there's the gnashing, cold but also cozy fear that after a while there'll be no *me* left, only *me chemically amalgamated with another*[.]" By contrast, "the proposition with Sally is that there's *just* me. Forever. I alone would go on being responsible for everything that had me in it; no *other*; only me and my acts, her and hers, somehow together—which of course is much more fearsome" (1995, p. 177).

Ford's narrator succinctly expresses both the vision that propels us toward marriage and the fear that sometimes awaits us when we arrive. We want to be partners in a relationship of shared meaning. We also, however, want to remain individuals with our own unique sense of identity. There may be less of a consensus on exactly what marriage means in the modern world, but this set of contending desires seems inescapable.

In this book, I suggest that appreciation of this tension can help inform our ideas about how law should deal with marriage. I will examine three issues in an effort to explore this theme in some depth: the use of economic concepts in legal analysis of marriage and divorce, the law governing the ability of one spouse to testify against another, and the rules governing financial rights and responsibilities at divorce. Each of these issues, I will argue, raises the question of the relative weight that we should give to spouses as individuals and as participants in a shared community.

As I will make clear, resolving these issues is not a matter of formulating a set of general principles and then applying them to particular cases. Rather, my analysis is meant to serve as an exercise in practical reasoning, which is sensitive to the many incommensurable values that we regard as relevant in the various contexts in which we think about marriage. It is for this reason that I confine myself to these three issues, rather than attempting to analyze a broad range of questions. Examination of them is meant to provide what scholars of practical reasoning call "exemplars." These offer guidance by illustrating practical reasoning in action rather than by pursuing the entailments of logical propositions.

The approach that I suggest will not speak to all aspects of marriage. That relationship has many dimensions, and therefore fruitfully can be seen from several different angles of vision. I do believe, however, that the framework I employ speaks to a deep ambivalence about marriage in an age that places a high value on both intimacy and individual autonomy. As such, it may shed light on the contradictory impulses that our legal treatment of marriage both shapes and reflects. In *Family Law and the Pursuit of Intimacy*, I suggested that we should not embrace in unqualified fashion a framework of individualism as the organizing principle of family law. That book was an effort to remind us of the important insights that a communal perspective on family life might offer. My emphasis on this dimension reflected not the belief that the communal paradigm alone should govern family law, but the sense that a restoration of balance was necessary. This book seeks to explore how such a balance might be struck in different settings with respect to the relationship of marriage. Marriage is particularly apt for such an analysis, since it is a relationship formed by individual choice that nonetheless generates a connection whose significance is not fully captured by the idea of consent. My hope therefore is to extend the ideas in my prior work by offering case studies of how we might maintain a dynamic equilibrium in family law by giving sufficient weight to both individual and communal dimensions of family life. More broadly, this exercise also may serve as an illustration of the complexity of any attempt to draw on both liberal and communitarian accounts of social life in addressing concrete questions of law and policy.

# Acknowledgments

I have been fortunate to have had insightful help from a number of people as I have worked on this book. Carrie Menkel-Meadow, Nancy Sachs, Jana Singer, Mark Tushnet, and Robin West have reviewed drafts and discussed with me on an ongoing basis the ideas that run throughout each chapter of the book. Molly Shanley not only provided important insights in our discussions, but graciously offered perceptive comments on the very last draft of the entire manuscript. In addition, conversations with Elizabeth Scott about her work and mine have been valuable occasions for assessing the significance of liberal and communitarian thought to family law. In preparing chapters 2, 5, and 6 I benefited from the scrutiny and comments of participants at a symposium on New Directions in Family Law at the University of Virginia Law School, including formal symposium commentaries by Dan Ortiz and Susan Williams; discussion with colleagues in the Georgetown University Law Center Faculty Workshop; and from the review of various versions of those chapters by Anita Allen, Bob Axelrod, Kate Bartlett, Gregg Bloche, Peg Brinig, Peter Byrne, Jules Coleman, Ann Laquer Estin, Steve Goldberg, Robert Post, Larry Rosen, Paul Rothstein, Elizabeth Scott, Mike Seidman, and Gerry Spann. Heidi Feldman also provided a helpful review of chapters 2, 3, and 4. Portions of the chapters 2, 5, and 6 have appeared in somewhat different form in "Spousal Privilege and the Meanings of Marriage," in volume 81 of the *Virginia Law Review*. In preparing chapters 3 and 4 I received valuable criticism and suggestions from participants in the Georgetown University Law Center Faculty Workshop and from June Carbone, Lisa Heinzerling, Avery Katz, Richard Posner, Steve Salop, Warren Schwartz, and Lynn Stout. My work on chapters 7 and 8 was greatly aided by the review and discussion of this material at the Georgetown University Law Center Symposium on Divorce and Feminist Legal Theory, including a formal commentary by Carol Rose; at a conference on "Families and Law: Changing Values, Rights, and Obligations," sponsored by the American Bar Association Commission on College and University Legal Studies; by comments from colleagues Richard Chused, Bill Vukowich, and Wendy Williams and by extensive discussions with Joan Williams. A portion of these chapters appears in somewhat different form in "Spouses and Strangers: Divorce Obligations and Property Rhetoric," in volume 82 of the *Georgetown Law Journal*.

I also would like to thank Jodi Short, Grace Won, and the research assistants under the direction of Karen Summerhill at the Edward Bennett Williams Library at Georgetown University Law Center for their valuable research contributions; Harriet Kaplan for her patient and skilled preparation of the manuscript for publication; Associate Deans Mark Tushnet and Anita Allen for providing the institutional support that helped this project come to fruition; and Dean Judy Areen for her extraordinary efforts in sustaining and strengthening a genuine community of teachers and scholars at the Law Center. Finally, I owe the greatest debt to my wife, Nancy Sachs, and to my children, Rebecca and Benjamin, for daily instruction in the rich and complex joys of family life.

# Contents

# PART I

# Spouses and Persons

The marital couple is not an independent entity with a mind and heart of its own, but an association of two individuals each with a separate intellectual and emotional make-up.

*Eisenstadt v. Baird*

[T]he precise nature of marriage is to begin from the point of view of contract—i.e., that of individual personality as a self-sufficient unit—in order to supersede it.

G.W.F. Hegel, *Elements of the Philosophy of Right*

ONE

# Introduction
## *Double Identity*

odern American attitudes toward marriage reflect
two competing commitments: that spouses are sep-
arate individuals with their own distinct interests, and that they are members of
a community who have special obligations to promote its welfare. I describe these
perspectives as the external and internal stances toward marriage, respectively.
This analytical framework, I will argue, offers useful insights into what is at stake
in debates over how law should conceptualize and regulate marriage. More generally, it also suggests that these debates represent but one instance in which we
address the question of how to accommodate individuality within community.

A good way to gain a clearer sense of how tensions in our vision of marriage
can have legal implications is to begin with the story of Arthur and Irene Seale.
Arthur and Irene were high school sweethearts who married at the age of 20 in
September 1967. He was the son of the deputy police chief of the Hillside, New
Jersey, police department. She was the daughter of a prominent local businessman.[1] Soon after their marriage, the couple began to encounter unexpected difficulties. Arthur joined the Hillside police force, but had several disagreements
with his superiors and was subjected to disciplinary action.[2] In 1977, he was injured
in an automobile accident and retired from the force with a disability pension of
$10,000.[3]

Arthur then obtained a job as a security guard with Exxon Corporation, but
three years later the Seales decided to "live their dream" and move with their
two children to Hilton Head, South Carolina.[4] There they bought a home, sail-
boat, and furniture shop. By the end of two years, however, they had lost all
three, as well as their life savings, and they were more than $700,000 in debt.
They then moved to Vail, Colorado, but left within a year when neither could
find a job.[5] Upon returning to New Jersey, Ms. Seale worked for a brief time, but
Mr. Seale was unable to gain long-term employment.[6] Eventually, the Seales and
their teenage children moved in with Arthur's parents in Changewater, New
Jersey.[7]

The couple burst into national prominence on June 19, 1992, when they were
arrested in connection with the kidnapping of Exxon executive Sidney Reso.[8]
Reso's disappearance on April 29 had prompted an intensive state and federal law
enforcement investigation. Since the disappearance, a ransom request for $18.5
million had been made for Reso's return.[9] During their arrest and arraignment

on federal and state charges, the Seales appeared supportive of each other; at one hearing, Irene Seale mouthed the words "I love you" to her husband.[10] Ten days after their arrest, however, Ms. Seale agreed to cooperate with law enforcement officials. She directed investigators to a grave in the Pine Barrens of New Jersey that contained the body of Sidney Reso.[11] She described how the couple had intercepted Reso as he left his driveway for work. The Exxon executive was wounded in the arm by a gunshot in a brief scuffle during his apprehension, and the Seales had tried unsuccessfully to attend to his wound. Eventually, they had bound Reso in a wooden box that was placed inside a storage locker, where he died on May 3, some five days after the kidnapping.[12]

In return for her information and her agreement to testify against her husband in federal court, Ms. Seale was permitted to plead guilty to two federal extortion charges and a state kidnapping charge. As a result, she would be eligible for release from her concurrent sentences within as few as 13 years.[13] Arthur Seale was then indicted on several federal counts dealing with extortion and threats of violence, and on state kidnapping and felony murder charges.[14] State prosecutors also indicated at one point that they had not ruled out a murder charge against him that would carry the death penalty.[15]

State prosecutors, however, faced a problem that federal prosecutors did not. While Ms. Seale was free to testify against her husband in federal court if she so chose, state law forbade her from incriminating him in state court. New Jersey prosecutors called upon the state legislature to change the law so that Ms. Seale could testify against her husband in the state prosecution. Mr. Seale ultimately pleaded guilty to the federal and state charges against him before the state legislature could act. He was sentenced in federal court to a 95-year prison term without parole and a $1.75 million fine, and in state court to a life sentence and a $220,000 fine.[16] The state and federal terms are to be served consecutively. Irene Seale received a 20-year concurrent federal and state sentence and a $500,000 fine.[17] The New Jersey legislature subsequently changed state law to permit one spouse to testify against the other in a criminal proceeding if the witness is willing to do so.[18]

How should we regard Irene Seale's decision to inform on and testify against her husband? Does it undermine marriage as an institution to permit, indeed to encourage, one spouse to help send the other to prison or the death chamber? Or do we undercut the real meaning of marriage by preventing a willing spouse from testifying against his or her partner? From one perspective, we might say that law should respect the fact that Ms. Seale is a distinct individual with interests of her own. She should be free to act on a belief that the interests of justice override any duty to honor the trust her husband placed in her. Furthermore, she is the only person entitled to decide whether being loyal to her husband is worth the personal cost of forgoing a plea bargain. On the other hand, we may feel something less than unqualified admiration for the decision that she made. An apparently willing partner in the couple's activity, she ultimately decided that the prospect of a relatively light sentence was worth incriminating her husband of 25 years. From this perspective, Ms. Seale violated perhaps the central norm of marriage by being willing to betray her husband for personal gain—and the law was an accomplice to her betrayal.

## External and Internal Stances Toward Marriage

Our ambivalence about Ms. Seale reflects appreciation of what I will describe in this book as two different moments of marriage that are in some tension with one another. One moment is characterized by a spouse taking what I call an "external" stance toward her marriage. This stance represents an individual's capacity to reflect critically upon, rather than simply identify with, her commitments and attachments. It enables a person to keep in focus the extent to which any given commitment serves her interests as a distinct individual. Insistence on the importance of the external stance toward marriage draws in particular on dissatisfaction with traditional gender roles, which encouraged married women to define themselves primarily as wives rather than as individuals with their own unique interests. In modern life, the external stance has become an increasingly important orientation toward marriage and family life in general.

While the external stance may represent a valuable moment of modern marriage, it is insufficient by itself to ensure full enjoyment of the distinctive good that marriage can provide. Most people likely would regard a continuous posture of critical distance, acutely sensitive to the individual costs and benefits of marriage, as inimical to the sense of shared experience that marriage at its best makes available. Adopting an "internal" stance toward marriage also seems important, from which marriage appears as a universe of shared meaning that serves as the taken-for-granted background for individual conduct. At this moment, a spouse stands "inside" the marriage as a participant who accepts its claims, not "outside" it as an observer who calls those claims into question. This stance makes possible the experience of lives lived in intimate concert, rather than mere parallel association.[19]

I will argue that the external and internal stances are fundamentally different orientations that are irreducible to one another. Each stance offers its own account of personal identity and of the claims and obligations that arise in human relationships. In the course of everyday life, spouses move back and forth between these stances, seeking to balance their status as separate individuals with their roles as members of a marital community. Law seeks implicitly to reconcile these visions of marriage. This perspective suggests that controversies over the legal regulation of marriage can be seen as conflicts over the relative weight that we should attach to each vision in a particular context.

Spouses' fluidity of perspective is underscored by research in social psychology that focuses on how partners in close relationships develop a sense of entitlements—of who owes what to whom.[20] This work suggests that individuals' perceptions are shaped by the degree to which each person has a sense of communal or individual identity in a given instance. These identities are evoked by situational cues that lead a person to interpret his or her partner's behavior according to certain schemas, which then determine the entitlement rule regarded as most appropriate in that context. An "identity" schema corresponds to the internal stance toward marriage: "it is commonly understood that there are times in nearly all marriages when the partners will feel merged with one another, when the pain or happiness of the one is experienced by the other."[21] In such instances, feelings of caring and closeness make need the primary consideration in determining what the partners owe one another.

By contrast, there are other occasions when awareness of oneself as distinct from the other is more salient. This corresponds to what I have described as an external stance. Such an orientation may lead to different entitlement rules depending on whether similarity to or difference from the other is felt as more significant. Predominance of the former perspective reflects a "unit" schema, in which partners are regarded as "distinct individuals who expect to be treated equally."[22] In such cases, entitlement expectations are based on the notions of equality, mutual respect, and the desire to cooperate in order to accomplish a common goal. This highlights a point that I discuss in more detail in chapter 2: that the external perspective is not simply an egoistic orientation. The sense of separateness among persons also can lead to appreciation of the importance of justice and respect for others. Finally, a "nonunit" schema is one in which "intimate partners will feel essentially different from each other and thereby promote their own individual goals and interests."[23]

Contextual cues between intimate partners thus elicit particular senses of identity, which in turn lead to different expectations in various situations. Researchers emphasize that persons in close relationships whom they have studied are very much aware that they experience these different orientations in the course of a single relationship. "The basic premise that one's feelings can, and often do, change toward the same partner seemed natural and familiar to them, as did the particular feelings they were asked to recall and the solutions they were to rate."[24] The analytical framework of the internal and external stances thus seems to capture a basic and important feature of an intimate relationship such as marriage.

## Why Marriage?

Some may ask why a family law scholar should devote so much attention to marriage. In an era that exalts emotional spontaneity and individual choice, this may seem a misguided focus on the form, rather than substance, of family relationships. Some contend that the criterion for identifying a family should be neither biological connection nor legal status, but love and support between and among individuals.[25] This is reflected in the rallying cry in some quarters that we need to place "families of choice" at the center of our conceptual family law universe.

One might claim that marriage therefore is of declining significance in a culture that emphasizes emotional rather than formal legal bonds. For support, an advocate of this position might point to our relatively high divorce rate, declining rate of marriage, increasing percentage of couples living together without marriage, and growing rate of childbearing outside of marriage. A critic also could take note of the suggestion by at least one set of family scholars that we take the "sexually based primary relationship," rather than marriage or conventional family boundaries, as the basic unit of analysis in what hitherto has been called "family studies."[26]

Furthermore, as a practical matter, many of the most vexing problems of modern family law arise in instances in which marriage cannot serve as the basis for rights and obligations. For instance, what are the rights of partners in unmarried relationships when they end? What are the respective rights of unwed mothers and fathers when a child is put up for adoption? What is the status of a same-sex partner with respect to his or her partner's child? What are the rights of the parties to a contract for a pregnancy and childbirth that occurs outside the marriage relationship? In these and other instances, the legal form of the relationships in question seems to offer little guidance on what we should do. Rather than looking ahead to the emerging cutting edge of family law, an emphasis on marriage may seem to be a nostalgic look backward to a supposedly simpler time in which marriage was the cornerstone of family life.

Marriage, however, still has powerful cultural power as the paradigm of intimate commitment. The companionate model of marriage that has become pervasive over the last two hundred years or so has created high expectations that marriage will serve as a source of personal fulfillment. In her book on divorce, Catherine Riessman notes, "The companionate ideal is stronger than it ever was. Recent evidence shows that spouses' reliance on one another—both for emotional reassurance and for companionship in leisure—is much greater now than even a generation ago."[27] As some have suggested, the very data that supposedly document the decline of marriage may in fact reflect its power. Some divorce scholars suggest, for instance, that a relatively high divorce rate may indicate that people have high expectations for emotional support from marriage and are unwilling to settle for anything less.[28]

Furthermore, a lower marriage rate and higher unmarried cohabitation rate may reflect the perception that marriage involves a qualitatively greater commitment than an informal intimate relationship. Certainly, marriage is a far less dramatic *legal* step than it used to be. Getting married in the modern age now has fewer significant legal consequences in itself, and obtaining a divorce is relatively easy. Those who eschew marriage nowadays thus are likely to be expressing the view that marriage is an important *emotional* step for which they are not prepared. Unmarried cohabitation, for instance, may reflect the desire for a "trial" marriage that will provide greater assurance that an eventual formal marriage will meet the high expectations that accompany it. Lower marriage rates and higher divorce rates may attest to the gravity, rather than the indifference, with which marriage is regarded. This suggests that, even for those who are not married, marriage may cast a large shadow on the psychological landscape.

Marriage thus is worthy of attention because of its continuing power as a symbol of enduring rather than transitory attachment. While we must confront the question of how to deal with relationships that are not organized around marriage, this should not obscure the fact that marriage continues to hold a distinctive place in the cultural imagination. In short, as David Chambers has put it, "after thousands of years of human history, the union of two people in a relationship called 'marriage' is almost certainly here to stay[.]"[29]

A second criticism of focusing on marriage might be that marriage historically has been closely associated with patriarchy, and therefore should be deemphasized as an element of family life. Much of the momentum for treating marriage and family life as a realm of choice rather than ascription has come from feminist critiques of the ways in which marriage has constructed and reinforced hierarchical relations between men and women.

The ways in which a marriage-based family law contributed to this system are numerous. Under the doctrine of coverture, women lost their legal identity when they married. This deprived them of basic rights to own property and to enter into contracts. Married women had no protection against sexual assualt by their husbands because a man could not be liable for raping his wife. Law enforcement authorities declined to respond to domestic violence on the ground that this would constitute unwarranted intervention into the privacy of the marriage. Furthermore, the doctrine of interspousal tort immunity effectively prevented a wife from bringing a private lawsuit to redress injuries suffered at the hands of her husband. Women generally were legally eligible to marry at an earlier age than men, based on the view that marriage and economic dependence on a man was the typical career path for women. All these disabilities rested on the more general notion that a married woman's destiny was to be confined to the domestic sphere, subject to the authority of her husband. Given this legal history, those who are sympathetic to feminism may be suspicious of family law scholarship that takes marriage as its focus. They may argue that sensitivity to women's concerns should lead us to emphasize individuals rather than husbands and wives, and relationships rather than marriages.

This argument, however, seems to assume that marriage has an essential un-alterable character that inevitably is disadvantageous to women. It ignores the tremendous changes in the law and in social attitudes toward gender roles over the past generation. The Supreme Court, for instance, has struck down a host of legal provisions on the ground that they reflect the view that a woman's place is solely within the home and not the wage labor workplace.[30] Furthermore, the argument ignores the trend that is the basis for the first criticism above—that marriage now is seen far more than before as an arena of choice. Powerful cultural assumptions still shape the opportunities of men and women and the sets of choices that they have.[31] Nonetheless, there is more negotiation between husbands and wives about the division of labor and other terms of marriage than tradi-tionally has been the case.

Ironically, one might argue that married couples have more freedom to order their relationship as they wish than do unmarried couples who desire some legal recognition of their intimate bond. Once a couple marries, they need conform to no particular model of behavior in order to receive the legal protections of that status. By contrast, those who are unmarried generally must act in a way that a court will regard as the substantive equivalent of marriage in order for any rights or obligations to flow from the relationship. Courts therefore must make inquiries into the intimate details of the partners' lives and tend to apply relatively conventional standards of what constitutes marriage in determining whether the relationship should enjoy any legal recognition.[32]

In addition, emphasizing "individuals" rather than "spouses" and "relation-ships" rather than "marriages" represents an abstraction from concrete daily ex-perience that some would argue is the antithesis of a feminist approach. Given the significance of marriage to many peoples' lives, ignoring it because of a less than perfect history risks an analysis that fails in important ways to capture the subtlety of intimate life. The challenge for those who are sympathetic to feminist concerns is not to abandon marriage but to reform it.

A final criticism is that directing attention to marriage artificially isolates it from the complex interdependence of family life. If we think about marriage in the broader family context, we will realize that our concerns about marriage flow primarily from the fact that it usually involves children. On this view, we have a social interest in marriage not for its own sake, but because marriage traditionally is the institution in which procreation has occurred.

Thus, for instance, some commentators suggest a two-tiered divorce system: relatively easy divorce for childless couples, but more difficult dissolution for marital partners with children.[33] Others argue that the law of divorce awards is misguided in implicitly focusing on marriage rather than parenthood as the basis for financial allocations. At least one scholar has suggested that the law should abandon the married couple as its fundamental unit and substitute in its stead the relationship between mother and child.[34] All these arguments are based on the notion that it is time explicitly to acknowledge that it is parenthood, rather than marriage per se, that underlies our legal interest in marriage. From this perspective, focusing on marriage mistakes what is of surface importance for what is of deep concern.

Focusing on marriage per se, however, does not simply reflect an artificial academic conceit. To be sure, we must always be attentive to the complex ways in which various relationships intersect within a family. All relationships can be seen as strands in a larger fabric. This does not mean, however, that we can gain no insights from studying any given relationship in its own right.

In particular, recent developments in family life make it quite reasonable to examine marriage apart from parenthood. The increasing emphasis on choice in family matters has attenuated, if it has not severed, the automatic link between being married and having children. Births out of wedlock have reached historically high rates in recent years, reflecting the idea that the choice to marry is seen as distinct from the choice to have a child.[35] Similarly, the rate of marriages without children has been increasing,[36] while the average number of children per marriage has been decreasing.[37] These data underscore that the choice to marry no longer necessarily involves a choice to have children. Furthermore, parenthood nowadays is less likely than before to be regarded as an obstacle to divorce. The quality of the relationship between the spouses is seen as an issue that is separate from the quality of the relationship between parent and child. In all these ways, decisions regarding marriage and those regarding parenthood are treated as distinct from one another, guided by different sets of considerations.

This suggests that the third criticism is not so much that marriage is not a coherent topic of analysis, but that we have little legal interest in it when it doesn't overlap with parenthood. The assumption that underlies this contention is that marriage is a relationship of choice whose purpose is to provide personal fulfillment for spouses. As such, it is essentially a private matter between husbands and wives. Thus, for instance, while we may have an interest in making divorce more difficult for spouses with children, divorce for childless couples ought to be relatively quick and easy. The basic argument is that marriage is a relationship whose rights and obligations ought to be determined by the partners, whose freedom of action society limits only because of the brute biological fact of children's vulnerability. On this view, family law scholarship that focuses on marriage alone is likely to yield few complex or subtle insights.

There is a certain irony in this criticism, which illuminates why marriage in fact is of significant analytical interest. Historically, marriage has been regarded as the cornerstone of family life and thus as the basis for numerous ascribed rights and duties. Now, however, it serves as an exemplar of a family relationship of choice, in which members are bound together by emotion and volition.

Marriage has been seen as a consensual relationship for quite some time, of course. Indeed, more than three hundred years ago John Locke characterized marriage as a "voluntary compact between man and woman."[38] For many years, however, religious belief in the sanctity of marriage and marriage's close association with parenthood obscured this feature. Locke, for instance, suggested that the reason why the partnership between humans tends to last longer than that of other creatures is the helplessness of human infants. Marriage, he argued, ought to last "so long as it is necessary to the nourishment and support of the young ones, who are to be sustained by those that got them till they are able to shift and provide by themselves."[39] Once the responsibilities of parenthood are discharged, however, "it would give one reason to inquire why this compact . . . may not be made determinable, either by consent, or at a certain time, or upon certain conditions, as well as any other voluntary compacts, there being no necessity in the nature of the thing, nor to the ends of it, that it should always be for life."[40] Locke thus saw marriage as a fundamentally liberal institution founded upon consent. Only when spouses became parents did the governance of marriage become more than a matter of individual choice.

In our day, with the waning influence of religion and severance of the automatic link between being married and having children, marriage has emerged more visibly as a consensual relationship. If family life is indeed evolving toward families of choice, then marriage may serve as a useful example of the dilemmas and concerns that we will confront in the family of the future.

In particular, how are we to accommodate two aspirations of family life that are in some tension? On the one hand, there is an intense desire that family relationships provide emotional support, unconditional acceptance, and steadfast commitment. On the other hand, there is a strong belief that family relationships must rest on personal satisfaction, individual choice, and freely assumed obligation. If we can no longer rely on ascription as the central principle of family life, to what extent can variable and contingent individual sentiment serve as the basis for the self-restraint, sacrifice, and forbearance that enduring relationships require?

In raising such issues, modern marriage may be of broader social interest as well. A central task in liberal society is to fashion bonds between and among individuals who are not bound by traditional moral norms. This raises a crucial question: How can we tame individual desire for the sake of communal stability when society regards individuals as "self-authenticating sources of valid claims?"[41]

Marriage has long been seen in Western culture as a symbol of this enterprise and the ambivalence that it provokes. It has served as a way of channeling powerful and volatile drives for sexual gratification and individual fulfillment into an arrangement that furthers interests in procreation and social stability. As such, it has carried significance as "the reconciliation of law and spontaneity" for at least the last century and a half.[42] This reconciliation is inherently unstable, however, given the urgency of both the felt social needs and the individual passions that it must accommodate. Thus, for instance, novels such as *Anna Karenina* and *Madame Bovary* depict the agonizing personal costs that enforcement of marital norms inflicts—yet each suggests that society's continued existence may rest on its ability to impose such controls.[43] Modern sensibilities might shift the weight attached to each set of interests, but cannot deny the force of both. Regarded at once as the most important source of adult intimate happiness and as the cornerstone of society, marriage crystalizes the tensions that we face as both distinct individuals and as members of a shared community. How law seeks to accommodate these dimensions of marriage thus may offer instruction in how to manage the inevitable dilemma of our dual existence.

I WILL EXPLORE THESE THEMES in the pages to come by examining specific instances in which different concepts of spousal identity are at stake. Chapter 2, which concludes Part I, sets forth the analytical framework for the book by elaborating on the external and internal stances toward marriage. The impetus for the external stance is the desire for what philosopher Jean Hampton has called "self-authorship." This principle demands that both individual actions and the trajectory of a person's life as a whole be based on reflection about her genuine interests and commitments. The external stance represents a vantage point from which an individual can engage in such reflection. Such a perspective has been particularly important for women. Many feminists have argued that the one set of attachments in women's lives that has not been subject to assessment from the external stance has been the family. They voice concern that the difficulty of women in taking this stance with respect to family relationships has led to self-effacement and, at times, to exploitation. In recent years, however, such reflection has become a more important aspect of family life, as individuals have begun to assert more control over decisions relating to sexuality, procreation, marriage, and divorce. Several scholars have suggested that the modern intimate relationship is characterized by increasing emphasis on negotiation, sensitivity to individual needs, and commitment conditioned on personal satisfaction.[44] As a result, both men and women have come to regard it as more legitimate to ask whether the benefits and burdens of family life are acceptable in light of reflection on their own needs.

The external stance therefore emphasizes the importance of recognizing that marriage is comprised of separate individuals with their own unique interests. This makes salient certain ethical concepts such as distributive justice, contract, and consent. Most of us have an intuitive sense, however, that this is an incomplete account of marriage. Even those who underscore the need for the external stance maintain that it provides a minimum safeguard against injustice, not a prescription for how to establish and sustain a satisfying relationship. At its best marriage offers a distinctive kind of good: the possibility of bridging the distance between separate selves. Genuine intimacy seems to require the ability to adopt the internal stance toward marriage, in which the relationship is taken as a given without reference to individual costs and benefits. This stance reflects a perspective from which the boundary between self and other becomes blurred. It focuses on the health of a larger relational unit whose viability is a shared concern.

Just as the external stance implicates distinct moral concepts, so the internal stance involves particular ethical concerns. One is recognition that individual maturity consists not simply in the ability to act autonomously from the external stance, but also involves the ability to foster and preserve relationships with others. This requires sensitivity to persons in their particularity, not simply as individuals who warrant respect by virtue of their status as human beings. The internal stance also highlights the importance of trust in personal relationships, those times when partners suspend their capacity for critical scrutiny and proceed on the basis of confidence in one another. Finally, a self proceeding from the internal stance acknowledges that obligation may arise not simply through consent, but from shared experience in relationship with another. This sense of responsibility reflects the awareness of a self whose identity emerges from the formation and maintenance of attachments. The course of these relationships is not completely subject to individual control. Yet involvement in them can create a sense of constraint. Appreciation of the nature of intimate connection thus reminds us that a satisfying marriage requires moments when spouses adopt an internal stance, from which their marriage appears as a relationship irreducible to the sum of individual interests.

The analytical framework of the external and internal stances can offer insight not only into marriage, but also into broader debates about social existence. As I have suggested, marriage is but a particularly stark example of a setting in which we seek both preservation of individuality and commitment to a shared purpose that transcends the self. I will argue that debates between liberals and communitarians, and between proponents of an ethic of justice and an ethic of care, also represent implicit discussions about the relative priority of the external and internal stances in social life more generally. This perspective underscores that the positions in these debates should not be seen as mutually exclusive dichotomies, but as complementary expressions of different dimensions of existence.[45] The analysis of marriage that I offer thus may have wider relevance as a case study of one particular attempt to accommodate individual and communal aspects of identity.

Part II: Markets and Marriage examines the debate over the role of economics in guiding legal and social policy toward marriage. Proponents of the economic approach argue that it offers a far more rigorous framework for analyzing family life and family law than any other contender. Indeed, they claim that economic analysis offers a universal theory of human behavior, of which family relations is but one instance. For this reason, some contend that economics offers a perspective that should guide our choice of legal rules to govern marriage and divorce. Critics, however, contend that the market and the family are and should remain different domains of life with their own distinct orientations. They suggest that applying the economic model to the family will tend to commodify relationships such as marriage, thereby undermining the altruism and empathy that characterize this realm of life.

My analysis contends that we can best evaluate the role of economic analysis of the family if we see it as an effort to express the priority of the external stance.

Viewed from this perspective, the economic approach offers distinct insights into certain aspects of marriage, but fails adequately to capture others. As such, it neither offers the universal language that its advocates claim nor represents the profanation of family relationships that its critics depict. The best way to think about economic analysis of marriage, Part II will argue, is as a metaphor whose desirability will depend upon how important we deem the normative concerns of the external stance to be in a given situation.

Part III: Trust and Betrayal returns to the issue posed by the story of the Seales that opens this chapter. This is the law governing the ability of one spouse to testify against the other in a criminal proceeding. There are two forms of spousal testimonial privilege. One, the communications privilege, prevents a spouse or ex-spouse from testifying about confidential marital communications in any proceeding, even if she wants to testify. The other, the adverse testimony privilege, traditionally precludes one spouse from testifying at all against the other in a criminal trial. There is an exception to this privilege for cases involving allegations that one spouse has injured the other or a child of either. More recently, the adverse testimony privilege has been modified in federal and some state courts to allow a spouse to decide for herself whether to testify in such a trial, as long as she does not reveal any confidential communications.

Part III examines why the communications privilege enjoys widespread support, while the traditional adverse testimony privilege is under attack. Commentators conventionally explain this difference by claiming that the rationale for the former privilege is more persuasive than for the latter. I argue, however, that this explanation is unconvincing. We can better understand the different reception accorded these privileges by recognizing that the communications privilege is more consistent with the increasingly influential external stance toward marriage. By contrast, the adverse testimony privilege largely is inconsistent with that stance. This suggests, however, that this privilege may be a way to express the importance of the internal stance toward marriage. I will explore some genuine concerns about this privilege, but will conclude that spousal privilege law may best vindicate our competing conceptions of marriage by providing a role for both privileges.

Part IV: Money and Divorce discusses one of the most controversial issues in modern family law: what financial claims one spouse may make on another at the time of divorce. How we address this issue has implications not only for divorce but for marriage as well. The law in this area helps construct our understanding of marriage by specifying the distinct rights and responsibilities that this relationship entails.

Numerous studies in recent years indicate that women suffer far more financial disadvantage from divorce than do men. Several analysts have suggested that the no-fault divorce reforms over the past 25 years have served to exacerbate economic disparities between men and women. There is some irony in this outcome, since the implicit model of marriage that animated such reforms is one that depicts husbands and wives as equal members of an economic partnership. Such a model, I will argue, gives priority to the external stance toward marriage. It conceptualizes spouses as parties who associate for mutual gain, each of whom makes his or her own distinct contribution to the common enterprise. When this enterprise ends, partners are liable to each other only for debts that arose from implicit exchanges between them during marriage.

I maintain that this view of divorce obligation reflects a reaction against a previous model that emphasized the internal stance toward marriage. That model posited that husbands had some continuing financial responsibilities to their wives after divorce. Critics argued, however, that it tended to treat divorce awards as assistance to needy and unproductive women. The economic partnership concept was intended to change this, by presenting divorce awards as the recognition of economic rights that women earned during marriage. A theory of divorce obligation based on the external stance, however, has its own limits in addressing the financial needs of women at divorce. I conclude that divorce law should preserve the emphasis on economic justice that characterizes the external stance toward marriage. At the same time, it should draw on the internal stance and an ethic of care to provide equalization of the post-divorce standard of living of the partners for a period of time related to the length of the marriage.

In the conclusion to the book, I identify some general considerations that should inform our analysis of the claims of the external and internal stances in any given context. These represent concerns that appear to emerge from our examination of the three issues in this book. As such, they are tentative guides for practical reasoning, not general principles that must govern all future analysis. I also discuss in the conclusion the extent to which the framework of the external and internal stances may shed light on family law issues more generally.Marriage is a particularly clear instance of a more general phenomenon: that many relationships we enter voluntarily can eventually link our lives with others in important ways. By exploring our ambivalence about this with respect to marriage, my hope is that this book will suggest how we might approach the task of balancing the claims of individuality and community in other settings as well.

TWO

# Moments of Marriage

The sense that we are capable of taking both an external and internal stance toward an attachment reflects the fact that, as Thomas Nagel has put it, we are "complex beings without a naturally unified standpoint."[1] Nagel suggests that desire for a sense of control over one's life leads a person to seek detachment from the pull of particular connections, in an effort to subject motives, values, and desires to "critical examination so that nothing moves me to action without my agreeing to it."[2] In this sense, the external stance can be seen as closely associated with the liberal ideal of autonomy. Despite this aspiration to gain critical distance from the particularities of our lives, however, "[w]e remain . . . creatures inside the world who have not created ourselves. . . ."[3] We can never secure a point from which we take an external stance toward the entirety of our concrete existence. The ground on which we stand in order to gain an external view of one set of commitments necessarily consists of other commitments toward which we take an internal stance. This inevitably embedded character of our existence has been emphasized by communitarian theorists.[4]

Recent developments in the debate between liberals and communitarians suggest that our task is not so much to choose between sharply different accounts of selfhood as it is to appreciate that different dimensions of identity may have more or less salience in particular settings.[5] The external and internal stances thus reflect two understandings of identity that are in some tension: that "an individual standing apart from all social relations is unimaginable," and that "it is a good thing that modern men and women feel able to distance themselves from, reflect upon, and consciously embrace or repudiate any or all of the relations that constitute their history."[6] The need to reconcile or mediate between these perspectives is particularly pronounced in family law. Appreciating their significance therefore should illuminate an important dimension of the choices that confront us in thinking about the relationship between law and family life.[7]

## The External Stance

The inspiration for the external stance is the search for a standpoint from which a person can independently evaluate the moral demands made by the relationships in which she is involved.[8] This self "acknowledges no a priori loyalty to any feature of [any] situation or role, and . . . claims the right to question the moral legitimacy of any contingent moral claim."[9] This stance has powerful roots in the Reformation and the Enlightenment, historical moments whose inspiration was a challenge to traditional civic authority in the name of the individual. Traditional authority relied heavily on the principle of ascription, according to which the location of an individual within a particular set of social relationships was a significant and largely ineluctable determinant of his or her share of the burdens and benefits of social life. Those who sought to affirm the inherent worth of the individual independent of social position faced the task of identifying an "external" vantage point from which to evaluate church, monarchy, and the systems of ascription associated with them. In order to be effective, this perspective had to be independent of the existing pull of attachment to those regimes, untainted by the tendency to grant them intrinsic normative force. A crucial move in this process was to distinguish between the contingent world of appearances and the universal realm of reason, and to demand that authority justify itself in the court of the latter. This required that the observer detach herself from the particular circumstances in which she found herself, which were simply an accident of history that tended to mire her in the status quo. The quest for an external stance was a feature of the *zeitgeist* that informed wide-ranging areas of thought beyond those explicitly concerned with the issue of political legitimacy. Descartes and Kant, for instance, sought with respect to epistemology and moral reasoning, respectively, to establish the sovereignty of the individual apart from the contingent material world.[10]

Social contract theory, at least in its Kantian form,[11] can be seen as an application of the external stance to the realm of civic authority. It asks that in evaluating basic social institutions we abstract ourselves from the structures of authority that we currently maintain, which are products of circumstance and fortuity that have no necessary normative claim. We must imagine a moment when society does not exist, when the only inhabitants of the world are solitary individuals possessing both the power of reason and their own distinct interests. Each individual has the capacity to devise and pursue certain ends, and each is capable of evaluating for herself what courses of action will promote those ends.[12] Appealing to reason in assessing social institutions means asking if the current terms of social life would be voluntarily accepted by all reasonable persons in this presocial state of nature.

From the external stance, consent therefore is the sine qua non of legitimate social and political authority. Respect for the equal value of each person requires that each decide on her own what obligations she will accept in return for the benefits of participation in social life. The requirement of consent dictates that the social contract must appeal to a person's interests as a discrete and separate individual, without regard for ties of sentiment or allegiance to others. Such attachments "become a source of exploitation if [they] induce persons to acquiesce in institutions and practices that but for their fellow-feeling would be costly to them."[13] As a result, "the contractarian insists that a society could not command the willing allegiance of a rational person if, without appealing to her feelings for others, it afforded her no expectation of net benefit."[14]

This emphasis on an appeal to each person's self-interest is not simply a rationalization for individuals to engage in the blind pursuit of egoistic objectives. Rather, by directing attention to the fact that every person has distinct and separate concerns, it requires that each individual both exhibit proper self-regard *and* acknowledge that others are just as valuable as oneself.[15] One who takes an external stance toward a given relationship need not be motivated solely by narrow self-interest. Ideally, appreciation that the other person in this relationship is a discrete individual also provides the basis for one to act as well out of a sense of justice. The external stance makes available moral resources that can constrain the tendency of egoism to seek advantage over another, because it directs attention to whether "the infliction of costs or the confiscation of benefits over a significant period . . . implicitly reveals disregard rather than respect for that person."[16] This stance therefore is not reducible to a posture of narrow self-interest. Its distinctiveness lies rather in its emphasis on the separateness of individuals—an emphasis that can lead to both self-and other-regarding behavior.

Social contract theory's abstraction of the individual from her relationships is regarded as crucial in providing the critical distance necessary for each person to act autonomously by engaging in the practice of "self-authorship."[17] Self-authorship demands that both individual courses of action and the trajectory of one's life as a whole must be the product of reflection about one's interests and commitments. This principle asserts that "no particular cultural practice has authority that is beyond individual judgement and possible rejection."[18] As a result, "we can and should acquire our tasks through freely made personal judgements about the cultural structure, the matrix of understandings and alternatives passed down to us by previous generations, which offers us possibilities we can either affirm or reject. Nothing is 'set for us,' nothing is authoritative before our judgement of its value."[19] The requirements of autonomy defined as self-authorship thus are satisfied only when an individual *subjectively* defines for herself "who she is, what she wants, and what she will pursue in her life."[20]

In this way, the external stance seeks to offer a vantage point from which we can become "the absolute source of what we do."[21] A proponent of self-authorship need not, however, assume the existence of a noumenal self defined solely by an abstract capacity for choice, but may freely acknowledge the constitutive character of social attachments and commitments.[22] What is crucial is that we reserve the right to question the desirability of any given attachment or commitment, even as we recognize that the self that does so will be embedded in other connections that for the moment are taken for granted.[23]

At least since John Stuart Mill, observers have criticized the failure to extend these liberal principles to women.[24] Many feminists have argued that the one set of attachments in women's lives that has not been subject to assessment from an external stance has been the family.[25] Historically, social contract theory explicitly applied only to the realm of "public" authority, characterized as a domain constituted by the voluntary consent of its participants. The "private" sphere of the family, however, was deemed inconsistent with this principle because of women's ostensible "natural" inclination to nurture and identify with others.[26] The result was that women were urged to define themselves largely in terms of their roles as wives and mothers. They were discouraged from taking an external stance that offered an independent vantage point from which to assess the costs and benefits of family relationships. Virginia Woolf succinctly describes this orientation: "She was intensely sympathetic. She was immensely charming. She was utterly unselfish. She excelled in the difficult arts of family life. She sacrificed herself daily. If there was chicken, she took the leg; if there was a draught she sat in it—in short she was so constituted that she never had a mind or a wish of her own, but preferred to sympathize always with the minds and wishes of others."[27]

The danger for women from this socialization has been the potential for uncritical acceptance of responsibility to provide for other family members, with insufficient attention to their own individual needs.[28] Assessment of a relationship solely from an internal stance can lead to a willingness to accept disadvantage and even abuse for the sake of preserving the attachment. As Lyn Mikel Brown and Carol Gilligan observe, sometimes "women silence themselves or are silenced in relationships rather than risk open conflict and disagreement that might lead to isolation or to violence."[29] Inability to take an external stance makes it difficult to acknowledge that self-respect and self-concern are morally valuable,[30] and to develop the competence in autonomy that comes from awareness of one's needs, values, and desires as a singular individual.[31]

Because of this potential for exploitation, some feminists have sounded a note of caution about the work of other feminists who seek to valorize women's nurture of relationships as a distinctly important moral orientation. Marilyn Friedman, for instance, suggests that partiality to particular relationships may create at most a prima facie duty, but this obligation must be assessed in light of the moral value of the relationship—that is, from an external stance.[32] Similarly, Jean Hampton argues that contractarian thinking can serve as a welcome contrast to women's traditional selfless orientation.[33] A contractarian approach asks whether the benefits and burdens of family life could be justified by appeal to the consent of each individual in light of reflection about her own interest.[34] Proponents maintain that application of these ideas to the family need not preclude orientations of altruism and care, but would ensure that such sentiments reflected an individual's genuine choice in light of her authentic values.[35] As Marilyn Friedman argues, "[t]here is room in care ethics for a cautious strain of individualism," which would emphasize that "[r]esponsibilities to care should not eclipse those features of the care giver that constitute her as an individual, nor should they obscure those dimensions of meaning in her life that are independent of her care-giving role."[36]

As should be apparent, an external stance toward marriage mirrors liberal emphasis on the normative priority of the individual and of principles of justice. Indeed, one way to describe liberalism is as an effort to work through the implications of the external stance toward social attachments more generally. Liberalism places emphasis on the fact that persons are separate individuals who have a variety of distinctive and potentially conflicting desires, values, and aspirations.[37] Each person has intrinsic value as an individual, regardless of her particular commitments or attachments.[38] She therefore must have the freedom to formulate and pursue her own life plan. An individual engaging in this process necessarily draws on cultural resources,[39] and her judgment is subject to assessment and criticism by others. This does not mean, however, that anyone can ever be justified in forcing her to adopt one option or way of life over another. Liberalism generally opposes paternalism, insisting that "[m]y life only goes better if I'm leading it from the inside, according to my beliefs about value."[40]

Nonetheless, the plurality of values that characterizes liberal society encourages an attitude of open-mindedness and a willingness to revise one's commitments in light of new information or different perspectives. Indeed, Stephen Macedo has suggested that liberalism conceptualizes autonomous individuals as those who have internalized the value conflicts of modern life.[41] Such individuals are acutely aware of the numerous incommensurable goods that exist in modern society, and of the impossibility of attaining or reconciling all of them. They also are sensitive to the possibility that their judgments may be mistaken or may change over time. As a result, the liberal individual "maintain[s] some distance from any single end, or the values of any particular community with which [she] happen[s] to identify; each of [her] ends and the whole set of [her] ends can be seen as less than absolute, and not simply fixed or given."[42] One likely result is "a kind of detachment or moderation of commitment"—a "certain uneasiness or alienation from our own ends and purposes."[43] The practice of critical reflection "may temper or attenuate the devotion to one's own projects and allegiances" by encouraging individuals to regard their lives as perpetually open to "criticism, choice, and change."[44] Liberalism thus insists that persons are both self-determining and "unpredictably self-transforming."[45]

What are the criteria that the liberal individual uses in determining the extent to which plans and projects remain worthy of commitment? The first is whether a given commitment is consistent with her deepest or most authentic sense of self. Since no aspect of identity is immune from criticism, this sense of self is necessarily provisional. Nonetheless, an individual cannot call all of her commitments into question at once, for this would deprive her of any basis for evaluation.[46] The set of values that she currently regards as unproblematic thus serves as the relatively stable background for her assessment. These values themselves are subject to the possibility of reevaluation in light of other commitments that the individual comes to regard as more fundamental. At least at the moment of choice, however, they represent a person's best sense of authentic identity.

A second basis for critical revision is the demands of justice. As the "first virtue of social institutions,"[47] justice enjoins us that we must be prepared to "put a brake on our own pursuits and respect the equal rights of others."[48] Liberalism's emphasis on justice flows from a conception of individuals as only contingently connected. Those who adopt a liberal attitude toward attachments always retain the possibility of severing them in light of the demands of critical reflection. Bonds of affection and sentiment therefore are unreliable as the basis for social order. Furthemore, the free exercise of reason that characterizes liberal society will inevitably result in disagreement over values, disagreement that is likely to remain a permanent feature of such a society.[49] As a result, "[t]he liberal project is to find regulative principles for people who disagree."[50] Given the multiplicity of conceptions of the good life in the modern world, it is highly unlikely that all persons in a liberal society would assent to any principles based on a judgment about which way of life is most valuable. A more realistic aspiration is to gain acceptance of prohibitions that represent minimum constraints on the pursuit of individual interests. Such constraints reflect the idea that all persons, regardless of their particular attributes or commitments, are entitled to pursue whatever values they choose as long as their pursuits do not interfere with the ability of others to do the same. Respect for persons rests on recognition of their universal character as human beings, rather than on appreciation of the particular attributes and attachments that make each person unique.

Liberal justice therefore requires that the individual stand back from her projects "and subject them to critical scrutiny from an impersonal, moral point of view."[51] A person must ask if her commitments are consistent with respect for other individuals as such, without reference to their particular characteristics. Such critical assessment necessarily treats all attachments and commitments as contingent and subject to revision. The logic of liberal justice "requires that one imagine oneself uncommitted to each particular value or allegiance in turn, for the sake of interposing impersonal liberal norms."[52] The only attachment that is unconditional is to "an overarching, abstract, universalistic community of all persons."[53]

The motif of distance is thus integral to the normative tenets of liberalism and to an ethic of justice: the distance among persons who are fundamentally separate, and the distance between the individual and her own values and commitments. Such a motif is consistent with what I have called an external stance toward social relationships: an appreciation of the distinct interest of the individual apart from any particular attachment or connection. Insistence on the importance of the external stance has steadily increased in Western culture both in society in general and the family in particular. David Gauthier has argued that "contractarianism has passed increasingly from covert to overt manifestation in our self-awareness. Institutions and practices which derive their rationale from noncontractarian considerations are being discarded or rejected."[54] Lawrence Friedman suggests that modern Western culture aspires to be a "republic of choice," organized around the ideas that "the *individual* is the starting point and ending point of life[,]" and that "a wide zone of free *choice* is what makes an individual."[55] He underscores the importance of the external stance when he argues that the law reflects "a pronounced bias against *irreversibility*—against choices and arrangements that cannot be undone."[56] Individuals may be capable of making commitments, but must retain the right to reevaluate them at any time from a perspective in which the commitment per se cannot justify its continuation.

The idea of personal choice is now a far more important aspect of family life, as individuals perceive themselves with more control than before over decisions relating to matters such as sexuality,[57] procreation,[58] marriage,[59] and divorce.[60] Changes in family law over the past two-and-a-half decades have reflected this shift in sensibilities.[61] Assessing these developments, Anthony Giddens has argued that modern intimate relationships tend to move toward an ideal type that he calls the "pure relationship."[62] A pure relationship is entered into "for what can be derived by each person from a sustained association with another; and . . . is continued only in so far as it is thought by both parties to deliver enough satisfactions for each individual to stay within it."[63] It is "reflexively organized," which means that it is subject to continuous ongoing monitoring by both parties so that the information that they exchange about the relationship in turn shapes their understanding and evaluation of it.[64] This information is crucial to the ability to assess the relationship from an external stance that focuses on the contribution of that relationship to the ends of the individuals who participate in it. Ongoing evaluation means that it is difficult for partners to "coast along" on the basis of past achievements.[65] Rather, commitment must be continually earned by virtue of a fair allocation of benefits that elicits the ongoing consent of the parties to the continuation of the relationship.[66] The stability promised by commitment thus is constantly vulnerable to disruption from reflexivity.[67] As a result, "trust is not and cannot be taken as 'given': like other aspects of the relationship, it has to be worked at—the trust of the other has to be won."[68] Giddens links the emergence of the pure relationship with its historical political roots by suggesting that this relationship parallels the emphasis on egalitarian political ideals that characterize modern democracies.[69] In this sense, the pure relationship represents "intimacy as democracy," according to which obligation depends on the ongoing ability of individuals to determine the conditions of their association.[70]

The greater prominence of individual choice in family matters is reflected in the increasing application of rational choice theory to family life. This school of thought reflects the external stance in its focus on an individual who possesses a discrete preference ordering, evaluating goods such as personal relationships in terms of the individual utility that they provide.[71] Similarly, the emphasis on reciprocity of benefits is underscored in the expanding application of social exchange theory to the family in recent years.[72] The premise of this theory is that individuals associate with others to the extent that they expect to receive benefits from such association.[73] The application of this analysis to marriage posits that "marriages are maintained by a balanced exchange of resources controlled by each partner and needed by the other."[74] The standard against which satisfaction is measured is the benefits available from alternative relationships;[75] on this view, "[c]ommitments themselves constitute opportunity costs," since they represent the decision to forgo those benefits in favor of the status quo.[76] This perspective is consistent with the idea of the pure relationship as subject to ongoing assessment. As I explore in more detail in chapters 3 and 4, economists have relied on rational choice theory to develop an elaborate account of marriage and divorce—an account that I will argue expresses the commitments of the external stance.

The organization of the pure relationship around the continuing consent of its participants makes communication crucial to its continuation. Partners need to express to each other their needs, desires, expectations, and feelings; such a process both serves as a vehicle for discerning one's deepest self and offers the opportunity to be responsive to the interests of the other. Giddens suggests that "free and open communication is the *sine qua non* of the pure relationship. . . . Self-autonomy, the break with compulsiveness, is the condition of open dialogue with the other. Such dialogue, in turn, is the medium of the expression of individual needs, as well as the means whereby the relationship is reflexively organised."[77] For partners faced with the constant possibility that each will be evaluating the relationship from an external stance, dialogue is necessary in order to ensure that both parties will continue to be satisfied.

Consistent with these dynamics, communication conceptualized as "continuing mutual revelation" has come to be seen as the cornerstone of the family, especially for spouses.[78] Recent years have seen a proliferation of research on the phenomenon of intimate personal disclosure. Studies have suggested that satisfaction with communication tends to be a crucial consideration in parties' assessments of their relationships.[79] Other work indicates that those who divorce and happily remarry emphasize better communication as a crucial factor in the success of their remarriage.[80] Furthermore, those persons now coming into adolescence and adulthood tend to "view intimate disclosure as an integral part of a close, opposite-sex relationship."[81] The importance of communication in the pure relationship also has been the subject of analysis by exchange theory. Theorists treat self-disclosure as a good that is exchanged by partners, and suggest that reciprocity of disclosure has come to be closely associated with satisfaction with intimate relationships.[82] As one study concludes, "[w]ith reciprocity being deemed an expected characteristic of self-disclosure, deviations from this norm can be viewed as resulting in feelings of inequity for members of a relationship."[83] Communication thus becomes not simply the vehicle for the ongoing monitoring of feeling and expectation, but a good in its own right whose terms of exchange affect the experience of the relationship.

The external stance therefore is a metaphor that reflects a constellation of interrelated concepts. These emphasize that "[w]e are not just what we discover ourselves . . . to be. We can, as autonomous choosers of our ends, ask ourselves what kind of person we want to become."[84] This moment represents the adoption of an evaluative stance external to a given attachment, in order to scrutinize it in light of individual interests distinctive from it. This perspective has gained increasing prominence in social life in recent years. As the next section indicates, however, it is incomplete. Particularly with respect to family life, the ability to take a stance internal to a given relationship may be crucial to the experience of genuine attachment with others.


## The Internal Stance

In a chapter in Amy Tan's *The Joy Luck Club*, Lena, a first generation Chinese-American married woman, is entertaining a visit from her mother. Her mother is peering with puzzlement at a list on the daughter's refrigerator. As the daughter tells us:

The list says "Lena" and "Harold" and under each of our names are things we've bought and how much they cost:

| *Lena* | *Harold* |
|---|---|
| Chicken, veg., bread, broccoli, | Garage stuff $25.23 |
| Shampoo, beer $19.63 | Bathroom stuff $5.41 |
| Maria (clean + tip) $65 | Car stuff $6.57 |

Groceries (see shop list) $55.15    Light Fixtures $87.26
Petunias, potting soil $14.11        Road gravel $19.99
Photo developing $13.83             Gas $22.00
                                     Car Smog Check $35
                                     Movies & Dinner $65
                                     Ice Cream $4.50

The way things are going this week, Harold's already spent over a hundred
dollars more, so I'll owe him around fifty from my checking account.[85]

Lena goes on to say,

And I feel embarrassed, knowing what she's seeing. I'm relieved that she doesn't
see the other half of it, the discussions. Through countless talks, Harold and I
reached an understanding about not including personal things like "mascara,"
and "shaving lotion," "hair spray," or "Bic shavers," "tampons," or "athlete's
foot powder."[86]

Lena goes on to elaborate on their arrangement:

When we got married at City Hall, he insisted on paying the fee. I got my
friend Robert to take photos. We held a party at our apartment and everybody
brought champagne. And when we bought the house, we agreed that I should
pay only a percentage of the mortgage based on what I earn and what he
earns, and that I should own an equivalent percentage of community property;
this is written in our prenuptial agreement. Since Harold pays more, he had
the deciding vote on how the house should look. . . . As for vacations, the one
we choose together is fifty-fifty. The others Harold pays for, with the understanding that it's a birthday or Christmas present, or an anniversary gift.
And we've had philosophical arguments over things that have gray borders,
like my birth control pills, or dinners at home when we entertain people who
are really his clients or my old friends from college, or food magazines that I
subscribe to but he also reads only because he's bored, not because he would
have chosen them for himself.[87]

Lena's mother asks, " 'Why do you do this?' " Lena tells us: "My mother has
a wounded sound in her voice, as if I had put the list up to hurt her. I think
how to explain this, recalling the words Harold and I have used with each other
in the past: 'So we can eliminate false dependencies . . . he equals . . . love without
obligation. . . . ' "[88]

Many of us are likely to share Lena's embarrassment and her mother's dis
comfort at such an arrangement, because we believe that there is more to marriage than distributive justice.[89] While the external stance tells us that each person
in a marriage is a distinct individual who must be treated fairly, Lena and Harold
have made an effort to adopt the external stance on an ongoing basis with respect
to the minute details of their daily lives. They are two spouses who seek continuously to preserve an acute sense of their distinct interests despite their marriage.
In Sartre's terms, they seek to avoid "bad faith,"[90] which leads people to "take
refuge in the belief that decisions of principle or commitments on prior occasions

hold sway over present choices. . . ."[91] Recourse to such a belief denies the existential truth that "we make ourselves anew on each occasion of choice."[92]

Even many who stress the importance of the external stance admit that it provides only a minimum safeguard against exploitation, not a prescription for how to form and sustain satisfying personal ties with others. Susan Moller Okin, for instance, suggests that while justice is essential in any relationship, virtues such as affection and generosity may have higher value.[93] Similarly, Jeremy Waldron argues that to stand on one's rights announces that "other warmer bonds of kinship, affection, and intimacy can no longer hold. To do this in a context where adversarial hostility is inappropriate is a serious moral failing."[94] A person acting from the external stance may conclude that commitment to another serves her interest and may fulfill that commitment on the basis of this assessment.[95] This is different, however, from carrying out one's commitment out of a sense of shared purpose that emphasizes collective rather than distinct individual benefits. An individual must reserve the right if necessary to evaluate a relationship such as marriage from the external stance. Genuine intimacy, however, seems to demand that she also be able to take an internal stance from which the relationship is taken as a given without reference to individual costs and benefits. This point is underscored by research that indicates that spouses with a pronounced tendency to regard marriage in exchange terms have lower levels of satisfaction with marriage than other spouses.[96] Solicitude for the internal stance reflects appreciation that "the perception of empathetic identification and unselfish concern by one's partner is central to a meaningful interpersonal relationship and the growth of love."[97]

The internal stance is not merely a pose that an individual might pragmatically choose to adopt on a given occasion. Rather, we must inevitably take at least some internal perspective, because we are always embedded in a network of relationships with others that is the very basis for our sense of our individuality and our capacity for meaningful choice.[98] Individuals' core attachments "are not merely externally related to their self-conceptions. They are constituents of their identities and as such function, so to speak, as premises of their agency."[99] The external stance itself thus is not a moment in which a radically disengaged self evaluates her commitments but is one in which a person weighs the claims of one self-in-relationship against the claims of another.[100]

Appreciation of our inevitable embeddedness has led some recent philosophers to question the claim that moral reasoning requires that an individual deliberate from a stance external to her concrete attachments.[101] These critics argue that "we cannot adequately understand our moral situation only in terms of individuals and their problems. We need to find moral guidance for the evaluation and shaping of relations."[102] Just as the external stance implicates concepts such as justice, contract, and consent, so we must identify those ideas that are salient to the ethics of the internal stance.[103]

First, recognition of the moral value of the internal stance means that individual maturity consists not simply in the ability to act autonomously from the external stance. It includes as well the capacity to form and sustain personal attachments from within the internal stance.[104] Emphasis on activities of care in actual relationships raises the question of how such relationships "can be kept in good condition or repaired if damaged."[105] This question directs attention to the ways in which the dynamism of daily life creates stresses, challenges, and opportunities for those who are participants in personal relationships. It calls for appreciation of shifting balances of power and vulnerability, different forms of responsiveness and neglect, and evolving patterns of need and obligation.

Second, a focus on sustaining connection emphasizes the way in which the internal stance tends to blur the boundary between self and other.[106] As Marilyn Friedman suggests, this generates a "moral attitude that is neither egoism nor self-denying altruism."[107] This conception of an expanded sense of self is in contrast, for instance, with schools of thought that treat other-regarding behavior such as altruism and cooperation as based ultimately on individual self-interest.[108] As James Coleman has observed, while approaches such as economic theory assume that a person will " 'act in his interest[,]' " sometimes persons "act *as if* the 'his' referred to some entity larger than themselves."[109] One extensive body of research, for instance, cites group identity as a crucial factor in prompting cooperation, a factor "which is independent of the consequences for the choosing individual."[110] Group discussions provide a means of building solidarity among members, and this solidarity in turn increases the willingness to forgo individual advantage for the sake of the larger group. While one can of course characterize a feeling of solidarity as providing a benefit to the individual, researchers point out that, unlike conventional egoistic incentives, group identity "cannot be *defined and characterized* independent of membership in the particular group with which the individual is identified."[111] Put differently, the relevant actor is not the individual whose identity is defined apart from the group, but the self whose identity is partly constituted by it.[112] This capacity for identification with others means that a relationship is not simply reducible to separate interacting individuals who use it to pursue their own distinct interests. Rather, there is a "larger relational unit"[113] that represents a shared way of life whose viability is a collective concern.[114] I explore this phenomenon in more detail in chapter 4, as part of my assessment of the role in economics in analyzing marriage.

A third concept that is salient for a morality of the internal stance is trust. Trust is basic to attachment from the very beginning of a person's existence. As Annette Baier observes, an infant has no choice but to trust in her caregivers if she is to form the bond with them that enables her to survive.[115] Furthermore, even trust between adults can occur without conscious deliberation. It can flow out of the progress of a relationship with another, as daily experience incrementally and almost imperceptibly creates a milieu in which persons come to trust each other as the implicit background against which they act.[116]

At the same time, we come to realize that the renunciation of critical assessment that characterizes the internal stance can leave us vulnerable to disadvantage and exploitation. As a result, we develop the capacity to take the external stance and to mistrust others. Maintenance of the external stance reflects the desire to limit this vulnerability by keeping close tabs on costs and benefits. This comes at the price, however, of precisely the special good that we seek in personal relationships—bridging the distance between ourselves and another so as to reduce our sense of separation.[117] Trust involves a willingness to eschew the use of our capacity for mistrust. We may choose deliberately to trust another, by using information about the past to assess the likelihood of what will happen in the future. In this sense, we may decide from the external stance to gamble on trust. Effectuating this decision, however, requires adopting the internal stance, taking confidence in the other as a given for some period of time. While the self of the external stance may choose to trust, actually trusting requires the self of the internal stance.

The moral considerations relevant to the internal stance therefore direct attention to the importance of trust in human relationships, the conditions under which it emerges, and the ways in which it is sustained. We need the external stance to tell us when trust is warranted; at the same time, we must recognize that the fragility of trust makes it particularly susceptible to destruction by the adoption of that stance.[118]

Fourth, a self proceeding from the internal stance acknowledges that obligation may emerge from the accretion of experience in a relationship of interdependence, rather than solely from consent. The view of autonomy from the external stance makes unchosen responsibility suspect because of its echoes of ascription. The latter reflects the notion that the family is separate from both the civic and the moral domain because it rests on ineluctable bonds that involve duties not readily conceptualized as voluntary.[119] One feminist response to this conventional dichotomy, of course, is to insist on the relevance of the external stance toward demands within the family.[120] Another, however, is to ask whether women's historical experience with responsibility in the realm of family relationships suggests that the external account of responsibility is incomplete.[121] Persons sometimes "recognize" obligation in circumstances not wholly of their own choosing, which suggests that we attribute moral responsibility in some instances in the absence of its voluntary assumption.[122]

This sense of obligation is characteristic of the internal stance because it reflects the deliberation of a "historical self,"[123] whose sense of identity is shaped by relationships with others over time. A shared way of life is not wholly chosen; participants in close relationships "first live all or part of their lives together and then come to recognize fully what (some of) their aims and interests are."[124] Awareness of this character of attachments, the vulnerability that they create, and the trust that they require can produce a sense of constraint with respect to a particular attachment that an agent acting from the external stance would not experience.

Indeed, a person within the internal stance regards such a feeling of constraint not as an obstacle to self-realization, but as a way to affirm it. Those who identify with particular commitments "identify themselves with their desire to do what they must and are expressing their authentic selves in the actions that they have no choice but to do."[125] This does not mean that they may not experience ambivalence, or even wish that the pull of their attachments were not as strong.[126] A sense of commitment, however, "place[s] constraints on our lives from which we may not be able to unbind ourselves without self-betrayal and personal disintegration."[127] In this way, attachments that are freely chosen can still impose responsibilities that are not purely consensual.[128] Having made a commitment to someone, "we now fall under certain special but non-voluntary requirements that we are not at liberty to negotiate away."[129] From the internal stance, the past has a moral weight in deliberation that it does not have for a person who adopts the external stance.

The internal stance therefore is an essential moment in our experience of connection with others. The relational sense of self that distinguishes this moment involves a distinct moral orientation that complements the one that characterizes the external stance. The importance of this orientation is underscored by the Altruistic Personality Project, perhaps the most extensive research directed at understanding what motivated both those who did and those who did not act to rescue Jews during World War II.[130] A conception of morality based on the external stance would suggest that rescuers predominantly were persons with "[h]igh independence from external opinions and evaluations" who acted on the basis of "a set of overarching axioms, largely autonomously derived."[131] This description, however, was applicable to only 11 percent of rescuers.[132] Some 37 percent of rescuers were motivated by empathy—the plight of a particular person in distress,[133] while 52 percent acted on the basis of their affiliation with a social group, such as family or church, whose norms they felt obliged to obey.[134] What most distinguished rescuers therefore were "their connections with others in relationships of commitment and care."[135] Rescuers fostered a sense of the importance of maintaining attachments with others,[136] and inclusiveness in defining those to whom they felt some ethical obligation.[137] By contrast, nonrescuers tended to be characterized by "detachment and exclusiveness."[138] For rescuers, helping Jews "was less a decision made at a critical juncture than a choice prefigured by an established character and way of life."[139] The groundwork for their actions was laid primarily in the ways that they "normally and routinely related to others and made their decisions."[140] The researchers conclude, "[i]f moral decisions arise as much out of affiliation as through autonomous reasoning, we need to cultivate varied forms of moral sensibilities."[141] Put differently, we must foster the opportunity for adoption of both the internal and the external stances.

An internal stance toward marriage has some affinities with both the communitarian critique of liberalism and with emphasis on an ethic of care in contrast to an ethic of justice. Communitarians point out that the individual inevitably is embedded in relationships with others, so that we "all approach our circumstances as bearers of a particular social identity."[142] These relationships are both a precondition for engaging in critical reflection and choice, as well as important sources of human value in their own right.

Liberals acknowledge that we cannot call all of our commitments into question at once when we scrutinize our lives. Some aspects of our identity must be taken as at least provisionally fixed if we are to have any ground for examining others.[143] Communitarians focus on this feature of deliberation to stress the way in which the self cannot coherently be conceptualized apart from particular attachments and connections with others. Furthermore, the sense that any given choice has meaning depends upon a "pre-existing horizon of significance, whereby some things are worthwhile and others less so, and still others not at all, quite anterior to choice."[144] Such a horizon is the product not of the individual but the culture in which she finds herself, which generates particular understandings of what is valuable in life. Attention to these ways in which individual reflection depends on a social matrix leads us to appreciate that attachments are a predicate for meaningful personal freedom, rather than merely an impediment to it.

Furthermore, communal ties have intrinsic value as important sources of human satisfaction. Much of value in life consists in taking these relationships for granted and devoting oneself to their nurture and preservation. They often provide occasions for the emergence of an expansive sense of self-understanding and identity that includes others within its orbit. It is important therefore not simply to subject these relationships to critical reflection by calling their value into question, but also to inquire about their meaning and the obligations that they imply. Doing so reveals that we often recognize attachments as sources of obligation that are not wholly voluntary in character. Egalitarian liberals, for instance, who insist that we have certain special obligations to fellow citizens, must implicitly posit some prior moral tie among such individuals to explain why such duties should not extend to humanity as a whole.[145] Similarly, we commonly regard family members as having particularly weighty responsibilities for one another, despite the fact that most family ties cannot meaningfully be regarded as purely voluntary.

Sensitivity to the ubiquity and importance of connection leads communitarians to stress that preserving and strengthening a sense of shared purpose and common good is as important a social objective as protecting individual rights. In essence, communitarians argue that our models of political and moral life should not be based solely on a vision of social distance—of separate individuals persistently distinguishing between themselves and others. Moments of shared experience must also figure into our perspective if we are to do justice to the full range of social life.

The emphasis on connection that characterizes the internal stance also has affinities with the position of those who argue that an ethic of care is a distinctive moral orienatation distinguishable from an ethic of justice. As we have seen, the moral demands of justice are predicated on the common humanity of individuals as such, rather than on their particular attributes or attachments. Reasoning about justice therefore is characterized by a posture of detachment and is prompted by the need to regulate interaction among individuals with separate competing interests. By contrast, an ethic of care directs attention to the moral requirements that can flow from involvement in concrete attachments. As Carol Gilligan describes it, "[f]rom a justice perspective, the self as moral agent stands as the figure against a ground of social relationships, judging the conflicting claims of self and others against a standard of equality or respect."[146] By contrast, "[f]rom a care perspective, the relationship becomes the figure, defining self and others. Within the context of relationship, the self as a moral agent perceives and responds to the perception of need."[147]

Thus, while detachment is the hallmark of justice, it is morally problematic under an ethic of care because it signifies a failure of responsiveness to the other as a unique human being. Attention to the specific characteristics of an individual affirms that she has value as a unique person, rather than as someone who has the universal attributes that characterize all human beings. This requires viewing her as a "concrete other," an individual "with a concrete history, identity, and affective-emotional constitution."[148] Such a perspective is of course crucial to love and friendship. As Martha Nussbaum notes, "Here the agent's own historical singularity (and/or the historical singularity of the relationship itself) enter into moral deliberation in a way that could not even in principle give rise to a universal principle," since acting morally requires that we treat a person as "a being not like anyone else in the world."[149] The ability to act in this morally responsible way is not dependent on first taking account of a person's universal qualities and the duties that these impose. As Bernard Williams suggests in a well-known example, for instance, the notion that it is moral for a man to save his wife over another person whom he could have rescued does not depend upon his reliance on the general principle that husbands have a duty to save their wives. As Williams observes: "[T]his construction provides the agent with one thought too many: it might have been hoped by some (for instance, by his wife) that his motivating thought, fully spelled out, would be the thought that it was his wife, not that it was his wife and that in situations of this kind it is permissible to save one's wife."[150]

By focusing on the self-in-relationship, an ethic of care represents that moment of social life expressed by the internal stance. One is not calling the relationship into question by critically reflecting on either its value to the individual or its conformity with impersonal principles of justice. Rather, one takes the relationship as a given and seeks ways to nurture and sustain it. This requires attention to the significance of individual action within the larger historical pattern of interaction between concrete individuals with their own unique needs. It may be that this perspective need not be confined to personal relationships but can be extrapolated to broader social situations.[151] There is also controversy about the extent to which an ethic of care is associated specifically with women's experience of moral deliberation.[152] However these issues may be resolved, the basic point is that the roots of this ethic lie in the experience of attachment with particular others that I have characterized as the internal stance.

## Conclusion

I have argued in this chapter that the external and internal stances toward marriage are fundamentally different orientations that are irreducible to one another. Each stance offers its own account of personal identity and of the claims and obligations that arise in human relationships. Furthermore, each stance represents an important moment of marriage. We want spouses to be able to reflect critically on their marriages in order to avoid being trapped in unhappy or harmful attachments. We also, however, want them to see themselves as defined in part by their commitment to their partner. In the course of everyday life, spouses move back and forth between these stances, seeking to balance their status as separate individuals with their roles as members of a marital community. Indeed, as a phenomenological matter, it may be that spouses occupy both these stances simultaneously. If this is so, any given "moment" of marriage reflects not a single pristine orientation, but an instance in which one perspective has somewhat more influence than the other. That is, deliberation likely is a complex process that does not involve simply adopting one stance or another. Nonetheless, I believe that the external and internal typology, stylized though it may be, helps clarify the distinctive kinds of considerations that are taken into account in such deliberation.

Law seeks implicitly to reconcile these competing visions of marriage. One way to think about controversies surrounding the legal conception and regulation of marriage therefore is that they are conflicts over the relative weight that we should attach to each vision in a particular setting. Frank recognition of our ambivalence should lead us to appreciate that the weight that we attach to each perspective will vary, depending on the concerns specific to a given context. This means that we cannot escape the need for close case-by-case analysis. Accordingly, the remaining chapters will focus on three controversies relating to marriage. These are the use of economic concepts to analyze marriage and divorce (Part II), the law of spousal testimonial privilege (Part III), and the law governing financial awards at divorce (Part IV). In each instance, I will argue that the debate can be seen as implicitly raising the issue of the relative salience of the external and internal stances toward marriage. This framework will help us appreciate that each controversy is an occasion for attempting to accommodate conceptions of marriage that are in some tension with one another. In the conclusion, I will suggest considerations that seem to emerge from this contextual analysis that may tentatively guide our use of this framework in approaching other issues regarding marriage and family law more generally.

Marriage is but a particularly stark example of an instance in which we seek both preservation of individuality and commitment to a shared purpose that transcends the self. As I have suggested, debates between liberals and communitarians, and between proponents of an ethic of justice and an ethic of care, also represent implicit discussions about the relative priority of the external and internal stances more generally. Rather than cast these debates as the clash of radically different assertions about identity and morality, we can see them as dialogues in which each side emphasizes a different but equally important dimension of experience. In examining closely issues dealing with marriage, we therefore gain a window onto law's attempts to capture the intricate rhythms of human connection.

# PART II

# Markets and Marriage

The Americans . . . enjoy explaining almost every act of their
lives on the principle of self-interest properly understood. It
gives them pleasure to point out how an enlightened self-
love continually leads them to help one another . . . I think
that in this they often do themselves less than justice, for
sometimes in the United States, as elsewhere, one sees people
carried away by the disinterested, spontaneous impulses natural to man. But the Americans are hardly prepared to admit
that they do give way to emotions of this sort. They prefer
to give the credit to their philosophy rather than to themselves.

Alexis de Toqueville, *Democracy in America*

# Economics, Marriage, and Divorce

The economic paradigm that is the foundation of law and economics has become a more prominent account of marriage and family life in recent years, as witnessed by Gary Becker's receipt of the Nobel Prize for Economic Science. Economic theorists in recent years have refined their models in various ways that seek to take account of the distinct characteristics of family experience. Some have drawn on these refinements to argue that economics should guide our choice of the legal rules that govern family life. At the same time, "[n]otwithstanding the economic importance of families and of family relations . . . the economic analysis of law so far has had relatively less influence in family law than in other fields."[1] This reflects wariness about applying to the family concepts more typically used in analyzing arms-length market transactions motivated by self-interest. Proponents and critics of economic analysis of the family sometimes seem to talk past one another, if they talk at all.

The analysis in the next two chapters is an effort to bridge this gap by focusing on those dimensions of marriage that economics does and does not seem able to capture. Chapter 3 sets forth a composite economic account of marriage and divorce drawn from various theorists, and describes the ways in which this account has been used in analyzing particular issues. It then suggests ways in which the economic approach is consistent with the external stance toward marriage. In chapter 4, I examine economic theory's efforts to encompass attitudes and behavior that typify the internal stance. I conclude for various reasons that such theory does not fully account for the expanded sense of self that characterizes this moment of marriage.

There are at least three reasons why an examination of the economic analysis of the family sheds light on our complex attitudes toward marriage. First, economics implicitly rejects the portrait of duality that I have set forth. It purports to offer a single analytical framework that explains all marital behavior. Seen through its lens, contradictions and tensions are only apparent, ultimately reconciled in a unitary account of human experience. If this account is plausible, it calls into question my contention that we place value on competing visions of marriage that are in irreducible tension.

Second, evaluating economics' claim provides the occasion for a detailed examination of the phenomenology of the internal stance. As we shall see, that stance is marked by distinctive cognitive, motivational, and affective states that are characteristic of the experience of attachment. By working through the ways in which economic analysis does not fully capture this experience, we gain a deeper appreciation of what is involved in taking an internal stance toward marriage.

Third, we must recognize that economic analysis is not simply an intellectual exercise of interest only to academics. Its influence reflects the increasing resonance of the market as a framework for interpreting contemporary experience. Market advocates often tell us not to worry—that a heightened sense of calculating self-interest among individuals is not incompatible with regard for broader communal welfare. Gaining a more sophisticated understanding of the premises of this claim should lead to a more discriminating assessment of the role of economic analysis in pursuing our complex desires both for marriage and for social life more generally.

WHAT ACCOUNT OF MARRIAGE does economic discourse offer, and what are its legal implications? While theorists are by no means uniform in their specific approaches, there nonetheless are several conceptual elements that are common to an economic analysis of marriage. These allow us to construct a composite account of how economics conceives of individuals' decisions to marry, the way that spouses relate to one another during marriage, and their willingness to seek a divorce. The result, theorists contend, is that economic analysis demonstrates a "growing capacity to generate hypotheses about both large and small questions concerning family behavior and its consequences within a theoretical framework that is a logically coherent part of the main corpus of neoclassical economic theory."[2]

## Rational Choice

Economic analysis of the family places considerable explicit or implicit reliance on rational choice theory.[3] This theory conceptualizes experience as a process in which individuals are continually confronted with a variety of options for behavior, each of which offers outcomes with differing amounts of costs and benefits.[4] An individual's assessment of the relative desirability of these options is determined by her preferences, which are positive or negative valuations of states of affairs that reflect personal desires and values.[5] The common basis on which this assessment is assumed to proceed is utility, the amount of net satisfaction that each outcome will provide.[6] The individual's ranking of options constitutes her preference ordering, which is assumed to reflect her determination of the amount of utility promised by each option.[7] Rational choice under certainty requires only an ordinal ranking, which indicates which options are preferred over others without specifying by how much.[8] Cardinal ranking permits construction of a utility function, which assigns a specific amount of utility to each option, thereby permitting trade-offs between or among them.[9]

The rational actor therefore must be able to compare the relative desirability of options and determine which combination of them will maximize her welfare.[10]

She will be more successful in this enterprise the better-informed are her beliefs about the satisfactions offered by each alternative. As a result, Jon Elster suggests, rational choice "involves three optimizing operations: finding the best action, for given beliefs and desires; forming the best-grounded belief, for given evidence; and collecting the right amount of evidence, for given desires and prior beliefs."[11] Once an individual has evaluated the options and ranked their desirability in accordance with her utility function, rational choice theory maintains that she will choose that option that promises the greatest utility. In sum, as Gary Becker puts it, "all human behavior can be viewed as involving participants who maximize their utility from a stable set of preferences and accumulate an optimal amount of information and other inputs in a variety of markets."[12] This formulation is both descriptive—individuals act so as to maximize their utility—and normative—if an individual is to act rationally, she must act in this way.[13]

## The Marriage Market

Economic theorists maintain that "[m]arriage is a relationship of exchange that can be modeled in economic terms even if neither spouse's motives are crassly pecuniary, or indeed pecuniary at all."[14] Economics characterizes individuals as participants in the "marriage market."[15] An individual will marry if a cost-benefit analysis indicates that his or her expected utility from doing so will exceed the utility derived from remaining single.[16] Marriage has the potential to offer superior net benefits because individuals may be able to combine their resources and efforts to produce more nonmarketable household commodities than either individual could produce alone.[17] In this setting, the term "commodities" includes anything of value—not only financial assets, but also items not conventionally included in economic output, such as the number and quality of children and sexual satisfaction.[18] Each individual seeks to "choose[] the mate who maximizes his utility"[19] by assessing potential partners in terms of those attributes that are relevant to productivity in the market and in the household, such as "intelligence, education, health, strength, fecundity, height, personality, [and] religion."[20] An efficient marriage market will develop "shadow prices" for such traits.[21] That is, the market will assign imputed values to characteristics that reflect their marginal productivity, thereby signaling the expected gains in utility that will accrue to someone who marries a person with such characteristics. Such a market will match up "superior" persons with one another, since these partnerships will produce the greatest joint output for the individuals involved and for society as a whole.[22] The optimal sorting in the marriage market occurs when "persons not married to each other could not marry without making at least one of them worse off."[23]

Each individual can be seen as a potential buyer as well as seller of spousal labor—that is, labor that would benefit one's partner in marriage.[24] Both men and women participate in the market for spousal labor; women demand male spousal labor and provide female spousal labor, while men demand female spousal labor and provide male spousal labor. Each person also has a supply of market labor, which may affect the value of the spousal labor that the individual can offer.[25] Single persons contemplating marriage thus "respond to market forces and decide on the basis of expected costs and benefits whether to marry and how much spousal labor to contribute or employ."[26]

One of the significant costs that influence decisions about marriage is the cost of searching for a suitable partner. Individuals compare such costs to the likely increase in utility produced by a continued search.[27] After each "drawing" of a prospective partner from the pool of eligible mates, a person is guided by this cost-benefit calculation in deciding whether to accept that drawing or to continue the search. Search costs may increase for a variety of reasons: as a person ages there are fewer available prospective partners; work or family demands may leave little free time; or disposable income may decrease. As search costs increase, a person lowers his or her "minimum offer," and is willing to take seriously those potential mates that previously were regarded as unacceptable.[28] This in turn means that the benefits of marriage compared to remaining single decrease, as a person becomes willing to marry persons who deviate more from the mate that he or she would obtain in an " 'optimal' sorting."[29]

## Marriage

Men and women who marry therefore maximize their expected utility by entering into a "long-term contract" in which they agree to "produce children, food, and other commodities in a common household."[30] As with any economic venture, partners may be able to engage in production of these commodities most efficiently through specialization. Each spouse may have a "comparative advantage" that makes it more worthwhile to assume primary responsibility for either household or market activity.[31] Specialization of tasks thus often reflects an optimal division of labor, because it ensures that each person works in the sphere in which he or she has the highest marginal productivity. Incentives to specialize may be especially strong if children exist or are contemplated. Many theorists have assumed that women have a comparative advantage with respect to household production, both because of biological differences and because women tend to invest most of their time on household tasks, while men focus primarily on market activities.[32] This assumption has been subject to criticism on the grounds that it fails to take into account the benefits of specialization among women,[33] as well as the psychic costs of specialization for both men and women.[34] Traditional scholars more recently have acknowledged that the rise in women's potential market earnings have increased the opportunity costs of their specialization in household work, thereby reducing their comparative advantage in performing these tasks.[35] Nonetheless, the costs of child care, transportation, and domestic services, as well as the fact that women still on average earn less than men, still often mean that a couple maximizes at least its financial output by having a wife spend more time on domestic matters than does her husband.[36] For this reason, the concept of comparative advantage remains an important element of the economic analysis of marriage.

A focus on specialization leads to the depiction of marriage as an implicit reciprocal employment contract between spouses. This contract ensures that the value of the spousal labor exchanged by the partners is equal, or that the spouse supplying a lesser amount of labor compensates the other by providing a transfer payment in the form of material and/or nonmaterial benefits.[37] Assurance of compensation is particularly important for the spouse who specializes in household labor, traditionally the woman. This is because her investment in "marriage-specific capital,"[38] such as knowledge of her husband and the provision of services especially for him and for their children, will have little value if the marriage ends. By contrast, the partner who specializes in developing market earning power, typically the husband, will continue to enjoy the benefits of this form of capital, even if the relationship does not last. The emergence of marriage as a formal commitment with certain legal consequences thus can be explained in economic terms as a mechanism to reduce the risks, especially for women, of entering into partnerships that otherwise would produce greater welfare than would the uncoordinated activities of individuals. Whether intimate partners enter into a formal relationship, and, if so, what the specific terms of their implicit employment contract will be, will depend on their relative bargaining power.[39]

Economic analysis thus generally conceptualizes marriage as a rational joint venture that involves bargaining over and implicit exchange of resources. While conceding the basic viability of this model, several economic analysts nonetheless point out that intimate relationships have certain distinct features that tend to justify more extensive state involvement than with respect to other contractual relationships. These analysts draw on "transaction cost" economics of the firm in elucidating these features.[40] Transaction cost theory observes that the acquisition of certain kinds of goods or services may require that one party become involved in an ongoing relationship with another, creating the need for investment that has value primarily in the context of that particular relationship. Such a relationship may arise because of the need for repeated interactions with another firm, as in a manufacturer-supplier setting, or by virtue of the need for a technological- or capital-intensive long-term project that requires certain expertise. The agreement between the parties in these instances is best characterized as a "relational" contract to cooperate on an ongoing basis, rather than as a discrete transaction with specifically delimited rights and obligations.[41]

The value of the venture for each party in such situations is significantly dependent on the actions of the other. The long-term nature of the relationship, however, means that each party must deal both with uncertainty and the possibility of opportunistic behavior on the part of the other. The existence of few if any readily available substitute partners means that competitive market pressures may not fully curtail such opportunism.[42]

One response to this situation is to rely purely on contractual arrangements as a way of limiting risk. A firm might, for instance, enter a series of short-term contracts as the need for each discrete transaction arises in an effort to preserve flexibility and limit opportunities for misconduct by the other party. This strategy can be costly, however. It involves incurring the costs of bargaining each time a separate contract is negotiated and creates the possibility that failure to reach agreement with respect to a specific transaction may jeopardize the overall enterprise. Alternatively, a firm may seek to enter into a detailed contract that specifies rules for dealing with all conceivable kinds of contingency and all possible forms of misconduct. Such contracts will be expensive to draft and negotiate, however, and almost certainly will be unable to encompass all possible risks that may arise.

The transaction costs of a purely contractual approach to reducing the risks of interdependence therefore may deter parties from entering into ventures that would maximize their welfare. In response to this dilemma, firms may agree to form a single organization, or otherwise formally affiliate in some way. This integration permits them to maintain an ongoing relationship when it is infeasible to do so through arms-length market transactions. Rather than specify particular outcomes and objectives, the organization can commit itself to general goals and then establish a decision procedure for dealing with specific issues as the need arises. Creation of a single unit can improve communication, as individuals united in a common work effort communicate more often and efficiently, thereby providing better information for decisionmaking.[43] An integrated organization also can inhibit opportunism by more effective monitoring of performance and by tying individual benefits to attainment of the organization's objectives.[44] Furthermore, avoiding frequent renegotiation and reducing the likelihood of interruptions in production may improve the general atmosphere in which participants operate, which may be important when the process of interaction itself is deemed to have intrinsic value.[45]

Some economic analysts argue that this perspective sheds light on the rationality of cohabitation and marriage. The kinds of goods that one desires from an intimate relationship, such as companionship and rearing children, require repeated transactions between parties over a period of time.[46] The value of these transactions tends to be highly specific to the particular parties involved, so that substitutes are not readily available. Such features of the goods that intimate relationships provide mean that individuals are unlikely to attain them through a succession of discrete transactions with others in the "spot market."[47] The practical necessity of pursuing these goods in the context of an ongoing relationship creates the same kind of interdependence and vulnerability to opportunism that occurs when firms must rely on one another for the success of their efforts.

As with firms, a rational response may be integration of separate interests into a single unit. Cohabitation, for instance, can reduce some of the uncertainty and risk of opportunism involved in an intimate relationship. The parties can gain more information about each other, thereby improving the quality of communication and enhancing their sensitivity to each other's distinctive desires and values. This enhanced communication and awareness can increase the welfare that each party receives from transactions with the other. Furthermore, living together can reduce opportunism by improving the ability of the partners to monitor each other's behavior, and by creating a closer bond that reduces the inclination to seek individual benefits at the other's expense.[48] In addition, one of the "goods" of the relationship may be a child, the welfare of whom provides utility to the parents. Cohabitation affords a chance for each parent directly to promote the child's well-being without excessive reliance on the other to do so. It also provides a means of monitoring the parental performance of the other partner.[49]

Cohabitation alone, however, still involves a risk of opportunism because it leaves open the possibility that one partner may leave the relationship at a time when he or she can capture a disproportionate share of the goods jointly produced by the parties. Rational individuals will want to protect themselves against such a risk by negotiating an agreement that provides some security in the event that the relationship ends. The transaction costs of reaching such an agreement, however, may inhibit its formation and deter persons from entering into a partnership that may be welfare-maximizing.[50] In light of this prospect, the state may significantly reduce the transaction costs of intimate relationships by regulating their creation and dissolution. Rather than simply enforcing whatever agreements individuals may reach, the state can specify a relatively uniform set of rights that attend entry into the legal status of marriage. Such specification obviates the need for each couple to bargain to a satisfactory agreement before making a commitment to pool their labor and resources in a common enterprise. The legal institution of marriage therefore can be seen as a way of increasing the gains from trade in long-term interpersonal transactions, encouraging productive relationships that otherwise might not be formed because of high transaction costs.[51] The degree of uniformity in marriage terms that the state should demand depends on the relative homogeneity of preferences regarding marriage. The greater that homogeneity, the lower the chance that a standard marriage contract will discourage many potential marriages. In such instances, we would expect reliance on standard terms to be welfare-maximizing. The greater the diversity of preferences, however, the larger the potential gains from private agreements and the higher the opportunity costs from a standard contract.[52] In these cases, permitting deviation from standard terms might be the most efficient policy.

## Divorce

Economic analysis maintains that implicit bargaining and exchange of resources continues between partners during marriage. A marriage is "maintained by a balanced exchange of resources controlled by each partner and needed by the other."[53] The net benefits resulting from marital exchanges are measured against a "comparison level,"[54] which is the "lowest level of outcomes (the ratio of rewards to costs) a relationship member will accept in light of alternative available relationships."[55] With the possibility of divorce and remarriage, an individual will compare the expected welfare from remaining married not only with the utility from becoming single but also with the expected gain from remarriage—a calculation that must take into account the search costs of finding another spouse.[56] Spousal decisions about continued commitment thus depend on "the degree of substitutability between one's current spouse and alternative spouses."[57] When remarriage is possible, "continued marital search" may be quite rational even after marriage, given the possibility that other partners may offer a higher level of net benefits from a different marriage.[58]

An individual will prefer a divorce when the expected returns from remaining married are less than those from available alternatives. In theory, a couple will dissolve their marriage only if their combined welfare when divorced exceeds their combined married welfare.[59] If one spouse derives more from marriage than the spouse who wants the divorce would gain by divorcing, the former can attempt to preserve the marriage by providing the latter with a larger share of their combined resources, broadly defined. If this exceeds the other spouse's gain from divorce, it would be rational for that spouse to accept the offer and for the partners to stay together.[60] If not, it is rational for them to divorce.[61] Various obstacles to such intramarital compensation may arise that complicate the analysis, which may justify allocating and protecting an "entitlement" to marriage in certain ways.[62] Nonetheless, the basic analytical point remains that spouses expect reciprocity of benefits at least over the long term,[63] and that they implicitly make decisions about remaining married in light of the comparative net benefits of other options.[64]

## Beyond Conventional Egoism

Self-interested rational choice aimed at maximizing utility in implicit market exchanges therefore is the underlying foundation for the economic analysis of marriage and divorce. This does not require, however, that we conceptualize individuals in this setting as stereotypical narrow egoists who move in and out of relationships based on continuous calculation of short-term costs and benefits. Proponents of economic analysis emphasize that the model is sufficiently refined to take account of phenomena such as altruism and commitment, that it can serve as a model for enforcing an ethic of spousal responsibility at divorce, and that the value of the model is not undercut by the fact that few people may deliberately act in accordance with it. Analysts concede that persons in the family context often behave altruistically—that a concern for others may lead them to act in a way that appears at odds with their own immediate personal interest. This is not inconsistent, however, with the assumption that individuals act in self-interested fashion to maximize their utility. First, the reward that the altruist anticipates need not take the form of short-term tangible benefits, but may be long-term or intangible. A person may be motivated by "reciprocal altruism" because she believes that altruism maximizes the possibility that at some later point someone will act the same toward her.[65] Similarly, Gary Becker's "Rotten Kid Theorem" posits that if the head of a household is an altruist whose utility is a function of both his own and other family members' consumption, other persons within the family will see that it is in their long-term interest to act as altruists because this maximizes household income available for distribution to them.[66] An altruist may enjoy the social benefits of praise and reputation that accrue to those who act altruistically,[67] or may seek to avoid the costs of social disapproval.[68] More subtly, the altruist may have developed a conscience that generates internal "side payments" so that she enjoys self-esteem if she acts altruistically and suffers guilt if she does not.[69] In each instance, other-regarding behavior is perfectly consistent with the proposition that individuals pursue their self-interest through efforts to maximize their utility.

Second, economic theory posits that an individual will seek to maximize the utility derived from the satisfaction of *whatever* ends she has, regardless of whether they are egoistic or nonegoistic. As rational choice philosopher David Gauthier puts it, individual interests are "interests of the self," not inevitably "interests in the self."[70] In economic terms, a person who derives satisfaction from the happiness of others has an interdependent utility function.[71] If a person "derives utility from giving his money away to others, this can be incorporated into the analysis, and the marginal utility that he gets from a dollar given away can be compared with the marginal utility that he gets from a dollar spent on himself."[72] Thus, for instance, William Landes and Richard Posner conceptualize the altruistic rescuer as someone who recognizes that her utility is affected by the utility of an endangered person, and who is motivated to act in order to preserve the value of her own "wealth."[73]

It also may be economically rational for an individual to make commitments that lead her to eschew opportunities for immediate gains, if pursuing those gains might be inconsistent with her long-term interests. Economic analysis suggests that perfectly rational behavior would take into account prospective utility over one's entire lifetime. In order to pursue a rational life plan, an individual must critically assess short-term preferences from this larger perspective.[74] Concern for satisfaction of her long-term preferences may lead an individual to adopt various strategies to lessen the pull of temporarily attractive options that an immediate cost-benefit ratio would indicate are rational to pursue.[75]

A stable marriage may be in a person's long-term interest because it maximizes expected utility over her lifetime. As a person spends more time in a given marriage, her welfare may become more closely tied to her relationship with the particular person who is her spouse.[76] As partners come to have greater knowledge of each other's interests and preferences, and as each comes more comprehensively to include the other's welfare in his or her own utility function, each individual derives value from being involved with a particular person in a particular marriage. To the extent that spouses are altruistic, for instance, they depend on continuation of the marriage in order to enjoy the rewards of their unselfishness.[77] Each thus has a rational interest in declining to pursue short-term rewards that might undermine a marriage that maximizes their utility over the long term.

Indeed, it may be irrational for partners to keep a precise "running quid pro quo account"[78] of the distribution of costs and benefits between them, or to engage in frequent calculation of the net benefits of the marriage compared to alternatives. Willingness to accept a "nonsimultaneous exchange relationship"[79] can foster an atmosphere that increases mutual attachment between partners: "the more they . . . both give and receive, . . . the more they will depend on the specific relationship with the specific companion to continue."[80] Insistence on precise cost-benefit accounting may hinder this process, thereby reducing the long-term utility that each party derives from the marriage. Frequent comparision of the net benefits of marriage to other alternatives may have the same effect. Furthermore, the process of constant reassessment itself involves its own distinctive cost: "To have a perpetual choice means that one must choose—not once but over and over again. And to do so one must continually expend time and energy in evaluating and reevaluating the wisdom of the choice[.]"[81] Continuous short-term maximizing activity therefore may be a short-sighted strategy with respect to marriage. Attachment to a specific person may generate a significant flow of expected long-term benefits; commitment is consistent with the rational pursuit of self-interest because it seeks to preserve a relationship with that person.

Even if an individual concludes that a divorce is the most rational course of action, economic analysis does not sanction purely egoistic conduct in pursuit of that end. An economic model does not imply, for instance, that a person should be able to walk away from a marriage without any obligations to a partner. Economists regard any given marriage as efficient to the extent that the net benefits accruing to the spouses from marriage exceed those available from other alternatives. If one partner would obtain slightly more benefits than costs from divorce, while the other would suffer considerable detriment, divorce then would be an inefficient option. Economic analysis suggests that we seek to ensure that only efficient divorces occur, by requiring a person seeking divorce to bear the costs of the costs, or externalities, that his or her action would impose. If an individual can compensate others in the family unit for their losses and still be better off by divorcing, he enjoys a net gain from divorce and the divorce is efficient. Indeed, we should encourage divorce in such cases, because no one will be worse off and at least one person will be better off.[82] Economics thus would apply the same principle of efficiency that governs, for example, liability of a factory for damages resulting from its operation. If the factory can internalize its externalities and still operate at a profit, then its operation is efficient and therefore desirable.

Economic analysts differ in the way that they would provide for such internalization of the costs inflicted by divorce. One group argues that the losses from divorce are best identified by the affected party, and so argue for requiring mutual consent for divorce. Others see problems with such an approach and argue instead for various methods for calculating damages that tend to provide greater compensation than typically is awarded in divorce actions. I will examine both the conceptual underpinning and practical consequences of these proposals at greater length in chapters 7 and 8. For now, the important point is that an economic model of marriage and divorce does not imply that a person should be able to walk away with no further responsibilities when his individual cost-benefit analysis makes it advantageous to seek a divorce. Economics' reliance on implicit market exchange does not simply vindicate Hobbesian egoism in the pursuit of self-interest, but offers a framework that can be used to justify imposing responsibility to mitigate the adverse consequences of the decision to pursue a divorce.

Finally, proponents of economic analysis do not regard the viability of their approach undermined by the fact that many, perhaps most, people do not engage in the kind of deliberation that the economic model describes. As Richard Posner puts it, "Economics is not a theory about consciousness. Behavior is rational when it conforms to the model of rational choice, whatever the state of mind of the chooser."[83] Even if persons as a phenomenological matter do not regard themselves as engaging in rational cost-benefit assessment, theorists argue that the model is vindicated to the extent that their actions can be reconstructed as if they do. Ideally, such reconstruction offers a parsimonious set of propositions that can be applied and tested in diverse settings, as well as a way of generating predictions about behavior under various circumstances. I will discuss this claim at greater length later, but for current purposes it is important to keep in mind that the validity of a theory need not depend wholly on its full congruence with the mental states of those whose behavior it describes and predicts.

## Applications

Scholars analyzing marriage and divorce have used the economic framework to generate theories, conduct empirical studies, and offer legal recommendations. A sample of these uses of economic analysis illustrates various ways in which an economic approach can be used for both descriptive and normative purposes.

Gary Becker's work reflects the most comprehensive attempt to fashion a theory of the family based on economic principles. One aspect of his theory that has particular relevance to marriage is the proposition that rising market wages for women increases the opportunity costs of their specialization in household production.[84] This means that contemporary marriages may involve a less specialized division of labor than traditionally has been the case. In turn, this may reduce the comparative advantage of marriage as a way of producing various household commodities. The prospect of smaller expected gains from marriage, argues Becker, is consistent with a declining rate of marriage. In addition, it may contribute to a higher divorce rate, since the net benefits of remaining in a marriage are less likely than before to exceed those available from other alternatives.[85]

Becker and his colleagues Elisabeth Landes and Robert Michael have used an economic model to analyze some of the factors influencing the probability of divorce.[86] They suggest that the probability of divorce may rise the higher the search costs of finding a marital partner and the less that spouses invest in marriage-specific capital. High search costs tend to increase the probability of divorce because they limit the ability to explore many alternatives before selecting a marriage partner. The less the amount of market information before making a choice, the greater the chance that there will be surprise about marital outcomes—that is, a discrepancy between one's expected and actual marital experience. The more likely this discrepancy, the more the net benefits from marriage will seem unsatisfactory compared to alternatives.

Marriage-specific capital, to reiterate an earlier point, reflects the ability to produce things of value for a particular marriage. Knowledge of the preferences of one's spouse and children, for instance, and cultivation of skills and talents that provide particular benefits to other household members are components of such capital. Such investment increases the value of marriage compared to alternative sources of household commodities, but, because of its specialized nature, may be of little use if the marriage ends. The more a person invests in such capital, the greater her incentive to preserve the marriage, since divorce may leave her with little in the way of tranferable market skills. Greater investment in marriage-specific capital also tends to increase the incentive of the beneficiary to stay in the marriage. The fact that this capital is tailored to his or her needs and interests tends to increase the amount of utility from staying in the marriage compared to that available from alternatives. Conversely, the less the investment in such particularized capital, the weaker the incentives for either party to remain married. Economic analysts observe that the relatively high contemporary rate of divorce may make individuals reluctant to invest in marriage-specific capital because of the risk of economic disadvantage in the event of divorce. According to the Becker, Landes, and Michael model, this in turn will increase the probability of divorce, creating even greater incentives to invest in labor market skills than in household capital, in a self-reinforcing cycle.[87]

Lloyd Cohen has offered a more detailed account of the risk that results from investment in marriage-specific capital for women.[88] Beginning with the economic model's characterization of a wife and husband as contributors to the production of household commodities, Cohen observes that the roles of men and women in this enterprise are asymmetrical. Specifically, because most cultures seem to place a great value on women's physical attractiveness and child-bearing ability, a wife tends to make her most highly valued contributions early in a marriage. By contrast, a husband's contribution in the form of earnings tends to be most valuable later in the marriage as he advances professionally. The result is that women lose value in the marriage market more rapidly than men. This means that a husband may have an incentive to reap the rewards from his wife's contributions early in the marriage and then divorce her before she is able to receive compensation in the form of his higher earnings later in the marriage. Cohen thus uses economic analysis to identify the potential for systematic opportunism in marriage by men who "terminate without completing the exchange"[89] of resources that spouses contemplate will occur.[90] This means that unilateral no-fault divorce may enhance the opportunity for men to exploit differences in the timing of marital contributions for individual gain.

As Martin Zelder observes, the Coase Theorem suggests that as a theoretical matter this need not occur.[91] Arguably, unilateral divorce simply changes the bargaining leverage between the spouses by requiring the party resisting divorce to compensate the one seeking it through a renegotiation of the marriage contract. Divorces that occur will be as efficient as under a mutual consent system if this compensation is insufficient to outweigh the gains from divorce. Zelder draws on the economic analysis of bargaining dynamics, however, to argue that the spouse who wants to continue the marriage may be limited in her ability to offer a greater share of household goods to induce her partner to stay. One important good in many marriages is children, who constitute a "public good," a greater amount of which cannot be transferred from one spouse to another. This constraint on renegotiation of the marriage contract, suggests Zelder, means that unilateral no-fault divorce results in more inefficient divorces than does a system that requires the party seeking divorce to compensate the other spouse in return for his or her agreement to end the marriage.[92]

Appreciation of these risks of specialization in household production lays the foundation for a coherent theoretical rationale for alimony, a practice that historically arose when divorces were rarely granted and was continued without explicit justification after divorce became more readily available.[93] Theorists begin with the idea that spouses seek a division of labor between household and market activity that maximizes joint expected marital utility. Wives typically invest more heavily in production of domestic commodities, the opportunity cost of which is the forgone development of market earning power. Because the risk of divorce creates the prospect that she will suffer labor market disadvantage if the marriage ends, a rational wife would demand compensation from her husband for this risk in return for her specialization in household investment. If current and future marital resources were divisible and transferable without cost, the spouses would bargain to an agreement on compensation that induced the wife to engage in an efficient level of specialization.[94] Various types of transaction costs may prevent such agreement, however, thereby leading to suboptimal specialization.[95]

Alimony can be seen as a response to this potential inefficiency. Ideally, an alimony award should equal the value of the opportunity a wife forgoes by increasing her investment in household capital above the level that she would choose in the absence of any compensation, less her share during marriage of income generated by the additional household output that results.[96] From this perspective, the availability of alimony serves to promote efficient resource allocation during marriage by reducing transaction costs associated with interspousal compensation necessary to induce an optimal division of labor.[97]

Alimony also can be conceptualized as a mechanism for ensuring that couples divorce in instances in which it would be desirable for them to do so. Transaction costs may prevent a spouse who desires a divorce from adequately compensating his partner for her losses from the end of the marriage, even though compensation would leave him better off and her no worse off. Alimony "increases the flexibility of the contractual agreement, by substituting an enforceable claim to future transfers for a current transfer," which thereby "reduces the cost of redistributing income."[98] The result is that "the dissolution of 'suboptimal' marriages [is] facilitated without adversely affecting the incentives for parties to enter marriage."[99]

Elisabeth Landes has suggested further that economic analysis offers a rationale for consideration of fault in alimony determinations. Without the prospect of a penalty, a spouse may be tempted to appropriate a greater share of marital resources than the parties originally agreed or to invest less in the marriage than would be optimal. If detected, the other spouse is likely to respond in kind, which might cause the spouses' combined expected welfare from marriage to fall to a level below their combined welfare from ending the marriage. Even if the parties divorce, the spouse who originally engaged in opportunistic behavior might still be better off than if he or she had not "cheated," and the innocent spouse is made worse off whether or not the marriage ends. Landes argues that an efficient alimony system would penalize the party more at fault in contributing to a divorce, thereby reducing the incentive to cheat. Doing so "economizes on the costs of enforcing the terms of the marriage contract within the marriage and increases the expected gain from investment in the marriage."[100]

Several analysts have conducted empirical studies of propositions generated by an economic approach to marriage and divorce. Margaret Brinig and Steven Crafton, for instance, have argued that unilateral no-fault divorce effectively makes the marriage contract unenforceable. They predict that this will increase the likelihood of opportunistic behavior during marriage and will reduce incentives to marry and to have children during marriage. Their research suggests that spousal abuse is higher and marriage and birth rates are lower in states in which unilateral divorce is available and fault is not taken into account in divorce allocation decisions.[101] Similarly, Elisabeth Landes reports that states in which alimony is unavailable or fault is regarded as irrelevant to property settlements at divorce have lower percentages of ever-married women between age 25–34 and lower marital fertility rates.[102] H. Elizabeth Peters argues that data from the 1979 *Current Population Survey* indicate that divorce settlement payments and remarriage rates were lower in states in which unilateral no-fault divorce was available.[103] Finally, Douglas Allen maintains that divorce rates were higher and property awards lower during the period in which states with unilateral no-fault divorce had not yet replaced their title-based property distribution systems with equitable distribution.[104] Empirical studies all rely on an economic model in which marriage may represent an opportunity for rational individuals to maximize their utility through combined production of various goods. They assume that parties respond to incentives that enhance or decrease the returns from cooperative behavior, and that decisions to remain married or to divorce reflect assessments of the net benefits from each course of action.

Theoretical and empirical work such as this has led many economic analysts to suggest alternatives to the current law governing divorce and its consequences. Some theorists suggest that mutual consent divorce should be required, so that spouses who have subordinated their own career advancement for the sake of the marriage will have enough bargaining power at divorce to ensure that they receive adequate compensation.[105] A second set of scholars emphasizes the need for more generous financial compensation than typically is provided at divorce. Several of these theorists draw on the economic justification for alimony to highlight the sacrifice of earning power, or "human capital," that a spouse suffers by specializing in domestic labor. They argue that divorce law should require compensation for such sacrifices.[106] Other analysts direct attention to some spouses' provision of financial and nonfinancial support for educational and professional training that enhances their partners' earning power. They emphasize the importance of reimbursement for these contributions.[107] Still other theorists propose compensation based on an analogy to the return that an investor receives on an investment. They maintain that a spouse who helps the other increase his earning power during marriage should be entitled to a share of the future earnings that are attributable to this enhancement of human capital.[108] While all these recommendations for divorce compensation draw in part on the economic justification for alimony, analysts would not impose the limitations on financial obligation that traditionally have characterized alimony. The spouse who sacrifices earning power or helps her partner enhance his own does so as part of a joint economic strategy from which she expects future benefits. If the marriage ends before she realizes these benefits, her spouse will receive a windfall at her expense.[109] In effect, he will be appropriating benefits that she rightfully has earned. Thus, unlike alimony, the rationale for financial compensation is not the need of the recipient but the existence of an outstanding debt. A recipient's change of circumstances, such as a better job or a remarriage, will not extinguish one partner's obligation to the other. Furthermore, the form of compensation may differ from alimony. Alimony traditionally involved periodic payments for some span of time after divorce. By contrast, compensation for contributions and/or diminution in human capital could occur in a lump sum at the time of divorce if sufficient liquid assets are available.

I will analyze various proposals based on human capital theory in more detail in chapters 7 and 8.[110] For now, the important point is that reliance on the economic concepts of human capital and efficient marital investment lead many scholars to criticize current levels of divorce awards as inadequate. More broadly, an economic approach to marriage and divorce has provided the basis for criticisms of current divorce law and recommendations for reform.

## Economics and the External Stance

I have summarized how economists use the concept of efficiency to analyze decisions to marry and to divorce. From one perspective, we can see this approach as purely descriptive or positive. Analysts use the methodology of economics to tell us how individuals act when confronted with a given set of constraints. This allows us to explain and predict behavior and to determine the extent to which it results in efficient marriage and divorce. Strictly speaking, however, one need not conclude that we *ought* to promote efficiency with respect to marriage and divorce. We might believe that efficiency is irrelevant to such matters, or that it is outweighed by other considerations. An economist might claim that such questions are normative and therefore beyond the province of economics. If economics is indeed purely positive, it would be unjustified to claim that its application to marriage and divorce expresses the normative commitments of the external stance.

In fact, however, description and prescription are not so easily distinguished in economic analysis. First, the notion of a strict distinction between positive and normative discourse is highly problematic in social science and philosophy.[111] Any theory, economic or not, necessarily must select a vantage point and object of attention from among numerous candidates. Analytical categories will be shaped by a particular account of what is significant in the world, and those categories in turn will influence one's perception of significance. Thus, economics takes the individual as its fundamental unit of analysis, regards preferences as unassailable reflections of value, and models interaction among individuals in accordance with principles of exchange. As Margaret Radin puts it, market rhetoric "invites us to see the person as a self-interested maximizer in all respects,"[112] and "stresses separateness both between ourselves and our things and between ourselves and other people."[113] Such an account may or may not be insightful or accurate, but it is not a mere neutral description.

Second, more specific to economics, efficiency is "a peculiar blend of the positive and normative."[114] As Avery Katz has pointed out, the description of a state of affairs as efficient tends typically to be made in an interpretive context that implies that this condition is desirable. "In such a context, to say something is efficient also implies the statement that it ought to be done, absent some countervailing reason."[115] Thus, it is not surprising to find that many economists at a minimum assume that efficiency is one among several values that we should seek to realize. For such theorists, economics is well-suited to analyze the extent to which a policy will promote or diminish attainment of this value. They acknowledge, however, that other values may outweigh it in a given instance.[116] Furthermore, the "most aggressive version" of the economic analysis of law regards efficiency as the central ethical value that the legal system should pursue.[117] Russell Hardin, for example, maintains that the normative strain of economic analysis of law "propose[s] that the moral purpose law should serve is some variant of efficiency."[118] The result, as Jules Coleman observes, is that "[t]he economic analysis of law has taken a decidedly normative turn, especially in the hands of its legally trained advocates."[119] This is particularly notable in family law, where several analysts have proposed changes in divorce rules that are intended to increase the efficiency of both marriage and divorce.[120]

For these reasons, the analysis below assumes that economic analysts of family law tend to regard efficiency as a value that we should promote in marriage and divorce. My argument is that this position can be seen as an expression of the commitments that animate an external stance toward marriage. In the following sections I will present this claim by focusing on economics' reliance on rational choice theory and the concept of utility, its emphasis on private ordering and consent, and the particular concept of efficiency that underlies its analysis of marriage and divorce.

## The Process of Rational Choice

The first way in which economic analysis is consistent with the external stance is that the rational choice theory that tends to be the analytical foundation of that analysis treats as the fundamental unit of analysis a discrete individual with a unique set of preferences and values.[121] This individual is regarded as sovereign in the sense that she is the only person deemed competent to determine what is of value to her. Other persons are in no position to criticize the worth of the ends that she has, because "value is created or determined through preference."[122] Economic analysis therefore represents a "subjectivist and individualist"[123] theory of value that leaves it to each individual to determine by her own lights what aspects of the world are desirable or undesirable.[124] We must respect and take as given whatever goals an individual seeks to pursue, rather than attempt to judge her by the standards of others or of society as a whole. We have "no ground for appeal beyond what a person acknowledges," because we lack any objective theory of value that would enable us rationally to evaluate an individual's ends.[125] In the face of the plurality of unique individual lives, reason is able only to ascertain whether a person is likely instrumentally to be effective in attaining what she seeks—not whether what she seeks is of value. This view of rationality is reflected in Hume's famous statement that it is "not contrary to reason to prefer the destruction of the whole world to the scratching of my finger."[126] By taking as fundamental the discrete and separate character of individuals *qua* individuals, an economic approach mirrors the insistence of the external stance that each individual has a distinct set of interests that distinguishes her as a unique human being. This perspective emphasizes the irreducible importance of each person's capacity to frame, pursue, and revise conceptions of the good life.[127]

The individual as rational chooser conceives of the world as constituted by various potential objects of choice. These promise different states of affairs on which she places a positive or negative valuation, depending on her particular preference ordering. In order to engage in such assessment, an individual at a minimum must be able to rank-order the options as more or less preferred compared to each other.[128] Such an ordinal ranking[129] requires some "scale of overall value"[130] on which the options can be treated as commensurable. Under conditions of uncertainty, rational choice must proceed on the basis of the expected values of the alternatives, which requires multiplication of the value placed on each by the probability of its occurrence. For this purpose, a cardinal ranking is necessary that draws on the common metric to assign a numerical value to each option. Furthermore, a cardinal ranking allows the construction of a utility function that permits us to analyze trade-offs between or among objects of choice.

Economic theory generally relies on utility as the standard of measurement that permits alternatives to be treated as commensurable and thus amenable to rank-ordering. In simplest terms, utility is the amount of satisfaction, subjectively defined, that each outcome will produce.[131] Utility is not directly observable but is inferred from whatever one's behavior may be interpreted as maximizing.[132] Thus, regardless of whatever diverse and distinctive characteristics any two options may have, one can extract from them the common feature that each offers a certain amount of utility. This approach reflects what philosophers call "monism": the view that the only relevant difference between or among options is their differing amount of a single value.[133] On this view, "the difference between pleasures such as that of sunning oneself on the beach and of discussing philosophy are differences simply of the source of the same thing."[134] As a result, the idiosyncratic particularities of options need not preclude us from predicting how an individual will react in a given situation. We know that she will seek to maximize her utility, so whichever alternative promises the greatest amount of this value will be the one that she will select.

This assumption of commensurability among options can be seen as consistent with the emphasis of the external stance on the importance of detached critical reflection on attachments and social practices. The concept of utility abstracts from the specific unique features of various objects and events—their history, their embeddedness in social networks, their association with particular persons—that have the potential to appeal to sentiment rather than reason in making their claims. The external stance insists that no attachment warrants a priori loyalty on the basis of such considerations; each must earn its way according to its contribution to the welfare of the individual. Conceptualizing alternatives as vehicles of utility thus ideally helps a person establish some critical distance from existing social norms and practices. The "single good-constituting property" of utility is "characterized and knowable independent of thickly described, plural evaluative standards."[135] As an element of consequentialism, utility seeks to offer a "dispassionate, ostensibly asocial method for criticizing emotions and social norms: see whether they produce the best consequences" according to a single standard of value.[136] The pursuit of utility therefore is an attitude that an individual can take up "independent of relating to others in particular social contexts."[137]

In the context of marriage and divorce, for instance, the perspective of the external stance insists that an individual should not succumb to social pressures to marry if she is not convinced that marriage will offer more utility than remaining single. She should not stay married because of guilt or concern about the reactions of others if she is convinced that divorce would offer greater utility than remaining married.[138] While every individual is a product of her cultural setting and the norms that it espouses, she should try as much as possible to reflect on the importance of those norms to *her* in terms of their contribution to her utility. She need accept as legitimate the claims of no social institution, including marriage, unless she is convinced that it will promote her welfare as she understands it.

This critical distance is reflected, for instance, in Becker, Landes, and Michael's criticism of the "common belief that marital dissolutions are evidence of marital failure that should be avoided if at all possible."[139] Instead, they argue, divorce should be seen simply as a response to new information about the gains from marriage compared to other alternatives.[140] Similarly, economic theorists emphasize that marriage is not unique but is governed by the same principles that apply to any other long-term contract.[141] This posture toward marriage and divorce is consistent with the view that allegiance to *any* attachment ultimately must rest on the individual's belief that it is utility-maximizing, regardless of whatever religious, cultural, or other imperatives have come to be associated with it. Viewing an actual or potential spouse as a source of utility that can be compared with other sources is not a particularly romantic perspective.[142] It is precisely romanticism, however, that creates the risk of blinding an individual to the fact that an attachment is not actually in his or her best interest.

Economic analysis does acknowledge that persons develop attachments to particular persons based on their specific characteristics, attachments that often are reinforced by a sense of participation in the shared history of a unique relationship. Partners are not fungible in the sense that one person may offer the same set of qualities as another. This phenomenon nonetheless can be analyzed in terms of the more general concept of utility. As individuals spend more time together and come to know each other better, the opportunity arises for the partners to refine their awareness of each other's utility function and thus to provide a greater amount of utility than someone else who lacks such familiarity. Furthermore, their utility functions may move toward greater interdependence, which means that each derives considerable satisfaction from meeting the needs of his or her particular partner. Each marriage may provide benefits to its members in a unique way, but those benefits nonetheless can be compared according to the common metric of utility. Such analysis is consistent with the fact that people involved with particular individuals in unique relationships nonetheless are capable of comparing the relative desirability of various actual and potential partners.[143] Economic analysis argues that such behavior indicates that persons seek the same general end from all relationships—utility—even though any given relationship offers its own particular way of providing it. Conceptualizing marriage in this way can afford a spouse the sense of critical distance necessary to enable her to assess the relative contribution of marriage to her individual welfare.

## Private Ordering

A second aspect of the economic analysis of marriage and divorce that is consistent with the external stance is the emphasis on private ordering as the preferred means of establishing the terms of social interaction.[144] As we have seen, the individual is the fundamental unit of analysis, best situated to determine those arrangements that are likely to be beneficial for her. Negotiation and voluntary agreement provide the best indication that the obligations to others that a person must discharge are acceptable to her, because they reflect her conclusion that such obligations are warranted in light of the overall rewards that she expects to obtain.

One basis on which analysts rely in justifying this deference to private ordering is practical acknowledgment of epistemological limitations. To the extent that utility is defined as an individual's inner state of satisfaction,[145] we have no way of ascertaining which arrangements are actually utility-maximizing for her. This assumption that other persons are discrete individuals who remain relatively opaque to genuine understanding leads in turn to serious skepticism about, if not outright rejection of, the possibility of comparing utility between or among individuals.[146] As a result, we have no firm basis for concluding that any given social practice is valuable to the individuals who participate in it beyond their own genuine consent to such participation. Rather than attempting from some privileged standpoint to determine the effect of each option on each individual, we need rely only on individuals' own judgments of whether they are worse or better off in making assessments about alternative courses of action.

A second basis for a preference for private ordering, however, is normative. Respect for an individual's capacity to choose and pursue her own vision of the good life requires that we defer as much as possible to her own assessment of what is in her best interest. Markets embody the modern emphasis on autonomy understood as independence from others, in that they leave a person "free from uncontracted obligations to others, free to disregard their desires and value judgments, and free to exclude them from access to what one owns."[147] Consent is the criterion for legitimate obligation; one is free to trade only on one's own terms, with refusal or withdrawal always a prerogative.[148] Conceptualizing interpersonal interaction as implicit market exchange thus draws upon the market's close association in the cultural imagination with a realm of individual sovereignty and uncoerced contractual agreement.[149]

Depicting marriage as a series of transactions over time in which spouses implicitly exchange resources of various kinds therefore can be seen as a way of keeping in focus the fact that marriage is comprised of two separate individuals, each with distinctive interests, preferences, and values. This portrait is consistent with the model of the "pure relationship," in which each partner engages in ongoing assessment of the relative value of involvement with the other.[150] Such assessment prompts periodic renegotiation of the terms of the relationship, with bargaining positions ultimately backed by the ability to exit. Conceptualizing marriage in this way implies that the role of law should be to "facilitate mutually beneficial interactions"[151] rather than to impose some purported social standard of how spouses should behave toward one another. Ideally, marriage would reflect

a contract in which the parties anticipated all possible contingencies and negotiated an agreement to which each person voluntarily gave her consent. Transaction costs theorists recognize that various obstacles may prevent such an ideal
from being realized in practice.[152] Their objective is to select legal rules that reflect
the bargain that parties would have chosen but for these obstacles. Doing so
encourages individuals to enter into efficient trading relationships with each other
by limiting opportunities for opportunism that otherwise might make persons
reluctant to marry. The concern about opportunism can be characterized as a
utilitarian injunction to promote trades that promote overall social welfare—but
also as insistence on the importance of protecting every individual's interests
against harm by others. This latter rationale reflects the emphasis of the external
stance on the separate ends of each individual apart from whatever attachment
she may have formed or commitment she may have made.

Economic analysis of marriage and divorce therefore is strongly antipaternalist,
insisting on the superiority of private ordering as the fundamental mode of social
interaction. Economic concepts may serve to justify more active regulation of
marriage than other contracts, but the justification for doing so is still couched
in the discourse of enhancing opportunities for private agreement and trade. Legal
rules often are described as "default rules," implying that they come into play
only in the instance in which the parties themselves have not already made their
own arrangements. The subordinate role of such rules is underscored by the fact
that most economic analysts would allow parties to contract around them.[153]
Finally, the content of the rules themselves is to be determined by imagining
those terms to which parties with perfect information would have agreed in a
hypothetical *ex ante* bargain.[154] The paradigm of private ordering thus provides
economic analysis with its standard of evaluation and its vocabulary of justification. Such an orientation relies heavily on the concepts of contract, consent, and
autonomy that are integral to the external stance.

## Concept of Efficiency

Economic analysis of marriage features much talk of efficient marriage and divorce. An ideal marriage market matches up partners whose union is more efficient than independent production by each partner alone. An ideal legal regime
will ensure that only those divorces occur that are efficient. What do economists
mean by the term "efficiency" in such contexts, and what conception of marriage
does it entail? As I elaborate in this section, the standard of efficiency that is used
in economic analysis of the family tends to be strongly associated with Pareto
efficiency, a criterion that has close affinities to the external stance toward marriage.

Economists in general tend to vary in the notion of efficiency that they employ.[155] The most demanding standard is Pareto efficiency. One state of affairs is
Pareto superior to another if moving to it makes no individual worse off and
makes at least one person better off, as judged by each person's assessment of
her own welfare.[156] A state of affairs is Pareto optimal if no Pareto superior moves
can be made from it: "any further reallocation of resources will benefit one person

only at the expense of another."[157] Because the Pareto standard defers to each person's judgment of the effect of a proposed course of action on her, it gives an individual the power to veto any proposal that she believes will affect her adversely. Put differently, each and every individual must consent to any change before it can be put into effect. Economists argue that the best indication of a Pareto superior move is an actual voluntary transaction.[158] Since each party had the opportunity to decline to trade with the other, we can infer from the fact of exchange itself that each believed herself better off by participating in the transaction. We are justified, in other words, in concluding that each consented to the reallocation of resources that occurred as a result of the exchange.

One rationale for reliance on the Pareto criterion is a practical one: it repre sents a way to compare the desirability of various social policies without the need to conduct interpersonal comparisons of utility.[159] We can also justify the Pareto standard, however, as a criterion that expresses respect for persons.[160] A move from one state of affairs to another is not Pareto superior if any person would object to it, regardless of her grounds for objection or the amount by which other people would benefit from the change. The Pareto standard thus requires that there be no objection from any affected person before a change can be made that affects any person's welfare. Each individual has discrete interests and values. Only she can say whether any given social arrangement produces more costs to her than benefits, or offers more net benefits than other alternatives. Each person has a right to be free from any harms that would be inflicted for the sake of advancing other persons' interests. Put differently, "[c]onsent, an ethical criterion congenial to the Kantian emphasis on treating people as ends rather than means, in a word, on autonomy, is the operational basis of Pareto superiority."[161] This perspective parallels the insistence of the external stance that an individual must retain the ability to make her own judgment of the desirability of any attachment or commitment, regardless of social convention or opinion. To say that a vol untary transaction is Pareto efficient thus is to justify it on both utilitarian and deontological grounds.[162] Such transactions maximize overall social welfare, while at the same time respecting the autonomy of each individual.

For public policy analysis of measures beyond individual transactions, however, the stringent Pareto standard is impractical. Virtually any large-scale social policy will produce losers as well as winners. To subject it to the test of Pareto efficiency would be to permit any single individual to veto on idiosyncratic grounds a change that otherwise would produce widespread benefits.[163] Furthermore, even if individuals would consent to a change if they were compensated for their losses, transaction costs typically make it infeasible to identify and make payment to all such persons. As a result, most economists use the criterion of Kaldor-Hicks efficiency when discussing broad policy alternatives. Under the Kaldor-Hicks test, a move from one state of affairs to another is efficient if those who benefit from the change could compensate the losers for their losses and still enjoy a gain.[164] Compensation in such an instance is theoretical, not actual. The test is satisfied when we can say that, if transaction costs could be surmounted, compensation would be sufficient to prevent any individual from suffering any loss. For this reason, Kaldor-Hicks is sometimes described as a "potential Pareto-superior" stan dard.[165]

Reliance on theoretical compensation, however, moves the normative basis of efficiency away from consent.[166] Kaldor-Hicks can be seen as recommending whatever alternative produces the largest amount of net utility—that is, the largest number of benefits once the costs of compensation have been subtracted.[167] As long as the gains are sufficiently large, losers simply must suffer whatever losses that occur for this greater good—an approach that is the antithesis of a strict deontological position.[168] Thus, Richard Posner, for instance, describes a Kaldor-Hicks approach as involving a "forced exchange" of resources.[169] To the extent that economic theorists of marriage employ a Kaldor-Hicks conception of efficiency in their analysis, such theory arguably would be at odds with the insistence of the external stance on the integrity of each individual.

While analysts are not always explicit, however, there is good reason to believe that the economic approach to marriage draws on a Paretian standard of efficiency. Marriage and divorce are actual, as opposed to hypothetical transactions, which means that they are amenable to application of the Pareto criterion. Marriage requires the consent of both parties, which permits us to infer that individuals choose to enter into marriage only when they conclude that they are better off than if they remained single. Assuming adequate information about alternatives and genuine consent, marriage can be justified as presumptively efficient on both deontological and utilitarian grounds. Each person improves her utility (or at least is no worse off) as judged from her standpoint, and society is better off because such transactions in the aggregate produce only gains and no losses.

A Pareto efficient divorce also would maximize overall social welfare, while at the same time ensuring that at least one of the partners gains from divorce while the other is not left any worse off than if the marriage had continued. The Pareto standard is difficult to satisfy, however, because in all but two states divorce is available at the request of one spouse over the objection of the other. This creates the prospect that one party will suffer losses from divorce that she has no power to prevent, because her consent is not required for the divorce to occur. In this instance, divorce will not be Pareto efficient. The divorce also may fail to meet the Kaldor-Hicks efficiency standard if the gain to one party from divorce is not larger than the loss to the other.

For these reasons, economists generally have been critical of unilateral no-fault divorce. One group has proposed the requirement of mutual consent as a way of promoting efficient divorce. This approach is explicitly Paretian, since it requires the actual consent of the party who stands to lose from divorce as a way of preventing such a loss. The assumption is that it is difficult to identify all the ways in which a person's welfare may be reduced by divorce, which makes it difficult for a court to determine what amount of damages would compensate a spouse for the loss of expected benefits from marriage. Given this problem, the best way to ensure that no one is made worse off is to require the parties to bargain over compensation. In effect, this approach is akin to awarding each spouse an "entitlement" to the continuation of marriage that is enforceable by a "property rule."[170] The formation of an actual agreement between the parties will allow us to infer that the person who otherwise would resist the divorce will be fully compensated for the losses flowing from it and now is indifferent between remaining married or divorcing.[171]

By satisfying the Pareto ideal, a mutual consent requirement would be consistent both with utilitarian principles and with the insistence on respect for individual autonomy that characterizes the external stance. Requiring that a party internalize the externalities of divorce as a condition of obtaining one would ensure that divorce represents a net gain for society. If that party can pay damages that make the other party whole and still enjoy a gain from divorce, the divorce represents an efficient breach of the marital contract that maximizes social welfare. Furthermore, respect for persons requires that each individual consent to any change in position that in her judgment would have adverse consequences for her. We thus can see a mutual consent requirement as an application of the liberal "harm" principle that serves to limit the exercise of autonomy by the spouse who desires a divorce.[172] In these ways, mutual consent would promote an ideal of efficiency with respect to divorce that reflects the emphasis of the external stance on the irreducible importance of each individual's interests.

Other economic analysts, however, have criticized reliance on mutual consent as a means of ensuring efficient divorce.[173] The fact that the parties are locked into dealing with one another creates a bilateral monopoly, which may give rise to strategic behavior that results in an inefficient bargain.[174] The spouse who is not seeking a divorce may hold out for compensation that exceeds the amount of her actual losses. Even apart from a desire to maximize financial gains, there is genuine potential for such behavior because of the emotionally charged nature of many divorce decisions. "Overcompensation" would be problematic from both utilitarian and nonutilitarian perspectives. First, it may deter efficient divorces. The partner seeking divorce might be able to pay compensation equal to the actual losses that the other would suffer and still enjoy a gain from divorce. She may, however, be unable or unwilling to pay compensation above that amount and thus be unable to obtain her spouse's consent to divorce. The parties therefore would continue in a Pareto inefficient marriage: they would remain married even though a divorce accompanied by compensation equal to actual losses would make one party better off while not worsening the condition of the other. In this way, a mutual consent requirement has the potential to limit possible gains in social welfare.[175]

This scenario also would infringe the autonomy of the spouse seeking divorce. Her freedom of action would be curtailed by more than the harm principle would require, since she would be forced either to remain married or to pay compensation that exceeded the amount necessary to mitigate the impact of her behavior on others. She therefore would suffer a loss of either liberty or property that would hinder her from pursuing her conception of the good life. For this reason, one might argue, a mutual consent requirement runs a significant risk of failing to respect the interests of the individual *qua* individual apart from the marriage in which she is involved.

These potential problems with mutual consent have led some economic analysts to propose the use of financial awards as a way to promote efficient divorce. In effect, such analysts would protect the entitlement to marriage with a "liability" rule.[176] This approach is recommended when there is concern that a property rule might lead to an inefficient outcome because of bargaining problems. "Efficient damage" theorists argue that imposing greater financial obligations at divorce would avoid bargaining problems by simply changing spouses' cost-benefit calculations. Many spouses who would seek an inefficient divorce under current law would not do so if they were required to internalize more of the costs of their action by paying financial compensation.[177]

The level of divorce compensation most consistent with Pareto efficiency is expectation damages. Notwithstanding divorce statistics, spouses generally expect from marriage those benefits that flow from being married to a particular person over the course of a lifetime.[178] Expectation damages would require the spouse seeking the divorce to provide to the other spouse the resources that would have been forthcoming over the life of the marriage had the partners not divorced.[179] A party awarded such damages theoretically is not made worse off by divorce, because she receives compensation that represents the benefits she would have received had she remained married.[180]

Efficient damage theorists who analogize a spouse to an investor in her partner's human capital come close to proposing expectation damages. They argue that a spouse is entitled to a share of the increased earnings that she anticipated would accrue to the marriage over its lifetime. These proposals fall short of expectation damages, however. This is because compensation for lost expectations would dictate that an ex-spouse receive a share of the *total* income stream available to the household over the course of the marriage, not simply a portion of the added increment that became available while the parties were married. Furthermore, full expectation damages also would include compensation for psychological and emotional injury from divorce, as well as the search costs of finding another partner. A second group of efficient damage theorists suggests compensation that would fall even further below expectation damages. They would require compensation for sacrifices in earning power made for the sake of the household. Some would also award reimbursement for a spouse's contributions that enabled the other to enhance his earning power, to the extent that such contributions have not been repaid by enjoyment of a higher standard of living during marriage.

Efficient damage theorists therefore deviate from strict Pareto efficiency because the compensation they propose may still leave one party worse off from divorce. For this reason, their recommendations might seem to rest solely on a desire to create incentives for spouses in general to engage in efficient specialization during marriage, rather than on a concern to avoid hardship in individual cases. Indeed, some theorists are explicit in their hope that the compensation they propose will remove disincentives for a spouse to sacrifice career advancement in order to assume primary household responsibilities.[181] As a result, one might be left with the impression that efficient damage theorists are animated by a utilitarian focus on maximizing social welfare, not by the concern for individual well-being that characterizes the external stance.

There is some tension, however, between ensuring Pareto efficiency at divorce and the commitment to individual autonomy mandated by the external stance. Full expectation damages may well be inconsistent with contemporary spouses' conception of modern marriage. This is because the availability of such damages could make each partner vulnerable to opportunism by undercutting incentives to make the marriage work, and could place a significant burden on individual liberty in intimate matters. A useful way to illustrate this point is to use a hypothetical bargain model to evaluate efficient damage theorists' compensation proposals. This approach seeks to construct "a hypothetical contract at the time that marriage is entered into," for the purpose of determining what level of divorce compensation spouses would have found acceptable had they contemplated this issue.[182] As I discuss in more detail below, there is reason to believe that parties contemplating marriage would not demand expectation damages in the event of divorce, but instead would insist on the kind of compensation suggested by many efficient damage theorists. If this is so, then we can say that any uncompensated loss at divorce represents the materialization of a risk to which the parties consented. As Jules Coleman has pointed out, consent to the risk of loss is not the same as consent to the loss itself. It does, however, allow us to say that the loss is a fair one—that is, that the party who suffers it has no grounds for complaint.[183] We also must keep in mind that hypothetical consent is not morally equivalent to actual consent.[184] Nonetheless, as David Charny has noted, a hypothetical bargaining approach can be justified according to principles of autonomy and distributive justice,[185] which are ethical concerns of the external stance. If we can say that the divorce compensation proposed by efficient damage theorists reflects the outcome that parties would reach under a hypothetical bargain, then we can say that these theorists' proposals are consistent with the commitments of the external stance—even if those proposals deviate from strict Pareto efficiency.

What would be the likely outcome of a bargain between ideally rational parties contemplating marriage on the subject of divorce compensation?[186] There is good reason to believe that the parties would not agree to liability for expectation damages in the event of divorce. First, such expected benefits would create the problem of moral hazard: each party would be indifferent between continuation of the marriage and divorce, because her level of welfare would be the same in either instance.[187] Prospective spouses likely would want to preserve incentives for each individual to make her best efforts to make the marriage work in spite of the inevitable difficulties that will occur in the future. Put differently, each would want the other to feel that he or she *would* be somewhat worse off by divorce, because that would make her want to do her best to make sure that the marriage lasted. This requires accepting some risk of loss from divorce, which means that the level of divorce compensation that the parties would negotiate would be some figure less than expectation damages.

Second, the parties probably would not agree to expectation damages because of a desire to preserve the possibility of changing one's mind. However deeply one may be committed to a prospective spouse, the thought of having to provide compensation to that person for the indefinite future in the event of divorce may seem to lock one in at an early age to a path from which one can never deviate. Regardless of her reasons for seeking a divorce, or her relative financial position vis-à-vis her partner, the spouse who requested a divorce would be treated as the breaching party, thereby liable for damages. Such curtailment of freedom is at odds with a contemporary sensibility strongly nourished by the external stance.[188] That stance emphasizes the capacity for critical reflection on attachments and the prerogative that one always must have to withdraw from commitments that no longer serve one's best interest. An entitlement to compensation that required us to characterize a spouse who wishes to leave a marriage as in breach of a contract would coexist uneasily at best alongside the universal availability of no-fault divorce.[189]

For what compensation would parties likely bargain if not expectation damages? There is a good argument that the individuals would want to protect themselves from being financially disadvantaged as a result of the marriage. If divorce occurs and a person must go it alone, an individual's market earning power is the most important determinant of her standard of living. A person contemplating marriage likely would want to ensure at least that she suffered no net loss in this human capital if she made sacrifices for spouse and children during the marriage. She also probably would insist that she be reimbursed for any resources that she made available to her spouse to enhance his earning power for which she hasn't been compensated in the course of marriage.[190] Thus, the minimum level of compensation proposed by efficient damage theorists—payment for sacrifices in human capital and reimbursement of contributions—can be justified as the compensation to which parties would agree under a hypothetical bargain structured to promote autonomy and fairness. This allows us to rebut the claim that these theorists' conception of efficiency is animated solely by the desire to maximize overall social welfare. It also is possible that prospective spouses might agree that a spouse who helped the other enhance his earning power during marriage would be entitled to compensation in the form of a share of future earnings. Since this level of compensation moves even closer to expectation damages, it is even less vulnerable to the claim that it is premised solely on utilitarian concerns. One might argue that emotional or psychological losses, however, seem an inherent risk of being in love, for which persons would not expect compensation or assume liability.

The standard of efficiency that underlies efficient damage theorists' proposals for compensation therefore can be defended as consistent with the ethical commitments of the external stance, even though these proposals do not strictly conform to the standard of Pareto efficiency. Furthermore, as a practical matter efficient damage analysis in this context provides a rationale for far more significant mitigation of losses than typically occurs in divorce cases, even though it does not justify preventing all losses from divorce. In chapters 7 and 8, I will explore in more detail the ways in which efficient damage theorists implicitly rely on accounts of identity, relationship, and obligation that flow from an external stance toward marriage. For now, however, the point is the consistency of these theorists' proposals with the principles of individual autonomy and distributive justice that are integral to the perspective of the external stance.

To summarize the argument in this section, the economic analysis of marriage and divorce relies primarily on the Pareto criterion of efficiency, which expresses the concern for individual welfare that typifies the external stance. An efficient marriage and an efficient mutual consent divorce both represent actual transactions that presumably leave each party better off or at least no worse off. A divorce that includes efficient financial compensation can be justified under a hypothetical bargain model that has been structured to reflect commitments to autonomy and fairness, even though that compensation will not necessarily be sufficient to ensure a Pareto efficient divorce. Furthermore, although the bargain may be hypothetical, the compensation itself is actual. In these ways, the concept of efficiency used in the economic analysis of marriage and divorce reflects a nonutilitarian concern for the welfare of the discrete individual.

## Summary

Economic analysis can be seen as an expression of the external stance toward marriage. It emphasizes the discrete individual who has no prior ties with another. This person uses the metric of utility to gain critical distance from any potential or actual attachment; her choice of being single, marrying, or divorcing depends on the comparative utility of other alternatives. The economic approach to marriage promotes the conception of marriage as a voluntary contractual arrangement, in which consent is the source of individual obligation. It highlights the ongoing explicit and implicit exchange of resources between separate spouses that continues during marriage. Finally, the concept of efficiency used in the divorce context is either explicitly Paretian or can be justified by a hypothetical bargaining model, both of which emphasize the importance of attending to the interest of each individual.

## Contributions and Insights

Because of its close affinity with the external stance toward marriage, economic analysis possesses the characteristic strengths of that perspective. It brings to the forefront the needs and interests of the unique individuals who participate in marriage, thus reflecting the greater contemporary emphasis on marriage as a source of personal fulfillment. Treating persons only as husbands, wives, fathers, or mothers neglects the discrete concerns that persons have as individuals apart from their family roles. Economic discourse insists on treating any social arrangement, marriage included, as a means to satisfy individual ends. Every individual has the capacity and the right to decide whether independent or cooperative action will be most beneficial for her. No one should be conscripted by law or social pressure to enter into or to remain in a marriage whose benefits are less than the individual could achieve on her own or in another partnership. Only the individual knows her preferences and only she is in a position to say what arrangements will maximize her utility. Her consent thus is the ideal basis for any surrender of sovereignty that she must suffer. We need not assume that the individual can subject all her commitments to such evaluation at once. We can concede that a self that occupies an external stance toward marriage may be taking an internal stance toward some other commitment. The important point is that she is as capable of subjecting marriage to a critical cost-benefit analysis as she is of any other relationship. Such a perspective emphasizes the importance of preserving a margin of individual freedom from social convention.

This orientation is particularly important for women within the family, who traditionally have been socialized to efface their individual interests for the sake of others.[191] Economic analysis is of particular relevance to three aspects of many women's experience in the family. First, it may offer a particular perspective in the debate about an ethic of care, which some suggest is distinctively associated with women, especially with respect to family matters. To the extent that this association exists, economic analysis would tend to explain an ethic of care as at least partially a rational response to women's opportunities, rather than solely a biologically rooted phenomenon. Women traditionally have been faced with limited options outside family roles and have possessed fewer forms of power within the family than have men. In the face of such circumstances, it may be rational to cultivate caregiving skills and sensitivity to the subtle emotional needs and moods of others. Given a gendered division of labor, such traits tend to elicit rewards in the form of social approval and material benefits. Furthermore, it is important for one in a position of relative dependence to be highly attuned to others, both to be able to render effective care and to sense the potential for danger from more powerful household members. Carol Rose also has used rational choice theory to suggest how women in turn may have had their material disadvantage reinforced by their actual or perceived greater willingness to cooperate with others.[192] Economic discourse as an expression of the external stance thus can highlight the structure of opportunities within which women have operated and may suggest how an ethic of care and women's disadvantage have been reciprocally linked.

This leads to a second way in which the economic analysis of marriage may be relevant to women's experience within the family. By sharpening the focus on the explicit and implicit exchange of resources that occurs during marriage, an economic approach can lay the foundation for greater attentiveness to economic justice between spouses.[193] Marriage ideally provides a rough balance of trade at least over the long term. This concept offers a standard for assessing the share of benefits and burdens borne by each spouse and a basis for criticizing that distribution. Furthermore, if a woman stays in a marriage that features a serious maldistribution of resources, that may be less a commentary on her satisfaction than an indication of the poverty of alternatives that she has available. This brings to the forefront the ways in which marriage may contribute to women's economic dependence. In particular, human capital theorists emphasize the loss of earning power that women often suffer during marriage, which forces us to confront the issue of what justice requires with respect to this transfer of resources from women. Furthermore, attention to economic dependence highlights the way in which unequal background entitlements may contribute to inequality of bargaining power during marriage and asymmetry of risk from divorce.[194] This may require that we ask whether those entitlements reflect the kind of marriage contract terms that rational parties would have chosen ex ante.[195] Characterizing marriage as a series of transactions thus can make us more sensitive to subtle forms of exploitation that may occur during marriage.

This is related to a final way in which economic analysis is pertinent to gender issues within the family. The assumption of the economic approach that individuals are motivated by self-interest may prompt a certain amount of healthy wariness toward others. Much economic analysis of divorce, for instance, focuses on the ways in which different legal rules affect incentives for opportunistic behavior during marriage. Similarly, the transaction cost explanation of marriage stresses the way in which fear of exploitation may inhibit willingness to marry when it is infeasible contractually to protect oneself from this risk. One can acknowledge that intimate relationships have the potential for immense satisfaction and still recognize that they also contain the potential for imbalances and abuses of power. In particular, wives' traditional lower financial status has been closely associated with asymmetries of spousal power that sometimes have had severely destructive consequences. By acknowledging the significance of self-interest within marriage, an economic approach can help us move beyond the idealized image of the family as a realm of unalloyed altruism, toward a more realistic and complex account of family life.[196] The economic emphasis on individual interest, consent, and fair exchange may offer a useful corrective to a language of sharing that sometimes has been used to cloak women's disadvantage.

Attention to individual satisfaction, personal autonomy, and distributive justice are all important dimensions of marriage to keep in mind for both men and women. As an example of the discourse of the external stance, economic analysis expresses the value of these normative commitments. As we've seen, however, the external stance is a partial perspective. It neglects a different but also important dimension of marriage: the internal stance. Can economic analysis also incorporate this stance, as part of presenting a comprehensive discourse of marriage? In the next chapter, I will argue that while it has made attempts to do so, those attempts at bottom are unsuccessful. Ultimately, then, economic discourse reflects not only the insights of the external stance but its limitations as well.

# Economics and Attachment

The internal stance would seem to offer an account of marriage that is at odds with economic theory. I have suggested that this moment of marriage is characterized by the understanding that one is part of a collective unit to whose welfare one may be committed quite apart from a calculation of individual costs and benefits. Such an orientation is associated with "prosocial" attitudes and behavior such as empathy and cooperation, which appear to prompt one person to forgo private advantage for the sake of another. Ordinary language, for instance, distinguishes between self-interested and other-regarding attitudes and commonly draws a distinction between selfish and unselfish behavior. Herbert Margolis's description of the way in which altruism seems to diverge from individual rationality serves also as a general description of the common understanding of a prosocial orientation: a person "could have done better for himself had he chosen to ignore the effect of his choice on others."[1] Such behavior would appear to be inconsistent with a portrait of persons as individuals inexorably devoted to maximizing their own utility. This raises the question whether economic analysis offers an adequate account of the internal moment of marriage.

As I have indicated earlier, however, economic theory purports to accommodate such behavior by emphasizing the ways in which prosocial or other-regarding conduct in fact provides individual rewards. One approach maintains the assumption of independent utility functions and narrowly egoistic benefits. It emphasizes the subtle and often intangible rewards that accrue to an individual as a result of altruism or cooperation, such as social approval, avoidance of guilt, or the satisfaction that comes from doing one's duty.[2] In addition, prosocial conduct may simply reflect enlightened self-interest, in the sense that an individual may anticipate reciprocal assistance and consideration from others in the future. In each instance, the action is self-interested because the discrete individual gains or expects an increase in her own consumption of goods independent of the consumption of any other person.

A second approach is to acknowledge that individuals sometimes have prosocial preferences, so that they gain satisfaction from the happiness of others. In such instances, persons' utility functions may be described as interdependent.[3] If I am generous to someone for whom I care, I forgo my immediate material self-interest for the sake of the joy that I gain from seeing their pleasure. Helping another therefore is a way of helping myself as well.

In sum, economic theory maintains that the various forms of prosocial behavior simply reflect subtle ways in which individuals pursue personal rewards. Put differently, economics posits that the account of the person provided by the external stance is fully able to subsume within it those instances in which a person seems to act out of a sense of attachment to others.

Recent empirical and theoretical work, however, calls into question the contention that economic theory entirely captures the phenomenon of other-regarding behavior. Several experiments in social psychology profess to refute the claim that cooperation and altruism depend on incentives for some form of egoistic gain, and to establish that individuals are not uniformly attentive to private costs and benefits in all kinds of relationships. These studies suggest that persons sometimes act on the basis of a social identity that goes beyond the discrete individual to include other persons as part of the self. Furthermore, refinement of public goods theory suggests that the concept of interdependent utility functions may not adequately capture what occurs when individuals forgo personal advantage for the sake of a larger collective good. This overall body of work thus makes a strong case that people are capable of both self-and other-regarding behavior, that the latter is not easily reducible to the former without a loss in comprehensibility, and that a sufficiently rich theory requires appreciation of both separation and attachment as basic dimensions of social existence.

## The Egoistic Reward Thesis

### Experimental Data

One version of the claim that a prosocial orientation is prompted by the prospect of subtle egoistic reward is the assertion that persons moved by empathy to help another are motivated by the desire to obtain various intangible benefits. A helper may seek, for instance, to relieve her own distress provoked by seeing another in need.[4] Another explanation is that the helper anticipates having to account to the other person for her failure to help.[5] Other theorists argue that the motive evoked by empathy is to gain social or self-rewards such as praise, honor, and pride or to avoid social or self-punishments such as censure, guilt, and shame.[6] Still others maintain that an empathic person is moved to help not so much in order to relieve empathic distress as to improve a "negative affective state" characterized by sorrow or sadness.[7] According to this theory, providing assistance can seen as based on "an entirely egoistic reason: personal mood management."[8] Finally, some researchers propose that empathically aroused individuals provide help in order to share vicariously in the needy person's joy at improvement.[9] Thus, "[t]he empathically concerned witness to the distress of others helps in order to be happy."[10] Each of these egoistic explanations therefore posits that an empathic individual gains some discrete private utility from providing assistance, and that the desire for this reward is what prompts her to extend help to another.

By contrast, the "empathy-altruism" hypothesis asserts that the motivation evoked by empathy is directed toward the ultimate goal of improving the situation of a person in need,[11] and that any personal benefits that accrue to the helping party are incidental.[12] A series of experiments over the last fifteen years has sought to isolate and determine the validity of the empathy-altruism hypothesis and its various egoistic rivals.[13] C. Daniel Batson, the principal scholar involved in this research, recently has concluded: "Results of these experiments have provided remarkably consistent support for the empathy-altruism hypothesis. None of the egoistic explanations proposed has received more than scattered support."[14] He suggests that while egoism does explain the motivation for helping others in certain circumstances, it does not in others. Individuals in fact proceed on the basis of a rich set of motives, each of which seems to have salience in different contexts, and each of which may interact with other motives in some circumstances.[15] Support for the empathy-altruism hypothesis is at least a step toward gaining a deeper understanding of this process, because it "contradicts the general assumption" that "all motivation, including all prosocial motivation, is ultimately egoistic."[16]Another set of researchers led by Robyn Dawes has conducted numerous experiments over the past several years that have sought to analyze the conditions under which individuals will cooperate in "social dilemmas."[17] Such dilemmas reflect instances in which individuals have incentives to choose courses of action that are privately rational, which nonetheless in the aggregate produce an undesirable result.[18] For virtually all potential contributors to public broadcasting, for instance, "defecting"—that is, not contributing—is a "dominating" strategy.[19] This means that regardless of how many others contribute, a potential contribution will almost always have greater utility for an individual if it is spent on private consumption rather than on public broadcasting. If all potential contributors follow this logic, however, the result is a "deficient equilibrium": an outcome that no individual desires.[20] A social dilemma thus represents a case in which "each individual's payoffs for chosing defection are higher than those for choosing cooperation, no matter what others choose; however, all individuals receive lower payoffs under universal defection than under universal cooperation."[21]

Economic theory posits that the only way to avoid a deficient equilibrium is to change the utility that each individual derives from the dominating strategy. Thus, for instance, someone must offer inducements or threaten penalties for defection, which alter the individual's cost-benefit calculation. Alternatively, we may attempt to "embed the dilemma in a larger context" by pointing out more subtle sources of utility, such as long-term individual benefit, or emphasizing psychological rewards or costs associated with cooperative behavior.[22] In these ways, cooperation can become the dominating strategy, and individually rational choices will also be collectively optimal. Economics therefore assumes that when cooperation does occur, it is "a byproduct of the individualistic pursuit of some goal other than collective success."[23] Put simply, people will not cooperate in the absence of some type of egoistic incentive to do so.

Dawes and his colleagues began their work as conventional rational choice theorists who sought to isolate the effect of various egoistic incentives on the willingness to cooperate. Over time, however, the results of their studies began to suggest that cooperation may occur even in the absence of such incentives. As a result, they developed and conducted several experiments designed explicitly to test the relative importance of egoistic and nonegoistic incentives on rates of cooperation. The experiments involve social dilemmas in which individuals are given sums of money and choose anonymously whether to keep or contribute it. If enough persons contribute their money, each participant gains more than her original individual share. If an insufficient amount contribute, contributors will lose their contribution but noncontributors will retain the sum that they were given. The individually rational course of action therefore is not to contribute, since that produces the largest gain both when a sufficient number of others contribute and when they do not. Conditions in experiments were manipulated in various ways to isolate and eliminate classic egoistic incentives. The basic study design provided for a single anonymous decision and precluded interaction among group members before or after the decision. In addition, participants in groups that engaged in a discussion session were prevented from interacting before or after the sesssion.[24] These provisions were designed to prevent incentives based on reciprocity, coercion, or reputation.[25] Furthermore, other experiments added features that were designed to eliminate the effect of conscience,[26] as well as the expectation that one's contribution is critical to achieving the collective good.[27] Participants in the groups that featured discussion generally were not told the necessary number of contributors until after the close of discussion.[28]

Researchers report that even in the absence of egoistic incentives, "group discussion was found to increase the rate of cooperative choices dramatically."[29] They reject the possibility that discussion induces cooperation simply because it affords an opportunity for the group to determine who should contribute in order to gain the collective good. In one experiment, the conditions in one group were structured so that all five subjects in the group were informed that it was necessary for everyone to contribute in order for the members to obtain the public good. No discussion was permitted among group members, but every person was aware that all knew that each member was critical. In this group, it therefore was clear that each member's self-interest would be maximized by contributing. The rate of contribution in this group nonetheless was significantly lower than in the group that engaged in discussion, and in no instance were contributions made at a rate sufficient to obtain the public good.[30]

Dawes and his colleagues suggest that the reason that group discussion elicits cooperation is that it induces individuals to identify with the group, and that this "group identity" then leads them to make choices that are collectively beneficial.[31] As they note, "[i]n discussion, people immediately start discussing what 'we' should do, and spend a great deal of time and effort persuading others in their own group to cooperate (or defect!), even in situations where these others' behavior is irrelevant to the speaker's own payoffs."[32] They suggest that this tendency to identify with group members is consistent with an evolutionary framework that emphasizes inclusive fitness, if we assume that sociality is the central feature of human existence.[33] Such an assumption is at odds with evolutionary theories that depict persons who begin in isolation and evolve to social groupings in order to achieve the same egoistic ends that they pursued in isolation.[34] Sociality reflects the fact that conditions of early human evolution were such that "group living was essential for individual survival."[35]

This is not to deny the influence of egoistic incentives for cooperation. Rather, it is to question that all motivations must be reducible to them. Dawes and his colleagues suggest that both "self-interest" and "fellow feeling" should be regarded as fundamental to human nature. They conclude that experiments involving 27 different no-discussion conditions with 1,188 subjects in 178 groups, and 12 different discussion conditions with 637 subjects in 95 groups all "lead to the same conclusion: with no discussion, egoistic motives explain cooperation; with discussion, group identity—alone or in interaction with verbal promises— explains its dramatic increase."[36] This suggests that the internal stance, with its identification with and orientation to collective welfare, has an independent significance that cannot be wholly derived from a model that adopts the perspective of the external stance.

Other research indicates that group identity that enhances cooperation can be elicited by means other than group discussion. One series of "comon fate" experiments, for instance, involved individuals who made decisions about resource depletion without any interaction with others.[37] These subjects first were given descriptions of the studies in which they were participating that were designed to emphasize identification with different subgroups or with the group as a whole. They then were told that they would be sharing with the entire group a resource pool consisting of a certain number of points, from which each member could take turns making withdrawals until the pool was depleted. Participants were told that their objectives were to accumulate as many points as possible and to make the resource last as long as they could. Subjects were given information before each turn that indicated the effect of each prior withdrawal on the amount of the resource left in the pool.

Researchers indicate that individuals were more likely to exercise restraint in their use of an endangered common resource when they identified with the group as a whole than when they identified with any of the subgroups.[38] They suggest that in such instances "[i]nclusion within a common social boundary reduces social distance among group members, making it less likely that individuals will make sharp distinctions between their own and others' welfare."[39] The result is that "outcomes for other group members, or for the group as a whole, come to be perceived as one's own."[40] Other studies reveal that persons contribute more points in a situation in which a single lottery determined the value of points for all group members than in a situation in which the lottery determined the value of points for members of a subgroup.[41] At the same time, those who were led to believe that members of their own subgroup were most responsible for overuse of the resource tended to compensate by limiting their own use.[42] Group identity that leads individuals to "attach greater weight to collective outcomes than they do to individual outcomes alone"[43] thus can be triggered by mechanisms in addition to group discussion.[44]

Studies such as these, which indicate that helping and cooperation can occur without the prospect of personal reward, suggest that economic theory does not fully capture the internal stance to the extent that it seeks to explain this moment as subtle egoistic behavior.[45] They are consistent with work in social and cultural psychology that emphasizes the capacity of individuals in certain circumstances to adopt an expansive self-concept that includes the interests and concerns of others. As I discuss in the next section, a significant body of research suggests that attachment to and identification with others is not derivative of a more fundamental individualistic orientation but is an equally basic human capacity.

## The Expanded Self

Work by social psychologists on "social identity" theory over the past two decades or so has focused on the different components of self-concept that are associated with various levels of social involvement.[46] A self-concept is "the set of cognitive representations of self available to a person,"[47] which is based on "cognitive groupings of self and some class of stimuli as identical and different from some other class."[48] Social identity theory has sought to analyze the cognitive processes that are involved in group membership and attachment and to explore their implications for self-concept in this setting. Conventional modern theory has conceptualized the group as a product of individuals' quest to satisfy their personal needs. Many of these needs can be satisfied by other persons, which leads to the formation of social arrangements in which persons expect to achieve mutual satisfaction from their association.[49] Members of these groups then develop attachments to one another based on their personal interaction, which may generate a certain amount of group loyalty and cohesiveness.[50] Such an approach treats the discrete individual as basic, in the sense that "it begins with the needs of people as 'givens' and therefore implies that they are individual properties and construes them as the instigators of social action, prior to and having precedence over collective life[.]"[51] This perspective is consistent with the notion that attachment to and identification with others in a collective unit is essentially the outcome of individual efforts to satisfy egoistic needs.

Social identity theory developed out of the conviction that "traditional theories assuming a dominant role for personal self-interest had reached the end of their useful life."[52] The notion that groups are nothing but aggregations of individuals neglects the fact that being in a group has psychological consequences that change the nature of the individual.[53] These consequences reflect the fact that individuals in a group setting are capable "of seeing themselves as joint members of a shared social field that exists independently of them as individuals, and of regulating their behavior in terms of these shared understandings "[54] Theory will not capture this phenomenon if it treats group life as simply an extension of purposive individual behavior, and if it regards a person's self perception in that setting as based merely on an individuated self-concept that has been supplemented by an awareness of other people. Such an approach fails to take sociality seriously, in that it overlooks the critical cognitive and emotional impact of group membership on individual functioning.[55]

Research in social identity theory posits that persons tend in different settings to define themselves at varying levels of inclusiveness. These "self-categorizations" range from perception of oneself as a human being (human identity), through self-definition in terms of various intermediate groups and relationships (social identity), to an understanding of oneself as a unique individual different from anyone else (personal identity).[56] Moving "up" the continuum reflects a greater level of abstraction in self-categorization, so that each "higher" category includes but is not exhausted by "lower" ones. Thus, for instance, perception of myself as a human being abstracts from those qualities that form the basis for my self-understanding as a member of a profession, which in turn abstracts from those qualities that form the basis for my concept of myself as a distinct individual. The "higher" the level on the continuum, the more one's identity is defined in terms of inclusive social units. Moving from personal to social identity thus involves a categorization of the self in terms of "more inclusive social units that *depersonalize* the self-concept, where *I* becomes *we*."[57] This depersonalization involves a shift away from the perception of the self as a unique person defined by individual differences from others, toward an understanding of oneself as exemplar of a broader social category.[58] Since the universe of possible social categories is quite large, social identity may involve any number of various reference groups, each of which abstracts from individual uniqueness in a distinct way. Thus, for example:

> when an individual man tends to categorize himself as a man in contrast to women, he (subjectively "we") tends to accentuate perceptually his similarities to other men (and reduce his idiosyncratic personal differences from other men) and enhance perceptually his stereotypical differences from women. His self changes in level and content, and his self-perception and behavior become depersonalized.[59]

This shift in perception is neither a loss of individual identity nor a submergence of the self into the group.[60] Rather, it is simply a change in self-concept. Indeed, this change in some respects can be seen as a gain in identity, in that it represents a mechanism whereby an individual is able to draw on cultural understandings of difference and similarity to navigate her way in a complex world.[61]

Self-concept thus is fluid and context-dependent, an expression of a dynamic process of social judgment.[62] At the same time, it is not infinitely elastic, since unique personal qualities and experiences place internal psychological constraints on the variability of self-categorizations.[63] Different reference groups have different importance in different situations; these elicit different social identities that bring into play distinct social norms.[64] Personal and social identity are not mutually exclusive, however, but operate simultaneously and in competition with one another. Self-perception varies along a continuum defined by their relative strengths. In any given instance, "what becomes salient is probably rarely a single category or level of self-category."[65] Talk of *the* identity that is relevant to a given setting rather is "simply a way of talking about the dominant self-category where self-perception reflects the conflicts and compromises among several competing, alternative ways of categorizing self in a situation."[66] Marilynn Brewer has suggested that this dynamic process reflects a tension between human needs for validation and similarity to others on the one hand, and uniqueness and differentiation on the other.[67] As self-categorization becomes more individuated, the need for collective identity becomes stronger; as it becomes more depersonalized, the need for individuation is intensified. Equilibrium, or "optimal distinctiveness," occurs at any given moment through attainment of an identity in which the pull of needs for differentiation and assimilation are roughly equal.[68]

As should be clear, the highly individuated personal identity has no privileged role in defining the self in social identity theory.[69] Personal identity does not represent the "true" self, but only one level of self categorization that is neither superior nor inferior to more abstract self-conceptions.[70] Social identities are not simply aspects of a more basic individual self-concept but reflect extensions of self-concept beyond the individual.[71] At certain times, the self is "defined and experienced *subjectively* as a social collectivity."[72] That is, it is defined and experienced as identical or similar to a particular social grouping of people in contrast to some other grouping.[73] Thus, as John Turner and his colleagues explain: "when we think of and perceive ourselves as 'we' and 'us' (social identity) as opposed to 'I' and 'me' (personal identity), this is ordinary and normal self-experience in which the self is defined in terms of *others who exist outside the individual person doing the experiencing* and therefore cannot be reduced to personal identity."[74] In such instances, social identity reflects the perception of "self and others as a cognitive unit" distinguished from other persons within the frame of reference.[75]

Social identity theory posits that it is this perceptual process, rather than attraction to others as a potential source of individual need satisfaction, that accounts for the formation and cohesion of social groups. A sense of social identity leads to a perceived identity of interests with the relevant social grouping; "[w]hen the definition of self changes, the meaning of self-interest and self-serving motivation also changes accordingly."[76] This perception in turn serves as the basis for the development of empathic altruism and a sense of solidarity that enhance the prospect of successful cooperation.[77] Such a theory presents a sharp contrast to economic theories of social behavior: "It can be concluded that social co operation does not arise in a straightforward way directly from the pursuit of individual self-interest. It seems to depend upon the development of individuals into something we call a joint or collective psychological unit."[78] Put differently, social identity theory implies that an approach that takes the separate individual as the basic unit of analysis, and attachment to others as derivative, seems unable fully to account for the kind of orientation and behavior that is characteristic of the internal stance.

Cultural psychology theorists have also emphasized competing perceptions of identity by differentiating between cultures that stress an independent and individualistic self-concept and those that promote an interdependent and collectivist one.[79] The former orientation assumes "the inherent separateness of distinct persons," and promotes the goals of becoming independent of others and developing one's unique attributes.[80] It conceptualizes collective behavior as "voluntarily and purposely and temporarily engaging the separate self" to participate in action with others for a particular objective.[81] By contrast, an interdependent self-concept proceeds on the assumption of the fundamental connectedness of human beings. It emphasizes one's status as a participant in a larger social unit, deemphasizing individual differentiation. Self-knowledge focuses less on unique personal attributes and more on "the self-in-relation to specific others in particular contexts."[82] Numerous studies indicate that each of these conceptions of the self shapes in important ways individual cognition,[83] emotion,[84] and motivation.[85]

Such work in comparative cultural self-conceptions is illuminating if we recognize that "every group can be considered an expert on some features of human experience and that different cultural groups 'light up' different aspects of this experience."[86] Cultural psychology underscores that the bounded separate individual extolled in Western culture is not simply a reflection of natural human self-understanding but is a construct that reflects selective attention to particular dimensions of experience. Empirical studies provide evidence, for instance, that individuals in both Western and Eastern cultures are capable of proceeding on the basis of both private and collective self-concepts, and that "[d]epending on the development of the two aspects of self and the situation, [a person] may refer to one or the other of these selves."[87] One set of researchers suggests that these self-cognitions are stored in separate locations in memory, and that experimental "priming" procedures are able to stimulate retrieval of either type of cognition.[88] In addition, the practical everyday fact is that many people in Western culture act in far less independent fashion that the prevailing model prescribes. Together, these considerations lead many researchers to suggest that Western models of the self "should be reformulated to reflect the substantial interdependence that characterizes even Western individualists."[89]

In sum, recent scholarship in social and cultural psychology puts in theoretical perspective the findings of numerous experiments that prosocial behavior can occur in the absence of egoistic incentives. This scholarship explicitly challenges the view that social behavior at bottom is the product of self-interested individual actions. It argues that people are capable of acting in both "sociocentric" and "egocentric" fashion,[90] and that neither phenomenon is reducible to the other.[91]

While much of this work focuses on attachment to and membership in groups of intermediate size, research on friendship and intimate relationships that I describe in the next section is consistent with its findings.

## Close Personal Relationships

One body of research on close personal relationships that is consistent with the model of an expanded sense of self is the work of Arthur Aron and his colleagues on the cognitive processes involved in falling in love.[92] They suggest that a particularly useful way to characterize these processes is that they blur the distinction between oneself and another, so that the other is included in a person's sense of self.[93] While "the precise nature of what it means to have included other into self, in terms of cognitive structure, is probably manifold,"[94] experiments indicate that this phenomenon is manifested in at least three ways. First, people in a close relationship make less of a distinction between self and other in allocating resources.[95] This appears to result from a perception that resources are communal, rather than from an expectation that generosity will be directly reciprocated.[96] Second, a participant in such a relationship tends to adopt much of the perspective of the other, so that observations of events by partners tend to move toward congruence.[97] Third, research indicates that persons in close relationships tend to identify with and attribute to themselves the characteristics of the other.[98] These findings indicate that inclusion of the other in the self influences the ways in which persons both process information and select behavior.

Aron and his colleagues have devised an "Inclusion of Other in Self" (IOS) scale that consists of a pictoral map depicting circles with various degrees of overlap. Subjects who were asked to discuss their relationship in terms of this map used terms indicating various degrees of connectedness more than any other characterizations.[99] In addition, research indicates that subjects generally did not see connectedness as associated with loss of unique identity, as this was the least commonly mentioned interpretation of the map.[100] Furthermore, the degree of inclusion of other within the self was significantly correlated with marital satisfaction, excitement, commitment, and communication,[101] was negatively correlated with marital boredom,[102] and significantly predicted whether a romantic couple would still be together after three months.[103] Researchers suggest that the pictoral representation of the IOS scale may elicit a deep nonverbal sense of self-other union that could have its roots in infancy.[104] Such a thesis is of course speculative, but it does make plausible a claim that sociality is at least as basic a dimension of human experience as separation. Indeed, Aron and his colleagues are explicit in presenting their approach as a sharp departure from the "exchange, psychoanalytic, role and systems approaches" that have had such influence in the study of close relationships.[105]

Consistent with the notion that intimate relationships involve deemphasis of the individuated self are studies indicating that persons distinguish between what researchers call "communal" and "exchange" relationships, and that they adopt different norms in each regarding giving and receiving benefits. Over the last two decades, for instance, Margaret Clark and her colleagues have conducted experiments designed to analyze the perceptions and behavior of persons who are or desire to be involved in one or the other type of relationship.[106] This research indicates that in communal relationships, persons feel a general obligation to be concerned about each other's welfare and tend to give benefits in response to the other's need or to please the other.[107] By contrast, in exchange relationships, persons give benefits with the expectation of receiving comparable benefits in return or as repayment for benefits previously provided by the other.[108] Researchers acknowledge that some theorists use the term "exchange" to refer to any mutually rewarding pattern of interaction.[109] They emphasize, however, that they use the term in a more limited way to refer to instances in which persons recognize that what is given and received is done so because of explicit expectations of reciprocity.[110] Notwithstanding the fact that an observer may attribute to the parties in a communal relationship an intention to engage in an exchange of benefits, the parties themselves proceed on the basis of a different norm that attributes different motives. Indeed, in this setting, "the idea that a benefit is given in response to a benefit that was received is compromising, because it calls into question the assumption that each member responds to the needs of the other."[111]

Clark and her colleagues thus maintain that the distinction between communal and exchange relationships is psychologically important.[112] This importance is reflected in the fact that several experiments indicate that an orientation toward each relationship leads to different perceptions and behavior. People who desire a communal relationship with another are more likely to keep track of the other's needs than are persons who desire an exchange relationship, even when there is no opportunity for the other to reciprocate,[113] or when the person is actually unable to offer any assistance to the other.[114] Similarly, persons oriented to a communal relationship with a person are less likely to keep track of that person's inputs into a joint task for which a reward will be provided than are persons who seek an exchange relationship with that person.[115] When one person provides a benefit to a subject in an experiment after the subject previously helped that person, this action decreases the attraction of the subject to the person when the subject seeks a communal relationship with her.[116] Such behavior increases the attraction of the subject to that person, however, when the subject desires an exchange relationship with her.[117]

Similarly, subjects exhibit different reactions when receiving a request for a benefit from someone who previously had assisted them. Persons oriented toward an exchange relationship reacted more favorably toward the person making the request than persons oriented toward a communal relationship with her.[118] A request for a benefit in the absence of prior aid from the other decreases attraction when an exchange relationship is expected.[119] When a subject provided a benefit to another, the failure of the other to offer repayment increased the other's perceived exploitativeness and decreased attraction to her when an exchange relationship was expected, but not when a communal one was.[120] Such studies have led researchers to conclude that communal relationships are not simply long-term exchange relationships[121] but involve a distinct set of norms that shape both perceptions and behavior in distinctive ways.

Other research underscores that close relationships are characterized at any given moment by an imbalance of benefits and lack of perfect reciprocity, and that the parties have only a very generalized understanding of eventual symmetry of costs and benefits. One study suggests that in kin and friendship relationships, the potentially disruptive effect of imbalance is blunted by norms of need and of noninstrumental concern for the other person.[122] The need norm serves to excuse a party who fails to repay a benefit that another provides her, while the noninstrumental norm operates to depreciate explicit efforts to balance exchange. The person who is advantaged generally feels an obligation to make an offer of at least nominal payment, but expectations are that this offer will be treated as a gesture of good faith that the other party will refuse as a way in turn of underscoring her altruistic motivation.[123] In such relationships, a lack of reciprocity actually fosters solidarity, as persons "deepen their relationship and interpret imbalance as a gesture of concern for the well-being of friends and relatives."[124]

This process is especially notable in intimate relationships:

> intimates, through identification with and empathy for their partners, come to define themselves as a *unit*; as *one* couple. They see themselves not merely as individuals interacting with others, but also as part of a partnership, interacting with other individuals, partnerships, and groups. This characteristic may have a dramatic impact on intimates's perceptions of what is and is not equitable.[125]

Studies indicate, for instance, that spouses in happy marriages avoid a "book-keeping"[126] perspective that emphasizes conceptions of equity and equality that are associated with exchange. As long as they see themselves as receiving sufficient reward from the marriage, they are quite willing to ignore the relative allocation of benefits between partners.[127] Such couples seem instead to use a "bank account" approach that focuses more generally on whether there are more "deposits" than "withdrawals," rather than on whether benefits given are reciprocated by benefits received.[128] Partners are more likely to respond to each other's needs as they occur, rather than to emphasize equal exchange.[129] Indeed, the problems associated with an exchange orientation have led many marital therapists to abandon earlier quid pro quo models of marriage and to stress a concept of generalized reciprocity that encourages unilateral initiatives that do not include explicit penalties or rewards.[130]

This is not to say, of course, that persons in intimate relationships never focus more precisely on the distribution of costs and benefits between partners. As the discussion of entitlement "schema" in chapter 1 indicated, they are likely to do so when a sense of the couple as a unit has diminished.[131] Furthermore, even happy relationships involve times when explicit attention to the balance of exchange can strengthen the relationship. In other words, as I have earlier suggested, intimate partners can and do take an external stance toward their relationship that heightens an awareness of each person as a separate individual. The research on communal norms, however, suggests that intimates are also capable of taking an internal stance toward their relationship, and that attempting to reconstruct this moment in exchange terms fails to capture the dynamics of this process. Those who take this stance operate on the basis of a distinct sensibility that not only is irreducible to an exchange perspective but in fact defines itself in opposition to it. Assuming that economic theory sufficiently accounts for this orientation is likely to leave us unable to explain or predict the nuances of this moment of marriage.

## Summary

To recapitulate, one way of arguing that economic theory can account for the internal stance toward marriage is to claim that persons who exhibit prosocial tendencies such as empathy, altruism, and cooperation are actually pursuing subtle and intangible egoistic rewards. Research on prosocial behavior, however, suggests that such behavior is a complex phenomenon. People sometimes engage in such activity for the sake of personal benefits of various kinds. Sometimes, however, they act in prosocial ways even with no prospect of such rewards. A considerable body of work indicates that the best explanation for the latter kind of behavior may be that a person identifies with others, adopting a more expansive and less individuated sense of self. In such instances, a person proceeds on the basis of norms that deemphasize attention to individual costs and benefits. This evidence of distinctive orientations in different moments of social life seriously undermines the argument that economic theory can capture the internal stance toward marriage by assimilating it into a conventional egoistic self-interest model.

## The Prosocial Preference Thesis

As an alternative to the egoistic reward thesis, one might claim that economic theory can fully account for prosocial orientation by expanding the concept of self-interest to include satisfaction of prosocial preferences. One could posit, for instance, that a person has an interdependent utility function, which reflects the fact that she gains utility from the welfare of others. Or one may argue that some individuals have a taste for identification with others. Such persons are willing to sacrifice some amount of narrow egoistic benefits in order to enhance the welfare of others because doing so increases their own satisfaction. Thus, while an actor may not pursue personal reward in a narrow selfish sense, her prosocial behavior nonetheless can be seen as directed toward the attainment of benefits to herself as a discrete and separate individual. By expanding the concept of self-interest to incorporate prosocial preferences, one might argue, economic theory is able to capture the underlying essence of behavior and attitudes that characterize the internal stance.

There are at least two problems with this argument. First, it takes as the relevant unit of analysis the separate individual and attributes to her cognitive and motivational processes characteristic of individual rationality. This neglects the insight of social identity theory that persons may be changed psychologically through identification with others, so that collectively oriented behavior cannot be treated simply as the aggregation of individual actions. Identification with another involves distinctive cognition, motivation, and emotion that shapes perception, feeling, and behavior in ways that differ from the effect on these faculties when such identification is absent. The protagonist in interdependent utility function analysis, for instance, is depicted as someone for whom promoting the welfare of another ultimately is a vehicle for enhancing her own.[132] Yet an understanding of behavior as noninstrumental, undertaken solely for the sake of the other, is perhaps the essential norm that guides the behavior of persons in close relationships.[133]

As John Turner and his colleagues emphasize, "social co-operation reflects not an interdependence of separate, personal self-interests, but a cognitive redefinition of self and self-interest, [which] hence has a strong element of altruism[.]"[134] Appreciation of this phenomenon allows us to recognize that "the postulate that psychological processes belong only to individuals is fully compatible with a psychological discontinuity between individuals acting as 'individuals' and as group members."[135] This need not involve any metaphysical assertion of a "group mind," but simply awareness of the fact that "the group has *psychological reality* in the sense that there is a specific psychological process, a self-categorization or grouping process, which corresponds to and underlies the distinctive features of group behavior."[136] Positing that the individual has an interdependent utility function or a taste for identification misses this point.

The limitations of the interdependent utility function concept are illustrated by contrasting it with Herbert Margolis's use of a "dual utility function" to depict individuals' support for public goods.[137] Margolis notes the persistent difficulty of rational choice theory in providing a nontautological account of why persons contribute to the acquisition of public goods, given that the marginal individual costs of such contributions typically exceed the expected marginal individual benefits.[138] As Margolis observes: "[E]mpirically, it is obvious that people do have preferences about budgets for public goods which turn on social judgments of costs and benefits to society as a whole (how much defense is enough and so on), not merely on how much an incremental aircraft carrier, for example, is personally worth to Smith."[139] He acknowledges that economic theory has attempted to explain such behavior by distinguishing between "selfish" or "narrowly self-interested" preferences and "personal" preferences, which may reflect satisfaction from doing good for others.[140] He argues, however, that a nontrivial theory of choice cannot simply posit that an individual's utility function reflects a taste for actions that benefit others. Rather, it "will have to say something about what governs the taste for or duty to perform altruistic acts."[141]

Margolis maintains that a useful way to capture prosocial behavior is to imagine that inside each individual there are two persons: one who values only self-interest and one who values only group interest.[142] He calls these individuals S-Smith (oriented to self-interest) and G-Smith (oriented to the interest of "a larger entity of which Smith feels he is a part").[143] Margolis acknowledges that individuals may identify with a variety of groups, and that group identity is a complicated phenomenon.[144] For simplicity's sake, he dichotomizes between Smith's self-interest and his interest in society generally. Since Smith is a member of the group in question, G-utility includes S-utility but gives no special weight to Smith's private interests.[145] Similarly, utility to G-Smith is included in S-Smith's utility function, but only to the extent that it serves Smith's pure self-interest.[146]

In a standard rational choice model, the preferences of S-Smith and G-Smith would be traded off against each other to reach equilibrium in a single overall utility function. The strength of one's preference for social goods would be calculated as the amount of private resources the person would be willing to pay in order to obtain a gain for society.[147] A person would maximize utility by selecting an allocation of resources such that the utility of the last dollar spent for social goods would equal that of the last dollar allocated to private goods.[148] In effect, the standard approach treats S-Smith as the "real" Smith and his utility function as the "authentic" one. It incorporates G-Smith as a taste for public goods that is taken into account only insofar as it contributes to S-Smith's utility.

Margolis maintains, by contrast, that "G-Smith is just as authentically Smith as S-Smith."[149] People have "*irreducibly* distinct social and private preferences" that cannot be reconciled within a single utility function in which social goods are traded off against private ones.[150] A person can rationally judge the social value of a given outcome to be more than she personally is willing to pay to bring it about. A person may not be willing to pay $5,000 so that her vote will ensure that the candidate she prefers for president wins the election, but she may well conclude that the country would be better off by at least this amount if the election turns out as she wishes. Smith therefore must mediate between rival claims of self-and group interest, neither of which can be conflated with the other. While S-Smith and G-Smith each can be treated as rational maximizers of a single utility function, Smith himself cannot.[151] Equilibrium in this model represents not a balance of marginal utilities within a grand preference function, but the point at which a person has a sense "that he is doing his fair share, so that he feels neither selfish nor exploited in the way that he allocates spending" on private and social interests.[152]

While Margolis's model is not free from criticism,[153] it brings into sharp focus how a theory would have to depart from conventional economic assumptions in order to capture more adequately the internal stance. Margolis does not treat prosocial behavior as reducible to self-interest. Group identity does not represent simply an instance in which the welfare of others affects an individual's utility. Rather, it causes actual internalization of others' utility functions, so that their ends become one's own. The model thus more aptly expresses the expanded sense of self that occurs through identification with others, and the distinct sensibilities associated with perception of oneself as part of a larger social unit. Furthermore, Margolis's suggestion that individuals seek a balance between competing demands for private and social spending is similar to Marilynn Brewer's suggestion that persons attempt to reach a point at which competing attractions of both private and social identity are reconciled. Finally, the model captures far more psychological dynamism than does the concept of interdependent utility functions. Margolis claims that individuals typically have mixed motives, so that "there will rarely be pure G-or S-spending."[154] As I have suggested, we continually move back and forth between the external and internal stances, experiencing a deep sense of incommensurability between these two orientations. The dilemmas we experience therefore are genuine and cannot be reconciled within some more inclusive perspective. In short, expansion of the concept of self-interest to include interdependent utility functions or a taste for group identification ultimately seeks to subsume the internal within the external stance and thus doesn't do justice to the former's distinctive character.

A second, broader, problem with extensive expansion of the concept of self-interest is that at some point economic theory runs the risk of becoming tautological and nonfalsifiable. This danger in large measure is a function of the elasticity of the rational choice paradigm. That paradigm does not specify preferences in advance, so any behavior in hindsight theoretically can be seen as rational.[155] Furthermore, given a lack of consensus about what it means to be a rational actor, it is not clear precisely what kind of behavior in theory could fail to be explained by some variant of rational choice theory.[156] Too often the result, as eminent game theorist Anatol Rapaport observes, is that those who subscribe to a theory of egoistic incentives "are always ready to retreat to previously prepared positions by extending the concept of 'selfishness' to include any demonstrable source of motivation not previously subsumed under the concept."[157] Thus, for instance, rational choice theory can explain why a person does not vote as a natural response to the relative insignificance of his single ballot, but can also explain why a person does vote by referring to the utility that she gains from doing her duty or appearing to be a good citizen.[158] In instances such as these, the theory becomes "trivially true, and never disconfirmable."[159] The more the theory strives to encompass all behavior within a universal model, the less distinctive analytical power it has.

Restricting the concept of self-interest to behavior commonly understood to be selfish has the advantage of offering a parsimonious model that can illuminate aspects of social life, often in empirically verifiable ways. A theory informed by this perspective can identify ways in which egoistic interests shape behavior in various domains and offer predictions about what courses of action would be consistent with persons acting on this motivation. As I have suggested, this approach may be especially valuable in the analysis of social arrangements such as the family, in which the assumption of altruistic motivation may serve to obscure injustice in the distribution of power and material resources.

We must keep in mind, however, the trade-off between scope and analytical power. If we acknowledge that there is some behavior that is not fully explicable in terms of a suitably delimited rational choice model, we then "can go about the business of examining the rich variety of sources of human motivation governing choices where the outcomes of those choices result in the distribution of costs and benefits to self and others."[160] This means taking seriously the distinction that we draw in everyday life between selfish and unselfish behavior,[161] which appears to be rooted in at least two equally basic modes of orientation in the world. Much work in social psychology, for instance, has generated testable hypotheses and verifiable propositions precisely because it accepts this distinction. Economic theory's efforts to explain all behavior in terms of an elastic concept of self-interest thus ironically may undermine that discipline's aspiration to scientific status.[162]

## The Role of Theory

At this point, one may assert that it is misguided to criticize economic theory on the ground that its assumptions are unrealistic—that is, that its model does not comport with how people actually understand themselves when they engage in much prosocial behavior. For instance, the influential approach known as "predictionism,"[163] most closely associated with Milton Friedman,[164] argues that the criterion for identifying a fruitful theory is the accuracy of its predictions, not the realism of its assumptions.[165] Friedman observes that a completely realistic theory would have to be so complex and encompass so many variables that it would be utterly useless as a tool of analysis.[166] Any valuable theory necessarily abstracts from experience and in that sense is unrealistic.[167] The real question is whether it is "realistic 'enough,'" and this must depend on whether it "yields predictions that are good enough for the purpose in hand or that are better than predictions from alternative theories."[168] If it does, we can treat phenomena "*as if* they occurred in a hypothetical and highly simplified world containing only the forces that the hypothesis asserts to be important," without worrying about whether there is a discrepancy between the model's assumptions and the real world.[169] Indeed, Friedman argues, the most productive hypotheses are those that are "wildly inaccurate descriptive representations of reality," because they explain much by using a small number of variables that have been abstracted from complex phenomena.[170] Thus, Friedman suggests, we can construct a theory of the density of leaves around a tree by hypothesizing that the leaves are positioned as if each leaf deliberately made the calculations necessary to maximize the amount of sunlight that it receives.[171] This theory offers an elegant model of leaf density that has great predictive power; the fact that leaves actually do not engage in such calculations is irrelevant.[172] Closer to home, we can predict the shots of an excellent billiard player on the basis of the hypothesis that he makes his shots as if he is aware of the mathematical formulae necessary to maximize his performance, or the actions of a businessman as if he engaged in complex computations based on perfect information about market conditions.[173] The fact that neither the billiard player nor the businessman understand their own behavior in such terms is irrelevant.[174]

The premise of Friedman's argument is that a social science such as economics must conform to the methodology of the physical sciences if it is to be truly scientific.[175] His view that predictive accuracy is the sole test of a theory, and that the realism of assumptions is irrelevant, is contestable even as an account of physical science.[176] Nonetheless, even if we accept *agruendo* the claim that prediction is the sole aim of physical science, it is far less plausible to assert that predictive accuracy in *social* science is unaffected by the realism of one's theory. In the physical sciences, one need not be concerned about the mental states of the inanimate phenomena under study because they have none. A theorist can safely exclude such a variable from her equation, or, as in Friedman's leaf example, attribute a fanciful internal state to an object, without concern that her failure to capture this variable "realistically" will diminish her ability to predict the behavior of that object.[177] Human beings, however, do have mental states, and we commonly regard such states as a crucial influence on human conduct.[178] Indeed, the assumption of mental phenomena is taken to distinguish behavior, which is common to all organisms, from action, which is distinctive to humans. "Human beings do not just *behave*. They *act*, and their actions occur with an understanding of their significance in a wider social context."[179] Mental states such as motive, purpose, and intentionality thus are essential features of human events.

This fact has at least two implications for social science. First, in order to determine the accuracy of predictions, we must be able to determine if what we observe conforms to what the theory leads us to expect. Yet social phenomena are not directly observable as brute facts about the world. What is directly accessible to our senses is a series of physical gestures and movements, which requires some understanding of relevant mental states in order to become comprehensible as human action. If we exclude any account of the meaning of behavior for those involved in it, we will not, for instance, know whether a person seated at a desk placing marks on a piece of paper is signing an invoice, a letter, or a death warrant.[180] The realism of one's account of relevant actors' mental states thus is directly relevant to the capacity to engage in social science observation.

Heightened appreciation of this fact has informed recent scholarship on close personal relationships and marital therapy. As I have discussed, one application of economic or rational choice theory to intimate relationships is an emphasis on the implicit exchanges that occur between partners. The working assumption in behavioral marital therapy based on this theory has been that "rewards and punishments could be 'pinpointed' objectively and that cognitive and interpretive processes were essentially epiphenomena."[181] Research indicates, however, that partners' motives and concerns serve as "interpretive filters" that determine the significance of behavior within the relationship.[182] Without appreciation of these mental states, observers may have a poor sense of what is actually occurring in marital interaction.[183] As a result, recent work has emphasized the need to focus on "the symbolic aspects of exchange"[184]—how parties themselves actually experience marital interaction—as the basis for their description of the situation.[185] A sense of actors' mental states therefore is necessary in order to engage in the fundamental scientific act of observation.

Second, social science predictions of the future also are heavily dependent upon an understanding of human motives, purposes, and intentions. An assessment of what is likely to happen relies crucially on appreciation of the meaning that different states of affairs are likely to have for relevant participants. To return to marital therapy for a moment, the failure of researchers to attend to the meaning of interaction for the spouses themselves tends to inhibit the ability to predict how partners will react to one another under various circumstances.[186] Similarly, the assumption of egoism may lead researchers erroneously to predict an absence of prosocial behavior in the absence of egoistic incentives because they fail to appreciate the mental states associated with identifying with others.[187] Furthemore, the ability to influence behavior, which conventional scientific theory regards as an important payoff from predictive accuracy,[188] may be frustrated by unrealistic assumptions about the meaning of events for those who participate in them. Marital therapists who proceed on the basis of an erroneous understanding of how spouses interpret each others' behavior, for instance, will be ineffective in helping couples deal with marital distress.[189] More generally, "[t]he man who expects to influence others must work more through their feelings and his own than through explicit stimulus and response."[190] Indeed, the emphasis in economic theory on devising effective incentives to encourage various kinds of behavior implicitly assumes that we have some realistic sense of what will motivate individuals in specific circumstances—not simply that they will pursue utility, but that they are likely to derive utility from particular sources.

In short, it is perilous to regard the realism of a theory's assumptions as irrelevant to social science, even if we regard predictive accuracy as the criterion for evaluating social science theory. As Frank Knight observed, the centrality of human desire and value means that "the method of social prediction and control is as closely akin to the method of art and of aesthetic criticism as to the method of laboratory science."[191] Appreciation of this fact has led to increasing attention in the social sciences to the importance of interpretation, as analysts of human events seek to comprehend the meaning of those events for the persons who participate in them.[192]

If predictionism has its problems, however, so does insistence that a theory is valid only if it captures the actors' own understandings of their action. As Alfred Schutz once suggested, "We should certainly be surprised if we found a cartographer in mapping a town restricting himself to collecting information from natives."[193] One of the most significant consequences of Freud's work, for instance, is to make us question whether an individual's explanation of her own motives is a complete account of the sources of a given instance of human action. Individuals have the capacity to delude themselves in a variety of ways, and observers may have a clearer perspective on underlying grounds of action than persons directly involved in events. Furthermore, individual action takes place within a dense field of social practices that are not reducible to individual mental states. Such practices "are neither subjective nor objective but what lies behind both."[194] They exert subtle influence of which an individual may be only dimly aware, creating patterns of interaction that may be best discerned by "outsiders."[195]

Is there a middle ground between predictionism and an exclusive focus on the correspondence of a theory's assumptions with the self-understanding of relevant actors? Debra Satz and John Ferejohn suggest that the best interpretation of rational choice steers a course between these two poles.[196] Satz and Ferejohn argue that in some contexts the best account of rational choice theory is that it offers an explanation that is plausible irrespective of its congruence with individuals' mental states.[197] They maintain that this is the case in situations in which actors are subject to significant environmental constraints, such as firms operating in a competitive market.[198] In these instances, the theory illuminates elements of social structure that tend to generate certain predictable patterns of behavior. Satz and Ferejohn argue that the insight provided by the theory in these cases illustrates that "mental entities need not figure in the best rational-choice explanations of human action."[199] In this respect, they reject an "internalist" interpretation of rational choice theory.[200]

On the other hand, Satz and Ferejohn reject "radical externalism,"[201] the notion that mental states are simply "theoretical constructs inferred from human behavior" that "entail no claim about the agent's psychology at all."[202] "Unless humans are blind automotons," they argue, "they must actually be motivated to act in the way that the theory predicts."[203] We thus cannot dispense with mental states altogether in rational choice explanations. A "moderate externalism"[204] "do[es] not deny that the explanation of human behavior goes through agent psychologies in some complicated manner."[205] At the same time, it posits that in some instances an explanation couched in nonpsychological terms will offer more insight.[206]

Two aspects of Satz and Ferejohn's position are especially relevant to our discussion. First, they suggest that the more constrained the setting in which individuals operate, the less we need to be concerned with an account of behavior that refers to mental states. This is the case when we are attempting to explain "social interaction in markets, governments, and other institutions."[207] Conversely, the fewer the constraints, the more we need to be concerned about the psychological processes of the individuals in question. Satz and Ferejohn suggest that this is the case with respect to the behavior of consumers,[208] voters,[209] and persons choosing a marriage partner.[210] The behavior of spouses falls much closer to the unconstrained than constrained end of the continuum, as does the behavior of persons in many instances that involve prosocial conduct. Our account of the behavior in these settings therefore needs to be at least amenable to plausible formulation in internalist terms. Second, Satz and Ferejohn emphasize that even when externalist explanation offers more insight, we cannot completely abandon attention to mental states. As two other scholars put it, in such cases explanations "must be compatible with, though not necessarily deducible from" the intentions of individuals.[211]

One way to understand this criterion is to draw on Alfred Shutz's concept of the "postulate of adequacy."[212] Schutz insisted that social science is done "on a level of interpretation and understanding different from the naive attitudes of orientation and interpretation peculiar to people in daily life."[213] At the same time, the postulate of adequacy demands that theory should be constructed such that "a human act performed within the life-world by an individual actor" in the way indicated by the theory "would be reasonable and understandable for the actor himself, as well as for his fellow-men."[214] We may wish to revise this standard slightly to avoid subjectivist overtones,[215] by positing that the account of events must be one that an individual could regard as a reasonable reconstruction of her experience after due reflection upon it. A theory thus must have at least some compatibility with participants' understanding of their own actions. At the very least, a theory that is radically divergent from deeply settled convictions about the significance of behavior is one of which we should be especially suspicious.

The question therefore is whether the assumptions of economic theory satisfy this standard with respect to behavior that I have described as characteristic of both the external and internal stance. The theory seems to offer a reasonably good fit with respect to the former. Milton Friedman's businessman may not engage in the subtle economic calculations contained in a model of profit-maximizing activity, but he likely would not take issue with that model's account of his basic motives and purposes. The portrait that the theory paints of him is one that he would find recognizable.[216] More broadly, a person engaged in the pursuit of egoistic interests of various sorts probably would accept rational choice theory's description of the project in which she is engaged, even if she herself has not conceptualized it in such terms. It is important to emphasize that in some instances this egoistic project will generate prosocial behavior. For instance, an individual involved in a long-term relationship, as trading partner or as spouse, is in a setting that features repeated interactions over time. This likely makes the anticipation of reciprocal benefits a contributing factor in the production of prosocial behavior. Even a spouse is likely upon candid reflection to admit that this offers a good account of at least some portion of her altruistic conduct. Economic theory thus offers a plausible account of behavior oriented to what I have called the external stance.

As my earlier discussion indicates, however, a considerable body of research suggests that actors in settings that we might describe as the internal stance proceed on the basis of a very different orientation. Furthermore, it is unlikely that upon reflection such actors would accept the economic account of their behavior. Indeed, most people probably would vehemently resist such an account, because the very meaning of their action is defined in explicit opposition to the premises of economic theory. Everyday accounts of behavior distinguish between selfish and unselfish conduct and regard as meaningful concepts such as sacrifice and altruism. These understandings of human action are deeply rooted in common language and social practice and offer comprehensible narratives of social life that have powerful cognitive, motivational, and emotional significance. In short, they seem both authentic and irreducible. There is no reason to believe that replacing them with the terms of economic theory will offer us better insight into the wellsprings of human behavior. Once again, we return to the idea that our analysis of social phenomena requires a "complicated pluralism,"[217] which treats economic behavior as only one instance of human conduct.[218]

One may concede that economic theory doesn't accurately capture all of social life, but argue that nonetheless it is realistic enough to serve as our basic model of human behavior. The human being that it depicts is an ideal type.[219] Treating people *as if* they pursued only self-interest is a useful simplication that enables us to make reasonably accurate predictions about both egoistic and prosocial behavior. Why bother with two theories when one will do the job? The first response to this argument is that economic theory in fact does not always offer a useful model for predicting prosocial behavior. As the earlier discussion indicates, it in fact has drawn criticism from many quarters for engaging in ex post explanation that uses elastic definitions of self-interest as ways of avoiding the implications of disconfirming outcomes.[220] Many experiments have produced cooperation or altruism in circumstances in which a straightforward account of self-interest would lead us to predict that it would be absent. Judging economic theory by the standard of predictive accuracy therefore gives us no reason to ignore the unrealistic nature of its assumptions in certain contexts of human experience.

Second, we may question whether a theory of human action is merely an instrument for prediction and control. Theory is also an attempt to understand ourselves, and such understandings enter in subtle ways into our sense of who we are and why we act. Accounts of human action "form our minds by habituating them to certain modes of attention, certain ways of seeing and conceiving of oneself and of the world."[221] Because we are "self-interpreting animals,"[222] the language that we use to describe what we do can't be regarded as simply a neutral tool that grants us insight into independently occurring phenomena.[223] Rather, our descriptions enter into our understanding of who we are, providing us with a "vocabulary of motives"[224] that offers a specific set of ways in which we can justify conduct to ourselves and to others.[225] Each motive offers a distinct account of human nature, social relationships, and what is of value in human experience. This account then can constrain behavior in that it establishes what can count as a good reason for acting. As Quentin Skinner puts it:

> the problem facing an agent who wishes to legitimate what he is doing at the same time as gaining what he wants cannot simply be the instrumental problem of tailoring his normative language in order to fit his projects. It must in part be the problem of tailoring his projects in order to fit the available normative language.[226]

Hilary Putnam illustrates this point by positing a country in which the inhabitants are "super-Benthamites" who resolutely adhere to a stringent utilitarianism. Their philosophy countenances, for instance, even torture of individuals as long as it maximizes social utility.[227] For these citizens, telling a lie in order to maximize social welfare would not have the pejorative connotation that it has for us. As a result, "after awhile the use of the description 'honest' among the super-Benthamites would be extremely different from the use of that same descriptive term among us."[228] The same transformation would occur with respect to terms such as "considerate," "good citizen," and even "torture."[229] As Putnam argues, eventually

[t]he vocabulary available to the super-Benthamites for the description of people-to-people situations will be quite different from the vocabulary available to us. Not only will they lack, or have altered beyond recognition, many of our descriptive resources, but they will very likely invent new jargon of their own (for example, exact terms for describing hedonic tones) that are unavailable to us. The texture of the human world will change. In the course of time the super-Benthamites and we will end up living in different worlds.[230]

Appreciation of theory as an act of self-interpretation with subtle consequences raises concern about using an economic model to describe both the external and internal moments of marriage. Research indicates that "exposure to the self-interest model commonly used in economics"[231] tends to increase individuals' propensity to act in egoistic ways.[232] In various studies, economists and economics majors are less likely to engage in forms of prosocial behavior than are other persons. Furthermore, one experiment indicates that this tendency is greater the more intensive a person's exposure to training in economics,[233] and that it is strongest among students in economics courses that emphasize that human behavior is fundamentally self-interested.[234]

Research suggests that individuals' adoption of a purely economic account of behavior in close personal relationships could have especially pernicious consequences. Partners' emotions and attitudes toward one another in such relationships reflect a process of "attribution," in which the behavior of both oneself and the other is interpreted as indicative of certain dispositions and motives. These interpretations then elicit emotional responses that motivate and guide both parties' future behavior, as the actions of oneself and the other acquire symbolic significance.[235] In close relationships, a crucial distinction in the attribution process is between behavior that is undertaken to benefit oneself and behavior that is done in order to benefit the other. The first is interpreted as driven by "instrumental" motives, while the latter is seen as prompted by an "intrinsic" concern for the welfare of one's partner.[236] Attributing an intrinsic motive or disposition to someone means that she is viewed as responsive to another's needs at some personal cost, in the sense that she is willing to sacrifice narrow selfish interests without any expectation of immediate reciprocation.[237] By contrast, an individual to whom instrumental or extrinsic motives are attributed is regarded as engaging in behavior primarily for the purpose of gaining personal benefits. She tends to monitor the terms of exchange with others more closely and to "make a more explicit accounting of the value of [her] actions[.]"[238]

Research indicates that the attribution of intrinsic motivation is crucial to the development of love. As one group of theorists suggests, "positive affect alone may not be sufficient to predict love."[239] Rather, love results from "the labeling of positive affect, attitude, and so on to intrinsic rather than extrinsic concerns."[240] Persons who are made aware of possible extrinsic reasons for maintaining a relationship, for instance, report less love for their partners and see marriage as less likely, than persons who are made aware of possible intrinsic reasons.[241] Similarly, those who attribute instrumental motives to themselves and others in intimate relationships tend to be less happy and to express less commitment than other individuals.[242] In addition, the more an individual perceives herself to be extrinsically motivated in a close personal relationship, the more volatile she expects her partner's behavior to be.[243] The importance of a perception of intrinsic motivation to satisfaction is also underscored by studies indicating that married couples with a high "exchange orientation" are less happy than other couples.[244] Researchers suggest that such an orientation can promote dissatisfaction because it focuses closely on proportionate costs and rewards between parties,[245] and encourages attention to running accounts that make momentary imbalances symbolically salient.[246] Such behavior undermines the perception of intrinsic caring because partners' behavior can be attributed to expected instrumental gains.[247]

Not only is the attribution of intrinsic motivation crucial to a successful intimate relationship, it is also fragile. Considerable research indicates that the existence of an extrinsic reward reduces the likelihood that a person will construe either her own or another's motivation for caring behavior as intrinsic, even if there is evidence that she or the other would have acted the same way in the absence of the reward.[248] The attribution of an extrinsic motive in turn makes a person less likely to engage in helping or caring behavior in the future in the absence of an external reward.[249]

The body of work on attribution theory suggests that reconceptualizing caring, responsiveness, and other forms of prosocial behavior as ultimately directed at gaining individual utility might well undermine satisfaction and stability in marriage. Economic theory makes salient the kind of reward that persons tend to regard as instrumental, which may diminish the extent to which they attribute responsiveness to their partners as intrinsic concern for the other person's welfare. This runs the risk of decreasing willingness to engage in such behavior when there is no perception that a personal reward will be forthcoming. This keener sensitivity to individual benefits in turn seems likely to enhance an exchange orientation among couples, as they attend more closely to the ratio of costs and benefits between them. Furthermore, it may increase the emphasis on short-term rewards, particularly in light of evidence that contemporary individuals tend to engage in steep discounting of longer-term benefits.[250] All these developments would increase the probability of attitudes and behavior that would be inimical to creating and sustaining satisfying intimate relationships.

One way to appreciate the importance of the distinction between intrinsic and instrumental motivation is to draw on Jon Elster's observation that certain states of affairs can only come about as the by-product of actions taken for other purposes.[251] Such states cannot be brought about intentionally "because the very attempt to do so precludes the state one is trying to bring about."[252] For instance, overcoming insomnia generally requires that a person relax and not focus on the need to sleep. Someone may believe that drinking herbal tea will produce such a state of mind. If, however, she drinks the tea instrumentally only in order to bring about this state, she is unlikely to be successful, because this keeps the need for sleep in the forefront of her mind. By contrast, she may succeed if she values the tea intrinsically, drinking it for the sake of the enjoyment that it brings. In such an instance, her immersion in the experience of tea-drinking may ultimately produce a genuine inattention to sleep that is sufficient to overcome her insomnia. Falling asleep in this instance, however, is a by-product of tea-drinking for its own sake, not an outcome that she directly sought to bring about by drinking tea.[253]

This example suggests the perils of internalizing the economic account of behavior as the only source of self-understanding. Economic theory asserts that all behavior is directed toward the attainment of personal utility or happiness. Achieving a sense of intimate union in a relationship of mutual care is an important source of satisfaction. Someone who accepted the portrait of herself as a utility-maximizer therefore would place instrumental value on a close personal relationship, regarding it as an intermediate state pursued for the personal happiness that it ultimately would bring. Cultivating a relationship for this reason, however, likely would be self-defeating. The failure to place intrinsic value on the other person and the relationship would prevent a sense of intimate union from occurring, thereby undermining the pursuit of utility. A better way to think of the way in which love produces happiness may be to regard happiness as a byproduct of genuine care for and commitment to another. Only if a person intrinsically values her partner and is genuinely responsive to her needs will she enjoy the satisfaction that flows from intimate union with another.[254] Motive therefore is crucial to the possibility of happiness in this setting. To the extent that a person internalizes the economic theory of behavior as a complete account of human experience, she ironically may proceed on the basis of motives that undercut her ability to maximize utility in a domain of life that most would regard as a source of profound gratification. The plausibility of economic theory rests in part on its common-sense assertion that we can model individual behavior on the assumption that human beings seek happiness. We can accept this assumption, however, while recognizing that directly seeking personal happiness in an economically rational way may be counterproductive in some circumstances. If we are to avoid this pitfall, we need a richer account of human motivation and experience that recognizes the limits of economic analysis.


## Conclusion

Despite claims by some scholars that economic analysis offers the framework for a comprehensive account of marriage and divorce, I have argued that this school of thought in fact is an expression of an external stance toward marriage. As such, it offers an insightful but partial perspective on spousal behavior. Its emphasis on critical reflection on attachments, the importance of individual welfare, consent as a prerequisite for the assumption of obligation, and distributive justice place it squarely within the mainstream of traditional liberal thought and its normative commitments. Situating law and economics within this tradition also illuminates its limitations. It is unable fully to account for all instances in which individuals act for the benefit of others. In particular, it does not capture the expansive sense of self that characterizes an internal stance toward marriage.

This suggests that our choice of an economic perspective on marriage and divorce in a given instance is particularly appropriate when we wish to underscore liberal concerns about the welfare of spouses as discrete individuals. This approach will be less successful, however, when we seek to understand and to reinforce the sense of communal attachment that marriage can involve. Any adequate account of marriage ultimately must speak to both sides of our ambivalence, capturing convictions about spousal identity that remain in irreducible tension.

# PART III

# Trust and Betrayal

PORTIA: Within the bonds of marriage, tell me, Brutus,
        Is it excepted I should know no secrets
        That appertain to you? Am I your self
        But as it were in sort or limitation?
        To keep with you at meals, comfort your bed,
        And talk to you sometimes? Dwell I but in the
            suburbs
        Of your good pleasure? If it be no more,
        Portia is Brutus' harlot, not his wife.

*Julius Caesar*

The secret puts a barrier between men but, at the same time, it creates the tempting challenge to break through it, by gossip or confession and this challenge accompanies its psychology like a constant overtone.

Georg Simmel, *The Sociology of Georg Simmel*

# FIVE

# Spousal Privilege

L et us return for a moment to the story of Arthur and
Irene Seale, the married fugitives whose story I related
in chapter 1. Recall that New Jersey's version of the adverse testimony privilege
prevented Ms. Seale from testifying at all against her husband in a criminal trial.
This privilege is over 500 years old but has been increasingly criticized as an
antiquated relic in recent years. Indeed, the privilege has been modified in federal
court and in several states to permit one spouse to testify against the other in a
criminal trial if she so chooses. New Jersey eventually changed its law to give a
spouse the option to testify in these cases. In doing so, it followed the modern
trend toward reducing the scope of the adverse testimony privilege. In federal
court and in most state courts, the adverse testimony privilege now protects a
defendant from the incriminating testimony of his spouse only if the latter
chooses not to testify. Less than a dozen states continue to retain the traditional
privilege, which protects the defendant from adverse spousal testimony regardless
of whether a spouse is willing to testify. By contrast, in federal and in all state
courts, a defendant generally has protection against disclosure of any confidential
communications that occurred between him and his spouse during marriage, even
if the witness and defendant are no longer married. This privilege appears to
enjoy wide support, and few have seriously questioned its desirability. The adverse
testimony privilege thus appears to be shrinking in significance, even as the communications privilege remains robust.

   In this and the next chapter, I explore this difference in support for the adverse
testimony and communications privileges. Marital intimacy gives rise to a host of
confidences and occasions for self-revelation. Why fully protect only those that
involve what we regard as communication but not other forms of intimate secrets? What is the implicit understanding of marital loyalty, trust, and betrayal
that seems to guide current attitudes? Few issues seem more at the heart of what
it means to be married. I believe that we can gain some insight into these questions by seeing spousal privilege law as an instance in which we must mediate
between internal and external stances toward marriage and the visions of marital
commitment that they involve.

   This analytical framework sheds light on the debate over spousal privilege in
a way that focuses attention on the complex relationship between law and culture. First, it helps explain why the communications privilege is widely accepted

and the adverse testimony privilege is widely criticized, even though the rationale for the former is no more compelling than the justification for the latter. The reason, I will argue in this chapter, is that the communications privilege is more amenable to reconstruction as an obligation that is consistent with the increasingly influential external stance toward marriage. In this sense, my focus is on the effect of culture on the law. Second, appreciating that the issue of spousal testimony raises questions about the meaning of marriage suggests a justification for the adverse testimony privilege that may be more persuasive than those traditionally offered on its behalf. As I suggest in chapter 6, this privilege is an expression of the importance of the internal stance toward marriage. As such, it may help preserve an understanding of marital obligation that has intuitive resonance but that cannot be expressed in the vocabulary of the external stance. In this sense, my focus will be on the possible effects of law on culture.

Even if we believe that the privilege expresses the importance of the internal stance, however, we must still ask whether we want to promote that stance in the context of a criminal trial. I address this issue in the last portion of chapter 6. My discussion suggests that the most serious concern about the adverse testimony privilege is one that is rarely discussed: its disparate gender impact. The plain fact is that in practice the adverse testimony privilege operates largely to prevent wives from testifying against their husbands. We therefore must confront the issue of whether the privilege serves to reinforce a traditional ethic of self-sacrifice for women within marriage. My tentative conclusion is that on balance the adverse testimony privilege is warranted, and that, by recognizing both forms of privilege, spousal privilege law can strike a balance between the different notions of obligation that underlie internal and external stances toward marriage.

## The Law of Spousal Privilege

The adverse testimony privilege is available in federal court and in the majority of state courts. It precludes any testimony by one spouse that may adversely affect the interest of the other[1] in proceedings that are criminal in nature.[2] The privilege is available only during marriage and therefore does not survive the dissolution of the marriage by death,[3] divorce,[4] or, as some courts have held, estrangement.[5] An exception to the privilege consistently has been recognized in both federal and state courts for testimony relating to any alleged wrong committed by one spouse against the other.[6] The logic of this exception has been extended in many instances to encompass any allegation of an offense against a child of either spouse.[7] A more controversial exception to the privilege has been for spousal testimony in cases in which the spouses are accused of being partners in crime. Federal Courts of Appeal for the Seventh and Tenth Circuits have adopted such an exception,[8] while the Second and Third Circuits have rejected it.[9] In federal court, twenty states and the District of Columbia, the witness spouse holds the privilege, and alone may determine whether to invoke the privilege.[10] In twelve states, the consent of both parties is necessary, so that one spouse can prevent the other from testifying, even if the latter is willing to do so.[11] When I refer to "the privilege" in this chapter, I will be discussing this latter traditional version unless I indicate otherwise.

As I discuss below, the marital communications privilege precludes testimony about any confidential communications between spouses during marriage. The adverse testimony privilege therefore serves to exclude testimony about noncommunicative matters—such as the conduct of a spouse; his conversations with others; her demeanor or reaction at a given time; and his habits or personal history that could be used against him.

The first reference to the adverse testimony privilege appears to be in the late sixteenth century, in a civil case recognizing a husband's right to keep his wife from testifying against him.[12] By the end of the seventeenth century, the privilege was well established in both judicial decisions and legal commentary.[13] The doctrinal origins of the privilege, however, are less clear. Some commentators have assumed that the privilege is rooted in the doctrine of spousal disqualification, which prevented husbands and wives from testifying either for or against one another.[14] Other scholars, however, point to the fact that the adverse testimony privilege was accepted almost half a century before any mention of the disqualification rule, and note that different reasons were given for exclusion of favorable and unfavorable spousal testimony.[15] Professor Wigmore offered as an alternative to the disqualification theory the notion that the privilege drew upon the doctrine of petit treason, which prohibited violence against the head of the household by one of its members.[16] Whatever the privilege's pedigree, its "modern" rationale has been regarded as the maintenance of marital harmony. As one court declared, the purpose of the privilege "is to preserve family peace by preventing husband and wife from becoming adversaries in a criminal proceeding."[17]

The second spousal privilege, for confidential marital communications, may be invoked in federal court and in all state courts. In federal court[18] and in many state courts,[19] the privilege is available in both civil and criminal proceedings. While some states allow either spouse to invoke the privilege, the more common rule vests this right in the communicating spouse.[20] Any form of expression or conduct is protected by the privilege,[21] if a spouse seeks thereby to transmit information[22] and intends that the communication not be disclosed.[23] The privilege survives the dissolution of marriage and thus precludes testimony about any confidential communication that occurred while the parties were married.[24] Like the adverse testimony privilege, the communications privilege is not available when one spouse alleges an injury inflicted by the other to herself or, in many cases, her child.[25] Federal courts generally agree that the communications privilege is unavailable with respect to spousal communication that concerns joint criminal activity,[26] a position that several states also have adopted.[27] The communications privilege is of more recent vintage than the privilege against adverse testimony. The need for it did not arise until the mid-nineteenth century, when courts and legislatures began to modify or abolish the spousal disqualification rule.[28]

There has been a striking difference in recent years in the degree of support for each spousal privilege. While the communications privilege is relatively uncontroversial, the adverse testimony privilege has been subjected to increasing criticism.[29] Indeed, the privilege for communications not only enjoys widespread acceptance in the marital context, but calls have arisen for its extension to other emotionally supportive relationships. Most states, for instance, now provide a privilege for communications between a psychotherapist and patient,[30] and between a physician and patient,[31] as well for communications between clergy and penitent.[32] Furthermore, in some states, the privilege has been extended to relationships with marital or family counselors,[33] school employees,[34] psychiatric and nonpsychiatric social workers,[35] and rape crisis or domestic violence counselors.[36] Indeed, one federal court has held that the privilege may be invoked by a scholar in a civil proceeding regarding information obtained during research with a promise of confidentiality.[37] The communications privilege thus seems to be the unquestioned paradigm for protecting the modern confidential relationship.

By contrast, disaffection with the adverse testimony privilege has intensified as the twentieth century has progressed.[38] Professor Wigmore, for instance, denounced the privilege as "the merest anachronism in legal theory. . . ."[39] Concern that testimony might promote marital disharmony was unfounded, he argued, because "[w]hen one thinks of the multifold circumstances of life that contribute to cause marital dissension, the liability to give unfavorable testimony appears as only a casual and minor one. . . ."[40] Wigmore further maintained that the claim that there is a *"natural repugnance* in every fair-minded person to compelling a wife or husband to be the means of the other's condemnation" served to "confuse sentiment with reason."[41] It reflected, he argued, a "general spirit of sportsmanship" inappropriate in light of the fact that "litigation is not a game. . . ."[42]

As early as 1938, the American Bar Association recommended abolishing the adverse testimony privilege entirely but retaining protection for confidential communications.[43] The American Law Institute's Model Code of Evidence did likewise in 1942, rejecting the argument that the adverse testimony privilege served to preserve marital harmony.[44] The Committee on the Federal Rules of Evidence took the opposite view in its Proposed Draft Rules of Evidence in 1969 and 1972.[45] Its proposed Rule 505 abolished the communications privilege but provided that a defendant had a privilege against adverse testimony in criminal proceedings.[46] After publication of the proposed rules, "there was an immediate and virtually unanimous outpouring of criticism of Rule 505 and the Advisory Committee's comments[,]" particularly with respect to spousal privilege.[47] Congress reacted by rejecting the Committee's proposed section on privileges. Federal Rule 501 was adopted in its place, which provides that, unless otherwise specified, privileges are to be "governed by the principles of the common law as they may be interpreted by the courts of the United States in the light of reason and experience."[48] Further indication of hostility to the adverse testimony privilege is the fact that the National Conference of Commissioners on Uniform State Laws originally recommended eliminating it and retaining the communications privilege, calling the former a "sentimental relic."[49] More recently, however, the Conference has amended its Uniform Rules of Evidence to include an adverse testimony privilege that may be invoked by the witness spouse in criminal proceedings.[50] The rule provides for an exception in cases in which there is an allegation either that one spouse has injured the other or that the married couple has jointly engaged in criminal activity.[51]

The Uniform Rules' designation of the witness rather than the defendant as the party who may invoke the privilege is consistent with the Supreme Court's decision in *Trammel v. United States*.[52] In *Trammel*, the Court confronted an instance in which the defendant's wife had agreed to testify against him as part of a plea bargain. The Court overruled its 1958 decision in *Hawkins v. United States*[53] by holding that "the witness-spouse alone has a privilege to refuse to testify adversely. . . ."[54] The Court noted that the existing privilege was far broader than the communications privilege that protected the confidences of husband and wife, clergy and penitent, physician and patient, and attorney and client.[55] The reasons advanced for such distinctive breadth, the Court found, were no longer persuasive. The concept of the unity of spouses had long since dissolved in light of the separate legal identity of married women.[56] As for the desire to foster marital peace, "[w]hen one spouse is willing to testify against the other in a criminal proceeding—whatever the motivation—their relationship is almost certainly in disrepair; there is probably little in the way of marital harmony for the privilege to preserve."[57]

Many critics continue to advocate complete elimination of the adverse testimony privilege,[58] and some states have followed this suggestion.[59] The most common expression of displeasure with the privilege, however, has been to give the potential witness the right to decide whether to invoke it. While twenty-four states permitted one spouse to prevent the other from testifying at the time of the *Trammel* decision,[60] only twelve now do so.[61] Furthermore, at least one federal appeals court has taken *Trammel* to indicate a preference for continuing restriction of the privilege.[62] It seems reasonable to wonder if, unlike the communications privilege, the adverse testimony privilege is on its last legs.

## Spousal Privilege as Cultural Narrative

Upon closer examination, the difference in acceptance of the two privileges seems puzzling. Criticisms of the adverse testimony privilege seem equally applicable to the communications privilege. First, the latter privilege contributes no more to marital harmony than does the former. In cases in which a spouse is willing to testify about marital communications, there is no more marital harmony left to protect than there is when a spouse is willing to testify about other matters. Second, each privilege seems equally to treat the spouses as a single marital unit rather than as individuals with their own interests. Just as with the adverse testimony privilege, a spouse barred from testifying by the communications privilege may be deprived of the possibility of a plea bargain in return for testimony, or prevented from effecting a sharp separation from her partner, or precluded from vindicating her sense of justice by cooperating with law enforcement authorities. The subordination of one spouse's interests to another's is no less pronounced with the communications privilege than with the privilege against adverse testimony.

One might argue that the communications privilege has distinctive value because it encourages confidential communication between spouses.[63] Because communication is a voluntary act, its frequency can be affected by legal assurance of confidentiality. By contrast, other intimate revelations—habits, demeanor, everyday conduct—are more spontaneous and less likely to require legal incentives for their occurrence. One response to this argument, however, is that, if anything, the latter forms of revelation seem more deserving of protection. Through sharing daily life, spouses reveal themselves in a variety of ways that transcend deliberate communication.[64] Coexistence makes possible a form of knowing in which silence can be as significant as speech. Those elements of ourselves that are so deeply ingrained that they escape conscious reflection would seem even more revelatory and deeply private than deliberate communication, and thus should be the core of what is protected from disclosure to persons outside the marriage.[65]

A second response is that it is hard to imagine that most spouses are even aware of the communications privilege, much less that they make conscious decisions about revealing information based on its availability.[66] Marital behavior is more likely to be based on an assessment of the quality of the marriage than the provisions of the law. In this regard, marriage is different from other relationships in which an assurance of confidentiality may be more important in establishing a milieu in which individuals are comfortable providing personal information. We may *need* a privilege for the attorney-client, physician-patient, clergy-penitent, and therapist-patient relationships in order to encourage the open communication necessary for those relationships to serve their purposes. The argument that the marital communications privilege encourages the transmission of confidences between husbands and wives, however, appears just as tenuous and speculative as the proffered justifications for the adverse testimony privilege that have attracted such vigorous criticism.

Indeed, it is puzzling not only that the two spousal privileges tend to differ in the amount of support that they garner, but that we have any spousal privilege at all. If it is unlikely that how people act within marriage is directly affected by privilege rules, it would seem that any marital privilege is unjustified because it sacrifices relevant evidence without providing any discernible benefits. Yet some form of a privilege for spouses has been recognized for over 400 years and is available today in federal court and in every state. It is not hard to imagine that any proposal to eliminate all spousal privileges would be met with hostility comparable to the reaction to the Advisory Committee's proposal two decades ago to eliminate the communications privilege. There seems to be a strong commitment to protection of marital secrets, even though such protection may be unnecessary to encourage spouses to repose their confidence in each other.[67]

This suggests that privilege law may be at least as important for its symbolic as its practical significance. In this respect, it is similar to many other family law issues, which often galvanize the public despite their minimal effect on the average person's daily life.[68] Such issues seem to serve as important reservoirs of meaning in which deeply rooted anxieties, fears, and hopes are played out. As such, they have symbolic significance as cultural dramas in which we confront, express, and reconcile the conflicting demands and aspirations of family life in a particular setting whose meaning has more general resonance.[69] They represent instances in which diverse aspects of daily life are presented in starker relief than ordinary experience often affords. Law symbolizes one way in which these aspects may be conceptually organized and reconciled, thereby contributing to a sense that existence has a meaningful order. From this perspective, in Clifford Geertz's words, adjudication involves "representing concrete situations in a language of specific consequence that is at the same time a language of general coherence. . . ."[70] For this reason, law cannot be judged solely as an effort directly to influence behavior but must also be seen as a form of communication that "point[s] to a presentational element in human behavior in which drama, symbol, and ritual are significant factors in the consciousness of social life."[71] This character of legal rules is not confined to family law[72] but does seem especially significant in that domain.[73]

One setting within family law in which this process occurs is the determination of the legal incidents of marriage. What it means to be married is constructed and reconstructed on an ongoing basis as the exigencies of daily life present legal issues that must be resolved. The law regarding eligibility to marry, the prerequisites for valid marriage, interspousal tort liability, spousal notice or consent requirements for abortion, the requirements for divorce, the division of property, child custody, and other aspects of married life all contribute to a cultural understanding of marriage. Each presents us with specific dilemmas and conflicts that implicate distinctive concerns and values in condensed form, not all of which can be harmoniously reconciled. Each is but one facet of a multidimensional portrait of what it means to be married.

We therefore can gain some insight into the debate over spousal privilege if we see it as an occasion for making a statement about the nature of marriage. One aspect of this narrative concerns the relationship between the married couple and the state: What is the relative priority of duty to the state and responsibility to one's spouse? My primary focus, however, will be on what privilege law says about the relationship between the spouses themselves: What is the relative priority of obligation to oneself and loyalty to one's partner?

I will argue that the communications privilege and the adverse testimony privilege can be seen as symbolic narratives about marriage that answer this question in different ways. More specifically, we can see each privilege as an expression of different stances toward marriage, which emphasize either individual or communal identity. This analytical framework sheds light on why there has been such a difference in support for the communications and adverse testimony privileges. Seeing the adverse testimony privilege as an implicit narrative about marriage suggests a rationale for the privilege that may be more persuasive than those typically offered on its behalf. At the same time, focusing on the symbolic significance of the privilege also raises a concern about its contribution to sustaining traditional gender roles that has not been addressed in the conventional debate. While ultimately we may conclude that cutting back the adverse testimony privilege is a desirable trend, my hope is that we will see this decision as harder and more complicated than the debate typically would have us believe. More broadly, by analyzing the law of spousal privilege in these terms, I seek as well to illustrate the power of Robert Cover's insight that "[o]nce understood in the context of the narratives that give it meaning, law becomes not merely a system of rules to be observed, but a world in which we live."[74]

## Spousal Privilege and the External Stance

### *The Communications Privilege*

As my earlier discussion has indicated, while the adverse testimony privilege has been subject to increasing criticism, there is widespread support for the marital communications privilege. In this section, I will argue that acceptance of the communications privilege reflects the fact that its implicit depiction of marriage, and of the obligations that accompany it, are more easily characterized as consistent with the external stance than is the account offered by the adverse testimony privilege. It is true that certain aspects of the communications privilege can be seen as part of a narrative in which responsibility flows from marital status. Other aspects, however, form the basis of a model that conceptualizes a spouse's inability to testify as a product of voluntary choice. By contrast, it is difficult to fashion a persuasive interpretation of the adverse testimony privilege that is consistent with the external stance. The different reception accorded each privilege thus can be seen as a reflection of the contemporary influence of the external stance toward marriage.

By arguing that the communications privilege is open to this characterization, I am not claiming that spouses self-consciously disclose and receive confidential communications in the way that I will describe. Marriage rarely plays itself out in such stylized fashion. The important point, rather, is that the inability to testify can be plausibly reconstructed as an obligation to which an actor occupying an external stance has consented. My analysis draws upon a long Western liberal tradition in which the theoretical possibility of consent, rather than its actual provision, has been used to justify moral and political duties.[75] The crucial assumption of this tradition is that individuals at least theoretically had the opportunity to engage in a deliberative process, culminating in consent to certain obligations were they so inclined, and that this opportunity makes legitimate the imposition of these obligations upon them. The existence of society and government can also be explained in noncontractual terms, just as the communications privilege can be seen as consistent with the internal stance toward marriage. The legitimacy of each within the dominant paradigm, however, rests on our ability to construct a narrative in which individual will is the source of a constraint on freedom—whether that constraint be the duty to obey the law or the inability to testify against one's spouse.

I want first to suggest the ways in which the communications privilege is open to interpretation as a vindication of the internal stance toward marriage. I then discuss two possible ways to construe the privilege as consistent with the external stance—constructive consent, which I argue is ultimately unpersuasive, and hypothetical ex ante consent, which is more plausible. I then offer an account of the privilege as consistent with the external stance that I believe is the best way of distinguishing the privilege from the one that precludes adverse spousal testimony.

The first sense in which the communications privilege can be construed as an affirmation of the internal stance is that the privilege is applicable only to spouses. Persons who have an intimate relationship cannot decide between themselves that neither partner will testify about confidential communications and then expect to have the law uphold that promise unless they are married.[76] Being a spouse therefore is demarcated as a special identity that is distinct from one's ordinary individual sense of self. This identity is consistent with the internal stance in that it cannot be defined in isolation but is meaningful only in relation to another. The desire to affirm this expansive understanding of marital selfhood leads to the notion that spouses have a particularly strong obligation not to injure one another through actions such as testifying about confidential communications between them.

A second aspect of the communications privilege that reflects an internal orientation is the fact that a spouse is precluded from testifying regardless of her personal wishes. This preclusion is inconsistent with the "reflexivity" of the pure relationship, a process in which the partners continuously monitor the extent to which personal satisfaction from the relationship justifies the demands that it imposes.[77] Someone taking an external stance toward marriage would insist on being free herself to weigh the costs and benefits of testimony, in order to determine whether a sacrifice such as the inability to strike an individual plea bargain is outweighed by the value of preserving her marriage. Preventing a spouse from engaging in such deliberation may force a potential witness to subordinate her interests to those of her spouse. This is precisely the kind of scenario that has prompted feminist criticisms of the internal stance toward marriage. The communications privilege thus requires a putative witness to operate from within the internal stance in the sense that she must assume the overriding value of continuing the marriage. It is her identity as a spouse, rather than as a unique individual, that determines her responsibility on this occasion.

Finally, the communications privilege is consistent with the internal stance in that it can be depicted as an effort to promote trust between spouses. Trust is a crucial prerequisite for the assumption of the internal stance, because the lessened attention to individual interest that characterizes that stance creates the risk of exploitation. The communications privilege ideally fosters trust by constructing a model of marriage in which spouses are assured that they may be open and candid without fear that their confidential communications will be used against them. This preclusion of testimony affirms the importance of building a shared life together in which marriage can be taken as the background for conduct and deemphasizes the need for the constant vigilance of the external stance.

This analysis suggests that the communications privilege has dimensions that are congruent with an internal stance toward marriage. Nonetheless, I believe that it is the privilege's amenability to characterization in terms of the external stance that accounts for the fact that it has tended to gain broader acceptance than has the adverse testimony privilege. Two conventional reconstructions of the privilege in terms of the external stance are plausible to differing degrees, but a third account seems most persuasive.

One way in which we might attempt to cast the communications privilege as the product of an external stance toward marriage is to apply the concept of constructive consent. Marriage, the argument goes, involves a discrete set of benefits and obligations whose terms theoretically are known to anyone contemplating entering it. If an individual decides to marry, she in effect has consented to the special rewards and responsibilities that constitute that relationship. Because one of them is the obligation to refrain from testifying about confidential communications that occur during the marriage, her eventual preclusion from offering testimony merely enforces a term to which she originally agreed. On this view, the communications privilege is simply a form of contract enforcement.

The problem with this account is its assumption that it is legitimate to impose standard obligations on all spouses. An emphasis on the importance of the external stance is designed precisely to challenge this assumption. Certainly nineteenth-century observers of family law, for instance, did not find persuasive the argument that the responsibilities of marriage should be conceptualized in contractual terms simply because the parties had voluntarily chosen to marry. Rather, as the Supreme Court emphasized in *Maynard v. Hill*,[78] "[t]he consent of the parties is of course essential to its existence, but when the contract to marry is executed by the marriage, a relation between the parties is created which they cannot change."[79] By contrast, the notion that persons should be able not only to decide whether to marry, but what the terms of their marriage will be, has become an influential tenet of contemporary life and has been the impetus for a variety of legal changes over the past two decades or so. This perspective insists that individuals need not assume only one valid model of marriage but should be free to repudiate traditional concept of how spouses should organize their lives together. Furthermore, marriage as an instance of the pure relationship requires that the partners be able to make an ongoing assessment of their obligations based on the most current information about spousal performance.[80] A spouse should not be able to point to the marriage itself as the basis for a responsibility not to testify, any more than he should be able to claim that being married for several years should automatically preclude his spouse from seeking a divorce. From the external stance, such a gesture represents an effort to enforce the demands of a relationship that can no longer rationally justify its claims.

A more promising effort to characterize the communications privilege as offering a depiction of marriage based on the external stance might be to argue that it represents the terms of a hypothetical ex ante bargain to which any rational spouse would agree.[81] The argument is that a self-interested prospective spouse would decide that the protection that the privilege provides outweighs the disadvantages of being unable to testify even when she would like to do so. If we can conclude that any rational person in this circumstance is likely to accept the obligation not to testify, we have a theoretical basis for arguing that the communications privilege represents not the imposition of an involuntary duty, but the enforcement of a responsibility that someone reasoning from the external stance would freely accept.

This argument seems a plausible reconstruction of the privilege. The privilege is applicable in all kinds of legal proceedings, so it might be difficult for a prospective spouse who is evaluating costs and benefits to calculate that in all possible instances she is less likely to need protection from disclosure than she is to need the ability to testify. As a result, she might well conclude that the advantage of being able to speak freely within marriage without fear of disclosure probably would outweigh the disadvantage of being unable to gain some benefit in litigation by testifying about her partner's communications.

At the same time, there are some complications that may muddy the waters a bit. First, it is conceivable that persons who are not very risk-averse might decide that they would be willing to take the chance that their spouse would testify against them because they would prefer to retain the prospect of securing the upper hand through testimony if discord in the marriage ever occurred. Indeed, someone who is not very optimistic about the future of the marriage, or who adopts an unqualified external stance that focuses relentlessly on individual costs and benefits, could decide that she will be circumspect in her communications so as to avoid the prospect that anything she says could be used against her. Such persons may be relatively rare, but we cannot necessarily say that they are irrational. The plausibility of this scenario might undermine some of our confidence that the privilege can be firmly justified from an external perspective.

A second complexity is that a prospective spouse may conclude ex ante that she is unlikely to require the protection of the privilege at least in criminal matters, and that she would want to retain the option of testifying if her partner became engaged in criminal activity. The use of the feminine pronoun here is significant, because it is men who commit the overwhelming percentage of crimes in this country.[82] A rational woman contemplating marriage who is aware of this fact might conclude that the potential benefits from the privilege in this context are outweighed by the disadvantage that she would suffer from being unable to testify. While she may not imagine herself as the instigator of a crime, for instance, she might foresee the possibility that her husband might involve her, willingly or unwillingly, as an accomplice. The privilege would then prevent her from striking a plea bargain in which she agreed to testify against her husband in return for lenient treatment. Alternatively, she might contemplate that if her husband engaged in behavior so offensive as to constitute a crime, she might well want to be able to testify against him to ensure that legal punishment would emphatically end the connection between them or in order to express her own moral convictions. Given the gravity of the possibilities presented in a criminal proceeding, a woman might rationally be willing to forsake the protection of the privilege in civil matters as the price for retaining the ability to testify in a criminal setting. As a result, while hypothetical-ex-ante-consent theory provides a plausible interpretation of the communications privilege in terms of the external stance, we might not be able to conclude quite as confidently as we would like that all rational persons would agree to the privilege as a term of marriage.

An additional account of the communications privilege is available, however, which offers a reconstruction of the privilege even more closely congruent with the emphasis on consensual obligation that characterizes the external stance toward marriage. I believe that this interpretation by itself is sufficient to support the argument that the privilege can be persuasively justified as consistent with the external stance. Nonetheless, at a minimum the combination of this theory and hypothetical-ex-ante-consent theory provides a convincing account of the privilege based on the external perspective.

This alternative account begins with the importance of intent in determining whether interaction between spouses will be protected from disclosure under the privilege. An act must both constitute "communication" and be "confidential" in order for the privilege to apply. Whether communication is deemed to have occurred depends on whether one spouse subjectively intended to convey information to the other.[83] For a communication to be privileged, the communicator must reasonably have intended that it be treated as confidential,[84] and reasonably have concluded that his partner would not disclose it.[85] The law generally adopts a rebuttable presumption that spouses intend that communications between them be treated as confidential.[86] If either party acts inconsistently with this imputed intent, however, the privilege does not apply. A spouse may make a communication, for instance, under circumstances that suggest that he reasonably could have expected others to learn of it. Similarly, a recipient may make clear that she is not willing to be held to a duty of confidentiality. The applicability of the privilege thus is triggered not simply by one's status as a spouse but by voluntary acts taken subsequent to marriage. A person who marries may be *eligible* for the protection afforded by the privilege. He must, however, take specific steps to gain that protection. First, he must choose whether to communicate with his spouse at all. Next, he must choose whether to do so in a way that signals an expectation of confidentiality. In turn, his partner must give him reason to believe that his expectation will be honored. If either party fails to make any of these choices, then no communication will be deemed to have occurred that warrants protection by the privilege. Furthermore, this meeting of the minds must occur with respect to each instance of communication, because it is discrete exchanges of information, rather than marital communication in general, that is protected by the privilege.[87] In this way, the voluntary conduct of the spouses themselves determines the scope of what will be protected from disclosure by the privilege.

Seen in this way, the privilege accommodates the desire for reflexivity in the modern pure relationship. When is a spouse likely to make a disclosure that he wishes to be treated as confidential? It is reasonable to assume that he will do so if his partner has indicated, either explicitly or implicitly, that she is likely to be receptive to a communication and can be trusted not to reveal it. In this sense, a communicator's decision whether to transmit a confidential communication depends on his current assessment of the value of the marriage. If he is not confident about his marriage, he may withhold his revelation or perhaps divulge it to a close friend. If, however, he believes that his wife is an important source of emotional and psychological support, he is likely to be willing to confide in her. Similarly, the recipient's willingness to accept the communication and to treat it as confidential depends on her assessment of the marriage at that moment. If she does not feel that her husband is responsive to her needs, she may not want to bear the burden of engaging him in communication at all. If she does listen, she may still wish to signal that the marriage is not sufficiently satisfying for her to make a promise of nondisclosure. If she fails to exercise this option to decline the duty of confidentiality, we may assume that she has willingly accepted it. She has done so because her spouse provides her with enough benefits that she is willing to pay the cost of a restraint on her freedom—the inability to disclose the communication even in circumstances in which disclosure might serve her own interests.

Each communication therefore can be depicted as a discrete exchange between the parties, a characterization that mirrors exchange theory's emphasis on "disclosure reciprocity" in intimate relationships. The communicator determines whether the marriage is rewarding enough that he would be better off making a confidential disclosure to his spouse instead of keeping the information to himself or revealing it to others. The recipient decides whether the marriage is fulfilling enough that she should accept the disclosure and treat it as confidential. Since the parties theoretically are free not to engage in such exchange if their assessments of the marriage are not comparable, the fact that a communication that warrants protection does occur indicates that both partners have voluntarily concluded that they are better off as a result of it.

Reconstructed in this way, the communications privilege is consistent with an individual's capacity for critical reflection on her attachments and the responsibilities that go with them. Partners in the pure relationship must earn each other's commitment on an ongoing basis in order to be able to make claims on each other. The past in itself—whether the agreement to marry or the previous willingness to make or accept other confidential communications—cannot serve as the source of obligation. Rather, each episode theoretically is the occasion for the exercise of individual freedom to accept or decline responsibility. Only an obligation to refrain from testifying that can be traced back to a moment of consent will be honored. The principle that a spouse is unable to testify if she implicitly has agreed not to is based on the universal capacity to make and fulfill voluntary promises, and therefore is likely to be acceptable to any reflective person occupying the external stance. In this sense, the communications privilege is consistent with liberalism's insistence on consent as the basis of obligation. It is just to impose a duty not to testify on spouses, because any rational individual abstracted from her role as spouse would agree that promises must be honored.

From this perspective, the versions of trust and loyalty that the communications privilege promotes are the type more closely associated with the external than the internal stance. The trust that the privilege declares is appropriate is not assurance that all the intimacies of marriage will be protected from disclosure. Rather, it is that certain discrete communications will not be revealed. A spouse theoretically earns the right to such trust on a case-by-case basis, by providing benefits to his partner that are sufficient to induce her to accept the responsibility of preserving each particular confidence. Similarly, the loyalty that one must exhibit represents fidelity not to the marriage itself, but acceptance of the duties that constitute the fulfillment of a specific promise. Neither trust nor loyalty can be taken for granted as the background for conduct in the future but must be achieved anew as that future unfolds. The partners cannot automatically rely on past commitment but must continuously renegotiate the terms of their contract as they receive new information about each other. Such an account reflects Annette Baier's observation that contractarian theory "treats lifelong mutual trust as iterated mutual delayed deliveries."[88]

The fact that it is *communication* that is singled out for protection, rather than the entirety of marital interaction, further underscores the plausibility of a reconstruction of the privilege in terms of the external stance. Communication plays a crucial role in promoting the reflexivity that characterizes the "pure relationship." It serves as an early warning system, indicating those areas in which the partners need self consciously to seek to improve the relationship. In addition, communication is crucial if marriage is to provide personal satisfaction for each spouse. Each person must be willing to reveal her most intimate fears, hopes, and desires so that her partner can be responsive to them. The privilege affirms the importance of such disclosure by declaring that what a spouse has said in confidence to her partner will remain between them, even if the marriage itself ultimately does not last. Such protection furthers liberal ends by enhancing the capacity of individuals to revise their projects and commitments.

As I have suggested, it is the theoretical opportunity for such deliberation regarding communication, rather than its frequent actual occurrence, that is crucial in justifying the privilege as a freely assumed obligation. It is true that much of the communication that takes place within marriage is more a product of the unself-conscious flow of everyday life than of explicit decisions about what will be revealed and what will not. Nonetheless, it is hardly unknown for spouses to have secrets from one another, which suggests that in each marriage there are some occasions on which each partner will engage in deliberation about what to disclose to the other.[89] Nor is it uncommon for a spouse to decide that she does not want the burden of listening to or keeping a particular confidence of her partner and to signal this in various ways. These common-sense observations lend plausibility to the argument that the communications privilege is acceptable from the external stance, because they suggest that it is always theoretically possible for any potential communication to be subject to this deliberative process.

In sum, the fact that we can plausibly conceptualize the communications privilege as consistent with the external stance is an important reason for widespread acceptance of that privilege. Indeed, the communications privilege seems to be the model for protecting any relationship of trust, because confidential communication can be abstracted as the element that is common to all such relationships. Protection of intimate disclosures affirms the value of the relationship, while nonetheless respecting the participants as individuals by imposing on them only those obligations of confidentiality that can be characterized as voluntarily assumed. By contrast, as I discuss in the next section, the relative disfavor into which the adverse testimony privilege has fallen reflects the fact that the implicit model of marriage on which it rests is at odds with the external stance.

## The Adverse Testimony Privilege

The adverse testimony privilege is inconsistent with the external stance in that marriage per se, rather than the voluntary conduct of spouses, is what triggers the protection of the privilege. The argument that a spouse constructively consents to be bound by this privilege by entering into marriage is no more persuasive in this context than it is with respect to the communications privilege. Persons adopting the external stance resist the claim that marriage automatically involves a standard package of benefits and obligations and insist instead on the right to arrange their marriages on terms that are most beneficial to them. Nor is an argument based on hypothetical ex ante consent as plausible as it is with regard to the communications privilege. The adverse testimony privilege is applicable only in criminal or quasi-criminal proceedings. A rational woman will be aware that it is far more likely that her husband will be involved in criminal activity than will she, and therefore that she probably would be the spouse whom the privilege prevents from testifying. She may well wish to preserve the opportunity to testify in return for lenient treatment if her husband has involved her as an accomplice, or because she could imagine that she might want to wash her hands of a husband who would engage in that kind of conduct. Unlike someone deliberating about whether to accept being bound ex ante by the communications privilege, she will not have to trade off the protection that she would receive in noncriminal matters as the cost of preserving her option to testify in criminal proceedings. A reconstruction of the adverse testimony privilege on the basis of hypothetical consent thus ultimately appears problematic.

By protecting all interaction within marriage whose disclosure might be adverse to a spouse, rather than simply confidential communication, the privilege imposes an obligation that cannot readily be conceptualized as voluntary. Unlike communication, it is difficult to characterize the transmission of noncommunicative information as the object of discrete exchanges between spouses. Spouses would find it difficult, if not impossible, to calculate the desirability of revealing every aspect of their daily lives in the way that is at least theoretically possible with respect to communication. Furthermore, spouses receive what the privilege treats as confidential information about each other without any opportunity to indicate their willingness to do so. As a result, they are deprived of the opportunity to decide whether the cost of nondisclosure of such matters is warranted by the benefits that they receive from the marriage. In this sense, the privilege is inconsistent with the reflexivity that ideally characterizes the pure relationship, because partners are deprived of the opportunity to use the most current information about the marriage as the basis for their assumption of obligation.

A spouse who is genuinely willing to testify against another has indicated that the marriage is providing insufficient current benefits to justify her continued loyalty to it. In exchange theory terms, she is running a deficit. The external perspective acknowledges that she should not be free to disclose confidential communications because the obligation to refrain from testimony in that instance can be conceptualized as voluntarily assumed. The inability to testify regarding other matters, however, imposes a duty on her whose desirability she previously has not had an opportunity to evaluate. This means that the putative witness incurs an involuntary cost and the defendant receives an unearned benefit simply because they are married to each other.

The adverse testimony privilege therefore treats the putative witness not on the basis of her universal identity as a reasoning individual but in terms of her particular identity as a spouse in a specific marriage. Put differently, it defines her not as an agent who is free to revise the terms of her interaction with others, but as the occupant of a status, to whom certain duties are ascribed regardless of her wishes. On this view, the privilege fails to honor the individual's capacity to reflect critically on her attachments and to accept only the claims of those that she herself regards as rationally justified. It forces her to play the role of loyal spouse, despite the fact that she may have concluded that her individual interest counsels otherwise. In these ways, the adverse testimony privilege is in tension with the more individualistic aspects of liberalism. Dissatisfaction with the imposition of burdens solely on the basis of one's social role was precisely the historical impetus for liberal emphasis on the individual as an autonomous chooser.

The adverse testimony privilege also is inconsistent with the claim that, aside from the obligation to keep one's promises, the past has moral force only insofar as the individual currently is willing to grant it such influence. The privilege precludes one spouse from testifying against another because of the claims that arise from a shared history. Deliberation from the external stance, however, focuses on the future. A spouse may rationally conclude that she should continue to acknowledge the claims of marriage because of the benefits that it promises. She also, however, must retain the freedom to disavow those claims and start life anew regardless of the pull of her history. The Supreme Court's opinion in *Trammel v. United States*[90] reflects this emphasis on the future. The Court characterized the adverse testimony privilege as an effort to preserve marital harmony, but concluded that any marriage in which one spouse is willing to testify against the other likely has little harmony left to preserve.[91] On this view, whatever shared experience has occurred up to the time of potential testimony exerts no moral force per se. Rather, the relevant question is whether the cost of the privilege is worth the benefits that it will bring in the future. *Trammel* says that it is up to the individual to make this decision. If she wishes, she may treat the marriage as having outlived its usefulness; if she desires, she is free to regard it as a source of future rewards sufficient to make testimony unwise. In this sense, *Trammel* affirms the reflexivity of marriage as a pure relationship. The protagonist of its story occupies the external stance, poised in a moment of calculation in which her attachments will be honored only to the extent that they offer reasons that can satisfy her.

Those who subscribe to the priority of the external stance nonetheless may believe that even *Trammel* does not go far enough, and that a witness spouse should not be able to refuse to testify about noncommunicative matters. The premise of this argument is that the benefits and burdens associated with any relationship should flow not from its legal status per se but from the voluntary actions of the parties. Critics may contend that marriage is only one of several forms of confidential relationship and therefore does not warrant uniquely broad protection. A person must not grant categorical allegiance to any association but should retain the opportunity on an ongoing basis to weigh the demands of confidentiality in each instance. No social attachment should have normative significance per se, because that would exalt convention over reason.[92] As I have suggested, the communications privilege can be construed as consistent with these ideas, but the adverse testimony privilege cannot.

An individual viewing marriage from the external stance therefore would likely regard the adverse testimony privilege as an antiquated relic inconsistent with the character of modern marriage. At a minimum, a spouse herself should be the one to decide whether to testify against her partner, because only she can authentically decide whether the value of the marriage is worth the possible sacrifice of her own individual interests. Furthermore, strict application of the external perspective counsels that even an adverse testimony privilege that may be voluntarily invoked by a witness is inadvisable. This is because mere involvement in a relationship should not itself be the source of distinctive protection and obligation. Attention to the increasing influence of the external stance toward marriage thus offers some insight into the growing chorus of dissatisfaction with the adverse testimony privilege.

In the next chapter, I will argue that the incompatibility of the adverse testimony privilege with the premises of the external stance in fact suggests a rationale for the privilege more persuasive than those traditionally offered on its behalf. The privilege precludes a spouse from adopting the external stance under circumstances in which self-interest may create great temptation for one spouse to betray the other. In this way, the privilege makes a statement about marriage that emphasizes the importance of the internal stance. Appreciating the privilege as a symbolic narrative about marriage, I argue, offers novel insight into both the contribution that it may make and the danger that it may pose with respect to our understanding of marriage.

# Adverse Testimony and the Internal Stance

In the first half of this chapter, I will describe the adverse testimony privilege as a legal rule that uses the setting of the criminal trial to construct a narrative about marriage that ideally encourages adoption of the internal stance. My emphasis will be on the terms of this story and its potential to foster such an orientation. This story is not necessarily the only one that we might infer from the privilege. I believe, however, that it captures an important aspect of the protection that the privilege provides and the duty that it imposes. In the next part of the chapter, I will examine the ways in which the privilege might serve to communicate the narrative I have described. How likely is it that anyone will actually "read" this story? My discussion here is more tentative, given the difficulty of describing how a specific legal provision might serve as an agent of socialization. I raise the possibility that the primary significance of the privilege may be that it prevents the transmission of a message that could undermine the influence of an internal stance toward marriage.

Even if there is a colorable argument that the privilege expresses the importance of the internal stance, however, the question remains whether we should affirm this stance in the setting of a criminal trial. I turn to this issue in the last part of this chapter. I examine the costs to the putative witness and to the state but conclude that the most serious concern may be the symbolic potential of the privilege to perpetuate an ethic of self-sacrifice for women within marriage. I conclude that on balance, however, the privilege is worth preserving. Even for those who disagree with this conclusion, my hope is that my analysis reveals that assessing the privilege is a more complex undertaking than the conventional debate suggests.

## Narratives of Marriage

### Loyalty and Trust

One theme in the account of marriage that is constructed by the adverse testimony privilege emphasizes the importance of loyalty and trust. Recall that the commitment that characterizes the internal stance is one that makes the self vulnerable.[1] Operating from within the internal perspective means suspending the capacity to differentiate sharply between the distinct individual interests of oneself and one's spouse. As the feminist critique of traditional female socialization instructs us, such an orientation can leave a person open to exploitation and abuse by her partner. Because the internal stance necessarily reflects a moment of unwillingness to monitor individual outcomes, such risk is inherent in this moment of marriage.

One who is willing to accept this risk for the sake of the distinctive good that the internal stance provides therefore must be able to trust her partner not to take advantage of her. She must be able, in other words, to assume that her spouse will be loyal. Trust and loyalty are mirror images of one another in that each reflects a willingness to rely on shared history, rather than calculation of individual advantage, as the basis for conduct. As Annette Baier puts it, "[t]rust is an alternative to vigilance and . . . to recurrent recalculations of costs and benefits."[2] Similarly, R.E. Ewin suggests that "[i]f I stick with the firm, or the football club, or whatever, only when reason makes it clear that that is the thing to do, then I am a fairly calculating person and not particularly loyal. The loyal person sticks in there in the bad times as well."[3] Trust and loyalty reflect acknowledgment that individual fates have become intertwined to some degree as a result of the past, a fact that places constraints on the range of behavior that is deemed acceptable.

As crucial as trust and loyalty are, they may be difficult to sustain in the modern world. To the extent that marriage comes to approximate the "pure relationship," it is characterized by the reflexivity of spouses. Each partner tends to monitor with increasing frequency the extent to which the marriage provides personal satisfaction and to base commitment on the relationship's continuing ability to do so. Neither spouse can assume that for any significant length of time one's partner will take the marriage for granted as the background for his or her activities. As a result, a spouse in self-defense constantly must be ready to take the external stance in order to minimize the chance of being disadvantaged by her partner. This creates the danger that spouses may not be able to sustain the internal stance sufficiently to create a sense of shared commitment. The kind of trust that emerges from reflexivity is circumscribed, tentative, and fragile, perpetually subject to disruption based on the use of new information that allows each spouse to reassess the desirability of continued involvement.

An understanding of marriage in which loyalty must be earned at every moment therefore likely will inhibit adoption of the internal stance. Willingness to take that stance requires reliance on a narrative in which marriage to some degree is a safe haven, where protection from betrayal does not depend on the relentless process of reflexivity. The law can't construct this story, however, simply by prohibiting and punishing all instances of marital betrayal. In practical terms, of course, it would be virtually impossible to enforce effectively such a legal regime. More important, the fact that the behavior that resulted would be seen as coerced rather than freely chosen would destroy much of its value. Ideally, we want spouses to *internalize* the ideal of loyalty, so that they refrain from betrayal because they want to, not because they have to. This will occur only if there are some settings in which their behavior is not subject to legal compulsion. Discretion is crucial to a sense of moral responsibility; "[t]he moral growth that comes from being held accountable for one's actions . . . derives at least in part from the perception that one's actions are voluntary."[4] Spouses come to internalize the ideal of loyalty by choosing to be loyal when they could act otherwise. Similarly, trust emerges only when betrayal is a possibility. If we know that someone cannot act to harm us, there is no need to trust her.[5] In this sense, legal duty substitutes for loyalty and obviates the need for trust.[6] Any effort to inculcate loyalty simply by requiring it in all situations therefore would be self-defeating.

At the same time, the law needs to require it in *some* instances, or there may be no ideal to internalize. Law can shape perceptions of morality in powerful ways.[7] Indeed, some have suggested that there is a particularly pronounced tendency in American culture to conflate the two.[8] If there were no legal protection from spousal betrayal in any form, the message might well be that spouses are free to act in whatever fashion their individual interests might dictate. In seeking to construct a story of marriage in which loyalty plays a central role, the law therefore must attempt to strike a balance between coercion and freedom. As Katharine Bartlett has said with respect to legal regulation of parenthood, "[s]omehow the law must contribute to the creation of high expectations for parents," while at the same time "leaving sufficient leeway so that parents are free to become responsible in the true sense."[9] So, too, with respect to the ideal of loyalty in marriage. We must decide how to communicate the ideal effectively without robbing it of value.

A criminal trial offers a particularly significant occasion for expressing in highly condensed form an ideal of spousal loyalty. As Thurman Arnold noted, the criminal trial has powerful significance as "the way in which society is trained in right ways of thought and action, not by compulsion, but by parables which it interprets and follows voluntarily."[10] A criminal trial that also raises the issue of what one spouse owes another has even more significance. The consequences of spousal betrayal in this setting are grave: a person may lose life or liberty as a result of his partner's testimony. The prospective witness may have a particularly strong interest in testifying, because doing so may gain her lenient treatment by the prosecution. For this reason, the temptation for betrayal may be especially acute. Finally, the state has an important interest in seeing that justice is done through the detection and punishment of criminal activity. The stakes are high; the interests are in sharp relief. Multiple and conflicting dimensions of selfhood—individual, spouse, citizen—call out for reconciliation. What the law does in this setting cannot help but send a powerful message about the relative importance of spousal loyalty. Completely abolishing the adverse testimony privilege—that is, compelling a spouse to testify about noncommunicative matters—conveys the idea that marriage alone cannot serve as the basis for protection from betrayal. Rather, marriage is a safe haven only insofar as the parties have engaged in activity that can be conceptualized as a deliberate request for and acceptance of the duty of confidentiality. As I have suggested, this is an account of marriage in which loyalty is contingent on the process of reflexivity.

Giving one spouse the choice whether to testify against the other at a criminal trial also provides a narrative of marriage that can undermine a norm of loyalty. At a minimum, the very act of providing a choice suggests that the state is agnostic about what a spouse chooses to do in these circumstances. It signals that even when the consequences of betrayal are momentous, a spouse need not be loyal if a current assessment of her individual interest suggests that testimony is advantageous. License to engage in this kind of calculation encourages a spouse to distance herself from the marriage by taking the external stance, explicitly distinguishing between her own interest and that of her spouse. Indeed, when a plea bargain is involved, she likely will see those interests as antagonistic. Not all who receive this invitation to adopt the external stance will accept it. Simply being granted a choice, however, may well subtly channel deliberation into this path. Furthermore, some who adopt the external stance may choose not to testify. That decision nonetheless will be based on an assessment of the likely future value of the marriage to the decisionmaker, rather than loyalty to a shared history in which two lives have become interwoven. Permitting a person to determine whether loyalty is advisable, even when the consequences of disloyalty are so high, suggests that spousal loyalty is primarily an individual, rather than a social, concern.

Furthermore, as a practical matter the state is more antagonistic than agnostic toward loyalty in this setting. Prosecutors will at least encourage, if not more vigorously seek to induce, one spouse to incriminate the other if they believe that the putative witness has relevant evidence.[11] When a spouse chooses to testify, betrayal occurs explicitly at the behest of the state. The witness is prompted by the government to use the intimacies of married life as the vehicle for criminal conviction of her spouse. Recognition of human frailty may lead us to refrain from relentlessly seeking to identify and punish all those who inflict injury by their disloyalty. Resigned acceptance of inevitable betrayal is different, however, from active official promotion of it.

By contrast, the adverse testimony privilege gives a spouse no choice about whether to testify in circumstances in which, unlike the communications privilege, the inability to make such a choice cannot be readily conceptualized as having been voluntarily accepted. The privilege thus expresses a vision in which marriage itself, not merely certain discrete acts within it, is the basis for protection against betrayal. The importance of this vision is underscored by the state's willingness to deprive itself of information that otherwise would assist it in the prosecution of justice. By depicting marriage in this way, the privilege constructs a narrative of marriage that ideally prompts spouses to "internalize high ideals for responsibility and voluntarily proceed to act upon them"[12] in other settings in which the law cannot control their conduct. To the extent that this occurs, trust within marriage can emerge because it is protected from the potentially corrosive effects of incessant reflexivity. By conveying a message about what loyalty requires in the setting of a criminal trial, the privilege is part of a "process of community norm-building"[13] about what it means to be married.

Jon Elster underscores the way in which adherence to a norm involves an attitude that differs from the rational calculation that characterizes reflexivity. Norms, suggests Elster, seem to preclude the kind of cost-benefit analysis that is characteristic of actors in conducting rational choice analysis. "Whereas rationality tells people, 'If you want y, do x,' many social norms simply say, 'Do x.' "[14] He illustrates this by the use of an example. Suppose, he says, that a homeowner is willing to pay his neighbor's son ten dollars but no more for the half hour required to mow his lawn. By rejecting the son's offer to mow for eleven dollars and mowing the lawn himself, he has indicated that a half hour of his time is worth no more than eleven dollars. Suppose now that another neighbor offers the homeowner twenty dollars to mow the neighbor's lawn. As Elster says, "It is easy to imagine that he would refuse, probably with some indignation."[15] Yet this response seems irrational. His refusal implies that his time is worth at least twenty dollars. This is inconsistent, however, with his earlier valuation of it at no more than eleven dollars.

After surveying various rational-choice explanations that don't seem fully to capture what is going on here, Elster suggests that a norm against mowing one's neighbors's lawn for money is part of the explanation. As he says, the man in his example "doesn't think of himself as the kind of person who mows other people's lawns for money. It *isn't done*, to use a revealing phrase that often accompanies social norms."[16] Elster suggests that the norm may implicitly reflect concern that a consequence of allowing what otherwise would be individually rational behavior "could be the loss of the spontaneous mutual-help behavior that is a main benefit of living in a community. By preventing deals, the norm preserves the community."[17]

Refraining from certain conduct because "it isn't done" is different from refraining because one has consciously chosen to do so. In the first instance, a particular course of action never becomes a viable option, while in the second it does. Socialization is never completely effective; some persons may resent the norm in question and others may even deliberately flout it. Nonetheless, a community in which most persons have internalized a norm against requesting or offering money for performing domestic tasks for neighbors will be different in character from one in which there is no such norm—even if individuals in the latter community rarely decide that it is advantageous to engage in such transactions. Similarly, our understanding of marriage will be different under a legal regime that expresses a norm against testifying against one's spouse than it will be under one in which such behavior is potentially an option—even if many spouses decide not to testify. Furthermore, Elster's comment that the person in his example doesn't regard himself as "the kind of person" who would accept his neighbor's offer underscores the way in which norms contribute to a distinct sense of self. Internalizing a norm of spousal loyalty makes commitment to one's partner a constituent of personal identity, so that disloyalty becomes a form of self-betrayal.

Elster also emphasizes the way in which behavior guided by a norm reflects acknowledgment of the claims of the past. He notes, "Rational actors follow the principle of letting bygones be bygones, cutting one's losses and ignoring sunk costs. In the operation of social norms, by contrast, the past plays an essential role."[18] Loyalty imposes obligations based on a conception of the person as a "historical self"[19] who makes "identity-conferring commitments"[20] that cannot easily be undone without damage both to oneself and to others. The constraint exerted by the past in this model of identity is at odds with the view from the external stance, which insists that all attachments are contingent and continually subject to rational assessment. As should be apparent, this set of concerns has affinities with communitarianism and an ethic of care. The relevant actor is the spouse situated within marriage, rather than the individual abstracted from it. The relevant obligation is rooted in the interdependence that arises between intimate partners, rather than in an act of consent. The substance of that obligation is to respond with care to need and vulnerability, rather than to abide by one's promises. The transgression that animates our concern is an act of betrayal, rather than a breach of contract. In these ways, the adverse testimony privilege underscores the embedded quality of both identity and responsibility.

How might the privilege's symbolic message foster adoption of the internal stance? Literally speaking, the privilege promotes neither loyalty nor trust with respect to criminal testimony but in fact precludes their emergence. This is because motive is crucial to the meaning of action in intimate relationships. We want people to act for our welfare not because they are forced to do so, but because they willingly make that choice.[21] In that sense, as I have suggested, loyalty and trust depend on the possibility of betrayal. A spouse who has the option to testify but chooses not to, despite personal disadvantage, powerfully affirms her loyalty. A spouse who is the beneficiary of such a decision will feel a particularly strong sense of trust. By prohibiting testimony, the privilege prevents this process from occurring. It sacrifices genuine loyalty in this setting in order to place the law's moral force behind an ideal that we hope will influence spouses when the law does *not* purport to control their conduct.

How can forced "loyalty" beget voluntary loyalty and the trust that accompanies it? This is difficult to specify with precision but at least two possibilities seem plausible. First, by expressing the idea that marriage involves certain expectations incumbent upon all spouses, the privilege can contribute to the internalization of a "role morality"[22] that may prompt a spouse to be loyal on occasions when disloyalty is an option. Social roles offer opportunities to seek personal fulfillment by identifying with the impersonal demands that devolve upon occupants of those roles.[23] Indeed, the perception that such demands originate in a source of value beyond the self, rather than solely in personal choice, is crucial to their potential to endow an individual life with meaning.[24] We have a sense of what it means, for instance, to be a "true" friend or a "true" spouse, so that not just any behavior that a person wishes to declare as consistent with friendship or marriage will be regarded as such.[25] The capacity of a social role to serve as a source of personal meaning thus depends in important ways on an individual's sense that he or she is able to live up to the special ideals that are associated with this role.

By prohibiting the incrimination of one's partner, the adverse testimony privilege expresses the importance of loyalty as a regulative ideal of the spousal role. Someone who wants to regard herself as a good spouse ideally will react with awareness of this obligation by seeking to act consistently with its underlying ideal of loyalty in instances in which the law does not constrain her behavior. In this way, sending the message that loyalty is required in one setting may induce loyal behavior in other circumstances. Such behavior is likely to elicit trust from one's partner, which in turn will strengthen a sense of commitment to the marriage that will make loyalty more probable on other occasions. By promoting a sense of "obedience to the unenforceable,"[26] the privilege may foster the kind of voluntary conduct that lies at the core of trust and loyalty.

Second, by reducing the risks involved with intimate self-revelation, the privilege may provide something of a "safety net" that prompts the kind of openness that can generate spontaneous loyalty and trust within marriage. Liberal theorists, for instance, make a similar argument when they emphasize the importance in intimate relationships of basic protections that do not depend on the goodwill of others. As Jeremy Waldron argues, "[h]aving something to fall back on if an attachment fails may be a *condition* of being able to identify intensely with one's attachments, rather than something which derogates from that intensity."[27] With respect to the possibility of adverse testimony, it may be most accurate to say that the privilege fosters trust in the future rather than trust in one's spouse.[28] This sense of security, however, may induce willingness to take those risks that furnish opportunities for the emergence of trust in one's spouse as well. Such opportunities will still arise with some frequency, because the adverse testimony privilege eliminates only one of the many risks that exist within a marriage. Spouses remain vulnerable to each other in numerous ways that the law can neither eliminate nor fully predict. Situations will recur in which partners must make choices that can either strengthen or undermine their marriage. In such instances, one party's trust in the future may prompt an expression of trust in one's partner, which in turn may elicit trust and a willingness to act loyally. By promoting confidence in the future, the privilege may lay the foundation for the kind of trust that emerges only when betrayal is an option that is not chosen.

This scenario seems plausible in light of suggestions that trust in some cases may be a product of, rather than the predicate for, cooperation.[29] Strangers, for instance, are far less inclined initially to trust one another than are spouses. They may be encouraged to cooperate in some circumstances, however, if they are given assurance of at least some protection against harm from the other.[30] In this way, legally imposed constraints on each party's conduct can serve as a substitute for the trust that otherwise would be necessary to motivate each party to take the first cooperative step. The cooperation that ensues then itself tends to foster trust, as the parties come to rely on one another in their common endeavor.[31] As Robert Axelrod says of one instance of cooperation that emerged in the absence of trust, "[t]he cooperative exchanges of mutual restraint actually changed the nature of the interaction. They tended to make the two sides care about each other's welfare."[32] Furthermore, trust tends to be mutually reinforcing, so that each instance of trust on the part of one person elicits trust on the part of the other.[33] Diego Gambetta describes the dynamics of this process: "When we say to someone: 'I trust you', we express both a belief in and an encouragement to commitment by the trust we place in the relationship. The concession of trust, that is, can generate the very behaviour which might logically seem to be its precondition."[34] This analysis suggests that, by obviating the need for trust with respect to betrayal through testimony, the adverse testimony privilege may encourage spouses to take the kinds of risks in other settings that can give rise to trust when there *is* the possibility of betrayal.[35]

One may question, however, how effective the privilege is in expressing the norm of spousal loyalty if a spouse is free to cooperate with the prosecution in other ways.[36] For instance, Irene Seale, the woman whose story begins this article, was barred from testifying against her husband in state court. She nevertheless led police to the grave site of Sidney Reso, the Exxon company executive whom the couple had abducted, and provided a detailed account of her and her husband's actions in perpetrating their crime. Such cooperation assisted prosecutors in obtaining a guilty plea against Arthur Seale and led to a relatively lenient sentence for her as part of a plea bargain. The fact that a spouse is free to offer such assistance arguably undermines the purported function of the adverse testimony privilege. One might claim that this effect of spousal cooperation makes the exclusion of testimony through the privilege an unjustifiable constraint on the receipt of relevant evidence in criminal proceedings.

One response to this argument is to accept its force, but to argue that it implies that a spouse should not be able to incriminate her partner through nontestimonial cooperation. Appreciation of the privilege as an effort to use the setting of a criminal trial to express the importance of an internal stance toward marriage prompts recognition that the norm of spousal loyalty can be violated both inside and outside the courtroom. If law enforcement authorities cannot enlist one spouse against the other on the public stage of the witness stand, they should not be able to abet disloyalty behind the closed doors of the police station. The concern in each case is identical: that the state seeks to pursue its objective by urging one spouse to draw on the intimate revelations of married life to betray the other.

Even if nontestimonial cooperation is permitted, however, the adverse testimony privilege still can be justified on the ground that a trial represents a public event that has especially powerful cultural significance. "It is in symbols, rituals, and ceremonies that societies reflexively perceive themselves[,]"[37] and legal trials in modern American culture represent a powerful ritual in which social meaning is conveyed in highly condensed form. The language in these proceedings is stylized and distinctive, and participants perform specific roles as part of the enactment of a larger drama in which cultural values are expressed and reinforced.[38] For this reason, permitting one spouse to testify against the other sends a particularly potent signal about the tractability of spousal loyalty, even when that same spouse may have cooperated with prosecutors outside the courtroom. Furthermore, participation in ritual can itself be transformative for those directly involved in it. A spouse who takes the stand in public to incriminate her partner may well be more likely to feel that she has taken a definitive step to end the marriage than if she had provided information to the police in a less formal setting. Testimony places her more starkly in the external stance, publicly signaling that she is someone who has concluded that the individual interests served by incrimination outweigh her attachment to the marriage. For these reasons, permitting out of court cooperation while prohibiting testimony may reflect a form of "acoustic separation."[39] We accommodate our ambivalence about spousal loyalty by officially preventing incrimination in formal public settings, even as we condone it in less visible surroundings.

Finally, to the extent that out-of-court cooperation undermines to some degree the objective served by the privilege, this does not distinguish the adverse testimony privilege from the communications privilege. A spouse generally is free to provide law enforcement authorities with information about marital communications that may greatly assist their investigation of a defendant.[40] The ostensible end of promoting intimate revelation between spouses would seem just as compromised in this instance as is the purpose of the adverse testimony privilege by nontestimonial assistance. One who is concerned about the effect of such cooperation therefore cannot point to it as a reason for condemning the adverse testimony privilege without calling the communications privilege into question as well.

In sum, the adverse testimony privilege can be seen as a way in which the law deploys the dramatic potential inherent in the criminal trial to construct a narrative of marriage in which loyalty is crucial. As such, it may provide a space for emergence of the trust that is necessary for a spouse to be willing to take an internal stance toward marriage.

## Responsibility and Identity

A second theme in the story of marriage that is told by the adverse testimony privilege is that it is important for spouses to see their identities as constituted to some degree by their relationship to each other. Such a focus is consistent with the communitarian emphasis on the importance of strengthening shared commitments as elements of a valuable human life. How does the privilege articulate this theme? Answering this question requires appreciation of Meir Dan-Cohen's suggestion that the legal assignment of responsibility can prompt an individual to construct the boundaries of the self in certain ways.[41] While Dan-Cohen's analysis focuses primarily on criminal and tort law, we can also apply it in a slightly different way to spousal privilege doctrine.

Dan-Cohen first observes that the predominant basis in Western culture for ascribing responsibility for the consequences of one's actions is the "free will paradigm," which focuses on "the agent's capacity to choose her actions freely."[42] This, of course, is a hallmark of liberal political theory. He argues that an alternative conception of legal responsibility is the "constitutive paradigm," which treats the ascription of responsibility as an occasion on which the boundaries of the self are negotiated and constructed.[43] This paradigm rests on appreciation of each individual's capacity for ongoing self-constitution through the process of either identifying with or distancing oneself from various elements of experience. One way in which this capacity is exercised is through the assumption of responsibility. When I assume responsibility for an event, I implicitly identify with some aspect of myself by virtue of which I am held accountable. Thus, for instance, to accept responsibility for drunk driving is to treat my intoxication as an aspect of myself rather than as some external agent over which I have no control.[44] Similarly, to accept responsibility for a child's destruction of a valuable piece of furniture is to treat my child as a part of who I am, rather than to emphasize the discrete bodily boundary between myself and him or her.[45] In each instance, drunkenness or the child serves as a "responsibility base" that identifies the events of which I will be held the author, and therefore those for which I will be regarded as responsible.[46]

Each occasion on which responsibility is at issue offers the potential for affirming or repudiating a different responsibility base and hence a different construction of the self's boundaries. If it was I who broke the furniture, rather than my child, my acceptance of responsibility would rest on a responsibility base that emphasized my authorship of events produced by bodily action, over which I could be expected to exert some control. If I damaged the furniture while subject to an epileptic fit, I might distance myself from the epilepsy, excluding it from the boundaries of my self by disavowing responsibility for the consequences that it produced. Furthermore, I may take a different attitude toward an item in different circumstances, depending on the "engagements of that moment."[47] If I participate with a friend in a prank in which another person is injured, I may feel responsible even if I did not directly inflict the harm. In this sense, I incorporate the actions of my friend within the boundaries of my self. By contrast, if my friend writes a bad check, I am far less likely to identify with his actions and accept responsibility for them. The assumption of responsibility in various contexts thus represents an ongoing process in which "I adopt a different source of objects and events as being the basis of *my* authorship of them and hence as a constitutive element of myself."[48]

As Dan-Cohen emphasizes, the assumption of responsibility is "shaped in anticipation of and in response to the ascription of responsibility by others."[49] Social conventions serve as the basis for this ascription, thereby representing "articulations of a shared public conception of the self."[50] This public conception helps shape the process of everyday self-constitution, encouraging persons to assume responsibility in certain settings. Law is an important way in which this articulation takes place. By "making an explicit public pronouncement regarding a certain instance of responsibility," law serves "to strengthen my identification with the appropriate responsibility base."[51]

This perspective on the attribution of legal responsibility illuminates that both the communications privilege and the modification of the adverse testimony privilege in *Trammel* reflect the use of free will as the relevant responsibility base in the context of spousal privilege. In each instance, the duty to refrain from testimony rests on an act of imputed or actual choice, an approach that represents a construction of the self's boundaries that excludes one's spouse as a constituent of identity. Implicit in this notion is the principle that a person is responsible only for the harm to her spouse that would result from the breach of a freely accepted obligation of confidentiality. If we appreciate the connection between identity and the assignment of responsibility, however, "candidates other than the will may be eligible as potential constituents of the self and therefore as bases of responsibility."[52] On this analysis, the adverse testimony privilege identifies marriage itself as a responsibility base. An individual is precluded from testifying because she is married to the person against whom she would testify, not because of an act of will on her part.[53] This encourages her to regard her spouse as a constituent of identity, rather than as a distinct person from whom she seeks to distance herself. This demarcation of the self's boundaries draws attention to the ways in which spouses' lives are intertwined and to the distinctive capacity for injury that such involvement makes possible.

The identification of marriage as a responsibility base means that a spouse would be held responsible for the harm resulting from any testimony against her partner, rather than simply the harm from testimony that can be construed as the breach of an agreement not to testify. The difference between these two approaches is reflected in the way in which critics of the adverse testimony privilege dismiss the argument that a spouse's testimony contributes to either marital disharmony or her partner's conviction. In both instances, critics argue that it is the defendant rather than the witness who is responsible for this state of affairs, by virtue of the former's allegedly criminal conduct. The constitutive paradigm helps us see that this conclusion implicitly reflects a construction of the self in which the defendant spouse is excluded from the boundaries of the witness spouse's identity. Because critics would not encourage the witness to identify with her partner in this instance, they resort to a narrow responsibility base in denying that she is accountable for certain consequences of her testimony. By contrast, a more expansive demarcation of the self's boundaries identifies a broader responsibility base that can serve as the ground for attributing blame to the witness spouse. The blameworthy character of spousal testimony then serves as the justification for its prohibition.[54]

The adverse testimony privilege's role in promoting identification with one's spouse is also illustrated particularly vividly in those instances in which the privilege has the effect of preventing a putative witness from testifying as part of a plea bargain. As Dan-Cohen has observed, one way in which the law expresses an expansive conception of identity in certain instances is the attribution of collective responsibility. To the extent that I am held responsible for the actions of others with whom I am associated, the law declares that my fate is to some degree connected with theirs—even if I may disapprove of their actions.[55] The effect of precluding a plea bargain for a potential witness who allegedly has participated in criminal activity with her spouse is thus a way of imposing some degree of collective responsibility. A spouse cannot sharply distinguish her fate from her partner's by incriminating him but must accept responsibility for having acted in concert with him. This suggests, for instance, that the coconspirator exception to the adverse testimony privilege serves to undermine this sense of collective responsibility and its attendant expansive understanding of spousal identity.[56] It encourages spouses to distance themselves from one another through their testimony, thereby implicitly denying responsibility for each other's actions. One may applaud or decry such a result,[57] but appreciation of the role of the privilege in constructing marriage offers a distinct perspective on the issues raised by the exception.

One might argue that the responsibility of one spouse to refrain from testimony is correlative with the right of the other to prevent it.[58] In this sense, the argument goes, the privilege expresses the importance of the internal stance only with respect to the putative witness; the defendant is treated as someone who is authorized to act in his own self-interest in precluding testimony by his spouse. Affording a defendant the right to preclude testimony if the need arises, however, at least leaves open the possibility that the right will never be asserted. Indeed, a defendant will invoke the right only if his spouse already has taken the external stance by indicating that she wants to testify. In this sense, the privilege has a potential to affirm the external stance that may never be realized if it is successful in promoting adoption of an internal stance. By contrast, granting the putative witness the right to choose to testify affirmatively authorizes a spouse to take the external stance, rather than holding the right to do so in reserve in case one's partner does so first. The privilege therefore may encourage the cultivation of loyalty and trust even though ultimate invocation of it by the defendant would reflect his adoption of an external stance.

Concern that granting the privilege to the defendant promotes a self-interested perspective can be addressed even more thoroughly, however, by making the privilege an absolute bar to testimony. In this vein, conceptualizing the adverse testimony privilege as a vehicle for expressing the importance of an internal stance toward marriage casts a different light on those versions of the privilege that take the form of a disqualification that cannot be waived by the defendant spouse. The disqualification for adverse testimony exists in only a handful of states[59] and has been described as based upon a principle of marital unity that reflects "archaic notions of the nature of the marital relationship and the role of women[.]"[60] If, however, the privilege represents an effort to impose responsibility in a way that promotes a certain understanding of the spousal role, it is best characterized not as a right that may be invoked or waived by an individual spouse, but as an essential element of that role. By precluding choice, disqualification avoids the necessity for a defendant to assume an external stance in which he weighs his own interests against those of his spouse. At the same time, an absolute bar would not preclude the defendant from having an opportunity to benefit the witness spouse. A defendant may prefer to waive the privilege in order to afford his spouse an opportunity to testify in return for a lighter sentence. He can achieve the same result, however, by himself providing the information in question in return for lenient treatment of his partner.

The constitutive paradigm of legal responsibility thus offers insight into one way in which the adverse testimony privilege constructs a narrative of marriage that expresses the importance of an internal stance. By imposing the duty not to incriminate one's partner, the privilege seeks to encourage development of the expansive sense of self that is characteristic of that orientation.


## The Question of Audience

I have suggested that the adverse testimony privilege can be seen as constructing a narrative of marriage that emphasizes the importance of the internal stance. How likely is it, however, that people are aware of this narrative? Instances in which the privilege comes into play are less frequent than, say, disputes over child custody or financial assets at divorce. Furthermore, when the privilege does become relevant it serves to shield disputes from public view rather than publicize them. In this sense, it is less visible than those areas of family law that galvanize the public because they require an explicit legal decision. For these reasons, one may question whether the privilege actually has much effect on our understanding of marriage.

At a minimum, of course, participants in criminal trials in which one spouse has information relevant to the prosecution of the other become aware of the privilege. This includes the spouses themselves, who may be learning of the privilege for the first time. One may contend that they become aware of the privilege too late in the game for its story of marriage to have much influence. This is not necessarily so, however. First, those spouses who wish steadfastly to remain loyal to each other will learn that the law ratifies this attitude by precluding testimony. In this way, they will receive reinforcement of their understanding of the meaning of marriage. Second, a potential witness who would like to protect her spouse but fears the effects of temptation and pressure will have her inclination toward loyalty insulated from contrary influences. In this way, the privilege may prevent the erosion of trust that might result were a spouse forced to choose whether to testify. Third, even if one spouse would be willing to testify if afforded the option, she need never indicate this to her spouse. Ambiguity about what she might have done may be enough to permit a marriage to survive the immediate crisis, affording spouses an opportunity to repair their relationship over a longer period of time. Finally, the privilege may have an effect, even if a spouse would be willing to testify, clearly conveys this to her spouse, and the parties eventually divorce. There is a good chance that each partner will remarry,[61] which means that there is the potential that their awareness of the privilege will have some effect on their understanding of their new marriages.

It is true that the number of spouses who will be in a situation in which the privilege is relevant is likely to be relatively low. We must add to them, however, others involved in the criminal justice system, such as judges, prosecutors, attorneys, witnesses, reporters, and jurors. When these persons are included, the total number of persons who become aware of the privilege probably will still be a small percentage of the population. Even a small proportion, however, may represent an absolute number that is not insignificant.[62] At the same time, one may question whether a legal rule of which only such a small percentage of the population is aware is likely to have much influence on how people view marriage.

There is some reason to believe, however, that the prospect that a broader segment of the public may become aware of the privilege is likely to increase in coming years. For better or worse, media coverage of criminal trials and family law controversies has considerably intensified in recent years.[63] Even a small list of the legal proceedings that have attracted national attention during this period includes those involving O.J. Simpson, Rodney King, Reginald Denny, Lorena Bobbitt, Erik and Lyle Menendez, Amy Fisher, Joel Steinberg, Baby M, Baby Jessica, Kimberly Mays, Tonya Harding, William Kennedy Smith, Gregory K., and Susan Smith. Forty-seven states now permit cameras in the courtroom.[64] Court TV has provided live coverage of legal proceedings since July 1, 1991, and local and national news teams have come to devote a substantial portion of their resources to covering high-profile criminal trials.[65] Court TV also produces "The System," a television show that uses extensive access to one New York City police precinct to "follow[] cases from arrests through prosecution and judgment[,]" with coverage of criminal investigations, plea bargaining, and sentencing decisions.[66] Time, Inc. is considering publication of *Eyewitness*, a true crime magazine that will include stories on courtroom trials.[67] Newspapers, magazines, books, and television talk shows offer additional avenues for publicizing legal events. Popular culture makes its own contribution to legal consciousness through the cinema, made-for-television movies, television series, and novels.[68] As one observer suggests, "the television courtroom, with its grisly diagrams and drooping flags, appears to provide one of the new forums where Americans come to find one another."[69] Conversations about matters such as jury instructions, the admissibility of evidence, the battered-woman syndrome, and expert testimony have become a common form of cultural discourse.[70]

In the midst of this climate, a criminal trial in which one spouse has information that could help convict the other seems a natural candidate for considerable media attention. One can easily imagine, for instance, that had Arthur Seale proceeded to trial, Court TV, television networks, and the press would have treated us to a steady diet of coverage of the proceedings—and that the ability or inability of Ms. Seale to testify against her husband would have been an irresistible aspect of the story. Indeed, even without a trial, newspaper stories discussed New Jersey privilege law,[71] and one show on National Public Radio was devoted primarily to the adverse testimony privilege.[72] We cannot predict with certainty whether or how often the privilege will arise as an issue, how well it will be covered by the media, or what kind of discussion it will provoke. Nonetheless, it seems reasonable to say that the potential for awareness of the privilege to increase has never been greater.

One still might claim that the incrimination of one spouse by another offers a more compelling drama than the absence of a spouse from the witness stand. For this reason, one might argue, heightened media coverage of criminal trials may not necessarily serve significantly to publicize existence of the privilege. This suggests, however, that an important function of the privilege may be to prevent transmission of the dramatic message that spousal testimony would send, rather than to send a powerful message of its own. While few may know of the privilege, the spectacle of spousal testimony is likely to make far more people aware of its absence.[73] We may be particularly concerned about the message that is conveyed when the weight and prestige of the law serve to condone spousal betrayal. By preventing this from occurring, the privilege may work interstitially, reinforcing a sense of spousal commitment that could be eroded were the state in this setting to ratify disloyalty for the sake of individual gain. In this way, the privilege may serve to buttress cultural attitudes already in place rather than to shape new ones.

We can liken this process to the expression and maintenance of a taboo. To echo Jon Elster's observation about norms, the message that the privilege sends with regard to testimony is " 'It isn't done.' "[74] By preventing the public event of spousal incrimination, the privilege seeks to make it unthinkable—conduct that evokes repulsion because it is inconsistent with what it means to be married. Wigmore therefore perhaps should have taken more seriously the "natural repugnance" that he suggested historically has prompted support for the privilege.[75] Had he explored the phenomenon more closely, he might have concluded that this repugnance is an indication of the effectiveness of the privilege in making shameful the prospect that one spouse might use the intimacies of married life to help the state convict the other. Such an attitude may well dissolve in the face of widespread legal approval of testimony. Even if some spouses choose not to testify, the formerly unthinkable will have become more possible. Even if spouses decide to be loyal, there will be less legal reinforcement for the kind of sensibility that leads to such a decision.

One way to appreciate this function of the privilege is to examine other in-stances in which the law serves primarily to reinforce certain values. Laws pro-hibiting the sale of children, for instance, also operate mostly invisibly, in that they seek to express a taboo about the commodification of children that prevents this behavior from ever occurring in the first place.[76] The objective is to make such conduct so unthinkable that, ideally, the need never arises to levy a more visible sanction through prosecution of transgressions and the imposition of pen-alties. As with any taboo, compliance will not be universal; indeed, the existence of a taboo reflects acknowledgment that the conduct that it attempts to make unthinkable may have powerful attractions.[77] Nonetheless, the relative rarity of the outright sale of children in American culture, and the intense disapproval that it evokes in most people when it occurs, suggests that commodification of children evokes repulsion that is both reflected in and reinforced by its legal prohibition. The prohibition contributes to a construction of the parental role in which such behavior is antithetical to being a parent. This process occurs even though it is likely that many people are unaware of these laws.

Were the laws repealed, however, attitudes could change. Many people might well continue to feel repugnance at the prospect of the sale of children. None-theless, this attitude no longer would be officially sanctioned by the state. Those transactions that occurred probably would receive more publicity than instances in which parents simply chose not to sell their children. It is at least plausible to suggest that over time our understanding of parents, children, and human nature might well change as a result of the mere possibility of sale.[78] Even those children who were not sold might well be more anxious and less secure about their relationships with their parents merely because this option was available.[79] The movement from prohibition to choice in this situation thus itself might send a message more powerful, and dramatically different, than prohibition sends on its own. Furthermore, to analogize even more closely to spousal testimony, active state encouragement of transactions likely would create even more momentum for reassessment, if not transformation, of sentiment. The law cannot affirmatively require parents to love and care for their children, just as it cannot ensure that spouses will be loyal to each other. It can, nonetheless, at least attempt to avoid contributing to an understanding of the parental or spousal role that may weaken these sentiments.

These suggestions about the extent to which the public is aware of the privilege or would notice its absence are necessarily speculative. Several other evidentiary rules, however, rest on assumptions that are arguably just as uncertain.[80] For instance, excluding evidence of post-accident repairs,[81] offers to pay medical ex-penses,[82] and offers of compromise[83] withholds potentially relevant evidence from legal proceedings for fear of discouraging salutary conduct. Yet it is likely that a survey of citizens would reveal that no more of them are aware of these eviden-tiary rules than they are of spousal privilege. Similarly, economic analysis of tort liability is premised on the notion that people will make rational choices in response to legal rules that will result in individuals taking an efficient level of care.[84] While this may be plausible with respect to large institutional actors, it is unlikely that the average person is either aware of tort rules in her state or bases her actions on them if she is. Skepticism about the direct effect of spousal privilege on behavior thus hardly distinguishes this body of law from many legal rules.

At the same time, it does seem fair to say that if one were setting out deliberately to devise a legal regime to encourage adoption of the internal stance toward marriage, an adverse testimony privilege might not be the first provision one would choose to serve this end. Other laws likely are more visible and directly relevant to spouses' everyday lives, such as provisions that treat all resources as shared marital property, or that authorize one spouse to make medical decisions for the other. Thus, the privilege probably is best seen as one piece in a larger mosaic. Each piece in isolation may not be crucial, but each contributes cumulatively to the achievement of a larger overall effect. In this regard, the privilege is perhaps similar to most laws dealing with the family and intimate conduct.[85] Evaluating a law in terms of its independent effect therefore risks neglecting the extent to which its significance lies in being part of a broader "socializing strategy."[86]

Consider, for instance, *Orr v. Orr*.[87] In that case, the Supreme Court was confronted with a state law that authorized alimony payments to women but not men. Probably few are aware of the particulars of alimony law, and the intimate choices of those who are likely are shaped by more powerful influences. Indeed, someone who specifically looked to the law to guide behavior would realize that only a small percentage of women ever received any alimony at all,[88] and therefore rationally would conclude that choosing a life as a homemaker was economically perilous. In isolation, therefore, the limitation of alimony to women probably has contributed little to the perpetuation of traditional gender roles. If we were seeking deliberately to dismantle a system of gender inequality, other legal rules would have far more priority than those governing alimony. Yet the Supreme Court had no trouble in striking down the law at issue in *Orr*. The Court said that the law risked "reinforcing stereotypes about the 'proper place' of women and their need for special protection."[89] In other words, when confronted with the law, the Court had to evaluate to what narrative about marriage and gender the rule would contribute—however modest that contribution might be.

Similarly, statutory rape laws in themselves probably have a marginal effect on most people's conception of gender roles. It is likely that few are aware of these laws, or that those who are act with reference to them. Furthermore, prosecutions under such statutes are relatively rare.[90] Yet many feminists argue that these laws should be invalidated or written in gender neutral language because they perpetuate the notion that males are sexual aggressors and females are sexually passive.[91] As with alimony, repeal of statutory rape laws likely would not be a top priority in a campaign that sought deliberately to use the law to promote gender equality. Nonetheless, when we consider such a provision we must necessarily attend to the message that it sends, notwithstanding the relatively modest force of that message in isolation.

These examples suggest that the expressive dimension of a legal rule may be important even when we cannot be certain that the message of the rule is transmitted to a large audience. This may seem puzzling and even mystical in an era in which we are accustomed to seeing law in instrumental terms as a vehicle for producing specific outcomes. The creation of meaning occurs less overtly and is difficult to grasp because it requires attention to the very background that makes evaluation and judgment possible. Recent work in a variety of disciplines, however, has emphasized the constitutive character of our discourse, social practices, and symbolic systems.[92] Attention to the implicit narratives embedded in legal rules is an effort to heighten awareness of the role of law in this process.

That said, we cannot necessarily conclude at this point that retention of the adverse testimony privilege is warranted. First, a rule whose significance is primarily symbolic is inherently vulnerable in that the benefits that it produces may seem vague and speculative compared with the more concrete costs that it imposes. Second, the internal stance is a partial perspective, not an unqualified good. Even if we accept the idea that the adverse testimony privilege serves to express its importance, we may still conclude that this is not a stance that a spouse should adopt when her partner is accused of a crime. In the next section, I explore some of the considerations that we need to take into account in evaluating the cost and desirability of the privilege. These include its impact on the potential witness, the costs to the state, and the direct and indirect effect of the privilege on women.

## Criminal Testimony and the Internal Stance

### The Potential Witness

I have suggested that the adverse testimony privilege uses the setting of the criminal trial to affirm the importance of an internal stance toward marriage. Would it be preferable, however, to encourage spouses to adopt the external stance in this context, so that they assess the desirability of testifying in light of their own individual interests? In answering this question, we must first consider the impact on a spouse who wishes to testify but cannot. The most significant cost to a putative witness will occur when she wishes to testify as part of a plea bargain that will provide her with relatively lenient treatment by the state. In that case, the privilege will preclude a deal, which means that she will be subject to prosecution to the full extent of the law. This may seem particularly unfair if the absence of her testimony leaves the state with insufficient evidence to convict the defendant. As the brief for the United States in *Trammel* put it, in this instance "instead of the witness-spouse having the option of earning her freedom by aiding in the conviction of her husband, the accused is in a position to subject her to punishment, while avoiding it himself."[93]

As Richard Lempert has suggested, however, it hardly seems unfair that a witness, unable to invoke the privilege, may be convicted of a crime that she has committed.[94] The offer of a plea bargain reflects not the judgment that one spouse is of such moral character that the punishment authorized by law would be unfair, but the instrumental conclusion that leniency is a means to obtain evidence against the other spouse. The fact that the state is unable to gather adequate evidence to convict other persons accused of criminal activity does not render unfair its conviction of those against whom sufficient evidence is available.

Furthermore, to the extent that a plea bargain reflects the belief that the defendant spouse is more culpable than the putative witness,[95] it is unlikely that the absence of spousal testimony will doom the prosecution's case against the defendant. In order for this to be so, we would have to assume that there is substantial independent evidence against the witness that would lead to her conviction, but that her testimony is the only evidence against the defendant. It is likely, however, given the spouses' joint involvement in criminal activity, that much of the evidence against the witness will also aid the prosecution's case against the defendant. In addition, if the government has enough evidence in the first place to reach the conclusion that the defendant is more culpable and therefore that a plea bargain is desirable, it would seem the rare instance in which the absence of testimony leaves the state bereft of sufficient evidence against the defendant to obtain any conviction at all.

In sum, a potential witness who is culpable may receive more severe treatment than she would have received had she been able to testify. She will not, however, be subject to prosecution for any more than that for which her own conduct has made her liable. Nonetheless, there may be a small number of cases in which her sentence seems harsh compared to a husband who goes free or is convicted of a lesser offense because of her inability to testify.

What about the impact of the privilege on a putative witness whose testimony would not be offered as part of a plea bargain? Prohibiting testimony may force her to lend support to someone of whom she has come strongly to disapprove and from whom she wishes to distance herself. Furthermore, it may prevent her from acting to affirm her own moral ideals by aiding in the prosecution of injustice. In these ways, the privilege may impose costs on a putative witness by requiring a stance of loyalty toward a spouse who does not deserve it. This may seem unduly to treat the person as purely a spouse without taking into account her capacity as an independent individual both to revise her commitments and to promote the cause of justice.

With respect to the first concern, it is true that testimony may afford a spouse an opportunity emphatically to repudiate a partner whose conduct is so reprehensible that a witness no longer wishes to be associated with him. For the spouse who desires to testify, the fact that a legal proceeding constitutes a public ritual makes testimony a particularly powerful way to communicate this repudiation. Precluding testimony deprives a spouse of this highly visible vehicle for declaring her emancipation from the claims of the marriage. It requires that by her silence she assist someone whom she may have come to loathe.

At the same time, the loyalty that the privilege demands consists of an act of omission rather than commission. A spouse is not compelled affirmatively to take steps to lend support to the defendant, nor is she forced to remain in the marriage. Someone who feels strongly about distancing herself from her partner can still do so to some degree. She can make clear to her husband that her silence should not be construed as devotion, by indicating that she would have testified against him had she been given the option. Indeed, the fact that the law has overridden her preference may reinforce the idea that marriage involves certain obligations that cannot be disavowed at will. Furthermore, she is free to seek a divorce, which is a public renunciation of the marriage, and to refuse to have any contact with the defendant in the future. While these actions may not have the immediate force of testimony, they nonetheless afford her an opportunity to communicate her disapproval of the defendant and to sever her relationship with him.

The privilege also prevents a spouse from expressing her commitment to moral principles by assisting the state in its prosecution of wrongdoers. As someone who has evidence that could lead to criminal conviction, a putative witness may believe that she has an especially important obligation to help rectify injustice. Her inability to fulfill this obligation may be a source of particular discomfort. Should we encourage spouses to adopt the external stance, so that they can achieve the critical distance necessary to decide whether the moral demands of justice should outweigh the claims of loyalty?

In assessing the dilemma of the putative witness in this situation, we must be careful not to conceptualize the privilege as an instance in which partiality to a particular attachment is taken to override a commitment to moral principles. Formation of and commitment to personal relationships is also an important element of moral sensibility.[96] Loyalty can be morally valuable and betrayal morally blameworthy.[97] As R.E. Ewin suggests, "willingness to stick with a group matters because it is the rawest expression of people's social nature: without such a willingness, groups would not be formed and we should all be isolated asocial atoms."[98] As a result, "[s]ociability, which is at the core of loyalty, is not just a good thing by-and-large . . . it is necessary to human life."[99] Indeed, Josiah Royce went so far as to suggest that loyalty is the ultimate moral principle.[100] With respect to marriage in particular, as I have suggested, loyalty seems integral to attainment of the distinctive good that the internal stance makes available.[101] The privilege therefore prevents a spouse from vindicating certain moral principles, for the sake of encouraging other moral sensibilities that are important to human relationships in general and marital intimacy in particular.

At the same time, however, loyalty per se is not necessarily a moral virtue. We would hardly, for instance, bestow moral approval on a loyal Nazi. The value of loyalty rather is ultimately dependent upon the value of its object.[102] Even if partiality to one's spouse is a good thing in general, surely there are certain marriages in which partiality is morally blameworthy. This suggests that a more discriminating analysis is preferable, in which we assess the character of the defendant to determine whether loyalty would be morally warranted in a given instance. At one end of the spectrum, we may argue that loyalty generally is justifiable if the defendant is innocent. The privilege does not serve to protect someone who has offended society's moral tenets in this particular instance. On the other end of the spectrum, a defendant who is guilty and who is committed to a life of wrongdoing would not seem worthy of protection. Even proponents of loyalty acknowledge that one has an obligation to withdraw support from someone who is dedicated to acting in a way that is inconsistent with basic moral principles.[103] In other words, we should encourage a spouse in this case to adopt the external stance toward her marriage, so as to realize that supporting her partner furthers an unworthy cause. Less clear, however, is the instance in which a person has committed a crime, but the misconduct is not necessarily the result of a depravity of character. The crime may, for instance, reflect a moment of weakness or a failure of judgment. In this situation, a spouse may disapprove of the behavior in question but remain loyal, seeking to influence her partner through constructive criticism and example.[104] As a general rule, loyalty may serve moral ends in this case, because it represents commitment to a flawed but redeemable person who may be receptive to moral improvement. Indeed, in this instance, understanding and support may provide a crucial human connection that helps a defendant right himself.

In an ideal world, we could identify each of these situations and limit the privilege to instances in which we could be sure that we were limiting our pursuit of justice for the sake of promoting another moral value. The problem, of course, is that we cannot confidently engage in such a discriminating assessment of the character of the defendant. We seem to have no choice but to make the privilege uniformly available or unavailable. It seems reasonable to believe that the number of cases in which loyalty would protect an incorrigible defendant is relatively low. If this is so, fidelity in most instances has at least the potential to serve moral purposes. The privilege will necessarily on occasion protect those whom we would deem unworthy of it, but this is the price for providing protection to those who are. Furthermore, we might console ourselves by noting that even a spouse who is prevented from testifying against an unworthy defendant would still be able to follow her moral principles and leave the marriage. The privilege would not require any additional affirmative acts of support from her, even if it required her to lend assistance by not testifying.

The person who is most knowledgeable about the moral character of a defendant in many cases will be his spouse. Why not let that spouse decide whether loyalty in a particular case is morally warranted? Can *Trammel* be defended on this ground? We would have to deny a choice to spouses engaged in plea bargaining, because their decision likely will be based on self-interest rather than on any disinterested assessment of the moral character of the defendant. Permitting other spouses to testify, however, perhaps would avoid the specter of betrayal for personal gain while withholding the privilege from at least some who do not deserve it.

Although this position has some appeal, on balance it seems inadvisable. First, we would have to be certain that implicit plea bargaining did not occur, in which assurances were offered that a spouse would not be prosecuted at all if she testified. Second, even if we could identify those witnesses who genuinely have no reason to fear prosecution, could we be sure that they would base their decision on assessment of the moral character of the defendant rather than animosity or spite? The mere fact of acrimony between witness and defendant does not necessarily mean that the latter is not an appropriate object of loyalty. Indeed, the law may send a particularly powerful message if it requires loyalty even when one spouse has come to dislike the other. Furthermore, deciding whether a defendant's moral character warrants protection by the privilege is both a momentous and highly subjective undertaking that admits few standards to guide the exercise of discretion. Although the stakes with respect to testimony here are smaller, one may draw an analogy to the decision whether a defendant should receive the death penalty. The simultaneous need for discretion and constraint in this setting has created a difficult conundrum for the law.[105] We may prefer to extend the privilege to some who do not deserve it rather than create the need to wrestle with a similar dilemma in this context.

The costs that a privilege imposes on a putative witness will be lower in those instances in which she is able to offer nontestimonial assistance. I have suggested that there is a good argument that such cooperation should not be permitted, but some may believe that it is justified as a way of lessening the consequences of a spouse's inability to testify. If so, we should be even less concerned about the impact of the privilege on a spouse who wants to testify.

A final point is in order with respect to the effect of the privilege on a putative witness. It seems quite plausible to believe that in many instances her psychological state will be complicated and conflicted. She may well be ambivalent about the prospect of testifying, torn between her own interests or principles and a sense of commitment to her partner. In such cases she likely will be beset by some amount of guilt and regret no matter which alternative she chooses. By depriving her of the need to make a choice, the privilege may protect a spouse from the considerable anguish that comes from knowing that she necessarily must betray herself, her principles, or her spouse. To the extent that this is the case, we must weigh this benefit against the costs that I have discussed above.

## The State

A second party on whom the privilege inflicts costs is the state. In instances in which a spouse is unwilling or unable to testify, the prosecution is deprived of evidence that otherwise might help it obtain a conviction. How significant a loss is this likely to be? Given that the confidential communications privilege already excludes a certain amount of evidence, we must focus on the increment that is lost beyond this by virtue of the adverse testimony privilege. As we have seen, courts sometimes construe "communication" broadly to encompass conduct that is deemed substantively to constitute a statement by the defendant. The adverse testimony privilege thus serves to exclude not all conduct by the defendant or all facts about him, but only those that cannot be characterized as communicative. In some cases, this conduct or these facts will themselves be incriminating, but it also will be the case sometimes that their incriminatory significance will depend on communications by the defendant as to which a spouse cannot testify. For this reason, some critics of the adverse testimony privilege argue that the privilege should be eliminated because it affects "relatively few couples."[106] This fact suggests, however, that the incremental cost to the state of precluding testimony may be relatively small.

An additional consideration is the quality of the evidence that the prosecution would receive if testimony were either compelled or optional. A spouse forced to testify against her will may well offer incomplete or even false information in order to protect her partner. An individual who testifies as part of a plea bargain may shade her testimony so as to make it seem worth the lenient treatment that she desires. In each instance, the failure of the privilege to preclude testimony will allow the introduction of information into a criminal proceeding that actually hinders, rather than furthers, the cause of justice. By preventing the possibility of such occurrences, the privilege affords some amount of benefit to the state that must be factored into the analysis of the costs that it imposes. In sum, while precise calculation is not possible, it seems reasonable to conclude that the privilege does not keep from the prosecution a large amount of trustworthy evidence beyond the amount already excluded by the communications privilege.

The state also has a broader interest in promoting justice that transcends concern about the effect of the privilege on the evidence available in actual prosecutions. One might argue that this interest justifies insistence that one's duty as a citizen must override one's attachments to particular individuals. On this view, even giving a witness the option to refuse to testify adversely is unwarranted, because it suggests that an individual legitimately may choose loyalty to others over devotion to justice. As Stephen Macedo suggests, liberalism in its strongest form implies that "[a] supreme political allegiance to 'impersonal' principles of justice might require that we part company with our friends or possibly even family if it should turn out that they have acted unjustly: liberal norms properly override and render subordinate all personal commitments, allegiances, and loyalties."[107] At a minimum, one might contend, we should give the witness the option to testify, so that the state has an opportunity to impress upon her the importance of her civic responsibility.

The relative weight of one's obligation to the state and to family members has been recognized as a vexing question at least as far back as *Antigone*,[108] and I cannot attempt a full-scale discussion, much less resolution, of this issue here. A few points, however, will at least suggest why an argument premised on the priority of civic duty need not automatically lead to elimination of the adverse testimony privilege. First, the force of such an argument is not confined to the adverse testimony privilege but extends to the communications privilege as well. To be consistent, one must be prepared to relinquish all family privileges on the ground that they foster a partiality inconsistent with the priority of social justice. To the extent that this application of the general principle results in an outcome that leaves us uneasy, the process of reflective equilibrium will suggest that we are not prepared to accept civic duty as a value that must be treated as superior in every instance.[109]

Even if we accept the view that social justice must override all other concerns, the capacity for justice may be dependent in important ways on personal relationships and the loyalty that they generate. Rawls, for instance, explicitly acknowledges the role of the family and other attachments in the development of a moral sensibility capable of acting on the basis of the principles of justice.[110] Relationships of care, and the orientations that characterize them, thus may be complementary, rather than antagonistic, to an ethic of justice. As Owen Flanagan and Kathyrn Jackson put it: "It is hard to see how we could teach children about kindness without teaching them certain things about fairness, but it is equally hard to see how we could teach them about fairness without teaching them certain things about kindness and sensitivity to the aims and interests of others."[111] The importance of loyalty in sustaining personal relationships may lead us to embrace rather than reject legal measures that seek to reinforce it, on the ground that such measures contribute to the cultivation of an appreciation of the importance of justice. I have maintained that spousal privilege law can be seen as one such provision. To the extent that it is, the adverse testimony privilege plays no less important a role in this process than does the communications privilege. Ultimately, an assessment of the force of the state's interest in reinforcing a commitment to social justice will depend on how persuasive one finds the argument on the role of the adverse testimony privilege that I have laid out above.

One may acknowledge the importance of loyalty to a capacity for justice and still contend, however, that it is only voluntary loyalty that warrants protection. For this reason, we should enforce only the communications privilege and the refusal to testify adversely when a spouse is given the option. If our aim is to express respect for volition, however, the prospect of plea bargaining may make it problematic to assume that every decision to testify reflects a voluntary choice to betray one's spouse.[112] In some instances, in fact, the state systematically seeks to undermine an inclination to act loyally. While a spouse's decision may be regarded as voluntary for legal purposes in these cases,[113] it is a harder question whether analysis from a broader moral perspective would yield the same conclusion.[114]

Even if we regard plea bargaining as an unproblematic instance of volition, we may also be concerned that voluntary loyalty is dependent to some degree on the willingness of the law to require loyalty in some instances. In particular, sanctioning betrayal in the context of a criminal trial may so severely undermine an ideal of spousal loyalty that a commitment to voluntary spousal loyalty would diminish. While definitive empirical proof is unlikely to be forthcoming, one must at least grapple with this question before concluding that permitting adverse testimony is consistent with preserving the viability of voluntary loyalty.

## Disparate Gender Impact

A final concern that we must address in analyzing the costs of the privilege is its impact on women. As I have indicated, the privilege for the most part prevents women, rather than men, from testifying. A more searching examination of the effects of the privilege, therefore, first must explore its consequences for "wives" rather than for the more general category of "spouses." This exploration seeks to be sensitive to the possibility that women's typical experience of marriage may be somewhat distinct from men's.[115] Second, less directly, does the disparate gender impact of the privilege reinforce the traditional notion that wives should subordinate their individual welfare to that of their husbands? This question requires that we consider whether the privilege is similar to other legal doctrines that have disadvantaged women by refusing to treat spouses as separate persons whose interests may diverge. Focusing on the impact of the privilege on women thus reflects appreciation that measures that draw on a certain strain of feminism to promote an ethic of care in marriage may run the risk of reinforcing gender stereotypes that disadvantage women.[116] This concern is consistent with liberalism's fear that failure to abstract persons from social context may lead to neglect of their interests as distinct individuals, thus violating the demands of justice.

With respect to the direct costs to the putative witness, I have suggested first that the inability to strike a plea bargain does not impose undue hardship, because the result is that the witness will be prosecuted for a crime that she has in fact committed. One may argue, however, that women may be susceptible to being coerced into criminal activity by their husbands because there often is an asymmetry of physical and economic power within marriage.[117] It therefore may seem especially unfair that a wife in such an instance receive a penalty comparable to or even more stringent than that received by her husband. The husband would be able to force her to participate in a crime, and then use the privilege to minimize or even avoid punishment while requiring her to face the full brunt of prosecution.

Such coercion surely occurs on some occasions. To assume that it inevitably occurs in all instances in which wives are involved in criminal activity with their husbands, however, would be to adopt the dangerous assumption that wives categorically are incapable of acting autonomously with respect to criminal behavior in which their husbands are involved. Recognition of the undesirability of denying women's agency in this way led the drafters of the Model Penal Code to abolish the presumption that a woman acting in the presence of her husband is coerced into criminal conduct.[118] Freeing all spouses to testify would potentially benefit wives who willingly engaged in crimes as well as those who were coerced to do so by their husbands.

One response might be to make the privilege available only to the latter group of women. This option, however, would require a full-blown inquiry into a wife's culpability prior to trial. Furthermore, if the facts indicated that a wife was in fact coerced, then the proper course of action would not be to let her testify in order to receive lenient treatment. Rather, it would be not to prosecute her at all, on the ground that she would be able to invoke successfully the defense of duress.[119] Instead of using privilege law to deal with instances of coercion, employing duress doctrine seems a more direct and sensitive vehicle for responding to the problem. Feminists might rightly be concerned that the "reasonable person" standard implicit in this doctrine may be insufficiently sensitive to women's experience, thereby making the defense unavailable in some instances in which women genuinely feared serious harm if they did not participate in their husbands' criminal schemes,[120] The best response to this possibility, however, is to challenge such insensitivity, rather than to permit testimony. The Model Penal Code section on duress, for instance, focuses on what a person would have done "in his [sic] situation."[121] The comment to this section indicates that this provision is meant to ensure that the standard for successful invocation of the defense is not "wholly external in its reference."[122] This suggests, for instance, that evidence relating to a particular wife's experience of coercion might be deemed relevant in the same way that testimony regarding the "battered-woman syndrome" has been treated by some courts as relevant to the issue of an individual woman's perception of imminent harm under the doctrine of self-defense.[123] It is true that the defense of duress is not available on uniform terms in all states, the most significant variation being its unavailability in murder cases in some jurisdictions.[124] Nonetheless, on balance it seems more responsive to concern about coercion of wives to seek to reform duress doctrine than to use privilege law to address the problem in more sweeping and overinclusive fashion.

Finally, it seems plausible that a wife's inability to testify against her husband in some cases may make him less likely to attempt to involve her in his criminal activity. One reason that a man may attempt to enlist his wife as an accomplice is the belief that doing so will make her less likely to turn him in, since she also will be implicated in the criminal scheme that she exposes. In this sense, the fact that she has a choice about whether to incriminate him makes it more likely that her husband will bring whatever possible pressure to bear on her. If she has no such choice, he may have less incentive to do so.

With respect to a putative witness not involved in a plea bargain, I have argued that the privilege does not force this spouse affirmatively to support her partner, and that there remain other ways in which she can distance herself from the marriage. Feminist scholarship, however, has made us more appreciative of the complex emotions that women may have even when they are involved in destructive relationships. Victims of abuse, for instance, may be unwilling to press charges against men who injure them because they feel that in some way they deserve the treatment that they receive, they retain a strong sense of attachment to their partner, and/or they feel guilty about being responsible for bringing any harm to him.[125] Testimony may have the effect of removing an abusive husband from a woman's life. It also may be a way in which she can assert her independence and emphatically terminate the marriage, in a context in which the support of law enforcement officials helps her take steps that she might not take alone.

As with coerced criminal activity, we know that some abusive marriages are characterized by a wife's complex emotional dependence. Again, however, it may be dangerous to assume that all wives who are potential witnesses are so incapable of ending such a marriage that we should make testimony available as a means of responding to their plight. There may be other measures that are more directly responsive to the difficulties of women in destructive marriages. More stringent punishment of spousal abuse, the availability of battered women's shelters and counseling, and temporary restraining orders may help women achieve both physical and psychological distance from their husbands.[126] Furthermore, a woman will be free to testify against her husband in any prosecution of him for abuse of her, since the privilege is inapplicable in cases in which one spouse is alleging injury by the other. Finally, we should realize that giving a wife in such a marriage a choice about whether to testify in fact may subject her to more abuse or eventual reprisal than if she were unable to testify, because her husband may attempt to influence her decision. As with duress doctrine, the measures that I suggest to help women in destructive marriages will not be fully responsive in all instances to the legitimate concerns raised by some feminists. These alternative measures do seem more directly focused on the problem, however, than making testimony available to all spouses, many of whom will not be confronting such abusive circumstances.

What of a wife who wishes to testify to vindicate her sense of justice? I have suggested that we should not regard the privilege as an instance in which non-moral considerations override moral principles. Personal attachments can make their own moral demands, and infidelity to them can be subject to criticism on moral grounds. Because of its disparate gender impact, however, one may argue that the privilege serves to promote a norm of spousal loyalty only for women. As such, it reinforces the traditional idea that a woman should stand by her man regardless of the personal costs that she incurs by doing so. One might claim that the privilege therefore is akin to other legal doctrines, such as the marital rape exemption and interspousal tort immunity, that we now realize supported a model of marital unity at the expense of women. On this view, the vision of marriage that the privilege helps to construct is one that ultimately is inconsistent with modern notions of gender equality. For this reason, we should promote an external stance toward marriage in the context of a criminal trial.

I believe that this concern warrants serious consideration. Family law can convey subtle messages that shape our understanding of the nature and possibilities of men's and women's lives. As one friend to whom I described the privilege said, "That sounds like something men thought of." The suggestion that the adverse testimony privilege contributes to an understanding of marriage that reinforces asymmetries of power and opportunity along gender lines should lead us to be cautious in embracing the privilege as a vehicle for fostering an internal stance toward marriage. The privilege does seem distinguishable, however, from legal doctrines whose ostensible vindication of marital unity left women vulnerable to exploitation by their husbands. The marital rape exemption and interspousal tort immunity, for instance, were premised on the assumption that permitting one spouse to assert legal accusations against the other would introduce a spirit of acrimonious contention into a realm that should be characterized by generosity and harmony.[127] The consequence, however, was that women in marriages that did not fit this ideal were afforded no legal protection from injury inflicted by their husbands. By contrast, the adverse testimony privilege is inapplicable in cases involving allegations that one spouse has injured another. A husband cannot use the privilege as a shield to avoid accountability for misconduct toward his wife. The privilege thus seeks to vindicate an internal stance without denying that in certain instances spouses' interests may be directly adverse to one another.

In addition, when the privilege *is* applicable it does not reflect the view that the law should affirm an internal stance toward marriage regardless of the costs to women. Compare the privilege, for instance, to the law reviewed by the Supreme Court in *Planned Parenthood of Central Missouri v. Danforth.*[128] That law required a woman to obtain the written consent of her husband in most instances in order to have an abortion during the first twelve weeks of her pregnancy.[129] This provision can be seen as an effort to promote an internal stance, in that it expressed the idea that spouses confronting major family decisions should act in concert rather than on the basis of individual interests. The Court acknowledged that a decision to undergo or to forgo an abortion "may have profound effects on the future of any marriage"[130] and conceded that such a decision ideally "should be one concurred in by both the wife and her husband."[131] It concluded, however, that when a husband and wife disagree, the wife's view should prevail because she is the spouse who is more directly and significantly affected by the decision.[132] In other words, the Court held that the costs imposed by an internal stance were too high in this case, and that it was more appropriate to affirm the viability of an external stance that distinguished "between women and the relational web in which they are located."[133] This seems the right result not only because the woman bears the physical costs of pregnancy and childbirth, but also, given the typical gendered division of labor, because a husband's refusal to consent to an abortion could well result in a wife's forced assumption of primary childrearing responsibility for an extended period of time, a burden that traditionally has been a major source of women's economic and professional disadvantage. In this way, the vision of marital unity promoted by the Missouri law would have the effect in many cases of reinforcing a system of gender privilege.

By contrast, as my earlier discussion suggests, the effects of the adverse testimony privilege on women are far less onerous. None of these effects reflects a disadvantage that traditionally has fallen distinctively on women. Nor do any seriously preclude a wife in most instances from distancing herself in other ways from her husband and her marriage, most directly by seeking a divorce. The privilege therefore does not express the view that it is important to affirm an internal stance toward marriage at whatever cost to women.

One may argue nonetheless that any attempt to promote an internal stance toward marriage usually requires women to sacrifice their interests for the sake of men, and thus is per se problematic because it reinforces gender stereotypes. The duty that the privilege affirms, however, is one that most people would say both wives and husbands should fulfill when a spouse's life or liberty is at stake. In this way, the privilege differs from other legal provisions that served to construct a separate spheres ideology. For instance, a title-based property allocation system, while facially gender neutral, left women with many fewer resources than men.[134] By reinforcing wives' economic dependence on their husbands, this regime represented but one element in a larger paradigm that expressed the notion that wives' primary responsibilities lay in the household. The ostensible gender-neutrality of the rule during its heyday could have been tested by asking a random sample of people whether they would support it if it tended to give women rather than men the lion's share of property. Most people likely would have been unwilling to accept this result, which indicates that it in fact was integral to a system of gender privilege. Were people who accept the adverse testimony privilege told, however, that it tends more to prevent husbands rather than wives from testifying, most people probably would still support it. For this reason, one might argue, the privilege is less likely to send a message about the obligation of a wife than about the obligation of a spouse.

It may be the case, however, that our ostensible acceptance of a gender-neutral duty in this situation is inescapably shaped by the fact that in practice its demands almost always have fallen on women. The idea that one spouse should not incriminate the other may be inextricably intertwined with the notion that wives must always be loyal to their husbands in these circumstances. A thought experiment that conjures a different world cannot free us fully from these assumptions, and therefore may be unreliable as an indication of how deeply gendered our conception of obligation is in this setting.[135] For this reason, the argument might go, there is a risk for women in fostering an internal stance toward marriage in any setting in which it has been mostly women who have been discouraged from acting on the basis of self-interest.

There is no easy way to answer this objection. Orientations that may have deeply gendered origins, such as sharing and commitment within the family, can still be valuable in their own right.[136] Although we may not be able to dissociate them completely from gender, this inability does not mean that fostering them will automatically reinforce gender privilege. There is, however, inevitably that risk. One plausible argument that the risk is worth taking with respect to the privilege relies on my earlier suggestion that, because of their difference in visibility, the ability to testify has more powerful significance than the inability to do so. If this is the case, we might conclude that the prospect of reinforcing gender stereotypes in this instance by preventing testimony is relatively low compared with the prospect of undermining the influence of an internal stance toward marriage by permitting it.

Concern about the disparate gender impact of the privilege illuminates that we can never feel completely comfortable about encouraging spouses to adopt the internal stance as long as there are systematic gender inequalities within marriage. Indeed, it would be entirely rational for many women to resist that stance, because the vulnerability that it involves would be exacerbated by the lesser amount of power and resources wives tend to possess compared to their husbands. This suggests that genuine equality between husbands and wives is necessary before women can embrace the internal stance without acute reservations. To the extent that the adverse testimony privilege reinforces gender inequality between spouses, it therefore could have the overall effect of undermining, rather than promoting, an internal stance toward marriage. I suggest that the danger of this is less than the danger that incrimination will undermine a norm of spousal loyalty. This conclusion, however, is admittedly tentative. My purpose, nonetheless, is not to resolve the matter definitively, but to suggest that we must take seriously the implications of the privilege for our understanding of the roles of men and women within marriage. In this way, attention to the symbolic significance of the privilege offers a vocabulary for discussing a set of concerns that traditionally have not been articulated.[137]

## Summary

On balance, there is a plausible claim that the benefits of using the adverse testimony privilege to express the importance of the internal stance toward marriage outweigh the disadvantages of doing so. The most serious cost to the putative witness will occur when her inability to testify prevents a plea bargain. The result, however, will be that she is prosecuted for a crime that she in fact has committed. Even so, we must acknowledge that there may be some instances in which the unavailability of her testimony means that she will be treated more harshly than a defendant who arguably is more culpable. The state will also bear some costs in cases in which the witness's testimony is crucial, but it seems unlikely, overall, that the privilege will exclude a significant increment of evidence beyond what the communications privilege already excludes. More broadly, the priority of loyalty to the state is a contested claim that in any event does not necessarily lead to the conclusion that the adverse testimony privilege should be abolished or that a witness should have the choice to testify. Finally, there is a stronger argument that the privilege is undesirable because of its symbolic potential for reinforcing a gendered view of marital obligation. Although we must take this concern seriously, I have suggested that on balance this potential may be less significant than is the prospect of undermining the internal stance toward marriage by permitting testimony.

One might argue that escalating criticism of the adverse testimony privilege indicates that there is little underlying cultural support for affirming the internal stance with respect to criminal testimony. After all, when it became apparent that the privilege would prevent Irene Seale from testifying against her husband in state court, the New Jersey legislature cut back the privilege. It seems at least premature, however, to draw that conclusion. The articulated rationale for the privilege in the modern era has been the preservation of marital harmony. Although this may be plausible in some instances, it clearly is difficult for this justification to carry the entire burden of defending the privilege. Given the acute vulnerability of this rationale, it is not surprising that its demolition results in the perception that the privilege simply has no coherent justification. Furthermore, while there is undoubted momentum to the external stance, recent critiques of unfettered divorce and the "clean break" philosophy suggest that we should be careful about automatically labeling as progress the hegemony of this stance in all aspects of family life.[138] Recognizing that we seem to have a commitment to two different conceptions of marriage that are in tension may lead us to question certain trends, attempt to counteract others, and more subtly accommodate our conflicting attitudes toward still others.

## Conclusion

I have sought in the last two chapters to move beyond the terms of the current debate over spousal privilege. Those terms cannot adequately explain why the communications privilege is so widely accepted and the adverse testimony privilege so vigorously criticized. Nor can they explain why the traditional adverse testimony privilege remains in place in several states despite its apparent lack of any persuasive rationale. I have argued that we can gain insight into these questions by focusing on issues that lurk beneath the surface of the debate: the relative importance of individual and collective orientations toward marriage and their respective accounts of spousal obligation.

While I cannot offer an unqualified endorsement of the traditional adverse testimony privilege, on balance I believe that it is worth preserving. The analytical framework that I have offered, however, does not necessarily dictate a particular outcome with respect to spousal privilege. It may be that once we appreciate the congruence of the communications privilege with the external stance, we will conclude that we have an even firmer basis for supporting that privilege and rejecting the one that precludes adverse testimony. Similarly, awareness of the centrality of individual choice to the external stance may provide an even stronger impetus for granting a putative witness the option to testify about noncommunicative matters. In other words, the external stance may be so dominant an orientation in modern culture that a clearer sense of the ways in which different spousal privileges are consistent or inconsistent with it will lead to steps that reinforce that dominance.

It also may be, however, that our embrace of the external stance is not without reservation. The adverse testimony privilege can be seen as one way to express this ambivalence. The external stance reflects a liberating moment, in which the claims of the past may be rejected for the sake of forging a new identity that offers greater fulfillment. It can also be a terrifying moment, in which much is up for grabs, the past is no guide to the future, and loyalty can turn to betrayal in an instant. We have gained much from greater emphasis on the external stance, but we also may be more vulnerable. In the realm of intimate relationships, few of us can earn our way all of the time. A wife who becomes disabled, for instance, may run a deficit in the balance of payments with her husband. Yet many a husband will be willing to devote himself to her care because she is his wife—a shorthand formulation for a moment of marriage in which account books do not tell the whole story. In a world in which the external stance becomes more prevalent, it may be harder to articulate why such a relationship should hold any special claim. The adverse testimony privilege may provide a language for doing so, providing a narrative of marriage in which responsibility arises from the demands of interdependence and history.

This suggests that spousal privilege law may implicitly reflect an effort to balance the claims of the external and internal stances. The communications privilege enforces a form of obligation that can be reconstructed as having been voluntarily assumed, based on specific exchanges between two independent individuals. The adverse testimony privilege imposes responsibility based on the interdependence that arises within marriage. Once persons divorce, they are no longer members of a community whose needs can give rise to duties regardless of consent. The adverse testimony privilege therefore no longer applies. They are still, however, subject to obligations to which they have consented, which means that they are not free to testify about confidential communications that occurred during marriage. From this perspective, law seeks to mediate the tensions between two different accounts of marriage and the stories about trust, loyalty, and betrayal that they entail

# PART IV

# Money and Divorce

It is acknowledged to be an unalterable law of nature that a man should have the free use and sole disposal of the fruit of his honest industry, subject to no control.

> Samuel Adams,
> 1 *The Writings of Samuel Adams*

[F]uture income is not marital property because it has not been acquired during the marriage. It is not, therefore, subject to equitable distribution.

> *Mocnik v. Mocnik*

SEVEN

# Divorce Awards and Property Rhetoric

$W$omen on average confront less favorable economic prospects than men.[1] Marriage often both exacerbates and obscures this condition. On the one hand, a woman's earning power may decline during marriage because she assumes primary domestic responsibilities. On the other hand, she may benefit because resources within the household generally are not allocated strictly according to financial contribution.[2] Divorce, however, often brings the economic disparity into sharp relief, as women's financial condition worsens considerably compared to men's. In a country in which the social welfare system tends be less extensive than in many other industrialized countries, it is natural that the extent to which a divorcing husband should have responsibility to alleviate his former wife's economic hardship is a subject that has received considerable attention. This debate has tended to focus on the issue of what economic resources should be characterized as marital assets to which a wife has a claim at divorce.

Consider, for instance, the stories of three women. The first, Dolores Wright, married at the age of 24, when she was a secretary and her husband was in dental school.[3] When they divorced eight years later, she had a salary of $15,600 per year, while her husband was earning $100,000 annually. Ms. Wright argued that she should receive some compensation for helping support her husband during dental school, thereby enabling him to increase his earning power. The court disagreed, stating that it was questionable whether she "did more than provide for her own support" at the time her husband was in school.[4] Accordingly, it ruled that the parties should divide marital assets equally, but that Ms. Wright was entitled otherwise only to alimony of $1,500 per month for a period of two years.

The second woman, Kathryn Postema, was married when she was working as a licensed practical nurse and pursuing an associate's degree in nursing, while her husband was employed as a cost accountant.[5] After the marriage, Ms. Postema worked full-time while her husband entered and eventually graduated from law school. Upon graduation, he accepted a position with a law firm, and she resumed pursuit of her associate's degree in nursing. Six months after Mr. Postema began with the law firm, however, the couple separated, which required that Ms. Postema support herself while finishing her education. At the divorce, she contended that her husband's law degree should be considered marital property, and that

139

she should receive a share of the increased future earnings made possible by its acquisition. The court agreed that she was entitled to compensation in light of the fact that the law degree was the product of a "concerted family effort" by the couple.[6] It rejected her claim, however, that she should receive a share of his future earnings. That approach, it said, would improperly treat the divorce as the loss of an investment. Rather, the court held, Ms. Postema should receive reimbursement for the contributions and sacrifices that she made in helping her husband obtain his degree.

Finally, Loretta O'Brien was married when she and her husband were working as teachers in a private school in New York.[7] About two years later, the couple moved to Mexico, where he attended medical school while she worked as a teacher. They then moved back to New York, where he finished the last two semesters of medical school and his internship training, while Ms. O'Brien resumed her former teaching position. A bit more than nine years after they were married, and two months after Mr. O'Brien obtained his medical license, he moved for divorce. The court found that, aside from a student loan, Ms. O'Brien had contributed more than three-fourths of the couple's income during the time her husband was in medical school, and that she had forgone the opportunity to obtain a permanent teacher's certificate during that time. It held that she was entitled to a share of the future earnings made possible by his medical license and awarded her $188,800, payable in annual installments. The court based this ruling on the idea that marriage is an economic partnership in which both parties make contributions to the welfare of the marriage.

These three cases explicitly raise the question of whether we should regard a spouse's increase in earning power during marriage as an individual or a marital asset. That increase may come about as a result of the acquisition of a degree but may occur under other circumstances as well.[8] The question of how to characterize it is crucial because, as I shall discuss, spouses' respective earning power often is the most significant financial asset that they have at the time of divorce.

In this and the next chapter, I want to explore the idea that the debate over what to identify as marital assets is driven by a more basic question: how to conceptualize divorcing spouses. At divorce, we tend to think of the parties as occupying an external stance toward their marriage. It is easy to regard divorcing spouses as individuals with distinct interests, who no longer see themselves as joined in a sense of shared purpose. At the same time, however, the claims that they assert and the obligations that they assume flow from the fact that these individuals in the past were members of a marital community toward which they took an internal stance to some degree. The issue is what relative priority should be given at divorce to these stances—that is, to individual and communal dimensions of identity. As I will discuss, this issue parallels questions about the merits of liberal and communitarian accounts of the self, and about the respective roles of an ethic of care and an ethic of justice.

Answering these questions requires that we articulate a vision of marriage. This is because understanding what it means to be a member of a community helps shape our sense of the terms on which individuals may leave it. At the same time, our view of divorce influences our conception of marriage. This is because the terms on which individuals may leave a community help constitute the meaning of membership in it. With respect to divorce awards, determining the rights and duties of ex-spouses thus implicitly demands that we reconstruct the economic relationship between spouses. That is, we must ask just how being a spouse can give rise to financial claims or obligations when one becomes an ex-spouse. Few if any issues are more controversial in modern family law.

I WILL ARGUE THAT UNTIL the 1970s, the law governing divorce awards generally emphasized an internal stance toward marriage. One way to put this is that for economic purposes divorce law tended to treat ex-spouses as spouses. This treatment rested on a view of marriage as a lifetime membership in a marital community. Such membership involved certain reciprocal duties of care, albeit deeply gendered, which served as the rationale for recognizing ongoing financial rights and responsibilities at divorce. In the past 25 years or so, the law of divorce awards has shifted to an emphasis on an external stance toward marriage. Divorce now ideally represents a "clean break" between spouses, which leaves no ongoing financial relationship between them. Divorce law thus tends to regard ex-spouses as strangers for economic purposes. This rests on a vision of marriage as primarily an arrangement to promote individual happiness, which generally may be dissolved at the request of either party.

On this view, any continuing financial rights or obligations after divorce cannot rest on the mere fact of prior marriage. Rather, as I will describe, they must reflect satisfaction of claims based on principles of fair economic exchange. On this view, divorce awards are premised not on special duties of care that community members have toward each other, but on a more general duty of economic justice that all individuals have toward one another. In sum, divorce law traditionally emphasized an internal stance toward marriage by treating ex-spouses effectively as spouses; it now tends to emphasize an external stance by treating them as strangers.

As I have suggested earlier, an external stance toward marriage has some affinities with the imagery of the market. Market metaphors are likely to seem especially salient when we conceptualize ex-spouses as strangers for the purpose of determining economic rights and duties. The result is that successful financial claims at divorce generally must be couched in what I call "property rhetoric." In the divorce context, property rhetoric sometimes is used to argue that attributes such as a professional degree or future income potential should be formally classified as property. This is not the only way in which property rhetoric can be used, however. Typically, an individual deploys property rhetoric when she frames her claim to resources as a request for the recognition of a right, arising either by virtue of her own efforts or as the result of a transaction that is supposed to involve an exchange for fair value. As a result, she tends to describe herself as someone who is entitled to a return on her investment, who has labored to produce something of economic value, who has not been fully compensated for her goods or services in trading with another, or who is an economic partner who is due a fair portion of the proceeds of a joint financial enterprise. Conceptually, even if not formally, such a person claims entitlement to a property right.[9]

Property rhetoric thus draws on the idea of fair economic exchange for its persuasive force. It has now become the dominant language in which to frame arguments about the economic relationship between divorcing spouses.

There are risks, however, in exclusive reliance on property rhetoric. This rhetoric in fact can be used to limit financial awards at divorce to a far greater extent than many who deploy it would find desirable. Women in particular have been disadvantaged by the family-market dichotomy because it reflects a hierarchy: market activity is privileged, while caregiving within the family devalued. Property rhetoric seeks not to challenge this hierarchy but to capitalize on it. It attempts to invoke on women's behalf the prestige of the market, by characterizing wives as individuals who are involved in implicit market transactions within the family. This conceptual universe is closely associated with what I will describe as the mythology of property: a set of images and metaphors that express certain norms concerning autonomy, obligation, desert, and economic inequality. These norms traditionally have served to construct a model of the ideal market actor, a model in many ways more congruent with men's typical experience than women's. Reliance on property rhetoric thus creates the risk that caregivers who do not conform to this model will be futher marginalized and their claims deemed even less worthy of financial recognition.

On the one hand, ex-spouses are persons whose lives have been intertwined in ways that can't be instantly undone at divorce. On the other hand, they are persons who must seek to construct a new life that is distinct from the one that they have shared. Neither the external nor the internal stance alone captures this complexity. Treating ex-spouses as strangers is as unrealistic as treating them as spouses. We should instead consider adopting a different approach to financial allocations at divorce. This approach would reject the "clean break" approach, drawing on the ethics of both justice and care to construct a richer account of the economic relationship between former spouses.

## Evolving Models of Divorce Obligation

### Fault-Based Divorce

Until the 1970s, divorce law was part of a legal regime that generally promoted an internal stance toward marriage, although to quite different degrees for men and women. Marriage was treated primarily as a lifetime commitment to the welfare of a marital community, rather than as an arrangement for promoting each individual's happiness. Legal rights and obligations were based on one's role within this community, rather than on one's identity as an individual citizen. These roles involved distinct duties of care for wives and husbands. Wives were expected to care for the community through acts of altruism whose value supposedly would have been tainted by explicit economic compensation.[10] In return for caregiving that left them economically dependent, wives were entitled to lifetime financial support from their husbands. This entitlement in part purportedly justified the transfer of ownership or control of her assets to him upon marriage.[11] Husbands thus had a duty of care, but it was more circumscribed than that of their wives. It consisted primarily of responding to the needs of economically vulnerable members of the community.

Alimony originally arose as a remedy during the period in which absolute divorce theoretically was unavailable, and divorce "from bed and board" was the only form of relief available to an aggrieved spouse. If a petitioning spouse could prove that her husband had engaged in specified forms of misconduct, a divorce from bed and board would permit the parties to live separately, although they remained formally married. In such circumstances, a husband continued to be held to his spousal obligation of providing for the financial needs of his wife. The payment of alimony in the event of a divorce from bed and board thus literally was the fulfillment of an ongoing spousal obligation.

Absolute divorce first became available under a fault-based system. Marriage remained a lifetime contract;[12] it could not be dissolved simply because either individual desired it. Nonetheless, when one member of the marital community could be blamed for the breach of communal duties, the innocent spouse could sue for divorce.[13] While absolute divorce made alimony more conceptually problematic,[14] such financial assistance continued to be justified on various grounds.[15] The most analytically coherent rationale was that a husband who had committed a breach of the marital contract sufficient to warrant divorce should not be permitted by his own wrong to escape his obligations under that contract.[16] The husband's misconduct might be regarded as a breach of duty that constituted tortious behavior[17] or as a breach of contract.[18] In either instance, damages consisted of the amount that was necessary to place the injured wife in the position that she would have enjoyed had not her husband wrongfully ended the marriage. As one court expressed it, an alimony award "should be so apportioned, as to secure to the wife the same social standing, comforts, and luxuries of life, as she would have had, but for the enforced separation."[19]

Alimony thus was the cornerstone of the traditional law of divorce awards. Since the husband had earned most if not all of the property acquired during marriage, he got to keep these assets. He had an obligation, however, to use part of them to ensure that his wife continued to have an adequate income after divorce. Even after divorce, men and women remained part of an ongoing community in which the more financially fortunate member had a duty to respond to the need of the less fortunate one. Such a system ideally served to reassure wives that they would not be economically harmed by their caregiving activity should the marriage end.

We should not overstate either the theoretical consistency or the practical effects of a legal regime in which alimony was the primary vehicle for financial claims and obligations at divorce. The rationale for alimony that I have described "was never universal, nor ever unquestioned."[20] Furthermore, the law of marriage and divorce promoted an internal stance toward marriage more thoroughly for women than for men. It was women whose lives were defined primarily by their responsibilities to the marital community, and whose interests as distinct individuals were most effaced. Men had economic duties to the community, but otherwise had relative freedom to pursue their own interests. The property that they acquired during marriage was legally theirs, not the community's—even though they had the duty to use a portion of it to satisfy obligations to their wives. In addition, perhaps only a third to a fourth of women ever received alimony under this regime, and the average award was not substantial.[21] Furthermore, although the wife typically was the party who moved for divorce, in some instances wives were adjudged the party at fault. The result in those cases was that the husband was absolved from any duty of support after divorce without consideration of the wife's financial need.[22] In addition, ex-husbands' financial hardship, practical difficulties in calculating and administering awards, and resistance in some quarters to imposing such an obligation on a former husband all qualified the application of its logic. Finally, there are indications that the model began to unravel even before the institution of no-fault divorce, as divorce came to lose the stigma with which it had long been associated.

Despite these qualifications, fault-based divorce featured a coherent discourse of divorce awards that expressed the importance of an internal stance toward marriage. Alimony represented an ongoing obligation of one member of the marital community to another, even after the marriage had officially ended. This financial responsibility represented the financial obligation that a husband had, in return for his wife fulfilling her own obligations during the marriage. The language in which divorce awards were justified thus was one of reciprocal communal duties of care. The advent of no-fault, divorce, however, undermined this conceptual model. The result has been acute awareness of the need to construct a new model based on premises quite different from those that underlay the fault-based divorce system.

### No-Fault Divorce

Beginning with California in 1970, states across the country began making available a no-fault divorce option. By 1985, it was possible to obtain a no-fault divorce in all fifty states and the District of Columbia. Some states revised their laws to make no-fault divorce the only basis for dissolution, while others added a no-fault alternative to existing fault grounds.[23] In all but two states, a spouse may unilaterally obtain a no-fault divorce over the objection of his or her spouse.[24]

The availability of divorce without proof of fault reflects a rejection of the concept of marriage as a lifetime commitment. As a result, in a no-fault divorce action, "[d]ivorce is no longer the unilateral release of a spouse from his or her marital obligations justified by the breach of the other spouse."[25] Rather, it simply represents the judgment of an individual that he or she would be happier elsewhere. In this sense, no-fault divorce reflects greater emphasis on the external stance toward marriage—a heightened sense of spouses as individuals entitled to pursue their own interests. If neither party can be regarded as having breached the marital contract, then alimony cannot be treated as a damage payment by a guilty party designed to compensate the other spouse for wrongfully depriving her of the benefits of marriage. No-fault divorce thus makes it problematic to base divorce awards on communal duties of care, as if ex-spouses continue to have the economic rights and obligations of spouses.

As a result, a new discourse of divorce awards has emerged that adopts what is primarily an external stance toward marriage. This discourse tends to conceptualize ex-spouses as strangers rather than as spouses. One influential metaphor is that marriage is an economic partnership, the assets of which should be divided between the parties to allow them to go their own ways after the dissolution.[26] Strangers can come together in a business enterprise, work together, decide to end their relationship, settle their accounts, and effectively become strangers again with no further obligations to each other. Similarly, financial adjustments at divorce have been strongly influenced by the idea that divorce should effect a "clean break" between spouses, obviating the need for ongoing contact between them.[27] The theory is that each spouse contributes a set of different but equally valuable resources toward the acquisition of assets and therefore is entitled to a portion of the fruits of this labor. In a traditional marriage, while the husband is the one who actually earns the income, the wife is seen as enhancing his ability to do so by assuming homemaking and child care responsibilities that he otherwise would have to perform or purchase. Many statutes reflect this logic, for instance, in expressly providing that the performance of homemaking responsibilities is to be regarded as a "contribution" for purposes of property distribution.[28]

Consistent with this theory, no-fault divorce reforms expanded the definition of property that is deemed available for distribution at divorce, treating most assets as marital property regardless of title. This approach was intended to draw on the model of community property states, which ostensibly utilized the concept of partnership to entitle spouses to an equal share of all assets acquired during marriage.[29] In addition, virtually all states have directed that this property be divided "equitably."[30] Finally, most states treat property division as the primary vehicle for financial adjustments, creating a presumption against alimony or maintenance that can be rebutted only by demonstrating that an equitable property division still leaves a spouse in dire financial condition.[31]

Equitable distribution statutes typically list several considerations that a court should take into account in allocating property, including financial need. As Martha Fineman has suggested, however, the economic partnership image places primary emphasis on the spouses' contributions to the acquisition of marital assets as the basis for their financial claims at divorce.[32] A spouse therefore will have the most success if she frames her claim to a financial award principally as a demand for recognition of an earned property entitlement, rather than as a request to alleviate post-divorce need. Need in itself has minimal significance under an economic partnership theory because, under a view of ex-spouses as strangers, there is no justification for holding an ex-spouse responsible for responding to a former partner's need.[33] Furthermore, as Fineman has observed, even those maintenance claims that are granted now tend to resemble property awards, because they are likely to be "based on modern perspectives of contribution to either the marriage or the career of the other spouse, or awarded in lieu of property."[34]

Divorce law therefore now regards divorce primarily as transforming spouses into strangers. By treating spouses as economic partners, it is possible to characterize their marriage as an implicit agreement to pool their resources for the sake of a joint financial endeavor.[35] Each partner constructively consents to share both the risks and rewards of this project, so it seems entirely reasonable that each should have a claim to a fair share of its assets should the partnership dissolve. Just as with strangers in the market, however, once these claims are honored there remains no basis for either spouse to have any further obligation to the other.[36]

The hope of many reformers has been that characterizing financial allocations as the recognition of earned property entitlements and deemphasizing maintenance would underscore the importance of domestic labor and thus affirm wives' status as equal partners within marriage. Reformers feared that a system in which maintenance was the primary form of financial award to women contributed to an assumption that women had made no significant economic contributions during marriage, and that they continued to be dependent on their former husbands after divorce. In this system, maintenance was a necessary concession to economic need, a payment based ultimately on largess and charity. Taken to an extreme, one result of this conception was the stereotype of the "alimony drone," who lived a life of leisure that was supported by the income of her ex-husband.[37]

Describing marriage as an economic partnership was meant to challenge the implicit devaluation of household labor that was the foundation of this stereotype. A theory of equitable distribution characterized wives as partners whose work during marriage contributed to household welfare just as much as that of husbands. At divorce, women could rely on this work in asserting a *right* to a portion of marital assets, rather than having to seek assistance as part of a plea to be taken care of after divorce. Women's financial claims no longer were dependent on the consciences of judges and ex-husbands but rested on the solid footing of their own labor. Property rhetoric thus had particular appeal to many as a language that affirmed the economic importance of domestic labor and based divorce awards on principles of justice. Indeed, this rhetoric's emphasis on marriage as an economic partnership echoes the claims of those nineteenth-century feminist reformers who argued that wives were entitled to joint rights in marital assets during marriage by virtue of the work that they performed within the household.[38]

Strict application of partnership theory would require that law rely on market principles to calculate the relative value of the spouses' contributions, as well as the balance of payments resulting from implicit economic exchanges between them, to determine each spouse's entitlement to a share of assets. Accordingly, nineteenth-century joint property advocates had to contend with arguments that their approach logically limited a wife's entitlement to a share based upon the market value of her domestic labor, rather than an equal share of marital assets.[39] Reva Siegel observes that antebellum feminists deflected this argument by asserting that the market itself reflected gender bias and therefore was an insufficient measure of women's economic contribution.[40] Later reformers claimed that work in the labor market and within the household were essentially incommensurable.[41] In fact, for at least some advocates, this early deployment of property rhetoric to justify a right to marital assets represented "an effort to secure equality in marriage without embracing norms of possessive individualism."[42] This effort had more resonance in the antebellum era before the emergence of a full-fledged industrial system in which the market became the pervasive standard for measuring economic value.[43]

More than a century later, there is some evidence that implicit reliance on market standards to evaluate husbands' and wives' contributions produces equitable distribution decisions that disadvantage women to some extent.[44] There is a tendency, however, at least to begin with the presumption that spouses are entitled to an equal share of marital assets at divorce.[45] As a result, the use of property rhetoric in this context does not fully reflect that rhetoric's implicit conceptual reliance on market principles as the basis for a claim on assets. An important reason for this is that the deployment of a property framework in divorce allocation is shaped powerfully by the desire to effectuate a "clean break" that transforms spouses into strangers after divorce. While the notion of equal shares is not completely consistent with the logic of property rhetoric, it is consistent with the clean break philosophy. It permits a distribution of assets that ostensibly gives each divorcing spouse an equal chance at succeeding after divorce, obviating the need for any further financial connection between the parties. In this sense, the conceptualization of ex-spouses influences the relative rigor with which the market principles associated with property rhetoric are applied. As I suggest in the next section, reform efforts based on human capital theory represent an even more rigorous application of property rhetoric based explicitly on market valuation of spousal contributions.

Despite hopes that reliance on the qualified market principles of equitable distribution would address women's financial needs at divorce, the years since the enactment of the initial no-fault divorce reforms have made it clear that women tend to fare far worse financially than men from divorce.[46] This state of affairs is particularly problematic in light of the fact that women overwhelmingly tend to be the custodians of children after divorce.[47] There is controversy about whether the legal changes connected with no-fault divorce have been responsible for women's financial distress.[48] At a minimum, however, we can say that the use of property rhetoric in the first round of no-fault divorce reforms has not significantly improved, and may have worsened, the financial condition of women after divorce. Entitlement to share in the division of assets at divorce regardless of title has had limited impact, because often little in the way of conventional liquid assets is available for division at divorce.[49] Courts have expanded the definition of property in some cases to include items such as certain types of pension benefits on the ground that these benefits constitute assets acquired during marriage.[50] These efforts, however, generally have been insufficient to change the economic impact of divorce for many women. As a consequence, "for the typical divorcing couple, no property division rule will make a substantial difference in economic well-being after divorce."[51] Genuine financial improvement would require some additional payments between ex-spouses. As Stephen Sugarman puts it, "if women generally are going to fare significantly better in the couple's division of their financial interests on divorce, a convincing case is going to have to be made that they are entitled to more of their former husbands' postdivorce income than they now obtain."[52]

The fault-based system provided a coherent justification for such a claim by treating ex-spouses primarily as spouses for economic purposes, but that rationale has been discredited in an age of no-fault divorce. Consequently, it has been difficult to establish a principled basis to determine when one ex-spouse is entitled to share in the other's post-divorce earnings. The conceptualization of ex-spouses as strangers does not readily lend itself to acknowledging ongoing entitlements after the marriage has ended. The economic partnership metaphor seems to authorize no assistance after the partnership has been dissolved and its assets distributed.

In the next section, I will explore human capital theory, which is the basis for some of the most prominent efforts to provide a coherent justification for recognizing post-divorce financial claims and obligations in an era of no-fault divorce. Proponents of this theory claim that divorce law can justify access to an ex-spouse's income by recognizing that each spouse's earning power is an asset that can be enhanced or diminished in value during marriage. As a result, human capital theory can be used in some instances as the basis for divorce awards that require financial payments from one former partner to another after the marriage has ended. If an ex-spouse is unable to discharge his obligation in one lump sum, the economic relationship between the parties may continue for some time after divorce. The payments in question, however, do *not* represent fulfillment of a special duty to respond to the need of a former spouse. Rather, they represent satisfaction of a debt incurred to an economic partner during the term of the partnership. The financial rights and obligations of ex-spouses therefore can be justified in terms applicable to any individuals who have engaged in a joint economic endeavor.

## Human Capital Theory

The concept of human capital refers to an individual's expected future earnings.[53] This capital can be seen as an asset that reflects a return on investments such as education, training, and work experience. As Allen Parkman suggests:

> parents can buy shares of common stock that they give to their child or they can pay for the child's education. The student is wealthier due to the education just as he or she would be wealthier on receiving shares of stock: The child will have a higher income in the future due to either of these investments.[54]

Appreciation of the ways in which human capital can be produced, enhanced, and diminished directs attention to the effect of a marriage on the earning power of each spouse. Seen as an economic partnership, marriage often reflects a joint effort to enhance the human capital of one spouse as part of a strategy to maximize total household income. On this view, a portion of the post-divorce earnings of the benefited spouse represents assets produced by the partnership that should be available for distribution between the spouses at divorce. Theorists adopt two basic approaches to determining the value of a claim that should be honored against a spouse whose human capital has been enhanced during marriage. One approach argues that an ex-spouse is entitled to the future financial gain that she expected to enjoy as a result of her efforts. A second school of thought maintains that she is entitled to compensation for her direct contributions and for the diminution in her own earning power that she suffered for the sake of enhancing her spouse's. In this section, I will examine in detail some examples of each of these approaches.

One reason for close attention to human capital theory is that it offers an integrated theory of divorce awards that is gaining acceptance from a broad spectrum of supporters. It is thus worth providing in one place an overview of the various major strands of this school of thought. A second, and more important, reason is that human capital theory in many respects represents the logical culmination of the use of property rhetoric to analyze financial relationships at divorce. Theorists explicitly rely on market metaphors closely associated with property rhetoric, and rigorously apply the logic of those metaphors in conducting their analyses. It is important, therefore, to appreciate how the growing influence of human capital theory presents us with a divorce reform option that reflects a particularly stark version of property rhetoric, premised ultimately on an external stance toward marriage. This development underscores how deeply this rhetoric shapes our thinking about financial allocation at divorce, even when analysts do not recommend formal classification of various resources as marital property. My hope is that once we understand this, and appreciate the elements of the mythology of property that I will describe, we will be in a better position to see that it is unwise to rely solely on property rhetoric and an external stance toward marriage in determining financial rights and responsibilities at divorce.

## Compensation for Expected Gain

One of the earliest and most influential comprehensive efforts to develop a human capital approach to financial allocations at divorce was Joan Krauskopf's analysis of the compensation due a spouse who has supported her partner during school.[55] While Krauskopf's argument is directed specifically at support for spousal education, her framework is logically applicable as well to any spousal contribution to the enhancement of a partner's earning power.

Krauskopf suggests that the human capital approach conceptualizes a family in economic terms as "a firm seeking to maximize its total welfare[.]"[56] Couples in which one spouse is employed while the other attends school are involved in at least four activities that have economic significance.[57] First, they both endure the loss of the student spouse's forgone earnings during the period of education. Second, the employed spouse provides the financial resources that permit the student to forgo those earnings. Third, the employed spouse may herself pass up opportunities to enhance her own earning capacity. Fourth, and most important, both spouses expect to enjoy a return on the full costs of their investment later in their marriage. Thus, the employed spouse is willing to sacrifice some current income and perhaps career advancement in the expectation that she eventually will share in the fruits of her husband's enhanced earning capacity. If the couple divorces, however, only he will continue to receive the benefits of this greater earning power. As a result, says Krauskopf, the employed spouse will be denied "a fair return on her investment," unless a court realizes that the case involves "investment by the marital unit in human capital," and therefore applies legal doctrine "honoring expectations of return for investment and preventing unjust enrichment."[58]

How might we calculate the expected return on the investment in a spouse's education? One standard approach is to determine the present value of the expected future earnings that are attributable to the education.[59] Krauskopf suggests that we first calculate the individual's earning capacity before the education in question. This involves a determination of those characteristics relevant to earning power, and the calculation of what an average person with those attributes would be likely to earn in the future.[60] Second, we can estimate the individual's earning capacity after the additional education by adding that education to the factors considered in the first step. Third, from these expected earnings we must subtract the "investment costs of the added education."[61] These include direct expenses such as tuition, books, and laboratory fees, as well as the earnings that are forgone during the period of schooling in question.[62] They do not include, however, daily living expenses, since a person would incur these costs regardless of whether he or she was investing in education. Finally, we subtract the present value of the expected earnings before the additional education from the present value of earnings after education, once investment costs have been subtracted from the latter. The difference is the expected return on investment, which is "the present value of the enhanced earnings attributable to the investment that exceed the cost of that investment."[63] Krauskopf maintains that, absent evidence about the couple's specific intentions, a court should assume that the partners expected to share equally the increase in earning capacity produced through the spouses' joint efforts.[64]

Krauskopf argues that a court can provide compensation for a spouse's expected gain from her investment without the need to classify the enhanced earning capacity itself as property.[65] An "in gross maintenance" award can be provided instead, which would be based on the theory that the amount of maintenance necessary to meet the reasonable needs of the spouse includes compensation for contributions to the other spouse's earning power.[66] In states in which in gross maintenance is unavailable, a spouse may claim that the increased earning power is marital property divisible at divorce.[67] Krauskopf concedes that this earning capacity traditionally has not been conceptualized as property. She argues nonetheless that it meets two requirements that conventionally have been regarded as essential to interests classified as property: alienability and valuation in monetary terms. She maintains that these criteria are satisfied because a person can hire out the skills and knowledge that constitute her human capital, and, as indicated above, standard methods exist that enable us to place a monetary value on the increment of capital created during marriage.[68] Ultimately, however, she argues that an in gross maintenance award is preferable to classifying increased earning power as property. This is primarily because many states have adopted strong presumptions of equal property division that limit a court's flexibility in determining the compensation that should be awarded a spouse who has invested in her partner's human capital.[69]

Krauskopf thus provides an argument for a claim on post-divorce income that is based on characterization of the claimant spouse as an investor. Framing the situation in this way allows us to see that "[t]raditional legal principles of honoring expectations of return for investment and of preventing unjust enrichment" dictate compensation measured by the gain that one spouse expected to enjoy from enhancing the other's earning power.

Cynthia Starnes offers a second theory in support of compensation for expected gain.[70] She suggests that principles of commercial partnership law should form the basis for determining financial allocations at divorce, especially when a woman has devoted most of her efforts to homemaking during marriage while her husband has concentrated on the paid labor market. In these cases, she argues, the marital unit makes an investment in the husband's human capital just as clearly as when one spouse enables the other to acquire an education. The result is the creation of what can be characterized as an "income-generating marital enterprise."[71]

Starnes maintains that conceptualizing marriage in this way highlights the ways in which the law governing commercial partnerships is relevant to marriage and divorce. Both commercial and marital partnerships seek to generate profits, although these may take nonfinancial form in the latter case.[72] Both often feature a specialized division of labor, in which one spouse primarily contributes capital while the other provides services.[73] Furthermore, the Uniform Partnership Act (UPA) establishes a broad fiduciary duty among partners, "a duty consistent with the social norm of reciprocal trust and love between spouses."[74] The Act also provides that all partners have equal rights in the management of the partnership, which is consistent with modern egalitarian notions of marriage,[75] and that a partner may dissolve the partnership at any time, a provision that is akin to the availability of unilateral no-fault divorce in most states.[76]

For these reasons, Starnes suggests that UPA rules regarding the dissolution of a partnership provide useful guidance concerning financial allocations at divorce. When partners dissolve a partnership a wind-up typically occurs, in which each partner's capital contribution is returned. This process may be analogized to statutes that require the return of spouse's separate property at divorce.[77] Of more relevance, however, is the instance in which partners in a fixed-term partnership may decide to continue the partnership after the withdrawal of one or more members. In this case, the remaining partners engage in a buyout of those who are departing, providing the latter with the value of their investment in the partnership.[78] Starnes argues that contemporary marriage can be seen as a partnership for a term, defined by the life of one partner, although spouses have the freedom to leave the relationship at any time. When spouses decide to divorce, each dissociates from the partnership. Nonetheless, the economic partnership continues "when the enhanced human capital of either spouse, attributable to education or labor force participation during marriage, generates income after divorce."[79] For this reason, a buyout is a more appropriate analogy for financial allocations at divorce than is a wind-up.[80]

Starnes illustrates the application of the buyout principle by examining what she describes as traditional, hybrid, and egalitarian marriages. In a traditional marriage, the marital unit has invested exclusively in the husband's human capital. When the parties divorce, the husband "takes the marital enterprise with him," in the form of enhanced earning capacity made possible by marital investment.[81] In this case, a wife should receive a buyout of her interest in this continuing economic enterprise. In a hybrid marriage, the wife assumes most of the homemaking and child care responsibilities, while also working to some extent in the paid labor market. In this marriage, the partnership invests primarily in the husband's human capital and secondarily in the wife's capital. When the wife leaves the partnership at divorce, she takes with her a portion of the marital enterprise, which is measured by her own enhanced earning power made possible by marital investment. If this share of the enterprise is less than her husband's, she also should receive a buyout.[82]

Finally, in an egalitarian marriage the marital unit makes equal investments in the human capital of both the husband and the wife. One might assume, Starnes observes, that in this instance each spouse should simply take one-half of the marital partnership, with neither receiving a buyout. Valuation of a continuing enterprise, however, is based not on the size of the investments that have been made but on the returns on them. In a commercial partnership, one investment may generate more income than another. The resulting gain or loss, however, is borne by the partnership rather than by the individual partners. In a marriage, an investment in a wife's human capital may result in a lower return, in the sense that it produces lower expected earnings than those of her husband at the time of divorce. Regardless of the reason for this difference, it also should be shared equally between the partners. For this reason, a divorcing wife should receive a buyout if her enhanced earning capacity is less than that of her husband.[83]

How should we calculate the value of this buyout? Starnes suggests that first we must estimate the future earnings of each spouse at divorce,[84] and subtract from that figure the estimated future earnings at the time of marriage.[85] The result of this calculation is the estimate of annual enhanced earnings—that is, the amount of post-divorce income attributable to marital investment. This figure in turn can be reduced to present value at the time of divorce.[86]

Once all these computations are done, it may be apparent that one spouse will be leaving the marriage with a greater share of the fruits of the partnership than the other. In these cases, the spouse with the lesser share would be entitled to a buyout of some percentage of the difference in earning power.[87] Starnes suggests that this percentage should vary depending on the length of the marriage. One model that may be adopted is the Uniform Probate Code, which provides that a spouse may have a graduated share in a deceased spouse's augmented estate based on the duration of marriage, with the maximum share of 50 percent available for marriages of 15 or more years.[88] Applying this approach to a buyout at divorce, we might first calculate, for instance, that the disparity in net enhanced annual earnings of the spouses is $50,000. If the marriage continued for, say, 15 years, the spouse with the lesser earning power would be entitled to 50 percent of this annual difference or $25,000 per year. In marriages of briefer duration, she would receive a correspondingly lower percentage of the annual difference. Starnes maintains that an increase in the income of the paying spouse after divorce should not trigger an increase in the buyout obligation, because generally it will be too difficult to establish that this increase is due to investment by the marital enterprise.[89]

Starnes' approach therefore extends the logic of Krauskopf's analysis of investment in education to the case of investment in earning power in general. Compensation at divorce reflects an economic partner's entitlement to a fair return on her investment. The amount of that return is based on the assumption that marital partners pool their resources and combine their efforts in an enterprise in which they expect to share equally in gains and losses. Financial allocations at divorce are a way of ensuring that neither spouse leaves the partnership with a significantly greater share of the benefits produced by the joint activity.

New York has been most explicit in adopting a policy of compensation for expected gain at divorce. In a series of cases, New York courts have held that various forms of earnings enhancement are marital property subject to division at divorce.[90] Only one other state court has followed New York in expressly holding that an educational degree or the like is marital property whose value should be measured by the expected earnings attributable to it.[91] There are, however, other instances in which courts implicitly have accepted the notion that a spouse is entitled to at least some portion of the expected gain from an investment made during marriage. Some courts in essence have been willing to provide compensation based on such an expectation when the portion of a professional practice or business attributable to goodwill is treated as a marital asset at divorce.[92] Still other courts have held that the anticipated earnings made possible by a degree obtained during marriage should be taken into account in determining an alimony award.[93]

The variant of human capital theory that focuses on expected gain expands the possibilities for compensation at divorce by asserting that a spouse may have a direct financial interest in a portion of the post-divorce income of her spouse. A second variant takes a somewhat different approach, by arguing that a spouse should be entitled to a return of the losses that she incurred for the sake of enhancing her spouse's income. These include any sacrifices she made that diminished her own stock of human capital.

## Compensation for Losses

One prominent human capital theorist who has focused on divorce allocations primarily as a means of compensating economic losses suffered during marriage is Allen Parkman.[94] Parkman argues that an increase in earning capacity that occurs during marriage typically is attributable more to investments in human capital that occurred before the marriage than activity during the marriage itself.[95] Thus, while he leaves open the possibility that an increase in earning capacity may constitute marital property in a few rare circumstances,[96] he maintains that in most instances it is more consistent with human capital theory to focus on the supporting spouse's loss of human capital during marriage as the basis for compensation at divorce.

Parkman argues that the rationale for this compensation is that "[t]he human capital that individuals possess at the time of marriage are separate property just as much as if they had owned portfolios of stocks and bonds."[97] The value of this property can decrease in the course of a marriage if labor market skills are not used or updated. The traditional assumption of primary household responsibilities by women, for instance, typically causes their capital to depreciate. This is reflected in the fact that such women can expect future earnings that are less than the income they could expect had they not curtailed their participation in the paid labor force.[98] If the marriage continues, a wife "is compensated for the reduction in her human capital by actions taken for her benefit by the other family members."[99] If the marriage ends, however, she will bear most of the long-term cost of the depreciation in her human capital.

Parkman argues that an appropriate response to this problem is to classify as separate property the human capital that individuals possess at the time of marriage. Any diminution in the value of that capital due to forgone employment or education opportunities for the sake of the household would be treated as a contribution of separate property to the marriage. The value of the contribution would be regarded as a debt of the marriage and an asset of the contributing spouse. Its amount would be determined by calculating "the difference between the earnings that the spouse could have expected after the dissolution without the limitations, in contrast to the earnings that the spouse can then expect."[100]

Parkman argues that appreciation of the way in which one spouse may enhance the value of the other's human capital also justifies compensation when one spouse serves as the main wage-earner while the other is in school. In these cases, part of the nonstudent's expected income stream is used to support the student spouse, based on an expectation that both parties eventually will benefit from this investment in the student's earning power. Parkman contends that, because of the student's prior investments in human capital and the availability of other sources of financing, this support usually "does not make the education possible, [but] simply reduces the burdens incurred during the educational process."[101] For this reason, the nonstudent spouse's contribution in most instances should be treated as a loan repayable at a market rate of interest, rather than as an equity investment that entitles her to a share of anticipated earnings.

The amount of this loan consists of the student spouse's living expenses, the direct cost of the education, and half the income forgone by the student spouse while in school.[102] If the marriage lasts sufficiently long, the supporting spouse will receive repayment of the loan in the form of a higher standard of living.[103] If divorce occurs before that point, however, Parkman argues that a nonstudent spouse should be entitled to reimbursement in an amount that represents "the unamortized value of the investment plus interest."[104]

Parkman thus suggests two instances in which financial compensation at divorce would be appropriate: when a spouse has sacrificed some of her human capital in order to assume domestic responsibilities, and when one partner has supported the other while the latter obtained an education. He suggests that these two occasions for compensation will tend to be "mutually exclusive."[105] If divorce occurs shortly after a student has completed his education, then reimbursement for support would be necessary because the nonstudent spouse has had insufficient time to recoup her investment. At the same time, however, she likely will have sacrificed little of her human capital due to an absence from the paid labor market. Conversely, the longer the marriage, the more opportunity for repayment of the loan, but the greater the likelihood that a woman has assumed significant domestic responsibility that has reduced her human capital.[106]

Ira Ellman also has offered a theory of compensation at divorce that focuses primarily on reimbursement for diminution in the human capital that each spouse brings to marriage.[107] Ellman argues that rational spouses will decide that the lower-earning spouse should assume primary responsibility for household tasks, since that strategy maximizes the income of the marital unit as a whole.[108] Women traditionally have had lower expected earnings on average than men. This means that women typically assume the majority of household duties. As a result, they usually make more investments that are of value to the specific marriage, such as rearing children and attending to the personal needs of household members. These investments have little general market value after divorce because they are so specialized, which means that the wife "depletes her capital assets" when she assumes primary responsibility for running the household.[109] By contrast, men's investment during marriage typically has taken the form of the enhancement of earning capacity, which does have significant general market value after divorce.[110]

The consequence of this division of labor is that divorce renders a wife's investment almost valueless, while the husband's investment retains its value in the paid labor market. The risk of divorce thus may make a woman less likely to engage in behavior during marriage that would benefit the household as a whole. A rational wife would only take on primary domestic responsibility if the expected return from that alternative exceeded the expected return on an investment in her own earning capacity.[111] Since the former figure must be discounted by the probability of divorce, there will occur many instances in which spouses adopt a division of labor that does not maximize the earnings of the marriage as a whole, because part of the husband's higher income potential will go unrealized in order to assume greater domestic responsibilities.[112]

Ellman argues that alimony should compensate a spouse for the loss of earning capacity that arises from concentrating on marriage-specific investments. This will ensure that neither party will enjoy a windfall nor incur a substantial loss as a consequence of divorce. Such compensation will serve to "protect[] marital decisionmaking from the potentially destructive pressures of a market that does not value marital investment as much as it values career enhancement."[113] By providing assurance that the lower-earning spouse will not be financially penalized at divorce for assuming primary responsibility for household matters, alimony will encourage spouses to make economically rational decisions about the division of labor within the marriage.

The amount of this compensation would be determined by the difference between (typically) a wife's actual earning capacity when the marriage ends and the earning capacity that she would have achieved had she remained single.[114] Ellman emphasizes that, with the exception of instances in which a spouse assumes primary responsibility for child care, a claim would be honored only when the sacrifice of human capital was "financially rational."[115] This means that the reduction in earning power was incurred with the expectation that the loss would be offset by a greater gain in the other spouse's earning capacity, thereby maximizing the human capital of the marital unit as a whole.[116] Thus, for instance, reductions in income prompted by nonfinancial lifestyle preferences would not qualify for compensation, nor in normal circumstances would the decision to stay home by one spouse in a childless marriage.[117] Furthermore, reimbursement would be due only when a financially rational sacrifice actually results in a financial gain. "If [a wife] invests in herself and does poorly, she has no one else to cover her loss. There is no reason why someone else should cover it if she invests in her husband and he does poorly."[118] Ellman suggests that an alimony system would create undesirable incentives if it made investment in one's spouse riskless but not investment in oneself.[119] The logic of Ellman's theory of alimony therefore is that a spouse should be required to compensate the other for a gain in income that is purchased with the other spouse's forgone opportunity to enhance her own earning power.[120]

Ellman justifies compensation for economically irrational decisions to assume primary child care responsibility on the ground that parental care is a "traditional ideal" that should be accommodated.[121] Thus, even if, for instance, child care services could have been purchased for less than the amount of income forgone by the primary caregiver, the spouse who provides this care would be eligible for compensation. The amount of this compensation, however, would be one-half the reduction in earning capacity, since the economic sacrifice was shared by both spouses, and since the higher-earning spouse received no economic gain from the loss of the other's earning power. When child care responsibilities are shared more equally, so that both spouses incur some loss in human capital, that loss should be shared at divorce by giving the spouse with the larger loss one-half the difference in the respective reductions in human capital.[122]

While no state has adopted an approach that would calculate compensation at divorce as precisely as Parkman or Ellman suggest, a few states have provided that one factor that a court should take into account in property division or alimony decisions is the extent to which the claimant sacrificed earning capacity during the marriage.[123] In addition, a somewhat larger number of states have declared that assistance in obtaining an education or enhancing earning power is a factor that should be considered in property or alimony determinations.[124]

The most explicit proposal to adopt a human capital focus on compensation for losses as the basis for divorce awards is contained in the chapter on "Compensatory Spousal Payments" in the Proposed Final Draft of the American Law Institute (ALI) Principles of the Law of Family Dissolution.[125] The Draft has not yet been finally adopted by the Council or membership of the ALI, but it represents a significant advance in the effort to provide a coherent and systematic analytical foundation for financial allocations at divorce.[126] Section 5.02 of the Draft states explicitly that the objective of the chapter is to "allocate financial losses that arise at the dissolution of a marriage according to equitable principles[.]"[127] The chapter does provide for financial awards in marriages of significant duration to avoid a precipitous loss in the standard of living of one of the spouses, an approach that is not based directly on reimbursement principles.[128] The drafters, however, see this as applicable in a relatively limited class of cases involving long-term homemakers.[129] The remaining provisions of the chapter provide for reimbursement for financial contributions to a spouse's education or training;[130] for a loss in earning capacity suffered because of care for children[131] or care for third parties for whom one has responsibility;[132] or to compensate a spouse in a short marriage who is unable to regain her premarital living standard because she made significant expenditures or gave up "specific educational or occupational opportunities" either to permit the other spouse to pursue such opportunities or to serve some purpose that the spouses regarded as important to their marriage.[133]

As with a theory that focuses on expected gain, the variant of human capital theory that emphasizes compensation for losses argues that an ex-spouse may have a financial interest in a portion of her ex-partner's post-divorce income. The assertion is that part of this income was obtained through the contributions and sacrifices of a supporting spouse, for which she should be compensated. At first glance, one might conclude that the argument by both branches of human capital theory that an ex-spouse may have to relinquish part of his post-divorce income reflects the view that ex-spouses are not strangers but have obligations toward each other that continue to some extent after divorce. As I will argue in the next section, however, human capital theory in fact conceptualizes ex-spouses as strangers, divorce as a clean break, and property rhetoric as the appropriate language in which to describe financial obligation.

## Human Capital Theory and Property Rhetoric

The rhetoric of human capital theory seems at first blush to respond to the inadequacies of the first round of divorce reforms by rejecting the idea of divorce as a clean break and of ex-spouses as strangers. The theory provides a basis for arguing that one ex-spouse may be entitled to a claim on assets earned by the other after divorce. This appears to imply that neither claims nor obligations of ex-spouses necessarily end at divorce, but may extend for some period afterward. Indeed, providing compensation for either expected gain or actual losses may require an individual to earmark a portion of post-divorce income for a former partner for a considerable time after the marriage has ended.[134] This ongoing financial relationship, in which the fates of the ex-spouses are intertwined for some period, seems at odds with the notion that divorce transforms partners into strangers who have no claims on each other once the marriage has ended. Rather than a property settlement that sends the parties on their way without the need for further contact, human capital theory often seems to justify a form of compensation that looks suspiciously like support, whatever formal name it might be given. Does human capital theory in fact reflect a departure from the "clean break" theory that was the basis for the initial wave of divorce reforms? Does it base financial claims and obligations of ex-spouses primarily on an ethic of care rather than of justice?

If we look closely at the logic of this theory, we will see that the answer to these questions is no. Human capital theory tells a particular story of marriage and divorce. That story begins with two individuals, each of whom independently owns a stock of property. A good portion of that property consists of human capital—a combination of education, skills, and training that has a value corresponding to the anticipated future income stream that it will produce. These property-holders may find it advantageous to combine their resources to form a marital "firm"[135] or partnership[136] directed toward maximizing the economic returns to the marital unit. Each partner makes contributions to this enterprise by providing assets that he or she brought to the marriage, as well as those earned afterward. In addition, the partnership may find it economically rational to invest more heavily in one of the partners' earning capacity, which may mean that the other spouse forgoes an opportunity to enhance his or her own. This opportunity cost must also be counted as a contribution of property to the marriage. All these assets are provided to the marital partnership by an individual with the implicit expectation that at some point he or she will enjoy benefits at least commensurate with, if not greater than, the value of the contributions. Thus, even though one spouse may temporarily reap a disproportionate share of rewards that are made possible by use of the other spouse's resources, in the long run one would expect a rough balance of trade between the partners to prevail.

On occasion, divorce may end this partnership before one spouse has received full compensation for her contributions. In this case, there is an imbalance in exchange. One partner has benefited from assets made available by the other, in the form of actual financial gain or at least an enhanced opportunity to obtain such a gain. In this sense, the benefiting spouse has accepted use of the property of the other without fully paying for it.[137] If all aspects of the marriage are to be resolved at divorce, this debt must be fully satisfied. Thus, for instance, one spouse may have suffered a depreciation in human capital because of forgone opportunity for advancement incurred for the sake of enhancing her husband's earning power. This depreciation represents a contribution of separate property for which she is due compensation. Some reimbursement may have occurred by virtue of the increased earnings that flowed to the marriage as a result of this investment.[138] If she has not received full compensation for the use of her property when the marriage ends, however, the remaining balance represents a debt for which her husband is responsible.

It should be clear that this description of the way in which financial obligation arises at divorce affirms that ex-spouses are strangers who have no obligations to one another once the marriage has ended. It should also be clear that this depiction of ex-spouses involves a reconstruction of marriage along specific lines. Being a spouse gives rise to financial claims and obligations after divorce only if there has been an unequal exchange of resources during marriage as determined by individual cost-benefit accounting.[139] This reliance on market principles as the basis of rights and duties emphasizes an external stance toward marriage and is consistent with a liberal ethic of justice. An ex-spouse may be entitled to a portion of the post-divorce income of the other as compensation for either expected gain or actual loss. She has that entitlement, however, because a portion of that post-divorce income represents enhanced human capital that was acquired with her property *during* marriage. This human capital asset was obtained while the ex-spouses were married, and could be assigned a value at that time reflecting the present value of the anticipated future earnings that would be enjoyed because of it. Even though some of those future earnings actually will be acquired after the marriage has ended, this future income represents a return on property in the form of human capital that was obtained during the marriage.

The compensation demanded by human capital theory thus represents the satisfaction of a debt that arose when the parties were married, not the fulfillment of any obligation that continues after divorce. Ideally, that debt will be paid in a lump sum at the time of divorce, but as a practical matter many ex-spouses may have to make periodic payments after divorce in order to satisfy their responsibility. Those payments, however, represent simply an accommodation to financial necessity, not any ongoing duty of support. Ex-spouses have only those obligations that they incurred as spouses, and these are confined to those that any market actor would have in abiding by principles of fair exchange. The fact that unequal exchange may have occurred in a *marriage* is of no significance in itself. A human capital approach thus is consistent with the aspect of liberal theory that abstracts individuals from particular relationships and emphasizes their universal features.

This is underscored by human capital theorists' rejection of need as a relevant consideration in determining post-divorce financial obligation. Ira Ellman, for instance, emphasizes that alimony is best conceptualized "not as a way of relieving need," but as a way to acknowledge "entitlement earned through marital investment" and to produce optimal financial incentives for spouses during marriage.[140] Similarly, the ALI Principles draft makes clear that the basis for post-divorce payments is "*compensation for loss* rather than *relief of need*."[141] While the ALI reporters suggest that their proposal might often reach the same outcome as cases in which financial allocations are based on need, they suggest that "[r]echaracterizing the award's purpose from the relief of need to the equitable allocation of loss transforms the claimant's petition from a plea for help to a claim of entitlement."[142] Unlike the principles of reimbursement and return on marital investment, emphasizing need would focus attention on the *post-divorce* situation of the parties. If ex-spouses are strangers, however, post-divorce need per se provides no more reason to require one former spouse to come to the aid of the other than there would be to impose that duty on someone picked at random from a crowd on a sidewalk. Marriage generates financial responsibility after divorce based on principles of fairness, not on an ethic of care. A divorcing spouse has a duty to remedy economic injustice, not to look after the welfare of the other partner.

For human capital theory, divorce therefore is a final settlement of economic partners whose responsibilities are limited to those arising from the exchange of resources during the marital partnership. We can infer that each party accepted the responsibility to compensate the other for benefits received from those exchanges. Enforceable obligations after marriage are confined to those that arise during marriage, and those that arise during marriage are limited to those that can be characterized as the result of an individual's free choice. By conceiving of ex-spouses as independent market actors who are obligated to each other only for benefits voluntarily accepted during marriage, human capital theory makes property rhetoric a natural language in which to describe financial responsibilities at divorce. Compensation for expected gain in post-divorce income represents a property right acquired through investment during marriage. Compensation for losses reflects the return of separate property contributed during marriage, payable from post-divorce income made possible in part by the use of that separate property. In each case, the claim of an ex-spouse is akin to the claim of a party demanding compensation on the basis of an arms-length market transaction. This emphasis on fairness between independent individuals with their own distinct interests is consistent with an external stance toward marriage.

## Conclusion

By conceptualizing earning power as an asset of each spouse, human capital theory offers a rationale for providing women with more substantial divorce awards than they now tend to receive. The theory furnishes rhetorical resources for a wife who has supported her husband during school, postponed or forgone her own education or training while her husband has pursued his, chosen a job with lesser benefits and prospects for advancement so as to be available for domestic duties, given up a well-paying job so that her husband can accept a job in another city, turned down a promotion so her husband would not have to move, or worked part-time while her children were in school. The traditional legal regime posited that a wife did such things altruistically out of an ethic of care. Her entitlement to financial assistance after divorce did not represent explicit financial compensation for her sacrifice but recognition of her ex-husband's duty to respond to her financial need. In this way, the law of divorce awards emphasized an internal stance toward marriage, particularly for women. In the first round of divorce reforms, wives' contributions and sacrifices were deemed to give them a claim on assets divisible at divorce but rarely a claim to the future earnings of their husbands. Recognizing human capital as an asset, however, provides the basis for acknowledging either a formal entitlement to a portion of a spouse's income after divorce, or a right of compensation that as a practical matter often must be paid out of such income.

Human capital theory therefore refines property rhetoric to furnish a coherent justification for granting divorced women greater access to the financial asset that has the most potential to alleviate their post-divorce hardship: their ex-husbands' earnings after divorce. Its ability to do so reflects the value of drawing on an external stance toward marriage in analyzing spouses' economic relationships. That stance insists that we attend to the implicit distribution of resources between spouses, rather than assuming that partners are joined by a complete harmony of interests. The genuine benefits that result from relying on the external stance and the property rhetoric associated with it might lead us to conclude that the law of divorce awards should be based solely on an external stance toward marriage. In the next chapter, however, I will suggest that this approach in fact provides rhetorical resources that can be used to restrict compensation more stringently than many of its proponents would find desirable. Property in American culture traditionally has been associated with conceptions of autonomy, labor desert, and market inequality that have marginalized caregiving activity. Relying on property rhetoric alone therefore will limit the extent to which we can address the dramatically different financial consequences of divorce for men and women.

I will argue that a fully adequate response to this problem requires drawing also on an internal stance toward marriage. This stance suggests that spouses have a special duty of care to each other that may entail some financial claims and obligations for a period of time after divorce—without any precise demonstration of the unequal exchange of resources during marriage.

EIGHT

# The Risks of
# Property Rhetoric

The conceptual underpinning of property rhetoric is of course the concept of property itself. In recent years, property has lost some of its ostensible rigor and unity as an analytical concept.[1] Furthermore, property rhetoric is comprised of diverse strands that co-exist in some tension, rather than forming a unified and harmonious whole. Nonetheless, certain strands have had particularly powerful influence on the cultural imagination, and together constitute what we might describe as the "mythology of property." Seen in this way, property constitutes a gestalt, a pattern of closely associated elements rather than a set of logically entailed propositions.

Within this gestalt, property has long occupied a position in American culture that is close to sacred. As deTocqueville observed early in the nineteenth century: "In no other country in the world is the love of property keener or more alert than in the United States, and nowhere else does the majority display less inclination toward doctrines which in any way threaten the way property is owned."[2] The images of property that come to mind for most Americans are based primarily on the cultural significance of property in the late eighteenth-and early nineteenth-century as the central source of freedom and independence.[3] Property has been regarded not as simply one of several types of legal entitlements, but as a distinctive right essential to liberty, which draws its authority more from natural law than civil society.[4] As Jennifer Nedelsky observes, such imagery persists despite more than a century and a half of legal developments that have undermined the notion that property is a uniquely stable and secure entitlement. The persistence of this vision reflects the fact that "[i]t is the *myth* of property—its rhetorical power combined with the illusory nature of the image of property— that has been crucial to our system."[5]

In this chapter, I want to explore the elements of this myth and their implications for the use of property rhetoric to conceptualize financial claims and obligations at divorce. I will argue that property is closely associated with three notions: (1) autonomy as independence from others, a formulation that limits obligations to those that can be characterized as voluntarily assumed; (2) property as a reward for economically productive labor in the marketplace; and (3) economic inequality as an acceptable and ineradicable feature of a market system that protects private property rights. As should be apparent, these tenets also have been central to liberal political theory.

In the section that follows discussion of this mythology, I will examine the ways in which these elements provide readily available rhetorical resources that can serve to justify legal outcomes that limit awards to financially dependent spouses at divorce. This is not to say that these outcomes reflect the straightforward application of the mythology of property. As observers have noted, the American legal system has tended to treat property rights as far more qualified and fluid than popular rhetoric would suggest.[6] The likelihood of reliance on the mythology of property to justify legal outcomes in any given instance therefore depends on a host of contextual considerations. Because gendered assumptions implicitly inform elements of the mythology, however, one context in which its metaphors are likely to seem particularly salient is when women assert property claims against men based on the value of their marital labor. Divorce reform efforts that use this rhetoric invite reliance on a conceptual universe that privileges what traditionally has been regarded as experience more typical of men than women. Exclusive reliance on an external stance toward marriage in this context thus may pose some distinctive risks.

## The Mythology of Property

### Autonomy as Independence

Property conventionally has been associated with the idea that a property right gives an owner, as Blackstone described it, "sole and despotic dominion which one man claims and exercises over the external things of the world, in total exclusion of the right of any other individual in the universe."[7] Blackstone's pronouncement was extravagant even in his own time as an accurate account of the right to property. Nonetheless, its imagery has had considerable influence on the typical everyday understanding of property, particularly in the United States.[8] As Joseph Singer has argued, property has been shaped by close association with a "free market model," which purports to promote autonomy by consolidating legal authority over resources in one owner who has the right to control them to the exclusion of others.[9] Such authority is designed to ensure not only that an individual is free from interference from others, but also that he is able to avoid dependence on them through the attainment of self-reliance.[10] Singer observes that, notwithstanding the legal realist challenge to the coherence of the free market model and its conception of property, "the model has a life of its own and continues to dominate legal discourse."[11] As a result, when we think of property, "[w]e still carry in our heads an image of the 'owner' as a person who has ultimate control over the disposition of a thing or a set of resources."[12] The right to control and to exclude others from the use of property thus establishes a boundary between oneself and others that demarcates a zone of ostensibly absolute autonomy. This image of property as the "cardinal symbol of individual freedom and independence in the United States"[13] has had particular appeal to those who see divorce as an opportunity for women to escape their traditionally constrained domestic role and become self-reliant actors in the market economy.

The association of property with independence has been particularly resonant with respect to the individual's right to be free from governmental intrusion. Jennifer Nedelsky has explored in some detail the way in which property has served as a metaphor for the vulnerability of minorities to the majority in a democratic government.[14] She argues that the framers of the Constitution, particularly James Madison, implicitly regarded property rights as unproblematic entitlements that would be in constant danger of usurpation by a permanent class of those who lacked a significant amount of property. In this way, "property was the central instance of rights at risk in a republic."[15] One consequence of this formulation was that property possessed the aura of a prepolitical right, which in turn meant that government would be exceeding the scope of its authority if it sought to engage in redistribution of property from one group of individuals to another.[16] In this way, property served to determine the very boundaries of legitimate state power, thereby affording the individual a haven from the demands of the collective.

Nedelsky notes that property never actually provided such invincible protection in practice,[17] and that the legal theories associated with the New Deal dealt a fatal blow to the notion of property rights as representing privileged prepolitical entitlements.[18] Yet, she observes, Americans nevertheless "have a strong sense of the naturalness of the entitlements of property and of the 'privateness' of the power those entitlements provide."[19] As a result, "[v]irtually everyone talks about . . . property ownership as free-standing, as a source of independence *from* the state, not a condition requiring the power of the state to give it its meaning."[20]

The significance of property as a barrier between the individual and the state stems from the resonance of property more broadly as a boundary between oneself and other people in general. As Nedelsky observes, property is a concept that serves to crystallize the desire of the self to utilize boundaries to avoid the loss of control and independence that are taken to represent a loss of autonomy in dealing with others.[21] An example of the perceived centrality of property ownership in the development of autonomy, she suggests, is child development theory that emphasizes the importance of possession to the emergence of a discrete sense of self.[22] One author, for instance, declares: "Possession is one device the young child uses to hammer out autonomy. Consequently, ownership takes on special meaning to the toddler set. To them, separateness *means* the right to possess."[23] As Nedelsky observes, such a formulation illustrates "the connection between private property, the notion of autonomy, and the self conceived of as essentially separate."[24] The child's understanding of herself as a property-holder provides the basis for the emergence of a sense of identity in which the self occupies a protected space free from intrusion by others. In this way, property provides a person a "bulwark of isolated independence from her fellows."[25]

This understanding of the relationship between property and autonomy entails a conception of obligation toward others that reflects the premises of social contract theory. As Nancy Hirschmann has noted, social contract theory takes isolated individual independence as the primal human state.[26] Consistent with their basic condition of freedom, persons in this state can be bound only by an exercise of individual will. Obligation therefore is the exception that must be justified in accordance with the general rule; the central problem for social contract theorists is "to understand how isolated individuals can develop and sustain connections and still be separate, how they can engage in relationships and still remain free."[27] The solution is that obligation must be conceptualized as voluntarily assumed if it is to be legitimate. Only such obligation is consistent with the control that is essential to genuine autonomy. Put differently, those persons whom an individual allows into her domain of private property are there because the owner has granted them access. This grant of access assumes the more fundamental right to exclude; it is an act of free will that expresses the individual's capacity to choose how much control over her dominion to exercise and how much to relinquish. Obligations between independent property owners therefore ideally arise only through "relationships of mutual agreement and gain."[28]

This paradigm of consensual obligation extends to the conceptualization of society itself by liberalism as the product of agreement among independent individuals. Persons in the presocial state of nature acquire property and seek to protect it more effectively by voluntarily entering into the social contract. As Hirschmann points out, the obligation that arises under this contract can be seen as based on a relationship of exchange: citizens surrender some of their freedom in return for the benefits of life in a more effectively ordered society.[29] This surrender itself affirms individual free will; as Locke argued: "*Law*, in its true notion, is not so much the Limitation as *the direction of a free and intelligent Agent* to his proper Interest."[30] The end of civil government is to protect the property that individuals bring to the social contract, since this is the purpose for which individuals voluntarily give up some of their autonomy in entering society.[31] Much work in social contract theory has been devoted to the task of demonstrating that, despite surface appearances, social and political obligation can be characterized as consensual and hence legitimate.[32]

Hirschmann argues that the coherence of this approach depends on the exclusion of family relationships from the model, relationships traditionally regarded as the domain primarily of women. This exclusion is necessary because relationships in this realm don't readily conform to the requirements of consent theory. Children have distinct needs, for instance, that arise from their vulnerability and dependence. While a couple or a woman may consciously choose to have a child, they do not choose to have the particular child who is born. If a child is born with severe disabilities, for instance, is it meaningful to say that the parents consented to provide around-the-clock care for this child throughout its life? One might attempt to rely on hypothetical consent theory in characterizing the obligations of parenthood as freely chosen. Yet if before birth the parents had been given this alternative or the alternative not to have this child, many, perhaps most, persons would choose the latter option. Furthermore, what of the couple who sought to avoid conceiving a child, and who believe that abortion is murder? Or the woman who cannot afford financially to have an abortion, or who lives in a state that restricts her ability to obtain one? Have these people consented to take on the burdens of parenthood? Hirschmann asks whether persons who become the caregivers for children in instances such as these "really consent to such situations, or do they recognize obligations of care that are not explicitly chosen?"[33]

Furthermore, the traditional assignment to women of primary responsibility for family matters has rested on the notion that women are naturally suited for such a role. This concept of natural suitability regards obligation as flowing not from explicit consent but from the ineluctable demands of biology.[34] The family thus poses a problem for social contract theory because the responsibilities that arise within that sphere can't be easily conceptualized as consensual. This in turn has the potential to undermine the paradigm of autonomy as independence from the will of others, because "the particular history and possibilities of women's lives generally foreclose the unconditional if not radical choice that liberal theory demands for male subjects."[35]

The consequence, argues Hirschmann, is that social contract theory requires the maintenance of a dichotomy between the public and private domains—that is, between the market and the family. The former is the realm in which all conduct conforms to the model of consent. "All things that do not or cannot fit this framework—that is, nonconsensual obligations—are consigned to the private realm."[36] Then, "since that is defined as the realm of the inessential, consent theorists do not have to worry about, or even include, such activities or considerations when thinking about and defining obligation."[37] The ideas of autonomy as independence and obligation as consensual rest upon the valorization of a realm in which men traditionally have been the primary agents, and the marginalization of a sphere in which women traditionally have been the primary actors. Relationships marked by personal dependence, vulnerability, care, and affection are taken as irrelevant in conceptualizing the fundamental terms of human interaction.[38]

While these models of human autonomy and obligation may seem axiomatic, some feminists argue that there are in fact alternatives that more fully incorporate insights from women's experience and therefore provide a fuller account of social life. These theorists assert that the traditional relegation of women to the domestic sphere has sensitized many women to the way in which personal autonomy is dependent on relationships with, rather than independence from, other persons. Similarly, immersion in family responsibilities has heightened awareness of how all persons are enmeshed in networks of connection that sometimes give rise to nonconsensual obligation. This emphasis on the experience of connection is useful in helping us think about how we might draw on an internal stance toward marriage in developing an approach to divorce awards in a no-fault era.

Jennifer Nedelsky, for instance, has observed that it is not isolation that enables individuals to become autonomous but nurture and support from others.[39] Everyone from the start is located within a web of relationships that he has not chosen, in which he is helpless and dependent.[40] Only gradually, through support and guidance from persons such as parents, teachers, friends, and loved ones, is he able to emerge as an agent capable of making choices that he can regard as his own. Thus, if we understand autonomy as conduct guided by a sense of one's genuine purposes and commitments, interdependence is an essential element of that process. This is because the capacity to deliberate and act in this way is cultivated through relations with others, and because the content of one's purposes "is comprehensible only with reference to shared social norms, values, and concepts."[41] The conception of autonomy as the power to exclude others, then, denies the very conditions necessary for its realization.

As a result, Nedelsky suggests that the most useful metaphor for autonomy is not the "isolated, distancing symbol of property,"[42] but childrearing, which expresses "the emergence of autonomy through relationship with others."[43] She argues that we need to think of interdependence as a constant condition of human existence, rather than as a product of individual acts of will. Within this framework, the central problem of autonomy is not how one may achieve distance from others, but what forms of relationship are most conducive to the development and flourishing of autonomy.[44] The focus, she maintains, should be on integration rather than isolation: on "autonomy within relationship"[45] instead of autonomy opposed to relationship.

Nancy Hirschmann also draws on the assumption of basic human connectedness in her argument for a reconceptualization of obligation. Acknowledging the inevitable fact of interdependence, she submits, can lead us to invert the premises of social contract theory. Rather than take isolated independence as a given and obligation as problematic, we might well take obligation as our point of departure, and isolation as the condition that must be justified. From this perspective, the basic question of social life is not how it is that obligations can arise in a world of separate individuals. Rather, "[t]he responsibility model, beginning with connection, tries to determine how to provide space for the self without violating the moral imperative of care."[46] Hirschmann elaborates:

This different orientation requires inquiry into the contextual conditions surrounding an obligation and an obligated person so we might understand the content of an obligation as well as the possible justifications for not fulfilling it. Such an inquiry would articulate not a justification for restraint of action but the conflicting pressures that lead to a particular action as the fulfillment of an obligation or that provide a reason for not fulfilling it.[47]

Beginning with the premise of interdependence thus leads us to realize that often we come to *recognize* obligation rather than consent to it. Again, Hirschmann suggests, women's experience can be useful in illuminating this point. Law and morality have regarded family responsibilities, for instance, as among the most powerful to which individuals are subject. As the earlier analysis indicates, however, most of these responsibilities do not satisfy strict criteria of consent. With respect to the care of children, for instance, one can make a strong case that it is the dependence and vulnerability of the child that gives rise to an obligation, rather than the parents' voluntary assumption of responsibility. Thus, while consent theory asserts that consent creates obligation, the concept of recognition involves "the admission of an obligation that *already* exists."[48]

It is of course possible to construct a rather complicated theory of consent even with respect to family responsibilities, much as social contract theorists have shown ingenuity in conceptualizing society as the product of consent, despite experience commonly at odds with that characterization. At some point, however, we have to wonder whether these elaborate formulations are merely attempts to evade the simpler truth that emerges from everyday life. As Hirschmann suggests, for instance, despite its formal assertions to the contrary, social contract theory in fact typically seems animated by the assumption that "humans have no choice:

government must exist."[49] Rather than take this as the starting point of analysis and then examine when the obligation to respect the social order may not apply, consent theory camouflages the way in which interdependence creates a strong presumption that some type of government must exist among human beings.

Hirschmann makes clear that she is not contending that women's experience involves the recognition of preexisting obligation, while men have been able freely to choose when to assume responsibility. Rather, her point is that both women *and* men already are subject to nonconsensual obligation in many ways, but that the dominant ideology denies this. By heightening awareness of the nature of responsibility in the realm that social contract theory has excluded from its analysis, we can fashion a much richer understanding of the complexity of human interaction and the obligations that it involves.

Property therefore is closely associated with a conception of autonomy as independence from others, which in turn entails the notion that obligation must be voluntarily assumed in order to be regarded as legitimate. This understanding of autonomy and obligation draws inspiration from the "public" world of the market, neglecting insights from experience in the "private" realm of the family. It should not be surprising, then, that locating ex-spouses within the market would lead to reliance on property rhetoric in conceptualizing financial claims and obligations at divorce. Nor should it be surprising that this rhetoric would be prominent in a regime that affirms the idea of autonomy as independence by characterizing divorce as a "clean break" between the spouses. In addition, it seems natural that the most prominent theory advanced to justify more generous financial awards at divorce would frame those awards as the repayment of obligations that were freely assumed during marriage.

The suggestion by some feminists that this model of autonomy and obligation marginalizes many women's experience should at least give us pause in relying on property rhetoric, and the external stance toward marriage on which it is premised, as the sole basis for contending that women should have greater claims on their husbands' post-divorce income. The image of ex-spouses as autonomous property-holders in the market, for instance, may well lead to a denial of the financial dependence of many women at divorce.[50] In addition, property's close association with negative liberty may well promote the idea that once assets are divided, spouses should be able to use their property to build new lives unencumbered by the past. The powerful symbol of property as a boundary that insulates the individual from others may prompt characterization of post-divorce income as property that should be protected from any obligations that have not been freely acknowledged by the property-holder. Furthermore, the traditional role of property as a source of independence from the state may provoke hostility to legal recognition of claims on future earnings, because enforcing such claims seems to represent state redistribution of an individual's private assets.

I will explore in more detail below the ways in which property's association with these images of autonomy and obligation may provide the legal basis for limiting women's financial claims at divorce. For now, the important point is that the rhetoric of property has tended to reflect a distinctive conception of social life that emphasizes certain dimensions of experience while neglecting others.

In the next section I explore labor desert theory, another significant element of property rhetoric. That theory, I argue, has been construed to provide rewards principally to those who labor outside the home in the market. Its deployment in the context of claims at divorce therefore may limit the amount of compensation that courts are willing to award women who have assumed primary responsibility for domestic tasks during marriage.

## Market Labor Desert

Labor desert theory, the idea that property rights are justified as a reward for the expenditure of one's labor, is perhaps "the principal normative theory of property[.]"[51] This theory has had particularly strong influence in English and American law. As Melville Nimmer has suggested, "It would seem to be a first principle of Anglo-American jurisprudence, an axiom of the most fundamental nature, that every person is entitled to the fruit of his labors unless there are important countervailing public policy considerations."[52] This principle finds considerable support in popular opinion. One extensive study of attitudes in the United States toward various features of capitalism and democracy, for instance, found overwhelming support for the proposition that it is fairer to base individuals' wages on "how hard they work," rather than "their economic needs."[53] Among those who classified themselves as "middle of the road," 82 percent agreed with the first criterion and only 2 percent with the second. Even among "strong liberals," the group with the most support for the second standard, 47 percent believed that wages should be determined by how hard someone works, and only 24 percent stated that they should be based on economic need.[54]

The seminal source of labor desert theory is of course John Locke. Locke asserted that every individual "has a *Property* in his own *Person*," so that "[t]he *Labour* of his *Body*, and the *Work* of his hands, we might say, are properly his."[55] Consequently, "Whatsoever then he removes out of the State that Nature hath provided, and left it in, he hath mixed his *Labour* with, and joyned to it something that is his own, and thereby makes it his *Property*."[56] This labor desert theory traditionally has been taken to refer principally to the rewards that accrue to those who work outside the home in the "public" sphere of the market economy. While but the rudiments of such an economy existed in Locke's time, Locke himself utilizes the conventional images of economic production, rather than domestic services, to describe the benefits produced by the expenditure of labor:

> For 'tis *Labour* indeed that *puts the difference of value* on every thing; and let any one consider, what the difference is between an Acre of Land planted with Tobacco, or Sugar, sown with Wheat or Barley; and an Acre of the same Land lying in common, without any Husbandry upon it, and he will find, that the improvement of *labour makes* the far greater part of *the value*.[57]

Furthermore, Locke's notion of the emergence of civil society through the social contract implicitly depended on the distinction between a "public" world of property-holders bound only by their consent, and a "private" domestic world populated by women whose responsibilities were dictated by nature.[58] Women's immersion in a realm of nonconsensual obligation, combined with their natural subordination to their husbands,[59] served to preclude their inclusion as direct parties to this contract. If society reflects an agreement made by signatories for the sake of protecting their property,[60] and if only men had capacity to be such signatories, then the strong implication is that it is primarily, if not exclusively, *men's* labor that creates the property rights that must be honored by the state.

This conclusion is underscored by the suggestion that Locke's labor desert theory is based on the belief that the expenditure of labor is essential to human moral development. As one commentator on Locke suggests, only through the act of appropriation, the "imposition of human Will upon the external world," can man "escape from his particular bodily needs, instincts, desires, and inclinations that were preventing him from abiding by the Law of Nature that his reason had discovered."[61] Women's labor in the domestic sphere ostensibly is governed by such "bodily needs, instincts, desires, and inclinations," and thus arguably could not be seen as an expression of human will that left its mark on the world through appropriation.

None of this is to suggest that the logic of Locke's theory inexorably leads to the valorization only of market labor as the source of property entitlements. Locke has many complexities with which one must grapple, such as a more expansive understanding of the term "property" than we have today, at least formal recognition of the ability of women to become property-holders in civil society, and rejection of traditional justifications for patriarchy. Nevertheless, his ideas have provided powerful support for a distinction between work done in the market that is rewarded by the acquisition of property and work done in the home that is motivated by nonpecuniary considerations. This is particularly the case in an American culture that has tended to embrace an absolutist strain in Locke that the author himself may not have intended.[62]

A testament to the strong influence of market labor desert as the justification for a claim on resources is the fact that traditionally the law has afforded no compensation for services rendered within the family, on the assumption that they are provided altruistically without expectation of financial remuneration.[63] The privileged status of market labor is also reflected in the fact that, as William Simon has observed, even supporters of social welfare programs have attempted as much as possible to defend benefits as simply the return of financial contributions made by the recipient.[64] The result has been that programs seen as offering social insurance benefits, such as Social Security, have obtained favored legal treatment and broad public support, while programs seen as providing benefits based on need have enjoyed far less favor.[65] As Simon indicates, advocates of public welfare programs "thought that conditioning benefits on work, and relating them to wages, would be enough to invoke among the public the liberal distributive values of effort and exchange, and, in particular, to deter association with need-based redistribution."[66] The valorization of market labor is also reflected in responses to criticism that the earnings-based Social Security program disadvantages women whose earnings are lower because they spend time caring for children.[67] Rather than base payments on some assessment of need or on the value of caring for children, reform proposals generally would provide wage credits based on a specified hypothetical wage rate for homemaker services or an approximation of the wage that a mother might earn were she in the labor market. As Simon observes, such proposals "assimilate childcare to services produced for exchange in the labor market, and they proportion benefits, not directly to need, but to the effort made by the beneficiary."[68]

Another example of the tendency to devalue domestic labor is the fact that its market value tends to be relatively low. Child care workers, for instance, have notoriously low salaries and minimal benefits compared to the value of the work that they perform.[69] Similarly, wages for those who provide other domestic services are among the lowest of any occupational group.[70] Furthermore, research indicates that persons who hold jobs that require "nurturant" skills similar to those that are utilized in homemaking and child care tend to suffer financial disadvantage from working in such positions when studies control for other relevant features of the job.[71] Not only are the wage returns to such skills lower than for other types of skills, but the returns are in fact negative. That is, being in a job that requires the exercise of nurturant skills actually reduces wages for both men and women below what persons earn in comparable jobs that do not involve these skills.[72] One study indicates that women in such jobs lose between 24 and 44 cents an hour, while men lose between $1.25 and $1.75 an hour.[73] The author suggests that this "nurturance penalty" reflects the fact that the kinds of skills traditionally deployed by women are valued less in wage determinations than are traditionally male skills.[74] This devaluation means that employers may tend to underestimate the contribution of work done in "women's jobs" to an organization's productivity.[75]

Recognition of the tendency to ignore or undervalue the performance of domestic responsibilities has prompted the directive in many recent statutes that homemaking be treated as a "contribution" to the acquisition of assets for purposes of property division. Without a claim on post-divorce income, however, this provision will have limited effect on the financial condition of women after divorce. Unfortunately, there is reason to believe that property rhetoric's close association with market labor may limit recognition of such claims.

First, thinking of post-divorce income as property may reinforce a tendency to regard that income as the product of labor expended after the marriage is over. It may seem plausible to a court to regard assets available for division at divorce as the product of comparable exertions of effort by the spouses during the marriage. The earnings of a spouse after divorce, however, may appear more naturally a function of and reward for the time and effort devoted to the job by the individual alone. The resulting visceral sense that the husband's income is property earned by the sweat of his own brow thus may lead a court to regard a claim on post-divorce income as a request for redistribution of property from one who has labored for it to one who has not. Such requests traditionally have been regarded with great hostility as efforts to "permit[] those who have done poorly to undo the results of past efforts and shift to themselves the benefits earned by those who have done well."[76]

Second, even if a court is willing to attribute a portion of post-divorce earnings as attributable to the efforts of a wife during marriage, there is a risk that the traditional devaluation of domestic labor will lead to low estimates of the value of those contributions to the acquisition of enhanced earning power. The performance of child care and homemaking responsibilities may be regarded as only marginally related to the kind of labor that typically brings rewards in the market. Even if a court treats a diminution in human capital as a compensable contribution, this approach will primarily benefit women who have invested in market labor skills. By valuing time spent in child care as an opportunity cost based on market wage rates, human capital theory provides little compensation for women who have invested primarily in domestic labor. A woman who had planned to devote most of her efforts to motherhood for the near future therefore would be disadvantaged by property rhetoric's close association with labor market desert. Furthermore, should she desire to engage primarily in care of her children after divorce, she may well be regarded as an able-bodied person who is not willing to make an effort to earn property in the market, and therefore as someone who should not be able to live off the labor of her ex-husband. This disparate impact of labor desert theory on different women bears resemblance to a phenomenon noted by Simon: reliance on private market analogies in defending public welfare programs has tended to produce the least support for public assistance programs that do not seem to condition benefits based on contributions by the recipient.[77]

Simon's analysis of the rhetoric of public welfare programs also may provide broader lessons. His study demonstrates the way in which private law norms strongly influenced by labor desert theory necessarily required framing justifications for entitlements in certain ways. Those norms were based on the image of a self-reliant individual whose claims on resources were defended as a return on market labor. This individual's claims against the state therefore could be conceptualized as the product of an exchange in which contributions were traded for eventual benefits. Simon argues that public welfare advocates were ill-equipped to defend welfare programs when public assistance came under more stringent attack, and when private pension plans seemed to offer income security even more congruent with labor desert theory than Social Security.[78] Their rhetoric prevented them from constructing a different vision of entitlement based on the theory that in an interdependent society we may have responsibilities to others that cannot be fully characterized by private law norms of earnings and exchange.

Similarly, property rhetoric's close relationship to labor desert theory may prevent those who seek reform from reconceptualizing the relationship between ex-spouses in a way that provides a defensible rationale for more generous financial awards at divorce. Claims on society of course are not the same as claims on ex-spouses. We may well justify entitlement to public benefits on the basis of need alone. We are unlikely to acknowledge a claim on post-divorce income, however, without a specific reason why an *ex-spouse* should be the one held responsible for responding to the need of his former partner. Nonetheless, we should be aware that property rhetoric, with its strong identification with market labor desert, is a language of earnings and exchange that minimizes the possibility that the interdependence of marriage may create at least some obligation for an ex-spouse to respond to a former partner's economic need.

### Economic Inequality

A final element of property rhetoric is the acceptance of economic inequality as an inevitable consequence of the protection of private property rights in a market system. To the extent that the relationship between individuals is seen as that of property-holders within the market, we may tend to regard any disparity in resources between them as the justifiable outcome of meritocratic economic processes rather than as a problem that may require redistribution of income.

Jennifer Hochschild underscores this point in her analysis of Americans' complex conceptions of fairness. Hochschild has suggested that Americans tend to apply distinctive norms of distribution to different domains of social life.[79] These domains represent conceptual devices for interpreting and organizing experience, and thereby provide general frameworks for sorting and analyzing various kinds of issues with which individuals must deal.[80] Hochschild argues that the principal domains that individuals utilize in this endeavor are the socializing, the economic, and the political domains. The socializing domain is the domain of " 'everyday life,' such as family, school, and friends."[81] The goods distributed in this realm tend to be "material goods, services, emotions, or authority, but seldom money."[82] The economic domain is the domain in which persons earn a living and find a place in the larger society. It involves issues relating to income and authority within the workplace and the social structure. The goods distributed within this domain are "pecuniary or obvious money substitutes,"[83] which means that the market is a prominent feature of this sphere. Finally, the political domain is the domain that involves issues of citizenship, governmental action, and national identification. The goods distributed in this realm tend to be both pecuniary and nonpecuniary, "since they influence rights, influence legal decisions, and authority over values."[84]

The two domains most relevant to my discussion here are the socializing and economic domains. Hochschild's work indicates that the predominant distributive principle in the socializing domain is equality.[85] Various kinds of equalitarian norms may express this principle, and different norms may be applied to different aspects of the socializing domain such as home, school, and community.[86] The norms that are regarded as most salient within the family, however, are those of strict equality and need.[87] Strict equality provides that "[a]ll community members deserve equal amounts of the good being divided. Alternatively, members should sacrifice equally when necessary."[88] A norm of need states that "[a]ll needs of community members deserve equal satisfaction. Alternatively, members should sacrifice equal amounts of satisfaction when necessary."[89] Hochschild observes that even within the family, different norms may be applied in different situations. Most parents, for instance, "leaven [their] focus on equality with discipline," by insisting on occasion that their children should earn the rewards that they are given.[90] Nonetheless, "strict equality and need predominate in family relations."[91]

By contrast, even individuals who rely on the principle of equality in the socializing domain tend to accept a principle of "differentiation" in the economic domain.[92] While a variety of norms may express this principle in particular situations, two particularly prominent norms associated with differentiation are investments and results. The former provides that individuals deserve rewards according to the efforts that they expend, while the latter dictates that persons are entitled to rewards "in proportion to their productivity or social contribution, usually, but not necessarily, measured by market value."[93] With respect to wages, for instance, individuals tend to insist that productivity should be the predominant consideration, regardless of need.[94] In addition, persons sometimes justify disparities in wealth by using a norm of ascription, which assumes that those who are wealthy must deserve their position because of their superiority.[95] When an issue is classified as falling within the economic domain, then, persons utilize a variety of distributive norms that tend to justify considerable tolerance of inequality.

Hochschild underscores the way in which solicitude for property rights is closely associated with commitment to differentiation in economic life. Those who claim that a norm of results best promotes individual freedom, she observes, "insist on the sanctity of private property."[96] Property is seen as both a reward and incentive for productivity, so that "[e]quality, or even a principle of prima facie equality, threatens property rights that are essential to liberty; therefore, it must be kept within strict conceptual and political bounds."[97] Solicitude for property is reflected in the fact that, while the principle of equality is generally accepted in the political domain, this principle finds least support with respect to the distribution of property.[98] Hochschild reports that attitudes regarding issues of economic distribution reflect ambivalence. On the one hand, viewed as an economic issue, redistribution "is wrong because it violates the principle of differentiation."[99] On the other hand, seen as an issue in the political domain, "it may be right because it satisfies the principle of equality."[100] Ultimately, however, while most persons would support intrusion on property rights in some instances, "[d]ifferentiation with regard to property seems as solid as a norm can be."[101]

Jennifer Nedelsky suggests that this close connection between solicitude for property and the acceptance of inequality has a long history in American society. She maintains that, for the framers of the American constitution, "[p]roperty was important for the exercise of liberty and liberty required the free exercise of property rights."[102] Since people necessarily will differ in endowments such as talent, perseverance, and other character traits, their pursuit of liberty will inevitably result in the acquisition of unequal amounts of property. Nedelsky argues in particular that James Madison regarded economic inequality as a constant feature of a society that prized personal freedom. Madison therefore believed that the recurring problem for a self-governing republic would be how to protect the rights of the propertied few from the demands of a permanent propertyless class.[103] The result, Nedelsky asserts, is that Madison's structural arrangement of power in the Constitution was animated to a considerable degree by the belief that "[t]he inequality of property had to be reflected in political inequality[.]"[104] In this way, acceptance of inequality has characterized the traditional American conception of the relationship between property and liberty.[105]

What might be the implications of this acceptance for the way in which we conceptualize financial claims and obligations at divorce? First, we can see that, in Hochschild's terms, traditional divorce located ex-spouses within the socializing domain. This is why need at least formally was a significant consideration in financial awards at divorce. It is why ex-husbands theoretically were obligated to continue supporting their ex-wives after divorce in order to avoid gross disparities in post-divorce economic condition. By contrast, contemporary divorce law locates ex-spouses within the market, a domain in which a variety of explanations are available to rationalize disparities in resources.[106] Once accounts are settled between economic partners at divorce, each person makes his or her own way in the market with different talents, skills, training, and other attributes relevant to economic success. We naturally would expect these individuals' economic fortunes to differ, because no two people will have the same endowments, work as hard, or make the same choices. An ex-spouse can't be held responsible for any disparities in the other's financial condition, because these simply reflect the meritocratic workings of the market.

This unwillingness to hold ex-spouses responsible for remedying inequality may be reinforced by human capital theory's conceptualization of spousal interaction as the exchange of resources between property holders, which may create accounts receivable for which compensation must be paid at divorce. Since persons enter into marriage with unequal endowments and resources, we might well expect that the results of these exchanges during marriage would not necessarily produce equal benefits for each partner. Thus, for instance, a woman can't expect much compensation for her lack of earning power at divorce if she entered marriage with relatively limited career prospects and devoted herself primarily to homemaking. As a result, inequalities after marriage may be seen as attributable to inevitable inequalities resulting from voluntary exchanges during marriage between spouses with different amounts of wealth. To the extent that we use property rhetoric to reinforce a vision of ex-spouses as market actors, we may be more willing to accept economic inequality between men and women after divorce.

## Legal Outcomes

How might current legal outcomes reflect the mythology of property? In this section, I will explore some of the ways in which the use of property rhetoric can serve to constrain decisions about financial allocations at divorce. I want to be clear that I am not arguing that property has essential characteristics whose logic inexorably must lead to certain outcomes. Property is a contestable concept. Indeed, as I will discuss at a later point, one reason that the issue of financial compensation at divorce is so controversial is that it is the occasion for struggles over the question of how property should be conceptualized. Nonetheless, as I suggested in the previous section, property traditionally has been closely associated with certain understandings that have powerful resonance in American culture. These understandings tend to shape in significant ways our sense of what it means either formally or effectively to characterize something as a property entitlement. Particularly in the context of gender relations, property rhetoric tends to call up particular images and metaphors that in turn seem naturally to lead to certain legal conclusions. Not all legislatures or courts reach these conclusions, but those who do not must struggle against the cultural current. My argument therefore is that the mythology of property provides a readily available rhetorical resource that can serve in many cases to justify limitations on financial awards at divorce. This suggests that it would be unwise to base divorce awards solely on an external stance toward marriage.

**Enhanced Earning Power as Property.**   The most direct deployment of property rhetoric to assert a claim to post-divorce income is the argument that the enhanced earning power reflected in that income is an asset acquired during marriage and thus constitutes marital property divisible at divorce. This argument is made perhaps most often with respect to an educational degree or professional license, but is logically applicable to any enhancement of earning capacity that occurs during marriage.[107] Courts have overwhelmingly rejected this claim,[108] with most states holding instead that any contribution to enhanced earnings is a factor that should be considered in property division and maintenance decisions.[109] The justifications for this rejection of the argument that enhanced earning capacity is marital property are worth exploring as useful illustrations of the ways in which property rhetoric may be used to limit financial compensation at divorce.

The most common rationale offered in denying the claim of a property interest in these cases is that degrees, licenses, and the earning power that they represent "ha[ve] none of the attributes of property in the usual sense of that term."[110] *Graham v. Graham*, for instance, the decision most often cited in reaching this conclusion, held that an M.B.A. degree is not property because it has no exchange value or any objective value on an open market; it is personal to the holder, uninheritable, and terminating on his death; and it cannot be assigned, sold, transferred, conveyed, or pledged.[111] A later Colorado Supreme Court reconsidering and reaffirming *Graham* noted an additional reason on which many courts rely: that valuation of future earning capacity is highly speculative, because it is dependent on myriad contingencies that might affect how much an individual might earn over the course of his lifetime.[112] In this sense, future earning power is deemed distinguishable from other assets, such as pension benefits, that accrue in the future. As one court explained, the latter have been earned during the marriage and have a definite ascertainable value, even if that value cannot be realized until certain conditions have been satisfied.[113]

For these reasons, courts tend to regard future income as a "mere expectancy,"[114] lacking the stable attributes that traditionally constitute a *res* that can be owned. As Jennifer Nedelsky has observed, "the most compelling part of the concept of property"[115] has been its "concrete, material quality" rooted in everyday experience.[116] As Nedelsky notes, traditional conceptions of property have not been exclusively material; indeed one characteristic of the legal understanding of property is that it consists of abstract divisible interests.[117] Nonetheless, property traditionally has had "a clear material base which is the core of both the legal and popular conceptions."[118] This material base contributes powerfully to the understanding of property as providing the stability and security that underlie the conception of autonomy as independence. The more indeterminacy and speculation that seems to attend a claim, the less likely that it will be regarded as a property interest.

This concern for relative certainty is reflected in the fact that property orders at divorce generally are unmodifiable.[119] This rule expresses the notion that property rights should be an absolute and unalterable source of security for the recipient, which cannot be undone by future judicial action. Several courts have argued that the inability to modify property awards in light of changed circumstances makes the classification of future earnings as property particularly problematic, since the valuation of that property would depend so heavily on speculation about an uncertain future.[120] Courts fear that a spouse thereby would be locked into a particular career path because of his financial obligations, severely restricted in the liberty to choose a more satisfying way of life.[121] This restriction would conflict with the notion that the earnings that eventually do constitute property as they are received by the wage-earner should provide him with the autonomy to live his life as he chooses without interference by others.

Courts are willing to engage in speculative calculations of future income in other instances such as tort cases. Damage awards in those cases, however, are regarded as necessary in order to affirm the autonomy of an individual upon which others have infringed. To the extent that the independence of the defendant is curtailed in these circumstances, that is deemed justified by his wrongful invasion of another's sphere of autonomy. Furthermore, there is no alternative to speculative calculations in such cases if a plaintiff is to receive redress. By contrast, courts in divorce cases assume that future earning power need not be considered property in order to take a spouse's contributions into account in maintenance decisions and in the division of conventional assets.

This solicitude for the ex-spouse's control over his earnings also reflects the notion that post-divorce income reflects property that is earned through the individual's market labor. As one judge put it, the value of an educational degree in the future is "entirely dependent on the efforts of the educated spouse."[122] Thus, even if it is property, it should be regarded as individual rather than marital property. This conclusion is lent support by the fact that state statutes explicitly provide that an individual's income after divorce is separate property not available for distribution between the spouses.[123] These statutes rest on the assumption that wages are earned by services rendered during the relevant pay period, so that classification of wages as separate or marital depends on the wage-earner's marital status at the time that income is earned.[124] As one scholar suggests, "[a] conclusion that all or a part of a spouse's post-divorce earning capacity at divorce is marital property is not consistent" with the approach of these statutes.[125] The same philosophy is reflected in cases that choose to value certain assets on the separation rather than divorce date, on the ground that any increase in value after the former reflects the efforts of only one of the spouses.[126] The association of property with relatively concrete attributes thus creates the tendency to assume that income earned after divorce is property that reflects a reward for contemporaneous effort. Granting an ex-spouse a claim on this income seems to take the fruits of an individual's labor and redistribute it to another person who has expended no effort to acquire it.

The same insistence that property have certain essential features, and the desire to shield future earnings from classification as property, are reflected in cases involving claims on the value of the goodwill of a business enterprise. Goodwill generally is defined as the value resulting from the tendency of customers or clients to do business with an enterprise because of its established reputation, rather than because of the specific individuals providing service.[127] Many courts hold that goodwill must be marketable in order to be treated as marital property at divorce.[128] In part, this requirement reflects the idea that legal interests should have certain characteristics, such as alienability, in order to be regarded as property. In addition, the marketability criterion serves to distinguish the portion of an enterprise that is considered marital property from the future earnings of the spouse associated with that enterprise.[129] The latter, courts insist, cannot be marital property because it is acquired after the marriage has ended.[130] Again, both autonomy and labor desert considerations inform this conclusion. If a spouse is subject to post-divorce obligations based on the value of illiquid goodwill, he will be forced to continue his current employment without the possibility of selling his business and choosing a different way of life. As one court declared:

> to award the value of an unmarketable asset to an ex-spouse might restrict the liberty of the spouse who possesses that asset. That spouse might want to leave the business, change careers, go into public service, return to school, or any number of other possibilities that could reduce one's income. However, that spouse will frequently be restricted from doing so because of large payments on a promissory note to the ex-spouse. The spouse possessing the goodwill asset, which might constitute a large portion of the value of the business, will not be able to sell the asset because it is unmarketable.[131]

In addition, the distinction between the firm's goodwill and the future earnings attributable to personal goodwill rests on the notion that the latter represents the fruits of an individual's labor after divorce. Indeed, the desire to protect future earnings on labor desert grounds is reflected even in one case in which the court held that goodwill existed in the husband's physical therapy practice.[132] The valuation of that goodwill, ruled the court, must be based on the past earnings, rather than the projected future earnings, of the practice because the latter reflects the "postmarital efforts of the professional spouse."[133]

The argument that enhanced earning power should be treated as marital property at divorce thus must contend with the association of property with relatively definite and concrete attributes, with its symbol as a source of autonomy and liberty for those who possess it, and with the perception that post-divorce income represents the fruits of labor expended after a marriage has ended. While courts need not and do not unanimously reach the outcomes that I have described in this section, property rhetoric provides a powerful language in which to justify them.

Concern that requests for formal classification of post-divorce income as property must face these obstacles has led some observers to argue that a claim for compensation for contributions as opposed to enhanced income is a preferable strategy. This argument rests on the assumption that the concept of human capital must be taken into account when defining the contributions that a spouse has made during marriage. While this approach may not couch its assertions as a demand for the formal classification of post-divorce income as property, it nonetheless relies on property rhetoric in framing its claims. In the next section, I will explore how this reliance may limit its effectiveness.

Return on Investment.   Several courts that refuse to treat enhanced earning power as marital property indicate that it is appropriate to take contributions to enhancement into account in maintenance decisions at divorce.[134] One approach is to conceptualize spousal compensation as a return on investment. This theory explicitly relies on a model of the supporting spouse as an investor who contributes resources that increase her partner's earning power, and who expects to share in the enhanced earnings that represent that enhancement of human capital. The first way in which the logic of property rhetoric may limit willingness to recognize such claims is that valuation of a degree, license, or other form of career advancement requires an estimate of future earnings. As a result, a claim for compensation in the amount of the expected gain from investment encounters most of the same difficulties that beset a claim that future earnings are marital property. The calculation will necessarily be highly speculative.

It is true that a maintenance order is more easily modified than a property award, so concern about locking the paying spouse into a specific career path arguably is less salient in these cases.[135] At the same time, there still may be concern that the provision of compensation from post-divorce income will restrict the autonomy of the paying spouse because he will have to petition for a modification of the original order if he does make a career change, and a court will scrutinize whether he has made this change in good faith.[136] Furthermore, the speculative calculation of future income remains in tension with the notion of property as a relatively definite, stable, concrete asset. In addition, a court may still tend to be protective of future income on the assumption that it reflects the fruits of labor expended after divorce. Thus, the conventional solicitude for shielding future earnings from claims against the wage-earner may well limit the success of a claim for compensation based on expected gain, even if that claim is not based on the argument that enhanced earnings are marital property.

A second limitation on the viability of a claim for expected gain is that human capital theory itself can be used to argue that such a claim should be honored only rarely. Allen Parkman's analysis of this issue is illustrative. Parkman argues that the argument for compensation based on expected gain typically is based on an overestimate of the increment of enhanced earning power attributable to contributions during marriage.[137] A common misperception, maintains Parkman, is that human capital is created when, for instance, a degree is received. In fact, the process of capital accumulation begins much earlier.[138] It consists of a package of investments that have been made over the person's lifetime up to that point, which includes elements such as prior education, academic performance, and sacrifices of leisure time and income by both the student and his or her family since childhood. Parkman argues that the greatest impediment to attaining a professional education is not the cost associated with attending school but the difficulty in gaining admission.[139] All these prior investments are crucial in overcoming this obstacle and constitute the vast bulk of costs incurred for the sake of enhancement of earning power. By contrast, tuition, books, and living expenses "are only a small part of these costs."[140] As a result, suggests Parkman, "[u]nder normal circumstances, the investment in human capital prior to marriage will be so large and essential relative to the investment after marriage that an individual's human capital should be treated as separate property."[141]

Furthermore, after admission to school several sources of funding for educational expenses are available: the student may work part-time, may leave school temporarily in order to work full time, or may obtain loans through government-subsidized programs, a university, or conventional market-rate sources.[142] Contributions from a spouse thus rarely are essential to the acquisition of a degree, but rather usually simply increase a student's standard of living while he or she is in school and/or reduce future indebtedness.[143] Parkman argues that Joan Krauskopf's proposal to compensate the supporting spouse for expected gain ignores this characteristic of spousal contributions and thus the difference between equity and debt financing.[144] Equity financing, says Parkman, provides funds that are essential, so that an enterprise cannot proceed without them. Because of the relatively high risk associated with such a contribution, an equity investor has a claim on a share of the proceeds generated by the enterprise.[145] For the reasons described above, spousal support usually does not fall into this category. Rather, it tends to constitute debt financing, providing funds that the student otherwise would have to acquire by loan. Persons with a debt interest are entitled not to a share of the proceeds of the enterprise that they funded, but to the return of contributions plus an agreed-upon rate of interest.[146] As a result, argues Parkman, the rigorous application of human capital theory in most cases will dictate that a spouse should receive reimbursement for the expenses that she incurred in providing support plus interest.[147]

The idea that spousal support often enhances the quality of life, rather than being essential to the enhancement of earning power, also likely has some force in cases that do not involve educational degrees. The logic of the economic partnership model is that a wife's homemaking and child care services make it possible for a husband to concentrate on his job, thereby enhancing his ability to generate income. The implicit assumption is that if she did not provide this assistance, the husband would have to spend more time on domestic and child care chores. One can argue, however, that this would not necessarily occur. Research indicates that work is highly significant to men's self-esteem.[148] Studies also suggest that husbands typically have little inclination to perform housework, even when their wives are employed full time in the paid labor market.[149] It seems plausible to predict that if their wives did little housework many men would simply tolerate a lower standard of domestic tidiness or would pay for someone else to perform housekeeping tasks. Similarly, evidence suggests that many fathers spend relatively small amounts of time with their children.[150] If mothers were not willing to provide the bulk of child care services, it seems plausible to predict that some men would simply choose not to have children or that a significant number would opt to purchase child care in the market rather than significantly curtail their work schedules to provide it. If this is true, then wives' homemaking and child care responsibilities may make life easier for a husband who works or may save the expense of paying someone else to perform those duties. It often may not, however, make it possible for him to earn more income than he would if she did not provide that assistance.[151] This suggests that a wife should be compensated for the value of the contributions that she has provided in the form of household goods and services, but should not share in any enhancement of income that occurs during marriage. As a result, rigorous application of the logic of economic exchange that underlies the financial partnership model would deny compensation for expected gain in many instances.

The metaphors and images of property rhetoric therefore can be used to undermine the argument that a spouse should be entitled to share in the gain in earning power that occurs during marriage. If we treat the spouse as an investor in her partner's human capital, in most cases the value of her investment is dwarfed by all the prior investments that have made an increase in future income possible. If we treat her as an economic partner, her contributions make life easier for her husband but often are not crucial to any enhancement of earning power. In each instance, property rhetoric suggests that at most she should receive the value of the resources that she transferred to her spouse plus interest. The implicit force of this logic may explain why most courts that have considered the issue tend to hold that one spouse who has contributed to the enhanced earning power of the other is entitled to reimbursement for the value of contributions,[152] even when, for instance, the court is willing to label a professional degree as property.[153]

Might property rhetoric and the model of economic partnership offer assistance by arguing that a diminution in the value of human capital should be recognized as a contribution that should be reimbursed? While this approach can be used to justify more generous financial awards in some cases, its logic also can be deployed to limit compensation in others. This suggests that the use of property and partnership metaphors as the foundation for reimbursement claims will not consistently avoid hardship for financially dependent spouses at divorce.

## Reimbursement of Contributions

Those who use the economic partnership model to justify compensation for contributions first must confront some difficulties under partnership law. Unless the parties agree otherwise, a partnership is terminable at will.[154] When a partnership ends, the partners are entitled to compensation only for their capital contributions.[155] They receive payment neither for the services that they have provided the partnership,[156] nor for any lost earning capacity that they may have suffered by virtue of participation in the partnership.[157] Once the required compensation is provided, "the partners have no further continuing obligations to one another."[158] Exceptions to this principle occur when one partner has wrongfully dissolved a partnership, has failed to serve the firm, or has provided extraordinary services to the partnership.[159] None of these exceptions, however, are readily applicable to divorce. If a partnership is at will, it can be terminated unilaterally "whatever the motive and whatever the injurious consequences to copartners[.]"[160]

Similarly, the availability of unilateral no-fault divorce means that either spouse has the right to end a marriage for any reason whatsoever, which insulates him or her from any claim that the termination is wrongful. Furthermore, as Ira Ellman notes, exceptions for failure to serve the partnership or for extraordinary contributions to it would require us to assume "the existence of accepted conventions regarding marital duties against which to test a spouse's performance."[161] Deriving these conventions by attempting to analogize the duties of parties in an economic partnership is of limited use. Furthermore, if these conventions are specific to marriage, why not simply say that marriage involves certain distinctive responsibilities, rather than seek to characterize it as an economic partnership? Reliance on the economic partnership model thus not only undermines a claim to compensation for a loss in earning power, but also makes problematic any sort of claim for compensation based on anything other than financial contributions.

As we have seen, Cynthia Starnes is more sanguine about the relevance of partnership law. She argues that we should regard divorce as giving rise to a right not of a wind-up of the partnership, with the distribution described above, but of a buyout of a partner's interest, which offers more generous compensation. The latter remedy is available when a partner withdraws prematurely from a fixed-term partnership, and the other partners elect to continue the business for the remainder of the term. Starnes argues that, in view of the typical vow of "till death do us part," marriage is a partnership for a term of the life of one of the partners.[162] When the spouses invest in one spouse's earning power, this is a marital enterprise that continues in the marketplace, even if one spouse leaves the partnership before the end of its term.[163] As a result, she argues, the buyout remedy entitles a spouse to compensation that reflects her share of the value of this enterprise. This analysis suggests that the economic partnership model need not lead to minimal financial compensation at divorce.

Starnes's argument, however, rests on a rather strained application of partnership law. First, it is difficult to argue that modern marriage is a partnership for a fixed term, given the widespread availability of unilateral no-fault divorce. The language of the traditional wedding vow is now precatory and aspirational, rather than an expression of the legally enforceable obligation that it once was. By contrast, the existence of a fixed term for a partnership gives rise to legal rights and duties. As Starnes herself observes, a partner can be liable for damages for wrongful dissociation from a partnership, and "[w]rongful dissociation usually occurs when a partner leaves the partnership before expiration of a definite term."[164]

Second, the notion that the marital enterprise continues after divorce is inconsistent with the common meaning of a partnership. A partnership requires more than one person for its existence. While a business partnership may continue after the withdrawal of one of its partners, a marital partnership *ends* when one spouse leaves. Indeed, Starnes implies this by her suggestion that a marriage runs its term when one of the spouses dies. The more natural application of the concepts of partnership law therefore suggests that divorce effects the dissolution of a partnership at will, with compensation only for financial contributions to the partnership. This provides scant comfort for those who argue that a spouse should be compensated for a reduction in human capital that occurs during marriage. Indeed, treating marriage as an economic partnership appears to lead to the much-criticized legal outcomes of the first wave of divorce reform: the return of separate property to the spouses, a division of common financial assets at the time of divorce, and a presumption against post-divorce obligation.

These limitations of the economic partnership model are consistent with property mythology's imagery of property holders as sovereign individuals who sometimes pool their resources for the sake of a joint enterprise. Partners in this venture relinquish their claim to absolute control of their property for its duration and agree to share those assets that they acquire through their combined efforts. When the association ends, however, they regain dominion over their property, are obligated to each other only by virtue of those duties that flow from their limited surrender of sovereignty, and go their separate ways in the market. Any inequality in their economic condition thereafter is attributable to market circumstances and differences in individual attributes. It therefore is not the occasion for requiring one former partner to come to the aid of the other.

A second difficulty that advocates may well encounter in pressing a claim for compensation for diminution of human capital is that the valuation of this contribution is extremely speculative. Consider, for instance, a woman who has a bachelor's degree in English who is working as an administrative assistant at the time of marriage. Suppose that the couple has a child, that she assumes primary responsibility for the child's care, and that the couple divorces after ten years of marriage. What would her earnings now be if she had not married and had a child? Are they those of an administrative assistant with ten years' of experience? Or would the wife have gone to graduate or professional school if she had not married and cared for a child? If so, in what field? If we can identify the field, how good a school would she have attended? How well would she have done in school? What would the job market have been like when she graduated? Would she have continued in that field or switched jobs? Or might she not have gone to school and instead married someone else? Even Ira Ellman, who believes in the necessity of such calculations, acknowledges the particular difficulty of determining how life might have been different without marriage:

> Of course, no adjudication is ever entirely certain, but perhaps there is a difference between the residual uncertain[t]y that usually remains in establishing an historical fact, and the uncertainty inherent in determining a "what if." The first uncertainty results entirely from limitations in the factfinding process: a real "fact" exists out there, if we can find it. The second seems more fundamental because we are not trying to establish what the real fact is, but what it would have been if the world had been different.[165]

The notion that a reduction in human capital represents a loss of property for which one spouse must compensate the other thus may require even more speculative calculations than are used in efforts to determine future earnings. In the latter instance, a spouse's profession is at least identifiable, even if other contingencies make the calculation uncertain. If, as I suggest, courts are reluctant to base claims to future income on such computations at least in part because of the necessity of speculation, then they are even less likely to do so when the determination of lost human capital requires far more elaborate assumptions. Regardless of economic theory, in such instances the asserted property interest seems only remotely to resemble the concrete, stable form of security that is an essential element in the mythology of property.

A third limitation of property rhetoric is that, even if we accept the idea that a spouse should be compensated for human capital losses incurred to enhance a partner's earning power, a spouse deemed to have suffered no such loss is entitled to no award. The logic of human capital theory thus may preclude financial assistance in cases in which a spouse is significantly disadvantaged by divorce. In

*Wright v. Wright*,[166] for instance, which I mentioned at the beginning of chapter 7, the parties married when the husband was in his first year of dental school. The wife was then earning $400 a month as a secretary, while the husband's parents provided him with tuition for educational expenses and $100 a week. At the time of divorce eight and one-half years later, the husband's annual income was $70,000, while his wife's annual income as a secretary was $15,600. The court rejected the wife's claim that she should receive compensation for her efforts in helping her husband obtain his dental degree. It limited alimony to the amount of the mortgage payment on the family home that she was awarded.[167] The court ruled that it was doubtful that the wife did more than provide her own support during the period that her husband was in dental school. Furthermore, said the court, since the husband was already in school at the time of the marriage, there was no decision to sacrifice income that the couple otherwise would have enjoyed in order for him to pursue his schooling. In addition, "[n]either did wife sacrifice her own career in order to make it possible for husband to achieve his career goal."[168] The court therefore rejected any claim on post-divorce income, despite the considerable disparity between the spouses in their economic prospects at divorce.

Similarly, in *Krause v. Krause*,[169] the wife worked full-time while the husband finished both his undergraduate and dental degrees. The couple lived for awhile with the husband's grandparents, who took care of a child born to the couple so that the wife could return to full-time work shortly after the child's birth. The husband filed for divorce five years after marriage, and the trial court awarded the wife alimony in the amount of $169,000 over 20 years in consideration of her efforts in helping her husband obtain his education. The appeals court reversed, stating that "we do not believe that [the wife] is entitled to a windfall merely by virtue of the fact that she was married to plaintiff while he earned his degree."[170] While she did provide some assistance, said the court, the majority of funds for education and household expenses came from loans secured by the husband, and a significant amount of additional support came from his relatives.[171] The court remanded for a recalculation of alimony with the directive that the trial court focus "solely on what is necessary to compensate defendant for the burdens on her or the sacrifices made by her so that plaintiff could pursue his career."[172] Thus, despite the fact that the parties had accumulated only a small amount of property during the marriage,[173] and that the husband's future income likely would be higher than his wife's,[174] the logic of the way in which the wife framed her claim on post-divorce income resulted in a reduction of her financial award by the court.[175] Those who are dissatisfied with results such as these must look beyond human capital theory in framing their criticism. The rationale for the denial of a claim in these cases is that there has occurred no sacrifice because no portion of post-divorce income has been earned by the supporting spouse through financial contributions or the expenditure of her own human capital. In the mythology of property, she has transferred no property to her husband, so he has no duty of compensation.

A fourth limitation on the effectiveness of human capital theory as the basis for a reimbursement claim is that, even if some sacrifice has occurred, that theory dictates that the compensation that is due depends on a spouse's lost earning capacity. Thus, even if a wife quits work and devotes herself completely to home-making and child care, she may receive little if any compensation if her opportunities in the paid labor market during marriage are not very lucrative. As Allen Parkman explains, "Some individuals have the prospect of flat income profiles over their lives because of limited investments in human capital before their marriage. They probably do not have the capacity to experience a substantial depreciation in their human capital during marriage."[176] For instance, says Parkman, a woman who at marriage "was and expected to continue to be a retail sales clerk" may not be made worse off by divorce than she would have been had she not married.[177] As a result, her human capital has not been adversely affected by marriage.[178]

This view is reflected, for instance, in *Cathleen C.Q. v. Norman J.Q.*,[179] a divorce case in which the court rejected the wife's claim that the court should equalize the income between the spouses after a 30-year marriage. In affirming an alimony award of $200 per month, the court noted that the wife possessed investment securities, and that there was no evidence that she had suffered any loss in earning capacity for the sake of her husband. "She was not employed at the time of her marriage and had no career plans or professional skills," said the court.[180] The wife's lack of significant earning capacity at the time of marriage meant that she was no worse off in human capital terms after 30 years of marriage than if she had never married.

A claim for reimbursement based on human capital theory thus is vulnerable to the tendency to valorize paid labor market activity that is so closely associated with property rhetoric. Women who receive the most financial assistance at divorce are those with the largest amount of paid labor market skills, and those who receive the least are women who have chosen a traditionally feminine path by concentrating on homemaking and child care or choosing jobs that emphasize caregiving. Mary O'Connell suggests that this approach to compensation tends to rely implicitly on a model that treats women as "damaged men,"[181] because "they have deviated from the male model of continuous participation in the labor force."[182] In this way, human capital theory marginalizes important aspects of many women's experience.[183]

Even if a court concludes that compensation is due for all contributions to a spouse's enhanced earning power, the logic of property rhetoric may limit an award in yet another way. That rhetoric characterizes a contributing spouse as a person who invests in her partner's earning power in the expectation that she will be paid back from increased household income over the life of the marriage. Compensation at divorce therefore may be necessary if the marriage ends before this repayment occurs. The logic of this theory is that the longer the marriage, the greater the likelihood that the spouse has been repaid for her contribution through an increase in her standard of living. California, for instance, explicitly provides that after a long marriage a supporting spouse is deemed to have received an adequate return on her investment in her spouse's earning power.[184] Similarly, some courts have declared that in cases involving enhanced earning power, the passage of time "reduces and eventually eliminates" the need to compensate for contributions, because the supporting spouse may well have realized "a return which may exceed the amount of her contribution to [her spouse's] education."[185]

This benefit may be reflected both in the consumption that occurred during marriage as well as the amount of property available for distribution at divorce.

Allen Parkman acknowledges that the need for reimbursement for direct financial contributions should decline as the length of the marriage increases, because the nonstudent spouse over the years will have received the benefits from her investment.[186] He suggests, nonetheless, that the longer the marriage the more likely a spouse has made a sacrifice of human capital that reduces her earning power. The need for reimbursement of *this* contribution, he argues, therefore increases over time.[187]

A court logically could find however, that an increased standard of living has provided adequate compensation for diminution of a spouse's human capital. Indeed, Parkman himself acknowledges that as a marriage continues, a partner will be compensated for a reduction in human capital by actions taken for her benefit by other family members.[188] Depending on a couple's standard of living, a spouse may well be compensated relatively early in a marriage for her direct financial contribution to enhanced earning power. Any increased income after that point would then serve to compensate her for her reduction in earning capacity. This reduction in some cases may be offset by the increased disposable household income made possible by her performance of domestic responsibilities. The extent to which this will occur will of course depend on the facts of each case. The broader point, however, is that the longer the marriage, the greater the chances that a spouse will have received compensation for the contributions that she has made, whatever form they may have taken.

Property rhetoric in this instance thus would suggest that those least deserving of financial awards at divorce are spouses who have been involved in long marriages—even though we know that those with the grimmest economic prospects at divorce typically are women who are in just this circumstance. In the mythology of property, these woman have received fair value for the resources that they have provided and therefore have no further claim on their former husbands.

Finally, aside from its logical implications, property rhetoric may be of limited effectiveness in securing reimbursement for contributions during marriage because of resistance to the application of its principles to marriage. Courts are more willing than before to provide such compensation, but even those that do so sometimes express the fear that a precise calculation of marital contributions and sacrifices is inconsistent with the spirit of marriage. *Mahoney v. Mahoney,*[189] for instance, adopted the concept of reimbursement alimony but cautioned that "[m]arriage is not a business arrangement in which the parties keep track of debits and credits, their accounts to be settled upon divorce."[190] Similarly, in *In re Marriage of Wisner,*[191] the court rejected the claim that a husband's medical license was marital property, stating that "unjust enrichment, as a legal concept, is not properly applied in the setting of a marital relationship. Marriage is by nature not an arm's length transaction between two parties."[192] The consequence is that some courts have held that a spouse is entitled to reimbursement at divorce only for those services that exceed the typical contributions that spouses make to the family during the marriage.[193] Another result may be that courts will be more willing to provide reimbursement of financial contributions, which most closely resemble market goods and services, while denying or limiting compensation for domestic labor, which traditionally has been regarded as gratuitously provided.[194]

This resistance of course reflects adherence to the belief that family and market activities should remain separate. Acceptance of this dichotomy is most pernicious to women when it assumes that spouses are involved in an altruistic communal economy during marriage but are transformed into independent market actors at divorce. Property rhetoric challenges this paradigm by arguing that spouses implicitly engage in market exchange during marriage and are entitled to compensation for any imbalance in trade. In this sense, property rhetoric and the external stance toward marriage that it reflects focuses attention on economic justice between spouses. This represents an improvement over approaches that maintain a sharp dichotomy between communal and individualistic domains. At the same time, however, a desire that marriage not be transformed into merely another sector of the market is based on a vision of marriage that has considerable resonance. For now, it is sufficient to observe that this sentiment may serve to limit willingness to provide the compensation that otherwise would be dictated by adherence to market principles. Later in this chapter, I will explore whether it can be utilized to fashion a different approach to financial awards at divorce that draws on appreciation of an internal stance toward marriage.

## Conclusion

I have suggested that property in American culture historically has been associated with certain distinct images and ideals that constitute a mythology of property closely aligned with liberal theory. The elements of this mythology include first the notion that the possession of property makes possible a form of autonomy characterized by independence from others. This independence entails that an individual is bound only by obligations that he has voluntarily assumed. Second, property entitlements typically are seen as earned by labor in the market rather than in the domestic sphere. Finally, because property rights are regarded as the fruits of talent and willingness to expend effort, and because these are unevenly distributed among individuals, inequality of property holdings is an inevitable feature of a regime that protects private property rights. Using property rhetoric to frame arguments about financial claims and obligations at divorce thus evokes a particular normative universe, populated by independent property-holders whose obligations to one another arise through the voluntary exchange of resources. This universe offers certain forms of argument and justification while precluding others.

I have explored the ways in which this rhetoric may create obstacles for those who seek to use it to argue for more generous financial awards at divorce. Those who seek to utilize property rhetoric to argue for greater financial compensation at divorce would find unacceptable most of the legal outcomes that I have described, even though these outcomes reflect a conventional application of the premises of that rhetoric. One reason for this is that many of these advocates in fact implicitly base their arguments on considerations that transcend this rhetoric, even as they profess to use it in framing their claims.[195] For many, denying financial assistance to a spouse with few market skills seems inequitable, even if she entered the marriage in the same condition. Similarly, rejecting the claim of a wife in a long marriage with few tangible assets seems unfair, even if there is an argument that she has been compensated for her contributions through a higher standard of living during marriage. These assessments implicitly reflect the use of a more expansive discourse than property rhetoric. That discourse regards marriage not simply as an economic partnership, but as a distinctive open-ended relationship of mutuality, interdependence, and care, in which responsibilities may arise without express consent and impacts may linger after divorce. As such, it expresses an internal stance toward marriage. From this perspective, the need of an ex-spouse is relevant because spouses have a special duty to avoid leaving their partners financially disadvantaged after divorce.

Reformers often tend to suppress this alternative rhetoric, however, because they believe that property rhetoric is the most persuasive language in which to justify divorce awards.[196] This prevents them from self-consciously fashioning the coherent rationale that is necessary to defend departures from the outcomes otherwise dictated by the economic partnership model.[197]

Why do reformers grant this privileged status to property rhetoric while suppressing their qualifications of it? One reason, I believe, is that their implicit account of marriage and divorce relies heavily on an external stance toward marriage. This stance presents marriage as an economic partnership that generates only those financial rights and duties that would arise between any two individuals who pool their assets in the hope of maximizing financial gain. Its depiction of divorce as a "clean break" characterizes ex-spouses as strangers who go their separate ways without any continuing economic ties. Property language *is* in fact the most persuasive language in which to describe the financial claims and obligations of individuals conceptualized in this way. Dissatisfaction with the outcomes produced by the logic of that rhetoric therefore should lead us to ask whether we should draw on an internal stance toward marriage to construct a more complex account of marriage and divorce to guide the law of divorce awards. In the next section, I sketch the form that such an account might take and speculate on its impact.

## Toward an Alternative Rhetoric

### Possibilities

The highly individualistic vision of marriage and divorce expressed by property rhetoric captures one dimension of marriage but fails to include another: the way that spouses' lives become intertwined psychologically, emotionally, and economically. Contemporary culture emphasizes the ideal of the companionate marriage, in which the spouses strive for intense intimacy and shared experience as part of a process of mutual personal growth.[198] In this way, marriage serves to construct a "nomos," an arrangement "that creates for the individual the sort of order in which he can experience his life as making sense."[199] The result is that marriage typically is a crucial constituent of a spouse's identity.[200] Indeed, most people probably believe that a person's sense of self *should* be changed by marriage. Someone who seemed psychologically unchanged by the experience, living his life and seeing the world no differently than before, likely would be regarded as unresponsive to his partner and insensitive to the emotional openness that marriage is seen to require.

Similarly, marriage typically involves sharing of financial resources. Not all spouses necessarily share all resources,[201] and disparities in income may produce disparities in power within a marriage.[202] Nonetheless, economic sharing is a powerful norm of married life, so much so that most spouses naturally adopt the presumption that they will pool their funds.[203] As one set of researchers puts it, "Pooling is part of the package of marriage."[204] Married couples are far more likely to pool their money, and to prefer to do so, than are unmarried couples.[205] This arrangement reflects the view that funds are available for individual family members' needs regardless of the extent to which they have contributed income to the household. The result is that "[i]n an ongoing marriage, the entire family shares in the salary advantages and job-related medical, insurance, and pension benefits that disproportionately accompany male jobs."[206] In important respects, spouses are participants in the closest thing to a communal economy that American culture is willing to sanction.

Marriage therefore tends to involve a relationship whose influence permeates virtually every aspect of a spouse's daily life. Furthermore, despite the fact that almost half of all marriages end in divorce, most of those entering marriage see it as ideally a permanent commitment to share one's life with another.[207] One study of applicants for a marriage license, for instance, found that the median estimate of the divorce rate in the United States was an accurate 50 percent. The median response when the applicants were asked the likelihood that they personally would divorce, however, was 0 percent.[208] In addition, contrary to actual practice, applicants were quite optimistic that a divorcing woman who requested alimony would be awarded it by the court.[209] Those entering marriage thus tend to have "thoroughly idealistic expectations about both the longevity of their own marriages and the consequences should they personally be divorced."[210] They see marriage as an open-ended commitment to a shared life that will endure. They expect not merely equal exchange but mutual care; not simply compensation for contributions but the enjoyment of a shared standard of living. They see their commitment as a pledge to look out for each other not only during marriage, but to some degree if the marriage ends as well. In reliance on these expectations, they make a host of subtle accommodations, sacrifices, and plans, not all of which can be readily identified as compensable contributions or opportunity costs.[211]

In view of spouses' intertwined lives, it should not be surprising that divorce is a wrenching experience for many, even when both spouses desire it. Divorce is the rupture of a nomic universe that has been a crucial source of meaning and identification for those within a marriage. "Loss of a marriage requires construction of a new sense of self. Myriad aspects of the self and the margins between the self and the world require enormous effort to regenerate."[212] While it is plausible to say that members of an economic partnership may regard themselves as strangers in the market after the partnership ends, it is far less reasonable to characterize ex-spouses solely in this way. Ex-spouses are not simply individuals who revert to the status of detached individuals. They have shared an experience that has affected them deeply, so much so that in a sense they are not the same persons they were when they entered the marriage. Rather than crossing immediately from the family to the market, they are poised uneasily at the border: caught in a web of lingering influences from the place they are leaving, knowing that they must begin to shape a new life in the unfamiliar territory they are entering.

Appreciation of this character of marriage and divorce calls into question the propriety of a clean break model of divorce and of property rhetoric as the exclusive way to describe the claims and obligations of ex-spouses. Sensitivity to the complexity of life at the border militates against relying exclusively on an external stance to characterize ex-spouses as strangers, and suggests that a vision of ex-spouses informed by an internal stance also should have influence. This stance provides that spouses have a special duty of care toward each other, whose demands at divorce are not limited to fulfilling only those obligations that can be conceptualized as voluntarily assumed. The standard for weighing financial claims at divorce is therefore the special responsibility of someone toward a former spouse, not simply the property rights that his partner may have earned.

At the same time, property rhetoric and an external stance toward marriage illuminate the ways in which exclusive reliance on an internal stance may perpetuate the devaluation of women's domestic labor, casting divorcing wives as dependents who must rely on the beneficence of their ex-husbands in order to receive financial awards. Property rhetoric focuses on the economic importance of homemaking, the financial sacrifices that women often make within marriage, and the economic inequalities that can result both during and after marriage. This perspective sensitizes us to ways in which marriage can create financial vulnerability and contains the potential for exploitation. Issues of economic justice thus come to the forefront in a relationship in which they have not always been regarded as salient.[213]

These insights of property rhetoric are best applied, however, not in a model of economic partnership but of *marital* partnership. Members of this partnership make a host of subtle contributions and sacrifices in reliance on continuation of a shared life together. Part of the special duty to one's spouse is to refrain from capitalizing on the economic vulnerability that this reliance often produces. Financial obligation at divorce thus rests not on the duty of charity to a dependent, but on the responsibility for economic justice toward a spouse. In this way, we acknowledge that market considerations should play some role in determining what ex-spouses owe to each other.

The internal stance, however, suggests that a precise accounting of contributions, sacrifices, and benefits is inconsistent with what should be the predominant spirit of marriage. Rather than attempt to engage in such calculations, we might seek simply to equalize the parties' standard of living for some period following divorce. This remedy would more closely match implicit spousal expectations of a shared standard of living than does an approach that seeks to provide compensation for benefits that one spouse has accepted but not paid for. Equalizing the parties' standard of living for some period after divorce affirms that spouses have a special duty to each other, that each has made valuable contributions to the marriage and to the other's welfare, and that reconstructing marriage on exchange terms generally is an undesirable basis for determining the amount of a divorce award. A requirement that spouses share equally the losses and gains from marriage thus reflects reliance on an ethic of care that draws on market insights to cast financial allocations as the achievement of economic justice. Justice between persons who have been married, however, may well require greater compensation than justice between economic partners. It is an ethic of spousal responsibility, not market entitlement, that is the governing principle.

This approach offers an opportunity to affirm conceptions of both autonomy and obligation that differ from those associated with property rhetoric. The conceptualization of ex-spouses' need for post-divorce autonomy, for instance, should reflect appreciation that autonomy emerges within relationships with others rather than merely through independence from them. Spouses' sense of themselves has been forged in important ways by marriage, and their autonomy has been nurtured in the context of their relationship with each other. The attainment of genuine post-divorce autonomy necessarily will be grounded in a process of gradually moving away from the influence of this familiar relationship to other supportive relationships. The future must be built on the past; the marriage that has ended will serve in part as the basis for the construction of a new identity and a different sense of agency. This suggests that divorce and some period of time that follows it is better seen as a transition rather than a clean break. An abrupt rupture of the relationship between the ex-spouses seems neither to correspond with common experience nor to lend any meaningful assistance in the effort to attain a new sense of autonomy.

Similarly, sensitivity to the ways in which spouses adopt an internal stance toward marriage helps us appreciate that the interdependence and vulnerability that marriage often creates can give rise to responsibility that is not adequately conceptualized as voluntarily assumed. Those in the realm of the family sometimes *recognize*, as well as consent to, obligation. Sharing one's life with another can create a special duty of care to ensure that one's partner is not seriously disadvantaged by the end of a relationship that so profoundly shapes a person's sense of identity and meaning. In this sense, the fact of the prior marriage itself can be a source of obligation, regardless of the discrete exchanges that occurred within it. Finally, to the extent that we are concerned with incentives, this approach encourages broad sharing in marriage, rather than preoccupation with identifiable contributions or sacrifices made in the context of discrete economic transactions.

At the same time, appreciation of ex-spouses as distinct individuals means that they cannot be expected to share post-divorce income indefinitely.[214] No-fault divorce has undermined the notion that divorce involves the breach of a lifetime commitment of care. Ex-spouses cannot be treated simply as spouses in determining their obligations after divorce. This means that there must be a limit to their claims on each other's income. The rationale for moving beyond property rhetoric is that spouses' lives have been intertwined in ways that the logic of this rhetoric cannot fully capture. The extent to which this has occurred is roughly a function of how long the individuals were married. As a result, we might require that ex-spouses share the same standard of living for some period of time corresponding to the length of their marriage.[215] One commentator has suggested, for instance, that we might provide for one year of sharing for each two years of marriage.[216] Treating ex-spouses as neither spouses nor strangers would lead us to eschew exclusive reliance on either an external or internal stance toward marriage. It would instead require us to devise an approach that was sensitive both to the claims of the past and the demands of the future.

The necessary calculations would be relatively straightforward and would be far more predictable than an approach premised on property rhetoric.[217] In addition, they would not require expensive expert witnesses whose cost may prevent many women from obtaining compensation.[218] We might want to deviate from the equalization requirement when one spouse can demonstrate that she has suffered a disproportionate financial loss as a result of the marriage. In this instance, a person has made a sacrifice that exceeds what we might reasonably expect a spouse to make. To the extent that an equal standard of living would not adequately compensate her for this sacrifice, it may be more fair to treat her as a property-holder whose individual interest must be vindicated. Thus, we might, for instance, base a divorce award on human capital theory when a spouse can specify with some precision that she has suffered a loss greater than the compensation that the equalization approach would provide.[219]

I would argue that appreciation of marriage as a special relationship, rather than simply an economic partnership, is the implicit theoretical foundation of scholarly arguments that ex-spouses should enjoy a comparable standard of living for some period after divorce.[220] Furthermore, I believe that it implicitly animates those courts who attempt to eliminate significant economic disparities between divorcing spouses by recognizing a claim on post-divorce income.[221] The most explicit expression of an alternative to property rhetoric can be found in the Reporters' Draft of the American Law Institute (ALI) Principles of the Law of Family Dissolution. As I have indicated, those principles reflect the adoption of provisions for compensation at divorce that rest on human capital theory in that they base awards on the principle of compensating losses in earning capacity. Section 5.05, however, provides a different approach for a spouse who has been married for a long time to someone with significantly greater economic resources. In that case, the spouse is entitled to compensation for the reduction in her standard of living if it seems fair to treat this reduction as the spouses' joint responsibility.[222] The less wealthy spouse in such cases would be entitled to a percentage of the difference in post-divorce income between the parties that would be based on the length of the marriage.[223]

The comment following this provision states that the long-term homemaker would be the primary beneficiary of the compensation provided by this section.[224] The draft explicitly rejects the idea that this compensation is based on any characterization of the marriage in exchange terms. This model seems inapt, says the draft, because "the parties define their relation by its nonfinancial aspects even though financial sharing is an important part of it. Spouses pool their financial affairs as part of a more general expectation of a shared life in which they have emotional and personal obligations as well as financial ones."[225]

The "principle of gradually merging responsibility"[226] recognizes that "[a]s the marriage lengthens, the marital living standard gradually replaces the pre-marital living standard as the appropriate measurement baseline," so that at some point "a loss that results from the joint relationship is a joint responsibility."[227] By contrast, the situation that faces each spouse at divorce after a one-year marriage is largely the product of choices and circumstances that existed before marriage. The transition from this point to the interdependence of a long marriage occurs gradually over time. As a result, "the share of the loss attributable to the spouses' joint undertaking is proportional to the marital duration," and at some point should be shared between them.[228]

Section 5.05 of the ALI draft reflects the view that the character of marriage as a shared way of life precludes treating ex-spouses as market actors in some instances. The drafters see this section as a limited exception to the general rule that the principles should provide compensation for lost earning capacity attributable to marriage. Yet there is no reason to restrict the philosophy of this section only to rare cases. Its insights are applicable to marriage in general. The idea that the extent of interdependence involved in a marriage is a function of its length can be accommodated, as I have suggested, by making the period in which ex spouses enjoy a comparable standard of living depend on the length of the marriage.

Furthermore, as the drafters themselves suggest, the approach of section 5.05 would justify an award in cases that seem to warrant assistance, but in which a theory of compensation for contributions or lost earning power is unavailable. Comment b to that section observes, for instance, that some argue that a long-term homemaker has a claim, even if she has not been responsible for child care, because she has helped her husband enhance his earning capacity. The comment states that wives do provide such assistance in some cases, but that this rationale is unavailable "when the facts do not suggest that the claimant in fact contributed to the potential obligor's earning capacity[.]"[229] Courts that nonetheless furnish awards in these instances thus implicitly must rely on some other theory to support their decision.

Similarly, section 5.06 establishes an irrebuttable presumption that a spouse has suffered an earning capacity loss when she has assumed primary responsibility for child care and her earning power at divorce is substantially less than that of the other spouse.[230] The comment justifies this presumption by noting that, while aggregate data indicate that child care responsibility has an impact on parental earning capacity, "it is often difficult to show in the particular case."[231] Furthermore:

> even where the fact of loss may be clear enough, its size often cannot often be established, because of the speculation inherent in comparing the actual facts with the hypothetical facts that would have developed had the parties behaved differently years earlier. Requiring specific proof of loss in each case would therefore result in the frequent rejection of claims that are in fact meritorious.[232]

In addition, the comment observes, "[e]arning capacity losses also arise from the expectation that one will in the future have primary responsibility for marital children."[233] Measuring this loss also is extremely difficult. For these reasons, a spouse who has assumed primary child care responsibility is entitled to an award "without individualized inquiry into whether the parental duty in fact led to a loss of earning capacity."[234]

The ALI draft justifies the presumptions contained in sections 5.05 and 5.06 as necessary accommodations to the practical problem of calculating a loss in earning power in these circumstances. Even were such calculations feasible, however, one might argue that conducting them would be inconsistent with the sense of shared fate that characterizes an internal stance toward marriage. Indeed, although the ALI characterizes awards under both these sections as compensations for lost earning capacity, the concept of "gradually merging responsibility"[235] arguably captures quite insightfully the phenomenon of two individuals who take on one another's broader burdens and satisfactions in the process of becoming a couple. Portions of the ALI draft on spousal compensation thus seem implicitly to rely on an internal stance toward marriage, even as the drafters feel compelled to frame their justifications in property rhetoric.

### Reservations

I have suggested that reliance on property rhetoric alone is a misguided approach to determining financial claims and obligations at divorce. One might voice concern, however, about deemphasizing a discourse that has powerful resonance in Western culture in general and American culture in particular. As C.B. Macpherson has suggested, "We have made property so central to our society that any thing and any rights that are not property are very apt to take second place."[236] Property rhetoric makes us more sensitive to the implicit economic exchanges that occur during marriage and to the opportunities that men often have to gain an advantage in this interaction. By demanding an accounting of these exchanges at divorce, property rhetoric affirms the idea that spouses are individuals whose interests cannot be compromised in the name of ostensible marital sharing. If a divorcing wife can be seen as earning through her labor the right to a financial award at divorce, a court is more likely to be responsive to her claim than if she is regarded as a supplicant seeking discretionary largess. By contrast, one might claim that drawing on an ethic of care in making divorce allocations risks reinforcing women's disadvantage, because marital sharing in the name of care often means a wife's uncompensated sacrifice. Reducing reliance on property rhetoric thus poses the risk that we will continue to regard the family as exempt from principles of justice and individual desert.

It is true that framing claims as the assertion of property rights has strong persuasive power in American culture. As we have seen, however, the mythology of property privileges market labor. Indeed, the strategic appeal of property rhetoric is that it invokes this mythology in attempting to characterize wives as implicit market actors who are entitled to a return on their investment or contribution. Exclusive reliance on this rhetoric, however, would extend to marriage and divorce the principle that obligation arises only through the consent of independent sovereign agents. This model of detached individual sovereignty creates the risk that caregiving activities would be even further marginalized than they are now. Women and men who fit the image of independent property-holders with contributions and losses of high market value would be regarded as the norm for purposes of compensation at divorce. Those who do not conform to this norm during marriage would receive little recognition of their efforts.

These concerns undercut the argument that the best strategy for divorce reform is to rely on the persuasive force of property rhetoric. While that rhetoric undoubtedly has potential to justify more generous awards in some cases, it seems most likely to help women with more economic resources than those with fewer. Those who would receive the highest awards would tend to be those who have provided the most financial assistance to their spouses and those who have suffered the greatest loss of earning capacity.[237] By contrast, those who have provided mostly homemaking and child care services, and whose earning power is relatively low, would receive the least compensation. The probability of this disparity is enhanced because the calculations necessary to determine the value of a degree or to estimate a diminution in human capital require expensive expert witnesses that relatively disadvantaged spouses cannot afford. Furthermore, the wide variations in these calculations make them relatively unpredictable, leaving courts with the ability to exercise considerable discretion that may be subtly influenced by more traditional conceptions of marriage.[238]

A concern more specifically about income equalization for some period between ex-spouses is that in some instances it ironically might undercut a sense of responsibility based on an internal stance toward marriage. One can imagine some cases in which the higher-income spouse treats marriage as an important commitment, but the lower-earning spouse acts irresponsibly to end the marriage. Providing a generous financial award for the latter at the expense of the former in this case seems to reward conduct that is antithetical to the idea of marriage as a relationship of care and interdependence. Indeed, one might argue that it subsidizes misconduct, making it easier for a lower-earning spouse to walk away from a marriage without regard for the impact of the divorce on the other spouse and possibly on children. The only way to avoid this paradox would seem to be to reintroduce an assessment of marital fault, which raises a host of other difficulties.

A first response to this argument is that it may be desirable in divorce proceedings to take into account egregious misconduct that violates widely accepted norms of marital behavior. I have written more extensively on this elsewhere[239] and will not recapitulate the argument here, except to say that this limited proposal need not reintroduce either a fault-based divorce regime or extensive intrusion into the particulars of every failed marriage.

The majority of divorces, however, will not involve such behavior. In these instances, we can regard post-divorce income equalization as equalizing the financial incentives that each spouse has for staying in or leaving the marriage. A higher-earning spouse, typically the husband, has more latitude to act in accordance with personal wishes in deciding whether to seek a divorce, because he is more likely to be able to enjoy a post-divorce stream of income that meets his needs adequately. A lower-earning spouse, typically the wife, has less freedom to act on the basis of personal desires, because her post-divorce economic prospects usually are grimmer. For this reason, she is more likely than her husband to stay in a marriage for financial reasons even when she would prefer a divorce.

It is true that income equalization may make it possible for a wife in this instance to act on a desire for a divorce that she would not able to effect if she had less post-divorce financial security. At the same time, however, her husband may be less likely to seek a divorce because income equalization makes financial considerations more prominent than they otherwise would be. The result is rough symmetry in the extent to which each spouse's decision about staying or leaving is affected by financial considerations. This relative equality in turn should help reduce disparities in power within marriage, which are to some degree a function of each partner's possibility of exit.[240] Some lower-earning spouses may use their increased latitude to act irresponsibly, but this is always a risk when we enhance an individual's freedom of action. In this context, promoting genuine choice for women and reducing differences in power within marriage make this a risk worth taking.

A second concern about income equalization is that it may force ex-husbands to compensate their ex-wives for economic disadvantage that is attributable not to the division of labor during marriage, but to society-wide gender discrimination in wage labor markets. To the extent that this occurs, the argument goes, a husband will be required to rectify a condition that he is not responsible for creating. Social welfare programs, rather than divorce law, should be used to address the problems stemming from unfair employment policies.

A first response to this argument is that it is difficult to isolate the effect of employment discrimination from the division of labor within the household. As Susan Moller Okin puts it, " [a] cycle of power relations and decisions pervades both family and workplace, and the inequalities of both reinforce those that already exist in the other."[241] Men and women make decisions about allocation of their time within a system in which the opportunity cost of women devoting more time to domestic tasks tends to be less than that of men, in large measure because the wage labor market features differences and occupational segregation by gender.[242] Similarly, the structure of the wage labor market is based in part on the belief that women's primary responsibility is in the home rather than a full-time career, or at least that women have distinct needs and desires regarding work that lead them to favor less renumerative but more flexible jobs that enable them to fulfill their domestic responsibilities.[243] It therefore may be unrealistic to attempt to distinguish economic advantage resulting from the division of labor during marriage, for which a husband presumably is responsible, from the disadvantage resulting from the broader structure of the wage labor market for which he obstentibly is not.

Even if we could make such a distinction, the longer the marriage the more likely it is that a wife's financial prospects have been shaped primarily by her assumption of major responsibilities for domestic tasks. At a minimum, her absence or lack of full-time commitment to the wage labor market will have deeply compounded whatever difficulties she might have confronted at the outset that might have been attributable to wage discrimination or segregation. It thus seems reasonable that those women who would receive the benefit of income equalization for the longest period of time would be those in the lengthiest marriages. Furthermore, in briefer marriages in which the structure of the wage labor market may be a more important reason for disadvantage, we must keep in mind that income equalization would not require ex-husbands to guarantee their ex-wives' standard of living for the rest of these women's lives, but only for some period related to the length of the marriage. Assuming that we could identify some portion of an ex-wife's economic disadvantage over the remainder of her life attributable to gender discrimination, it is probably unlikely that post-divorce payments would come close to providing compensation for this deficit.

Finally, even if some portion of post-divorce payments served to compensate for economic disadvantage that is socially imposed rather than attributable to the division of labor during marriage, we can regard this as consistent with the commitment entailed by marriage. The influential companionate ideal of marriage depicts it as a relationship in which each partner helps the other overcome the disadvantages that flow from the vicissitudes of daily life. In this sense, marriage is an agreement to share both the risks and rewards that otherwise would be borne individually. The longer a person is involved in such a relationship, the more she has made innumerable life decisions in reliance upon it. Income equalization for a period related to the length of a marriage takes the strength of this reliance into account and can be seen as a responsibility that one spouse necessarily assumes by virtue of the interdependence that typically characterizes marriage.

## Conclusion

Eschewing property rhetoric as the dominant language of divorce obligation would not necessarily leave us with an alternative of inferior persuasive power, or one that perpetuates women's economic disadvantage by continuing the devaluation of domestic labor. I must emphasize that I believe not that we should abandon all use of property rhetoric, but that we should weave its insights into a broader paradigm that focuses on marriage as an undertaking that creates distinctive responsibilities. That is, we should draw on both the external and internal stances toward marriage in thinking about what divorcing spouses owe one another. Such an effort seeks to build on the idea that orientations of care and justice can be complementary rather than antagonistic.[244] Marriage ideally involves altruism and sharing— but that does not mean that it is insulated from principles of economic justice. Occasions of justice may arise because parties make contributions to each other's welfare during marriage that have not been adequately reciprocated by the time of divorce. In such instances, care demands responsiveness to the other's claim of entitlement to a fair share of resources— but that share is not based on a precise accounting of contributions and exchanges governed by market calculation.

Care also requires awareness of the needs and vulnerability of a partner—but this does not dictate that we abandon the language of rights for purely discretionary awards.[245] One of the problems with alimony was that in practice it tended to be an allocation based in large measure on a legal decision-maker's assessment of the needs of a divorcing wife. This promoted perception of the award as charity to a dependent recipient and reinforced gendered relationships of power and powerlessness. By contrast, a divorcing spouse under my proposal would have a clear entitlement to equalization of her standard of living for a specific period of time. This bright-line standard would obviate the need to rely primarily on others' sympathy in obtaining a financial award at divorce. By acknowledging this right as arising within a broader context of the interdependence of marriage, however, we "treat[ ] rights rhetoric as a particular vocabulary implying roles and relationships within communities and institutions,"[246] rather than simply as an occasion for affirming autonomous individualism.

This hybrid approach seeks in a sense to offer a system of checks and balances. The danger of property rhetoric, as I have described in some detail, is that its association with possessive individualism will devalue caregiving traditionally done by women and slight the vulnerabilities arising in relationships of interdependence. My proposal attempts to temper this tendency by insisting on the importance of caregiving, rejecting the idea that it must be evaluated in market terms, and by imposing obligation on the basis of interdependence rather than pure consent. The danger of an ethic of care is that it may ignore economic inequalities within marriage and reinforce women's dependence on men. I seek to blunt this tendency by emphasizing the economic importance of domestic labor, making economic justice an important element of obligation at divorce, and establishing a clear nondiscretionary entitlement for a financially disadvantaged spouse. In these ways, my proposal represents an effort to hold in dynamic tension our commitments to both the internal and external stances toward marriage.

# Conclusion

In the preceding chapters, I have directed attention to the tension between our simultaneous commitments to individual and communal identity in marriage. I have used this analytical framework to examine the economic analysis of marriage and divorce, spousal privilege law, and the law governing financial rights and responsibilities at divorce. As I indicated at the outset of this book, my analysis has not been intended to reflect a deductive process in which I formulate general principles and then apply them to particular cases. Rather, it represents an attempt to proceed inductively. I have sought to look closely at the particular set of concerns that are relevant in each context and, informed by this examination, to determine the relative weight of the external and internal stances with respect to each issue. Chapters 3 through 8 thus are meant to serve as exemplars of practical reasoning, exercises in using the analytical framework in a fashion that is sensitive to its implications in specific instances.[1] Analyzing a handful of questions in some depth better fulfills this purpose than constructing a theory and applying it to a wide range of issues. My approach is premised on the belief that we value many conflicting things in many different areas of life, and that no single algorithm or metric can enable us to reconcile them all.

Nonetheless, it would be useful at his point to assess whether the analysis of these issues suggests any general considerations that can guide our case-by-case examination. Such generalizations should serve only as a rough rule of thumb rather than as a definitive exposition of relevant rules. Even in that capacity, however, they may serve to direct attention to concerns that seem to recur and considerations on which we appear consistently to place weight. What, then, might guide our assessments of the extent to which law should promote individualistic or communal dimensions of identity with respect both to marriage and to family law more generally?

The first is an understanding of the other considerations that have prompted the evolution of the law on a given subject. Legal rules rarely if ever reflect only one concern or value. They arise and develop in particular historical circumstances as responses to felt needs of the time, rather than simply as efforts to promote an individualistic or communal understanding of spousal identity. Thus, for instance, spousal privilege emerged in an era in which husband and wife were regarded as a single unit, in part because of the political and economic significance of the family at that time. As we have seen, the legal fiction of marital unity under this regime was so strong that spouses were precluded from testifying on behalf of one another as well. The extent to which the family continues to play this historical role in social life therefore is relevant in assessing at least one set of justifications for the privilege. Similarly, the law governing financial awards at divorce has been shaped by shifting understandings of the nature of the commitment that marriage involves, the appropriate division of labor within it, and the propriety of making moral judgments about marital conduct.

In short, expressing the value of an internal or external stance toward marriage may be one aspect of the law, but it is hardly the only one. Appreciation of the historical background of legal doctrine is important in helping us identify the distinctive concerns and interests to which law is a response. To the extent that those concerns have changed or law no longer is effective in addressing them, the weaker is the justification for preserving a legal rule. I have suggested, for instance, that the traditional rationales for the adverse testimony privilege are no longer persuasive. At the same time, I have suggested an alternative justification that is sensitive to different concerns. In the absence of such an alternative, we might well conclude that the privilege has outlived its usefulness in light of other interests that we want to vindicate.

Second, we need to take account of the impact of a legal rule on children. Some, for instance, may believe that permitting divorce only on fault grounds would reinforce the idea that spouses should see themselves as members of a shared community. Would such a rule, however, harm children by fostering acrimony and bitterness in protracted divorce proceedings? Belief that ex-spouses should be able to begin a new life after divorce may lead us to authorize reductions in child support if a parent changes careers or lessens time spent on work. We need to balance this, however, against the impact that such a reduction will have on the opportunities and life chances of the child. Similarly, we may regard it as important for a custodial parent as a distinct individual to be able to move to accept a more satisfying job offer. At the same time, we need to consider the effect of such a move on the children's relationship with the noncustodial parent. Imposing greater financial obligations toward an ex-spouse at divorce may strike some as inconsistent with respect for the ability of a spouse to take an external stance toward marriage. The immediate beneficiaries of such a rule, however, will mostly be women, and women overwhelmingly obtain custody of children after divorce. While child support represents an award specifically earmarked for children, making the mother more financially secure also will help children by, for instance, affording the mother greater choice in selecting employment that is compatible with her parental responsibilities. For the reasons given in chapter 1, I have focused in this book on the relationship between spouses, rather than between parents and children. We need to keep firmly in mind, however, that most marriages involve children. Legal rules that govern marriage therefore likely will have an impact on children as well.

Third, we must ask what the gender implications are for any given resolution of an issue. By this I mean both differences in the concrete effects of a rule on men and women, as well as the broader question of the vision that the law expresses and promotes. We cannot evade the fact that the external and internal stances historically have been coded in gender terms, or that law sometimes has drawn on this coding to establish and reinforce a system of male privilege. Thus, for example, we must take account of the fact that the adverse testimony privilege predominantly prevents women rather than men from testifying. We must also take seriously concerns that the privilege might reinforce the view that women should invariably subordinate their own interests to those of their husband. With respect to financial awards at divorce, we need to acknowledge that divorce tends to disadvantage women more than men, that a "clean break" policy may express a conception of human relationships more attuned to men's than to women's experience, and that rules governing rights and obligations may implicitly devalue caregiving within the family that traditionally has been conducted by women. Similarly, we need to appreciate the ways in which feminists both draw on and criticize law and economics in analyzing marriage and divorce. To the extent that a legal rule or an analytical approach would serve in important ways to perpetuate gender privilege, that should lead us to reject it.

Fourth, we need to consider the fairness of the distribution of burdens and benefits that would result from promoting the internal or external stance in a given instance. The adverse testimony privilege, for instance, may prevent a spouse from striking a plea bargain or vindicating her sense of justice. Permitting testimony, however, could cost an accused his liberty or life by virtue of incrimination by someone he trusted. Requiring a woman to obtain the consent of her husband to obtain an abortion would benefit the husband by acknowledging his interest in the child. At the same time, it may impose on a woman a profoundly life-altering event against her will. She may have to bear the physical and psychological strain of a pregnancy that she does not want, and, given the traditional division of labor, to assume primary caregiving responsibility that inhibits her personal or professional development. Requiring income sharing for some period of time after divorce may reduce a man's freedom to enter new relationships or to pursue different personal goals. This cost seems less weighty, however, than the benefit of providing a woman with adequate compensation for sacrifices made during marriage, sufficient funds to raise the children of whom she has custody, and enough resources to be able to make genuine choices about her life course. In short, it is important to be sensitive to the vision of marriage that a legal rule expresses, but we cannot lose sight of its practical impacts as well.

Fifth, we should take into account the extent to which a particular legal approach would require intrusive state involvement in family matters. I have suggested, for instance, that the adverse testimony privilege seeks to prevent spousal betrayal of trust. There are other forms of betrayal, however, that may be just as searing. Adultery, for instance, can be a source of great anguish that destroys a marriage. We may want society to discourage such conduct. Using the law to do so, however, may pose problems. Recriminalizing or vigorously enforcing laws against adultery would require state monitoring and investigation of sexual matters on a scale that most people would regard inappropriate and threatening.[2] Similarly, making divorce available only on fault grounds may send a message that marriage is an important commitment. Such a legal regime, however, would require state inquiry into and assessment of marital conduct in intimate detail. By contrast, I have argued that the adverse testimony privilege promotes an internal stance toward marriage by depriving the state of an opportunity to foment discord between spouses. We must be sensitive to ways in which foreclosing state involvement in marriage on privacy grounds can reinforce oppression, such as in domestic violence cases. Nonetheless, while the line between public and private is contested, it still speaks to important concerns.

Sixth, we need to consider whether a legal rule will be ineffective because it runs counter to a deep and relatively permanent shift in public opinion. Some may feel, for instance, that severely restricting the availability of divorce would powerfully express the desirability of taking an internal stance toward marriage. Current social attitudes, however, seem firmly to accept divorce as a necessary and at times desirable option that should be available without significant restriction. As a result, it is likely that any serious curtailment of divorce would be met with powerful resistance and with informal circumvention of the rules. Similarly, one may contend that imposing an obligation of lifelong alimony would reinforce the notion that marriage involves a distinctive ethic of care. This rule would run counter, however, to the entrenched view that divorce should afford ex-partners an opportunity to build a new life without serious burdens from a former marriage, and that both parties eventually should be financially independent of one another. We should not lose sight of the potential for law to influence social attitudes, but at the same time must recognize that legal rules that deviate too far from public opinion likely will be ineffective.

Finally, we need to consider the incentives that a law is likely to produce. For instance, economic analysts suggest that divorce awards that provide minimal compensation for women's contributions to the household may create incentives for husbands to behave opportunistically by seeking divorce after they have reaped the benefits of such contributions. At the same time, others express concern that generous compensation will disincline women to develop their earning power. Requiring that fault be established before divorce is granted may induce unhappy couples to collude in fabricating the necessary evidence. Compelling spouses to testify against one another may increase the likelihood of perjured testimony. We should be dubious about enacting a law if we can reasonably predict that parties will either circumvent it or behave in undesirable ways in response to it.

These considerations can inform our assessment of the relative desirability of promoting an internal or external stance with respect to a given aspect of marriage. It is important to reiterate that these are tentative generalizations, not formal principles. They are meant to offer preliminary guidance in analyzing particular cases, but must also be open to refinement in light of such analysis.

While I have sought to examine only a few issues in depth, I believe that appreciation of the internal and external stances directs attention to an important dimension of many issues regarding marriage in particular and family law more generally. Consider, for instance, the issue of the extent to which one spouse should be deemed responsible for the medical expenses of the other. This issue implicates the legal doctrine of "necessaries." Under this doctrine, a husband traditionally has been financially liable to third parties for the provision of goods deemed necessary for his wife's subsistence. Courts and legislatures have had to determine how, if at all, this rule should be modified in light of modern aspirations to gender equality.

One approach would make neither spouse liable for the expenses of the other, on the ground that the necessaries doctrine is based on an antiquated view of gender roles and spousal unity. We can see that this approach implicitly depicts marriage in terms of the external stance. That is, spouses have their own separate interests and should not be held liable for financial duties that the other may incur. Another approach would make both husbands and wives responsible for all expenses of the other. This reflects the view that each spouse occupies an internal stance toward marriage, so that financial expenses of either are regarded as incurred for the benefit of both. Once we view the necessaries doctrine through the lens that I propose, we can see that various possible legal rules assign different weights to the external and internal stances. For instance, we might require that spouses are responsible for each other's expenses, but require that creditors exhaust the assets of the spouse directly benefited before proceeding against the other spouse.[3] Alternatively, we could exempt certain expenses, such as for terminal illness, from liability.[4] Each of these rules reflects a different balance between the notions that spouses are both individuals and members of a community. The framework of this book thus can clarify one dimension of what is at stake in this debate, even if it is not our sole concern.

Similarly, the issue of what standards should govern the ability of one spouse to authorize termination of life support systems for the other implicitly requires us to consider different accounts of spousal identity. On the one hand, we want to encourage a spouse to take an internal stance toward marriage when considering what is in the best interest of her terminally ill partner. A rule that grants her discretion to make decisions in conjunction with physicians as long as they are made in good faith expresses this aspiration.[5] Law seeks to promote altruism by expressing confidence that one spouse will subordinate her own interests in this situation in order to promote the welfare of the other. On the other hand, we are committed to the idea that all persons, spouses or not, have an inviolable right to life. This means that ideally only the ill spouse's wishes should determine when life support is removed. Appreciation of the distinct individuality of each spouse also may make us wary of bestowing broad discretion on a healthy spouse, because her decision may be unduly influenced by her own interests. This perspective may lead to a rule that requires that a patient's desire to end treatment be ascertainable through clear and convincing evidence.[6]

The framework of the internal and external stances also has salience for family law issues beyond marriage. I have already alluded, for instance, to questions of the extent to which a divorced parent should be able to reduce child support payments, or a custodian should be able to move with children far away from the noncustodian, because of choices about personal objectives. All parents, married or not, are distinct individuals in their own right, yet simultaneously members of a community for whose welfare they have especially grave responsibility. Furthermore, consider the issue of the extent to which a parent's remarriage should affect his or her obligations to children from a previous marriage. Here we must balance not only individual concerns but the claims of two conflicting communities: the parent-child relationship from the prior marriage, the spousal relationship in the later marriage, and possibly a stepparent-stepchild relationship as well. Here we cannot escape deliberation about the contours of community membership and its complicated implications for both individual and communal dimensions of identity.

Issues under the Indian Child Welfare Act raise a similar set of concerns.[7] The Act provides, for instance, that American Indian tribes have jurisdiction over adoptions involving parents domiciled on a reservation, even if the parents wish to avoid such authority.[8] In addition, the Act requires that, absent good cause otherwise, children of American Indian heritage must be placed with Indian parents, even if the biological parent(s) wish otherwise.[9] Cases under the Act therefore force us to contend with notions of the child as a distinct individual in her own right, as a member of a community involving her biological parents, and more broadly as a member of the American Indian community. We must take account of similar dimensions of identity with respect to the parents as well. Furthermore, one parent may be a member of both a marital community and the community of American Indians, while the other may be a member of the first but not the second.

Appreciation of the internal and external stances toward human relationships certainly will not lead to a determinate resolution of the issues raised by these and other cases. With respect to necessaries, for instance, we will want to ask questions like: How often does this situation arise? What are the financial consequences of different rules for the healthy spouse? What effect would each rule have on the provision of health care? On the availability of health insurance? What sorts of incentives would different rules create? We will need to confront similarly detailed questions when deliberating about other issues. Furthermore, the analytical approach that I offer necessarily will illuminate some dilemmas and controversies better than others. It does not purport to present a framework that will encompass all instances of legal conflict between spouses. Inevitably, for instance, there will be some cases in which both spouses seem to assert interests that represent an external stance toward marriage. In some such cases, the relative weight of the competing individual claims may be the most important consideration. Even in cases in which purely individual concerns seem to be at stake, however, we need to be attentive to the extent to which a given legal rule may send signals about the relative importance of the internal stance. For instance, a lengthy marriage or one marked by a spouse's especially significant sacrifices may mean that one spouse's claims at divorce implicitly require judgments about the relative importance of a communal orientation toward marriage.

Marriage is, of course, but one of many communities to which we may belong. It is important to reiterate that when we take the external stance toward marriage, we occupy an internal stance with respect to other commitments not then called into question. As Michael Sandel has observed, modern life requires "the capacity to negotiate our way among the sometimes overlapping, sometimes conflicting obligations that claim us, and to live with the tension to which multiple loyalties give rise. This capacity is difficult to sustain, for it is easier to live with the plurality between persons than within them."[10] Law sometimes is called upon to play a role in reconciling these different claims of identity. The analysis I have presented is meant to illustrate that such reconciliation cannot succeed purely on a theoretical level. Rather, it requires attention to the distinctive concerns that arise with respect to particular communities in specific contexts. We must assess considerations such as the history of each community in question; the practical and symbolic functions it serves in individuals' daily lives; the opportunities for participation or exit that it makes available; relationships of power within the community; its relationship to other communities; and its broader social meaning.[11]

In this book I have suggested how, for one community, on a handful of questions, we might engage in such contextual assessment. Marriage continues to be not simply one of several communities to which we might belong, but a relationship that most believe should engage our being more fully than any other adult attachment. With such an aspiration, it is not surprising that marriage evokes profound ambivalence: a desire both to transcend and to protect the boundaries of the self. As a voluntary association in which lives can become intimately interwoven, it powerfully expresses a prominent feature of the current age: that we live with a heightened sense of both individual choice and of being situated selves. The external stance emphasizes the self who navigates among these choices; the internal stance the grounded attachment that makes such navigation possible. This analytical framework will not neatly resolve all the dilemmas that we must face. It will, however, inform our deliberation by leading us to appreciate the contradictory commitments that we seek to hold in uneasy balance.

# Notes

## One

1. John T. McQuiston, "Details Given on Suspects in Abduction," *N.Y. Times*, 12 June 1992, at A25, A29.

2. Evelyn Nieves, "Portrait of 2 Accused of Kidnapping: Ardent, Hapless Pursuit of Affluence," *N.Y. Times*, 28 June 1992, at A28.

3. Evelyn Nieves, "Murder Charges Expected This Week in Reso Case," *N.Y. Times*, 30 June 1992, at B4.

4. Nieves, *supra* note 2, at A28.

5. *Id.*

6. *Id.*

7. Charles Strum, "Neighbors Say Suspects Lived Quiet Rural Life," *N.Y. Times*, 20 June 1992, at A29.

8. Joseph F. Sullivan, "Couple Arrested in Kidnapping of Exxon Official," *N.Y. Times*, 20 June 1992, at A1.

9. Robert Hanley, "Couple Indicted in Kidnapping of Exxon Executive," *N.Y. Times*, 26 June 1992, at B4.

10. Robert Hanley, "Officials Say Body in Forest Is Sidney Reso," *N.Y. Times*, 29 June 1992, at B1.

11. Wayne King, "Suspect Changes Plea to Guilty in Kidnapping of Oil Executive," *N.Y. Times*, 9 Sept. 1992, at A1, B2.

12. Joseph F. Sullivan, "Woman Pleads Guilty to Lesser Counts in Kidnapping," *N.Y. Times*, 1 July 1992, at B4.

13. Associated Press, "Suspect in Exxon Kidnapping Seeks Trial Delay," *N.Y. Times*, 12 Aug. 1992, at B5.

14. Robert Hanley, "With Eye on Reso Case, Witness Rule Is Attacked," *N.Y. Times*, 20 July 1992, at B4.

15. Jan Hoffman, "When Love Is Blind, but So Is Justice," *N.Y. Times*, 12 July 1992, at D2.

16. Sullivan, *supra* note 12, at B4.

17. *Id.*

18. N.J. Stat. Ann. § 2A:84A-17 (West 1994). The law also permits a spouse to testify about marital communications in a criminal proceeding if she so chooses. N.J. Stat. Ann. § 2A:84A-22 (West 1994).

19. By arguing that a person "adopts" or "takes" these stances, I am not suggesting that the relevant agent is an individual who is independent of social practices and attachments. Rather, I mean to describe the actions of a socially constituted self who nonetheless

has the capacity to call certain practices and attachments into question while taking others for granted. For a discussion of the inadvisability of investing the self with an ontological status prior to the community, see Daniel R. Ortiz, "Correspondence: Saving the Self?" 91 *Mich. L. Rev.* 1018 (1993).

20. This research is summarized in Serge Desmarais & Melvin J. Lerner, "Entitlements in Close Relationships: A Justice-Motive Analysis," in *Entitlement and the Affectional Bond: Justice in Close Relationships* 43 (Melvin J. Lerner & Gerold Mikula 1994).

21. *Id.* at 48.

22. *Id.*

23. *Id.* at 48–49.

24. *Id.* at 58.

25. *See, e.g.,* Barbara Cox, "Love Makes a Family—Nothing More, Nothing Less," 8 *J. Law and Politics* 5 (1991).

26. John Scanzoni, Karen Polonko, Jay Teachman, & Linda Thompson, *The Sexual Bond: Rethinking Families and Close Relationships* (1989).

27. Catherine Kohler Riessman, *Divorce Talk* 67 (1990).

28. *See* William O'Neill, *The Road to Reno* (1962); Roderick Phillips, *Putting Asunder: A History of Divorce in Western Society* 640 (1988); Glenda Riley, *Divorce: An American Tradition* 185 (1991).

29. David Chambers, "What If? The Legal Consequences of Marriage and the Legal Needs of Lesbian and Gay Male Couples," 95 *Mich. L. Rev.* 447, 448 (1996).

30. *See, e.g.,* Kirshberg v. Feenstra, 450 U.S. 455 (1981) (management of community property); Wengler v. Druggists Mutual Ins. Co., 446 U.S. 142 (1979) (welfare benefits); Orr v. Orr, 440 U.S. 268 (1979) (eligibility for alimony).

31. *See* Amy Wax, *Bargaining in the Shadow of the Market: Is There a Future for Egalitarian Marriage?* (unpublished manuscript).

32. *See, e.g.,* Braschi v. Stahl Associates Co., 543 N.E. 2d 49 (N.Y. 1989).

33. *See, e.g.,* Elizabeth Scott, "Rational Decisionmaking About Marriage and Divorce," 76 *Va. L. Rev.* 1, 90–91 (1990).

34. *See* Martha Fineman, *The Neutered Mother, the Sexual Family and Other Twentieth-Century Tragedies* (1995).

35. *See* Paul Taylor, "Nonmarital Births: As Rates Soar, Theories Abound," *Washington Post,* January 22, 1991, at A3.

36. *See Statistical Abstract of the United States 1997,* p. 64, Table 77 (1997, 117th ed.); *Statistical Abstract of the United States 1980,* p. 48, Table 67 (1980, 101st ed.).

37. *See* James Sweet & Larry Bumpass, *American Families and Households* 397 (1987).

38. John Locke, *Two Treatises of Government* 155 (Peter Laslett ed. 1988) (3d ed. 1698).

39. *Id.*

40. *Id.* at 156.

41. John Rawls, *Political Liberalism* 32 (1993).

42. William Stacey Johnson, *Sex and Marriage in Victorian Poetry* 113 (1975) (discussing Tennyson's conceptualization of marriage). For a discussion of the way in which sexual relationships were seen in the nineteenth century to raise profound questions about the dynamic between self and society, see Louis J. Kern, *An Ordered Love* 19–33 (1981).

43. *See also* Sigmund Freud, *Civilization and Its Discontents* 60 (James Strachey ed. & trans. 1960).

44. *See, e.g.,* Anthony Giddens, *The Transformation of Intimacy* (1992); Scanzoni, et al., *supra* note 26.

45. For recognition of this point with respect to justice and care, see Robin L. West, *Caring for Justice* (1997).

# Two

1. Thomas Nagel, *The View From Nowhere* 4 (1986).

2. *Id.* at 119.

3. *Id.* at 118.

4. *See, e.g.*, Daniel Bell, *Communitarianism and Its Critics* (1993); Alasdair MacIntyre, *After Virtue* (2d ed. 1984); Michael J. Sandel, *Liberalism and the Limits of Justice* (1982); Charles Taylor, *The Ethics of Authenticity* (1991) [hereinafter Taylor, *Ethics*]; Charles Taylor, "Atomism," in 2 *Philosophical Papers: Philosophy and the Human Sciences* 187–210 (1985).

5. Several liberal theorists have either accepted or not contested the premise that the self is socially constituted, but insist that this does not undermine the normative importance of individual critical reflection on social attachments. *See, e.g.*, David Gauthier, *Morals by Agreement* 349–53 (1986); Will Kymlicka, *Liberalism, Community, and Culture* 47–73 (1989); J. Donald Moon, *Constructing Community* (1993).

6. Jeremy Waldron, "When Justice Replaces Affection: The Need for Rights," 11 *Harv. J.L. & Pub. Pol'y* 625, 645 (1988) (footnote omitted).

7. For a helpful discussion of the implications of the liberal-communitarian debate for family law, *see* Elizabeth S. Scott, "Rehabilitating Liberalism in Modern Divorce Law," 1994 *Utah L. Rev.* 687.

8. Marilyn Friedman, "Feminism and Modern Friendship," in *Feminism & Political Theory* 143, 149 (Cass R. Sunstein ed., 1990) [hereinafter *Feminism and Political Theory*].

9. *Id.* at 150.

10. *See, e.g.*, Rene Descartes, "Discourse on the Method," in *The Essential Descartes* 106, 128 (Margaret D. Wilson ed., 1969) (AI knew that I was a substance the whole essence or nature of which is to think, and that for its existence there is no need of any place, nor does it depend on any material thing. . . ."); Immanuel Kant, *Foundations of the Metaphysics of Morals* 5 (Robert P. Wolff ed. & Lewis W. Beck trans., 1969) (stating that the individual is a moral agent capable of apprehending the demands of the moral law "freed from everything which may be only empirical").

11. On the difference between Hobbesian and Kantian social contract theory, *see* Jean Hampton, "Feminist Contractarianism," in *A Mind of One's Own: Feminist Essays on Reason and Objectivity* 227, 233–38 (Louise M. Antony & Charlotte Witt eds., 1993).

12. *See* John Rawls, *Political Liberalism* 19 (1993). Rawls argues that this capacity and the capacity for a sense of justice constitute the moral powers of individuals in a society conceived of as a fair system of social cooperation. *Id.*

13. Gauthier, *supra* note 5, at 11; *see also* Hampton, *supra* note 11, at 240 (explaining that in the contractarian approach, "self-interested motivation is assumed for purposes of testing the moral health of the relationship; one is essentially trying to put aside the potentially blinding influence of affection or duty to see whether costs and benefits are distributed such that one is losing out").

14. Gauthier, *supra* note 5, at 11.

15. Hampton, *supra* note 11, at 241.

16. *Id.* at 240.

17. Jean Hampton, "Selflessness and the Loss of Self," 10 *Soc. Phil. & Pol'y* 135, 149–51 (1993).

18. Kymlicka, *supra* note 5, at 50.

19. *Id.* at 50–51.

20. Hampton, *supra* note 17, at 150.

21. Nagel, *supra* note 1, at 117–18. Nagel uses this phrase in describing the aspirations of one who seeks a successively more "objective" point of view that includes a greater number of the particulars of one's life, so that in our deliberation we are able to "encom-

pass ourselves completely." *Id.* at 118. While he concedes that such a perspective is impossible to obtain, he suggests that the desire for it creates dissatisfaction with anything less. *Id.*

22. *See* Hampton, *supra* note 11, at 249 (arguing that contractarian conception of the person need not "deny our deep sociality"); Waldron, *supra* note 6, at 645 (stressing that a rights orientation does not necessarily adopt ontological individualism, but merely contemplates the possibility of alienation from social roles).

23. *See* Kymlicka, *supra* note 5, at 51 (arguing that in making personal judgements, "we must take something as a 'given'; someone who is nothing but a free rational being or a freely creative being would have no reason to choose one way of life over another"); Friedman, *supra* note 8, at 150 (emphasizing the importance of questioning various norms and practices while acknowledging that "it would be impossible for the self to question all her contingencies at once"). The ground from which one engages in such scrutiny may also be conceptualized as a unique biography comprised of a singular configuration of social roles and experiences. *See* John P. Hewitt, *Dilemmas of the American Self* 178–90 (1989); *see also* John Cottingham, "The Ethics of Self-Concern," 101 *Ethics* 798, 798 (1991) ("[T]he exploding of the Cartesian myth cannot entirely defuse that sense of the primacy of the subjective which the phenomenologists and the existentialists and the poets insist on.").

24. *See* John Stuart Mill, *The Subjection of Women* (M.I.T. Press 1970) (1869).

25. *See, e.g.*, Susan M. Okin, *Justice, Gender, and the Family* 25–40 (1989).

26. *See* Nancy J. Hirschmann, *Rethinking Obligation: A Feminist Method for Political Theory* 35–76 (1992); Carole Pateman, "Feminist Critiques of the Public/Private Dichotomy," in *Feminism and Equality* 102 (Anne Phillips ed., 1987).

27. Virginia Woolf, "Professions for Women," in 2 *Collected Essays* 284, 285 (1967).

28. *See* Lyn M. Brown & Carol Gilligan, *Meeting at the Crossroads* (1992); Marilyn Friedman, *What Are Friends For?* 50 (1993) (creating "myths and idealizations" of relationships prevents critical assessment); Diana T. Meyers, *Self, Society, and Personal Choice* 152 (1989) (describing ways in which female socialization tends to encourage "receptivity to others' needs and desires").

29. Brown & Gilligan, *supra* note 28, at 3; *see also* Soren Kierkegaard, *The Sickness Unto Death* 80–81 n. (Alastair Hannay trans., Penguin Books 1989) (1849) (A[T]he fact that devotedness is woman's nature, recurs in despair as the mode of the despair. In her self-abandonment she has lost herself, and is only happy when having done so, this being the only way she can be herself."); Larry Blum, Marcia Homiak, Judy Housman & Naomi Scheman, "Altruism and Women's Oppression," in *Women and Philosophy* 222, 228–29 (Carol C. Gould & Marx W. Wartofsky eds., 1976) (asserting that altruistic qualities can become distorted in relationships based on lack of autonomy); Hampton, *supra* note 17, at 136 (suggesting that selfless women may be "in danger of losing the self they ought to be developing").

30. *See generally* Hampton, *supra* note 17, at 164 (arguing that where the duty to others and the duty to self conflict, the self-regarding choice may be morally superior). On the moral aspects of self-concern, see Cottingham, *supra* 23, at 802.

31. On women's potential difficulties in developing autonomy competence, see Meyers, *supra* note 28, at 141–71.

32. Friedman, *supra* note 28, at 40; *see also* Claudia Card, "Gender and Moral Luck," in *Identity, Character, and Morality* 199, 215 (Owen Flanagan & Amelie O. Rorty eds., 1990) [hereinafter *Identity, Character, and Morality*] (arguing that not all attachments are valuable per se). For additional discussion of the implications of women's identification with an ethic of care, see Joan Tronto, *Moral Boundaries: A Political Argument for an Ethic of Care* (1993); John Exdell, "Ethics, Ideology, and Feminine Virtue," in *Science, Morality and Feminist Theory* 169 (Marsha Hanen & Kai Nielsen eds., 1987) [hereinafter *Science, Morality and Feminist Theory*];

Barbara Houston, "Rescuing Womanly Virtues: Some Dangers of Moral Reclamation," in *id.* at 237; Pamela S. Karlan & Daniel R. Ortiz, "In a Diffident Voice: Relational Feminism, Abortion Rights, and the Feminist Legal Agenda," 87 *Nw. U. L. Rev.* 858 (1993); Joan C. Williams, "Deconstructing Gender," 87 *Mich. L. Rev.* 797 (1989).

33. Hampton, *supra* note 11, at 245; see also *id* at 239–40 (arguing that a contractarian test should be applied to relationships to determine whether the distribution of costs and benefits is motivated by self-interest in order to avoid exploitation); Okin, *supra* note 25, at 122–24 (feminists must surmount resistance to a contractual approach to the family).

34. *See* Hampton, *supra* note 11, at 240.

35. *See* Marilyn A. Friedman, "Moral Integrity and the Deferential Wife," 47 *Phil. Stud.* 141 (1985) (adopting ends of others is legitimate as long as not done uncritically); Hampton, *supra* note 17, at 156 (recognizing that service to others is acceptable when it represents an "authentically defined preference ... undertaken by one who pursues her legitimate needs").

36. Friedman, *supra* note 28, at 162; see also Hampton, *supra* note 17, at 160 ("Commendable, effective love does not mean losing oneself in a union with others; instead, it presupposes that all parties to the union have a self ... which they share with one another.").

37. "There are only individual people, different individual people, with their own individual lives." Robert Nozick, *Anarchy, State, and Utopia* 33 (1974).

38. "Each person possesses an inviolability founded on justice that even the welfare of society as a whole cannot override." John Rawls, *A Theory of Justice* 3 (1974).

39. Kymlicka, *supra* note 5.

40. *Id.* at 12.

41. Stephen Macedo, *Liberal Virtues: Citizenship, Virtue, and Community in Liberal Constitutionalism* 235 (1990).

42. *Id.* at 239.

43. *Id.* at 241.

44. *Id.* at 267.

45. *Id.* at 204.

46. "Critical reflection on some aspect of one's identity is possible because other aspects are not presently being questioned." *Id.*, at 247.

47. Rawls, *supra* note 38, at 3.

48. Macedo, *supra* note 41, at 245.

49. Rawls, *supra* note 12, at 36–37.

50. Macedo, *supra* note 41, at 203.

51. *Id.*, at 243.

52. *Id.*, at 244.

53. *Id.* at 239.

54. David Gauthier, "The Social Contract as Ideology," in *Moral Dealing: Contract, Ethics, and Reason* 325, 350 (1990).

55. Lawrence M. Friedman, *The Republic of Choice* 2 (1990).

56. *Id.* at 101.

57. *See, e.g.,* Theodore Caplow, Howard M. Bahr, Bruce A. Chadwick, Reuben Hill, & Margaret H. Williamson, *Middletown Families* 161–94 (1982); Arland Thornton, "Changing Attitudes Toward Family Issues in the United States," 51 *J. Marriage & Fam.* 873, 883–85 (1989).

58. *See* James A. Sweet & Larry L. Bumpass, *American Families and Households* 397 (1987); Thornton, *supra* note 57, at 881; Jane R. Wilkie, "The Trend Toward Delayed Parenthood," 43 *J. Marriage & Fam.* 583 (1981).

59. *See* Sweet & Bumpass, *supra* note 58, at 397; Graham B. Spanier, "Married and

Unmarried Cohabitation in the United States: 1980," 45 *J. Marriage & Fam.* 277, 287 (1983); Thornton, *supra* note 57, at 880; Paul Taylor, "Nonmarital Births: As Rates Soar, Theories Abound," *Wash. Post,* 22 Jan. 1991, at A3.

60. Estimates are that two-thirds of all first marriages will face disruption through separation or divorce. Teresa C. Martin & Larry L. Bumpass, "Recent Trends in Marital Disruption," 26 *Demography* 37, 49 (1989); *see also* William J. Goode, *World Changes in Divorce Patterns* 144 (1993) (reporting that most Americans now believe they have a right to end an unhappy marriage and that legal obstacles to the exercise of this right are unfair).

61. *See generally* Mary Ann Glendon, *The Transformation of Family Law* (1989) (noting that recent changes in family law have merely formalized social trends); Jana B. Singer, "The Privatization of Family Law," 1992 *Wis. L. Rev.* 1443 ("[P]rivate norm creation and private decision making have supplanted state-imposed rules and structures for governing family-related behavior.").

62. *See* Anthony Giddens, *Modernity and Self-Identity* 89–98 (1991) [hereinafter Giddens, *Modernity and Self-Identity*]; Anthony Giddens, *The Transformation of Intimacy* 49–64, 134–56, 188–203 (1992) [hereinafter Giddens, *Transformation*].

63. Giddens, *Transformation, supra* note 62, at 58; see also Giddens, *Modernity and Self-Identity, supra* note 62, at 89–90 (arguing that as marriage becomes less anchored in external social and economic conditions, it "becomes more and more a relationship initiated for, and kept going for as long as, it delivers emotional satisfaction").

64. Giddens, *Modernity and Self-Identity, supra* note 62, at 91. On the concept of reflexivity more generally, see Anthony Giddens, *The Consequences of Modernity* (1990).

65. Giddens, *Modernity and Self-Identity, supra* note 62, at 90.

66. "[C]ommitment must almost always be part of an effort-bargain; the pure relationship cannot exist without substantial elements of reciprocity." *Id.* at 93; *see also* Mary Lund, "Commitment Old and New: Social Pressure and Individual Choice in Making Relationships Last," in *Cooperation and Prosocial Behavior* 212, 213 (Robert A. Hinde & Jo Groebel eds., 1991) (finding that commitment in contemporary age "depends more on the individual's decision-making about a given relationship in which rewards, investments, and alternatives to the relationship are weighed").

67. Giddens, *Modernity and Self-Identity, supra* note 62, at 92; *see also* Giddens, *Transformation, supra* note 62, at 137 (highlighting the riskiness of unconditional commitment in the modern relationship).

68. Giddens, *Modernity and Self-Identity, supra* note 62, at 96.

69. *Id.* at 184–203.

70. *Id.* at 184.

71. For overviews, see Gauthier, *supra* note 5, at 21–59; *Rational Choice* (Jon Elster ed., 1986); Robyn M. Dawes, *Rational Choice in an Uncertain World* (1988). For applications to the family, see Gary S. Becker, *A Treatise on the Family* (enlarged ed. 1991); Shoshana Grossbard-Schechtman, *On the Economics of Marriage* (1993). For analyses of family law issues, see Allen M. Parkman, *No-Fault Divorce: What Went Wrong?* (1992); H. Elizabeth Peters, "Marriage and Divorce: Informational Constraints and Private Contracting," 76 *Am. Econ. Rev.* 437 (1986); Martin Zelder, "Inefficient Dissolutions as a Consequence of Public Goods: The Case of No-Fault Divorce," 22 *J. Legal Stud.* 503 (1993). For feminist critiques of economic analysis, see *Beyond Economic Man: Feminist Theory and Economics* (Marianne A. Ferber & Julie A. Nelson eds., 1993). For a feminist analysis of the law-and-economics approach to alimony, see Jana B. Singer, "Alimony and Efficiency," 82 *Geo. L.J.* 2423 (1994).

72. *See, e.g., Family Relationships: Rewards And Costs* (F. Ivan Nye ed., 1982) (compiling various studies). The pioneering study in this vein was Robert O. Blood, Jr. & Donald M. Wolfe, *Husbands and Wives: The Dynamics of Married Living* (1960). For examples of social exchange

theory generally, see *Social Exchange in Developing Relationships* (Robert L. Burgess & Ted L. Huston eds., 1979); *Social Exchange Theory* (Karen S. Cook ed., 1987); *Social Exchange: Advances In Theory and Research* (Kenneth J. Gergen, Martin S. Greenberg & Richard H. Willis eds., 1980). Seminal works in the field are Peter M. Blau, *Exchange and Power in Social Life* (1964) and George C. Homans, *Social Behavior* (rev. ed. 1974).

73. See Blau, *supra* note 72, at 20.

74. Christine S. Sexton & Daniel S. Perlman, "Couples' Career Orientation, Gender Role Orientation, and Perceived Equity as Determinants of Marital Power," 51 *J. Marriage & Fam.* 933, 933 (1989) (citations omitted).

75. Timothy D. Stephen, "A Symbolic Exchange Framework for the Development of Intimate Relationships," 37 *Hum. Rel.* 393, 394 (1984).

76. Blau, *supra* note 72, at 160.

77. Giddens, *Transformation, supra* note 62, at 194.

78. See Ann Swidler, "Love and Adulthood in American Culture," in *Family In Transition: Rethinking Marriage, Sexuality, Child Rearing, and Family Organization* 231, 235 (Arlene S. Skolnick & Jerome H. Skolnick eds., 5th ed. 1986).

79. See, e.g., Irwin Altman & Dalmas A. Taylor, *Social Penetration: The Development of Interpersonal Relationships* (1973); Caplow et al., *supra* note 57, at 125–26; Stephen R. Jorgensen & Janis C. Gaudy, "Self-Disclosure and Satisfaction in Marriage," 29 *Fam. Rel.* 281 (1980); Susan S. Hendrick, "Self-Disclosure and Marital Satisfaction," 40 *J. Personality & Soc. Psych.* 1150 (1981).

80. Frank F. Furstenberg, Jr. & Graham B. Spanier, *Recycling the Family: Remarriage After Divorce* 66–67 (1984).

81. Zick Rubin, Charles T. Hill, Letitia A. Peplau & Christine Dunkel-Schetter, "Self-Disclosure in Dating Couples: Sex Roles and the Ethic of Openness," 42 *J. Marriage & Fam.* 305, 313 (1980).

82. See, e.g., John H. Berg & Ronald L. Archer, "Responses to Self-Disclosure and Interaction Goals," 18 *J. Experimental Soc. Psychol.* 501 (1982); John K. Butler, Jr., "Reciprocity of Dyadic Trust in Close Male-Female Relationships," 126 *J. Soc. Psychol.* 579 (1986); Hunter A. McAllister & Norman J. Bregman, "Reciprocity Effects with Intimate and Nonintimate Disclosure: The Importance of Establishing Baseline," 125 *J. Soc. Psychol.* 775 (1985); Dalmas A. Taylor & Faye Z. Belgrave, "The Effects of Perceived Intimacy and Valence on Self-Disclosure Reciprocity," 12 *Personality & Soc. Psychol. Bull.* 247 (1986).

83. Bernard Davidson, Jack Balswick, & Charles Halverson, "Affective Self-Disclosure and Marital Adjustment: A Test of Equity Theory," 45 *J. Marriage & Fam.* 93, 101 (1983) (citations omitted).

84. Jeffrey Blustein, *Care and Commitment* 4 (1991).

85. Amy Tan, *The Joy Luck Club* 160 (1989).

86. *Id.* at 161.

87. *Id.*

88. *Id.* at 162.

89. See, e.g., Susan K. Whitbourne & Joyce B. Ebmeyer, *Identity and Intimacy in Marriage* 57 (1990) (mutual accommodation in marriage involves willingness to "give more than 50%" and "going that extra half of the distance").

90. See Jean Paul Sartre, *Being and Nothingness* 47 (Hazel E. Barnes trans., Philosophical Library 1980) (1943).

91. Blustein, *supra* note 84, at 99.

92. *Id.*

93. Okin, *supra* note 25, at 28–29.

94. Waldron, *supra* note 6, at 628; *see also* Hampton, *supra* note 11, at 250–51 (concluding

that justice and contract are but the beginning of guidance on how we should relate to others; they do not tell us all the ways we should cultivate emotions in order to "develop enriching ties to others").

95. For an illuminating discussion of the ways in which marital commitment may be individually rational, see Elizabeth S. Scott, "Rational Decisionmaking About Marriage and Divorce," 76 *Va. L. Rev.* 9 (1990).

96. *See, e.g.*, Gary L. Hansen, "Moral Reasoning and the Marital Exchange Relationship," 131 *J. Soc. Psychol.* 71 (1991); Joan E. Broderick & K. Daniel O'Leary, "Contributions of Affect, Attitudes, and Behavior to Marital Satisfaction," 54 *J. Consulting & Clinical Psychol.* 514 (1986); Margaret S. Clark & Judson Mills, "Interpersonal Attraction in Exchange and Communal Relationships," 37 *J. Personality & Soc. Psychol.* 12 (1979); John G. Holmes, "The Exchange Process in Close Relationships: Microbehavior and Macromotives," in *The Justice Motive in Social Behavior* 261 (Melvin J. Lerner & Sally C. Lerner eds., 1981); Bernard I. Murstein, Mary Cerreto, & Marcia G. MacDonald, "A Theory and Investigation of the Effect of Exchange Orientation on Marriage and Friendship," 39 *J. Marriage & Fam.* 543 (1977).

97. John K. Rempel, John G. Holmes, & Mark P. Zanna, "Trust in Close Relationships," 49 *J. Personality & Soc. Psychol.* 95, 110 (1985); *see also* H.H. Kelley, *Personal Relationships: Their Structure and Processes* (1979) (perception of partner's unselfish care is crucial to development of intimate relationship). For a discussion of the ways in which a persistent emphasis on fair exchange inhibits the attribution of motives to oneself and one's partner that are crucial to the viability of a personal relationship, *see* Holmes, *supra* note 96, at 279–81.

98. As Will Kymlicka observes, for instance, "[i]f at one time we make choices about what's valuable given our commitment to a certain religious life, we could later come to question that commitment, and ask what's valuable given our commitment to our family." Kymlicka, *supra* note 5, at 51.

99. Blustein, *supra* note 84, at 231; *see also* Philip Selznick, *The Moral Commonwealth* 193 (1992) (the self "is not free-floating: it emerges from and is sustained by specific personal relationships"); Annette C. Baier, "The Need for More than Justice," in *Science, Morality & Feminist Theory, supra* note 32 at 41, 49 ("[Individuality] is not something a person *has*, and which she then chooses relationships to suit, but something that develops out of a series of dependencies and interdependencies, and responses to them."); Lynne McFall, "Integrity," 98 *Ethics* 5, 13 (1987) (discussing "identity-conferring commitments[,]" which "reflect what we take to be most important and so determine, to a large extent, our (moral) identities"); Bernard Williams, "Persons, Character and Morality," in *Moral Luck* 1, 12–14 (1981) (person's sense of having a life worth living depends on "ground projects" that represent commitments to which she seeks to be faithful).

100. *See* Virginia Held, *Feminist Morality* 74 (1993).

101. For examples of the traditional view, *see* Lawrence Kohlberg, *Essays on Moral Development: The Philosophy of Moral Development* (1981); Stephen L. Darwall, "Autonomist Internalism and the Justification of Morals," 24 *Noûs* 257, 265 (1990).

102. Held, *supra* note 100, at 78.

103. *See, e.g.*, Lawrence A. Blum, *Friendship, Altruism & Morality* (1980); Blustein, *supra* note 84; Carol Gilligan, *In a Different Voice* (1982); Held, *supra* note 100, at 66; Nel Noddings, *Caring: A Feminine Approach to Ethics & Moral Education* (1984); Sara Ruddick, *Maternal Thinking* 6–7 (1989); Tronto, *supra* note 32; Annette C. Baier, "Trust and Antitrust," in *Moral Prejudices* 95, 115–17 (1994). Marilyn Friedman observes that this enterprise is consistent with the communitarian challenge to abstract individualism. *See* Friedman, *supra* note 28, at 161.

104. *See* Held, *supra* note 100, at 60.

105. *Id.* at 66; *see also* Owen Flanagan & Kathryn Jackson, "Justice, Care, and Gender: The Kohlberg-Gilligan Debate Revisited," in *Feminism and Political Theory, supra* note 8, at 37, 39 (finding that care focuses on the interconnections among people).

106. See Blustein, *supra* note 84, at 151; Friedman, *supra* note 28, at 224; Held, *supra* note 100, at 60; John Hardwig, "Should Women Think in Terms of Rights?" in *Feminism & Political Theory*, *supra* note 8, at 53, 57–58; June Jordan, "The Relational Self: A New Perspective for Understanding Women's Development," in *The Self: Interdisciplinary Approaches* 136 (Jaine Strauss & George R. Goethals eds., 1991).

107. Friedman, *supra* note 28, at 69.

108. This self-interest may reflect interdependent utility functions, see Becker, *supra* note 71, at 173; William M. Landes & Richard A. Posner, "Salvors, Finders, Good Samaritans, and Other Rescuers: An Economic Study of Law and Altruism," 7 *J. Legal Stud.* 83, 94–95 (1978); a concern to ensure assistance from others in the future, see Robert L. Trivers, "The Evolution of Reciprocal Altruism," 46 *Q. Rev. Biology* 35 (1971); a desire for social approval, see Robert B. Cialdini, Mark Schaller, Donald Houlihan, Kevin Arps, Jim Fultz & Arthur L. Beaman, "Empathy-Based Helping: Is It Selflessly or Selfishly Motivated?" 52 *J. Personality & Soc. Psychol.* 749 (1987); David A. Kennett, "Altruism and Economic Behavior: I," 39 *Am. J. Econ. & Soc.* 183, 188 (1980); a desire to support an associate, James R. Meindl & Melvin J. Lerner, "The Heroic Motive: Some Experimental Demonstrations," 19 *J. Exp'l Soc. Psychol.* 1 (1983); or the desire to avoid guilt, see Donald T. Campbell, "On the Conflicts Between Biological and Social Evolution and Between Psychology and Moral Tradition," 30 *Am. Psychologist* 1103 (1975); Robert C. Ellickson, "Bringing Culture and Human Frailty to Rational Actors: A Critique of Classical Law and Economics," 65 *Chi.-Kent L. Rev.* 23, 47 (1989).

109. James S. Coleman, "Individual Interests and Collective Action," in *Papers on Non-Market Decision Making* 49, 55 (Gordon Tullock ed., 1966).

110. This work is summarized in Robyn M. Dawes, Alphons J.C. van de Kragt & John M. Orbell, "Cooperation for the Benefit of Us—Not Me, or My Conscience," in *Beyond Self-Interest* 97, 99 (Jane J. Mansbridge ed., 1990).

111. *Id.* at 100.

112. For other research that suggests that group identity is a significant determinant of cooperation, see *Social Identity and Intergroup Relations* (Henri Tajfel ed., 1982); R.M. Kramer & M.B. Brewer, "Social Group Identity and the Emergence of Cooperation in Resource Conservation Dilemmas," in *Experimental Social Dilemmas* 205 (Henk A.M. Wilke, Dave M. Messick & Christel G. Rutte eds., 1986); see also Kristen R. Monroe, Michael C. Barton, & Ute Klingmann, "Altruism and the Theory of Rational Action: Rescuers of Jews in Nazi Europe," 101 *Ethics* 103 (1990) (suggesting that an expansive sense of self characterized those who helped save Jews during the Holocaust). For an argument questioning the emphasis on an enlarged identity among rescuers, see Neera K. Badhwar, "Altruism Versus Self-Interest: Sometimes a False Dichotomy," 10 *Soc. Phil. & Pol'y* 90 (1993). As Dawes and his colleagues remind us, "group identity does not equal morality," since it may be manipulated for a variety of ends. Dawes, et al., *supra* note 110, at 110. This is why an individual must also retain the capacity to take the external stance.

113. Held, *supra* note 100, at 60.

114. See Blustein, *supra* note 84, at 165 (persons "as a community can be said to have an interest in certain states of affairs"); John Hardwig, "In Search of an Ethics of Personal Relationships," in *Person to Person* 63, 77 (George Graham & Hugh LaFollette eds., 1989) (In a close personal relationship, "I see myself, in part, as part of a larger whole that is *us*.").

115. "Some degree of innate, if selective, trust seems a necessary element in any surviving creature whose first nourishment (if it is not exposed) comes from another. . . ." Baier, *supra* note 103, at 107; cf. R.E. Ewin, "Loyalty and Virtues," 42 *Phil Q.* 403, 419 (concluding that emotional ties between people lead parents to care for an infant, not because their child has contracted to care for them in old age).

116. *See* Baier, *supra* note 103, at 105 (finding that a person rarely makes up her mind to trust).

117. "[I]t is unity, a sense of community, and personal affirmation that we want in personal relationships." Hardwig, *supra* note 114, at 60.

118. "Trust is a fragile plant, which may not endure inspection of its roots, even when they were, before the inspection, quite healthy." Baier, *supra* note 103, at 129.

119. *See* Held, *supra* note 100, at 33 (recognizing that the conventional view of autonomy disapproves of relationships such as family ties that are permanent and not chosen).

120. Okin, *supra* note 25.

121. *See* Baier, *supra* note 103, at 114–20 (discussing the "male fixation on contract" as a paradigm of morality).

122. *See* Hirschmann, *supra* note 26, at 21–22; *see also* Held, *supra* note 100, at 70–73 (focusing on mother-child relationship as basic to social life raises the issue of whether ostensibly chosen obligations beyond the family may in fact more closely resemble non-chosen family obligations).

123. George P. Fletcher, *Loyalty* 3 (1993).

124. Blustein, *supra* note 84, at 165.

125. *Id.* at 115. *See also* Selznick, *supra* note 99, at 205 (one understanding of self-assumed obligation, different from explicit decision to be bound, is that responsibility is accepted because doing so is consistent with the self with which one identifies).

126. Consider, for instance, Irish actor Stephen Rea's simultaneous repudiation of and identification with violence-torn Northern Ireland: "Obviously I care about the place. I wish I didn't." "Irishman Stephen Rea's Transatlantic Splash," *Wash. Post*, 17 Dec. 1992, at D3.

127. Blustein, *supra* note 84, at 49–50; *see also* Fletcher, *supra* note 123, at 5 (loyal attachment reflects relationship as an "external force" that holds partners together during temporary dissatisfaction).

128. Blustein, *supra* note 84, at 5; *see also* Fletcher, *supra* note 123, at 39 (historical self may acknowledge "a duty to stand by those who have become a critical part of one's biography").

129. Friedman, *supra* note 28, at 216.

130. *See* Samuel P. Oliner & Pearl M. Oliner, *The Altruistic Personality: Rescuers of Jews in Nazi Europe* (1988).

131. *Id.* at 209.

132. *Id.*

133. *Id.* at 189.

134. *Id.* at 199.

135. *Id.* at 259.

136. *Id.* at 173.

137. *Id.* at 165.

138. *Id.* at 251.

139. *Id.* at 222.

140. *Id.* at 221.

141. *Id.* at 258.

142. Alaisdair MacIntyre, *After Virtue* 204 (1981).

143. *See* Kymlicka, *supra* note 5, at 51.

144. Charles Taylor, *The Ethics of Authenticity* 38 (1991).

145. Michael Sandel, *Democracy's Discontent: America in Search of a Public Philosophy* 14 (1996).

146. Carol Gilligan, "Moral Orientation and Moral Development," in *Women and Moral Theory* 19, 23 (Eva Feder Kittay & Diana T. Meyers eds., 1987).

147. *Id.*

148. Seyla Benhabib, "The Generalized and the Concrete Other: The Kohlberg-Gilligan Controversy and Moral Theory," in Kittay & Meyers, *supra* note 146, at 154, 164.

149. Martha Nussbaum, "The Discernment of Perception: An Aristotelian Conception of Private and Public Rationality," in *Love's Knowledge: Essays on Philosophy and Literature* 54, 72 (1990).

150. Bernard Williams, "Persons, Character, and Morality," in *Moral Luck* 1, 18 (1981).

151. For an argument that it can, *see* Tronto, *supra* note 32. For skepticism about this possibility, *see* Linda McClain, "Atomistic Man Revisited: Liberalism, Connection, and Feminist Jurisprudence," 65 So. Cal. L. Rev. 1171 (1992).

152. *See Science, Morality, and Feminist Theory, supra* note 32; Kittay and Meyers, *supra* note 146.

## Three

1. *Foundations of the Economic Analysis of Law* 372 (Avery Katz ed. 1998). Sustained economic analysis in family law casebooks, for instance, tends to be conspicuous by its absence. *See An Invitation to Family Law* (Carl Schneider & Margaret F. Brinig eds. 1995).

2. Robert J. Willis,"What Have We Learned from the Economics of the Family?" 77 *Amer. Econ. Assn. Papers & Proceedings* 68, 78 (1987).

3. Richard Posner has described economics as "the science of rational choice in a world—our world—in which resources are limited in relation to human wants." Richard Posner, *Economic Analysis of Law* 3 (4th ed. 1992). With respect to the family, see Gary Becker, "Nobel Lecture: The Economic Way of Looking at Life," 101 J. Pol. Econ. 385 (1993). Among the scarce resources that constrain satisfaction of our preferences is time. *See* Gary Becker, "A Theory of the Allocation of Time," 75 *Econ. J.* 493 (1965).

4. For overviews, see Robyn Dawes, *Rational Choice in an Uncertain World* (1988); *Rational Choice* (Jon Elster ed. 1986); David Gauthier, *Morals by Agreement* 21–59 (1986); Donald P. Green & Ian Shapiro, *Pathologies of Rational Choice Theory: A Critique of Applications in Political Science* 14–17 (1994).

5. "The theory of rational choice is . . . primarily concerned with preferences between states of affairs conceived as alternative possibilities realizable in action." Gauthier, *supra* note 4, at 22. *See also* Jon Elster, *Nuts and Bolts for the Social Sciences* 23 (1989).

6. Paul Samuelson & William Nordhaus, *Economics* 447 (13th ed. 1989).

7. Jack Hirschleifer, *Price Theory and Applications* 58 (1976). *See also* Green & Shapiro, *supra* note 4, at 14 (rational choice theory requires that "it must be possible for all of an agent's available options to be rank-ordered").

8. *See* Gauthier, *supra* note 4, at 24. Preferences in this ranking must be transitive. That is, if a person prefers A to B and B to C, then she must prefer A to C. *See id.* at 40; Herbert Margolis, *Selfishness, Altruism, and Rationality: A Theory of Rational Choice* 6 (1982).

9. Cardinal ordering also is required for the analysis of rational choice under risk, in which probabilities are assigned to the outcomes, and rational choice under uncertainty, in which even the probabilities are unknown. This is because in these instances the actor must proceed on the basis of the expected value of the options, which requires multiplication of the expected utility times the probability of occurrence of that outcome. *See generally* Gauthier, *supra* note 4, at 24–25; 42–46.

10. Elster, *Nuts and Bolts, supra* note 5, at 23 n. 4.

11. Jon Elster, "When Rationality Fails," in *The Limits of Rationality* 20, 21 (Karen Schweers Cook & Margaret Levi eds. 1990).

12. Gary Becker, *The Economic Approach to Human Behavior* 14 (1976).

13. "Rational choice theory is normative, in that it tells us what we ought to do in order to achieve our aims as well as possible." Elster, "When Rationality Fails," *supra* note 11, at 20.

*See also* Debra Satz & John Ferejohn, *Rational Choice and Social Theory*, 91 *J. Philos.* 71, 73 (1994) (to the extent that rational choice theory focuses on the reasoning process of individuals, it is "a normative as well as an explanatory enterprise"). Rationality is thus a "blend" concept, which simultaneously describes a state of affairs and implies that it is desirable. *See* Heidi Li Feldman, "Objectivity in Legal Judgment," 92 *Mich. L. Rev.* 1187 (1994). For an argument that "efficiency" is also such a concept, see *infra* notes 114–120 and accompanying text.

14. Richard Posner, *Sex and Reason* 112 (1992).

15. Gary Becker, *A Treatise on the Family* 110 (Enlarged ed. 1991).

16. *See id.*; Shoshana Grossbard-Shechtman, *On the Economics of Marriage* 55 (1993).

17. Gary S. Becker, Elisabeth Landes, & Robert Michael, "An Economic Analysis of Marital Instability," 85 *J. Pol. Econ.* 1141, 1143 (1977); Becker, *Treatise, supra* note 15, at 83. Household production transforms purchased goods into ultimate consumption goods. *See* Posner, *Economic Analysis of Law, supra* note 3, at 139; Reuben Gronau, "Home Production—A Forgotten Industry," 62 *Rev. Econ. & Stat.* 408 (1980).

18. Becker, *supra* note 15 at 112. *See also* Willis, *supra* note 2, at 73 (children can be seen as a collective good produced by marriage).

19. Becker, *Treatise, supra* note 15, at 110.

20. *Id.* at 115.

21. *Id.* at 81.

22. *Id.* at 108–109.

23. *Id.* at 110.

24. Grossbard-Shechtman, *supra* note 16, at 27. Examples include cooking, child care, household maintenance and repair, and emotional support.

25. *Id.*

26. *Id.* at 34.

27. Becker, Landes, & Michael, *supra* note 17, at 68. The costs of continuing a search include both direct search costs incurred and the income forgone by remaining single rather than accepting an available match. The expected benefit is "the probability of finding a preferable mate times the expected increase in wealth from finding him." *Id.* at 1148.

28. *Id.* at 1149.

29. *Id.* at 1147.

30. *Id.* at 43. *See also* H. Elizabeth Peters, "Marriage and Divorce: Information Constraints and Private Contracting," 76 *Amer. Econ. Rev.* 437, 438 (1986) (marriage is a "long-term match between two individuals that produces a valuable, though partially intangible, output. Examples of this output include children, love, security, companionship, money income from market work, and household goods from home production") (footnote omitted).

31. Becker, Treatise, *supra* note 15, at 33; Posner, *Economic Analysis, supra* note 3, at 140.

32. Gary Becker, for instance, claims that

> women invest mainly in human capital that raises household efficiency, especially in bearing and rearing children, because women spend most of their time at these activities. Similarly, men invest mainly in capital that raises market efficiency, because they spend most of their working time in the market. Such sexual differences in specialized investments reinforce any biologically induced sexual division of labor between the market and household sectors....

Becker, *supra* note 15 at 33. *See also* Gary Becker, "Human Capital, Effort, and the Sexual Division of Labor," 3 *J. Lab. Econ.* S-33 (1985).

33. That is, women with higher earning potential have begun more frequently to employ for domestic tasks those women with fewer market skills. *See* Margaret F. Brinig, "The Law and Economics of No-Fault Divorce," 26 *Fam. L. Q.* 453, 456–457 & nn. 20–22

(1993); June Carbone & Margaret F. Brinig, "Rethinking Marriage: Feminist Ideology, Economic Change, and Divorce Reform," 65 *Tul L. Rev.* 953, 990 & n. 168 (1991).

34. For women, these include restrictions on the ability to pursue a satisfying career outside the home; for men, they involve attenuated contact with their wives and children. See Margaret F. Brinig, "Comment on Jana Singer's Alimony and Efficiency," 82 *Geo. L. J.* 2461, 2472 (1994).

35. *See, e.g.*, Becker, *supra* note 15, at 54–79. To the extent that this is the case, these theorists suggest that the expected gains from marrying compared to remaining single have decreased. For a discussion of the asserted implications of this development, see *infra* notes 84–85 and accompanying test.

36. Even a small comparative advantage can produce large differences in productivity, thereby promising substantial gains from specialization. *See* Ben Yu & Yoram Borzel, "Effect of the Utilization Rate on the Division of Labor," 22 *Econ. Inq.* 18 (1984).

37. Grossbard-Shechtman, *supra* note 16, at 55.

38. Becker, Landes, & Michael, *supra* note 17, at 1152.

39. Grossbad-Shechtman, *supra* note 16, at 166–167.

40. *See, e.g.*, Oliver Williamson, *Transaction-Cost Economics: The Governance of Contractual Relations*, 22 *J. Law & Econ.* 233, 239 (1979).

41. *See* Ian Macneil, "Contracts: Adjustment of Long-Term Economic Relations Under Classical, Neoclassical, and Relational Contract Law," 72 *Nw. U. L. Rev.* 854 (1978); Robert Scott & Charles Goetz, "Principles of Relational Contracts," 67 *Va. L. Rev.* 1089 (1981).

42. *See* Timothy Muris, "Opportunistic Behavior and the Law of Contracts," 65 *Minn. L. Rev.* 521 (1981). As Oliver Williamson describes it, "[o]pportunism is a variety of self-interest seeking but extends simple self-interest seeking to include self-interest seeking with guile." Williamson, *supra* note 40, at 234 n. 3.

43. *See* Arthur B. Cornell, Jr., "When Two Become One and Then Come Undone: An Organizational Approach to Marriage and Its Implications for Divorce Law," 26 *Family L. Q.* 103, 111 (1992).

44. *Id.*

45. *Id. See also* Oliver Williamson, *Markets and Hierarchies* 37–38 (1975); Anthony T. Kronman, "Contract Law and the State of Nature," 1 *J. L. Econ. & Organiz.* 5, 21–22 (1985).

46. *See* Cornell, *supra* note 43, at 113. Yoram Ben-Porath, "The F-Connection: Families, Friends, and the Organization of Exchange," 6 *Popul. & Devel. Rev.* 1 (1980).

47. Douglas Allen, "An Inquiry Into the State's Role in Marriage," 13 *J. Econ. Beh. & Organiz.* 171, 171 (1990).

48. Cornell, *supra* note 43, at 117; Allen, *supra* note 47, at 171; Robert A. Pollak, "A Transaction Cost Approach to Families and Households," 23 *J. Econ. Lit.* 581, 585 (1985).

49. *See* Allen, *An Inquiry, supra* note 47, at 174.

50. *Id.* at 177–178.

51. *Id.* at 190; Cornell, *supra* note 43, at 119.

52. Allen, *supra* note 47, at 176.

53. Christine S. Sexton & Daniel Perlman, "Couples' Career Orientation, Gender Role Orientation, and Perceived Equity as Determinants of Marital Power," 51 *J. Marr. & Fam.* 933 (1989). *See also* John Scanzoni, Karen Polonko, & Jay Teachman, *The Sexual Bond: Rethinking Families and Close Relationships* 138 (1989) (in intimate relationship, "commitment is based on the ratio of gratifications (extrinsic/intrinsic) and costs (constraints, punishments, duties, obligations"). Robert A. Lewis & Graham B. Spanier, "Marital Quality, Marital Status, and Social Exchange," in *Family Relationships: Rewards and Costs* 49 (Ivan F. Nye ed. 1982).

54. H. Kelley & J. Thibault, *Interpersonal Relations: A Theory of Interdependence* 8–9 (1978).

55. Timothy D. Stephen, "A Symbolic Exchange Framework for the Development of Intimate Relationships," 37 *Human Rel.* 393, 394 (1984).

56. Becker, Landes, & Michael, *supra* note 17, at 1143–1144.

57. Grossbard-Shechtman, *supra* note 16, at 34.

58. Becker, Landes, & Michael, *supra* note 17, at 1154.

59. *Id.* at 1144; Elisabeth M. Landes, "Economics of Alimony," 7 *J. Legal Stud.* 35, 36 (1978) (if marital income is divisible and spouses can costlessly transfer income between themselves, a couple will decide to divorce if "their combined income from remaining married falls short of their combined expected income from dissolution") (footnote omitted); Peters, *supra* note 30, at 438 (efficient divorce occurs when "the joint value of the marriage is less than the sum of the values of opportunities that face each spouse at divorce").

60. *Id.*

61. Becker, Landes, & Michael, *supra* note 17, at 1144, 1153.

62. Becker, Landes, and Michael suggest that if all compensations between spouses were feasible and costless, divorce would be an illustration of the dynamics of the Coase Theorem, which asserts that under such conditions the allocation of legal entitlements will have no effect on ultimate ownership of those entitlements. *Id.* at 1144. One example of attention to the difficulties of interspousal transfers in the context of bargaining over divorce is Martin Zelder's observation that children are an important source of marital welfare. Because children constitute a "public good," however, it will be difficult for the spouse who desires continuation of the marriage to transfer a greater share of this good to the spouse who wants a divorce. *See* Martin Zelder, "Inefficient Dissolutions As a Consequence of Public Goods: The Case of No-Fault Divorce," 22 *J. Legal Stud.* 503 (1993). For a more extensive discussion of Zelder's thesis, see *infra* notes 91–92 and accompanying text.

Economic theorists of divorce emphasize that calculation of the net benefits of divorce for the party who desires it must take into account the externalities inflicted on other family members by dissolution of the marriage. For a discussion of how this point affects economic analysis of financial allocations at divorce, see chapter 7 notes 94–133 and accompanying text.

63. *See* Ronald C. Fish & Linda Stone Fish, "Quid Pro Quo Revisited: The Basis of Marital Therapy," 56 *Am. J. Orthopsych.* 371, 373 (1986).

64. This approach is reflected in those schools of marital therapy directed at helping the couples make more explicit the implicit bargains that they have struck with each other. *See, e.g. id.* at 383 ("the *quid pro quo* concept is the basic rule that binds both marriages and marital therapies"). *See also* R.L. Weiss, "Contracts, Cognition, and Change: A Behavioral Approach to Marriage Therapy," 5 *Couns. Psychol.* 15 (1975). For more recent qualifications to the quid pro quo model, see the discussion in chapter 4 at notes 126–130 and 189–190 and accompanying text.

65. On the concept of reciprocal altruism, see R.L. Trivers, "The Evolution of Reciprocal Altruism," 46 *Q. Rev. Biol.* 35 (1971). *See also* Garret Hardin, *The Limits of Altruism* (1977); Jeffrey Harrision, "Egoism, Altruism, and Market Illusions: The Limits of Law and Economics," 33 *U.C.L.A. L. Rev.* 1309, 1338–1339 (1986).

66. Becker, Treatise, *supra* note 15, at 183. *See also* Becker, *supra* note 3, at 398–401 (parental care of children conceptualized as investment that enhances prospect of assistance by children in old age). For an economic critique of the Rotten Kid Theorem, see B. Douglas Bernheim & Oded Stark, "Altruism Within the Family Reconsidered: Do Nice Guys Finish Last?" 78 *Am. Econ. Rev.* (1988).

67. David Collard, *Altruism and Economy* 4 (1978); C. Daniel Batson, "Prosocial Motivation: Is It Ever Truly Altruistic?" in 20 *Advances in Experimental Social Psychology* 65 (L. Berkowitz ed. 1987); R. B. Cialdini, M. Schaller, D. Houlihan, K. Arps, J. Fultz & A. L. Beaman, "Empathy-Based Helping: Is It Selflessly or Selfishly Motivated?" 54 *J. Person. & Soc. Psychol.* 749 (1987);

David Kennett, "Altruism and Economic Behavior: I," 39 *Am. J. Econ. & Sociol.* 183, 188 (1980); J.R. Meindel U M.J. Lerner, "The Heroic Motive: Some Experimental Demonstrations," 19 *J. Experiment. Soc. Psychol.* 1 (1983).

68. Kennett, *supra* note 67, at 192.

69. *See* R.L. Archer, R. Diaz-Loving, P.M. Gollwitzer, M.H. Davis & H.C. Foushee, "The Role of Dispositional Empathy and Social Evaluation in the Empathic Mediation of Helping," 40 *J. Person. & Soc. Psychol.* 786 (1981); D. Campbell, "On the Conflict Between Biological and Social Evolution and Between Psychology and the Moral Tradition," 30 *Am. Psychol.* 1103 (1975); J.F. Dovidio, "Helping Behavior and Altruism: An Empirical and Conceptual Overview," in 17 *Advances in Experimental Social Psychology* 361 (L. Berkowitz eds. 1984); Robert Ellickson, "Bringing Culture and Human Frailty to Rational Actors: A Critique of Classical Law and Economics," 65 *Chic.-Kent L. Rev.* 23, 46 (1989).

70. Gauthier, *Morals by Agreement, supra* note 4, at 7.

71. *See* Becker, *Treatise, supra* note 15, at 173; Richard G. Lipsey & Peter Steiner, *Economics* 142–143 (4th ed. 1975); Bernheim & Stark, *supra* note 66, at 1034; William M. Landes & Richard A. Posner, "Salvors, Finders, Good Samaritans, and Other Rescuers: An Economic Study of Law and Altruism," 7 *J. Legal Stud.* 83, 83–128 (1978).

72. Lipsey & Steiner, *supra* note 71, at 142–143.

73. Landes & Posner, *supra* note 71, at 94.

74. *See* Jon Elster, *Ulysses and the Sirens: Studies in Rationality and Irrationality* 36–47 (1979); Richard Thaler & H. M. Shefrin, "An Economic Theory of Self-Control," 89 *J. Pol. Econ.* 392 (1981).

75. For an excellent exploration of this phenomenon with respect to marriage and divorce, see Elizabeth S. Scott, "Rational Decisionmaking About Marriage and Divorce," 76 *Va. L. Rev.* 9 (1990).

76. *See* Cornell, *supra* note 43, at 113 (in marriage, "the value of the companionship is specific to the individuals in the transaction. We prefer specific persons to be our companions").

77. *Id.* at 116.

78. Ben-Porath, *supra* note 46, at 3.

79. Cornell, *supra* note 43, at 113.

80. *Id.*

81. E. Bernscheid & B. Campbell, "The Justice Motive," in *Times of Scarcity and Change* 23–24 (M. Lerner & S. Lerner eds. 1981).

82. This is of course the definition of a Pareto superior move. *See* the discussion *infra* at notes 156–162 and accompanying text.

83. Posner, *Economic Analysis of Law, supra* note 3, at 4. *See also* Vernon L. Smith, "Rational Choice: The Contrast Between Economics and Psychology," 99 *J. Pol. Econ.* 877, 880–882 (1991) (experimental economics indicates that persons consistently produce rational outcomes without being aware of rational choice principles).

84. Becker, *supra* note 15, at 54–79.

85. *See also* Willis, *supra* note 2, at 74.

86. Becker, Landes, & Michael, *supra* note 17.

87. Becker, Landes, & Michael, *supra* note 17, at 1152. *See also* Willis, *supra* note 2, at 74. For other models of divorce that rely on economic or rational choice analysis, see Stan L. Albrecht & Phillip R. Kunz, "The Decision to Divorce: A Social Exchange Perspective," 3 *J. Divorce* 319 (1980); John N. Edwards & Janice M. Saunders, "Coming Apart: A Model of the Marital Dissolution Decision," 43 *J. Marr. & Fam.* 379 (1981); Joan Huber & Glenna Spitze, "Considering Divorce: An Expansion of Becker's Theory of Marital Instability," 86 *Am. J. Soc.* 75 (1980).

88. Lloyd Cohen, "Marriage, Divorce, and Quasi-Rents; or 'I Gave Him the Best Years of My Life,'" 16 *J. Leg. Stud.* 267 (1987).

89. *Id.* at 289.

90. *See also* Allen Parkman, *No-Fault Divorce: What Went Wrong?* (1992); Ira Mark Ellman, "The Theory of Alimony," 77 *Calif. L. Rev.* 1 (1989).

91. Zelder, *supra* note 62, at 505.

92. *Id.* at 516–517. *See also* Landes, *supra* note 59, at 39–40 for discussion of public goods and general obstacles to interspousal transfer of resources.

93. On the absence of an explicit historical rationale for alimony, see Judith Areen, *Family Law: Cases and Materials* 712–713 (3rd ed. 1992).

94. Landes, *supra* note 59, at 45.

95. *Id.* at 45–46.

96. *Id.* at 46.

97. *See also* Carbone & Brinig, *supra* note 33.

98. Landes, *supra* note 59, at 40.

99. *Id.* at 46–48 (footnote omitted).

100. *Id.* at 49.

101. Margaret F. Brinig & Steven M. Crafton, "Marriage and Opportunism," 23 *J. Leg. Stud.* 869 (1994).

102. Landes, *supra* note 59, at 52–62. Two other scholars, however, found little difference in divorce settlements between states that do and do not take fault into account. *See* Yoram Weiss & Robert Willis, "Transfers Among Divorced Couples," 11 *J. Lab. Econ.* 1 (1993).

103. H. Elizabeth Peters, "Marriage and Divorce: Informational Constraints and Private Contracting," 76 *Am. Econ. Rev.* 437 (1986). While Peters concluded that the availability of unilateral no-fault divorce had no discernible effect on the divorce rate, *id* at 446–448, other scholars have reached a different conclusion. *See* Douglas Allen, "Marriage and Divorce: Comment," 82 *Am. Econ. Rev.* 679 (1992); Margaret F. Brinig & Michael V. Alexeev, "Trading at Divorce," 8 *Ohio St. J. Disp. Res.* 279 (1993).

104. Allen, *supra* note 47, at 185.

105. *See, e.g.,* Parkman, *No-Fault Divorce, supra* note 90, at 137–140; Allen Parkman, "Reform of the Divorce Provisions of the Marital Contract," 8 *B.Y.U. J. Pub. L.* 91 (1993); Gary Becker, "Finding Fault with No-Fault Divorce," *Bus. Week* 22 (Dec. 7, 1992).

106. *See, e.g.,* Ellman, *supra* note 90; Cornell, *supra* note 43, at 130–135; Michael J. Trebilcock & Rosemin Keshvani, "The Role of Private Ordering in Family Law: A Law and Economics Perspective," 41 *U. Tor. L. J.* 533, 555–558 (1991). Allen Parkman regards mutual consent as the best approach to divorce, see Parkman, *No-Fault Divorce, supra* note 90, at 137–140, but argues that the next best approach would be compensation for diminution in human capital. *See id.* at 123–127, 140. In addition, the American Law Institute (ALI) Reporters' Principles of the Law of Family Dissolution adopts compensation for human capital as the centerpiece of its proposed statute. *See* American Law Institute, *Principles of the Law of Family Dissolution: Proposed Final Draft* (February 4, 1997) 257–406. The Principles have not yet been formally adopted by the ALI itself and are still under consideration. For an excellent discussion of the different economic approaches to divorce reform, see Ann Laquer Estin, "Economics and the Problem of Divorce," 2 *U. Chi. L. Sch. Roundtable* 517 (1995).

107. *See, e.g.,* Allen Parkman, "Recognition of Human Capital as Property in Divorce Settlements," 40 *Ark. L. Rev.* 439, 445 (1987).

108. *See, e.g.,* Joan Krauskopf, "Recompense for Financing Spouse's Education: Legal Protection for the Marital Investor in Human Capital," 28 *Kan. L. Rev.* 379 (1980); Cynthia Starnes, "Divorce and the Displaced Homemaker: A Discourse on Playing with Dolls,

Partnership Buyouts, and Dissociation Under No-Fault," 60 *U. Chi. L. Rev.* 67 (1993); Katharine K. Baker, Comment, "Contracting for Security: Paying Married Women What They've Earned," 55 U. Chi. L. Rev. 1193 (1988).

109. This asymmetry in the timing of spouses' contributions is emphasized by Cohen, *supra* note 88.

110. For a cogent feminist analysis of these proposals, see Jana Singer, "Alimony and Efficiency: The Gendered Costs and Benefits of the Economic Justification for Alimony," 82 *Geo. L. J.* 2423 (1994).

111. *See* Roger Trigg, *Understanding Social Science: A Philosophical Introduction to the Social Sciences* 21–40 (1985).

112. Margaret Jane Radin, "Market-Inalienability," 100 *Harv. L. Rev.* 1849, 1885 (1987).

113. *Id.* at 1907.

114. Avery Katz, "Positivism and the Separation of Law and Economics," 94 *Mich. L. Rev.* 2229, 2243 (1996).

115. *Id.* at 2244.

116. Posner, *Economic Analysis of Law, supra* note 3, at 23 (economics shows the trade-offs between efficiency and other values); Katz, *supra* note 114, at 2240 n. 22 (non-Chicago economists tend to endorse efficiency in combination with other goals).

117. Posner, *Economic Analysis of Law, supra* note 3, at 23.

118. Russell Hardin, "The Morality of Law and Economics," 11 *Law and Philos.* 331, 334 (1992). *See also* Lloyd Cohen, "A Justification of Social Wealth Maximization As A Rights-Based Ethical Theory," 10 *Harv. J. Pub. Pol.* 411, 411 (1987)(criteria of morality and efficiency lead to the same outcomes); Katz, *supra* note 114, at 2240 n. 22 (Chicago school economists "tend to endorse efficiency as an exclusive goal").

119. Jules Coleman, "The Normative Basis of Economic Analysis: A Critical Review of Richard Posner's *The Economics of Justice*," 34 *Stan. L. Rev.* 1105, 1107 (1982)(Review Essay). Coleman includes in this turn both those who propose changes in legal rules to promote efficiency, as well as those who explore the normative basis of efficiency itself. *Id.*

120. *See, e.g.,* Parkman, *No-Fault Divorce, supra* note 90; Brinig & Crafton, *supra* note 101; Cohen, " 'I Gave Him the Best Years of My Life'," *supra* note 88; Ellman, *supra* note 90.

121. *See* Donald Green & Ian Shapiro, *Pathologies of Rational Choice Theory* 15 (1994) (there is widespread agreement among rational choice theorists that "the relevant maximizing units are individuals").

122. Gauthier, *supra* note 4, at 47. *See also* Elster, "When Rationality Fails," in *The Limits of Rationality, supra* note 11, at 21 ("Desires are the unmoved movers" of rational choice theory); George Stigler & Gary Becker, *De Gustibus Non Est Disputandum,* in *id.* at 191, 191 ("[t]astes are the unchallengable axioms of a man's behavior; he may properly (usefully) be criticized for inefficiency in satisfying his desires, but the desires themselves are *data*") (emphasis in original).

123. Trebilcock & Keshvani, *supra* note 106, at 533–534. *See also* Katz, *supra* note 114, at 2239 (one basic normative axiom of economics is "subjective utilitarianism," the view that individuals are the best, or even only, judges of their own interests).

124. Posner, *Economic Analysis of Law, supra* note 3, at 263; Richard Epstein, "Postscript: Subjective Utilitarianism," 12 *Harv. J. Law & Pub. Pol.* 769 (1989); Gary Lawson, "Efficiency and Individualism," 42 *Duke L.J.* 53, 65 (1992) (focus of economic analysis is on satisfaction of preferences rather than on measures of well-being); Gauthier, *supra* note 4, at 25 (rational choice theory "treats value as a subjective and relative measure").

125. Gauthier, *supra* note 4, at 34.

126. David Hume, 2 *A Treatise of Human Nature,* pt. 3, ect. iii 416 (L.A. Selby-Bigge ed. 1888). *See also* Elizabeth Anderson, *Value in Ethics and Economics* 129 (1992) ("Welfare economics identifies rational preferences with actual preferences").

127. On the importance of this capacity in liberal thought, see John Rawls, *Political Liberalism* 19 (1993) (capacity for a conception of the good is one of the basic human moral powers).

128. Green & Shapiro, *supra* note 121, at 14.

129. "An ordinal ranking says that either A is better than B, B is better than A, or they are equal in value. Unlike a cardinal ranking, it doesn't say how much more valuable one good is than the other." Anderson, *supra* note 126, at 46.

130. *Id.*

131. "The utility of a state of affairs is its value, to a person, as a possible outcome—as an alternative, therefore, to certain other possible states of affairs." Gauthier, *supra* note 4, at 54. *See also* Paul Samuelson & William Nordhaus, *Economics* 447 (13th ed. 1989).

132. Gauthier, *supra* note 4, at 27.

133. *See* Michael Stocker, *Plural and Conflicting Values* 169 (1990).

134. *Id. See also* Richard Pildes, "Conceptions of Value in Legal Thought," 90 *Mich. L. Rev.* 1520, 1530–45 (1992) (Review Essay) (discussing trend in legal theory to treat value as commensurable).

135. Anderson, *supra* note 126, at 118.

136. *Id.* at 44–45.

137. *Id.* at 118. This is not to say that an assumption of incommensurability is inconsistent with critical reflection. Rather, it is to acknowledge that the premise of commensurability is consistent with an understanding of reflection as abstraction from particularity than is especially influential in the Western tradition. While psychological and emotional distance continues to serve as the control metaphor for critical reflection, work by communitarian and feminist theorists can be seen as a challenge to this imagery. *See, e.g.,* Michael Sandel, Liberalism and the Limits of Justice (1982); Carol Gilligan, In A Different Voice (1982).

138. She may count guilt or concern for others, of course, as sources of disutility that affect her calculation. *See* Robert Ellickson, "Bringing Culture and Human Frailty to Rational Actors: A Critique of Classical Law and Economics," 65 *Chi.-Kent L. Rev.* 23, 47 (1989). Ideally, however, she should ask herself how important these considerations are to her in light of the advantages of divorce, rather than conclude that they automatically preclude leaving the marriage.

139. Becker, Landes, & Michael, *supra* note 17, at 1151.

140. *Id.* at 1151–52.

141. Allen, *An Inquiry, supra* note 47, at 172; Becker, Landes, & Michael *supra* note 17, at 1142; Cornell *supra* note 43, at 116–117.

142. *See* Becker, *Treatise, supra* note 15, at 96 (economic analysis "do[es] not assume that [spouses] value [one another] for their own sake, but only considers the value of the output produced by husbands and wives"); Grossbard-Shechtman, *supra* note 16, at 33 ("choices [in the marriage market] are available, which means that actual or potential spouses are substitutable").

143. Research indicates, for instance, that satisfaction with one's marriage is only one variable in predicting marital stability; the availability of alternatives is also a significant consideration. *See, e.g.,* George Levinger, "A Social Psychological Perspective on Marital Dissolution," in *Divorce and Separation: Context, Causes, and Consequences* 37, 42–43 (George Levinger & O. Moles eds. 1979); Udry, "Marital Alternatives and Marital Disruption," 43 *J. Marr. & Fam.* 889 (1981).

144. Trebilcock & Keshvani, *supra* note 106, at 535; Michael Trebilcock, *The Limits of Freedom of Contract* 1–22 (1993).

145. *See* Lawson, *supra* note 124, at 65.

146. *See* Hirschleifer, *supra* note 7, at 59; Richard Posner, *The Economics of Justice* 79 (1981).

147. Anderson, *supra* note 126, at 144. *See also* Jules Coleman, *Risks and Wrongs* 67 (1992) (free markets embody the liberal value of autonomy).

148. *See* Anderson, *supra* note 126, at 146 (market emphasizes exit rather than voice as a means of influencing the provision of commodities).

149. Posner, *Economic Analysis of Law, supra* note 3, at 265 (market economy rests on the principle of consent).

150. *See* Chapter 2 at 20–21 (discussing work of Anthony Giddens).

151. Hardin, *supra* note 118, at 381.

152. For at least one pair of economic analysts, those obstacles include significant asymmetry in the background entitlements of the parties to the contract. *See* Trebilcock & Keshvani, *supra* note 106, at 551.

153. *See, e.g.,* Trebilcock & Keshvani, *supra* note 106, at 556. Douglas Allen also suggests that the more diverse that marriages become, the less efficient will be a generic legal regime that limits alternative arrangements. Allen, *An Inquiry, supra* note 47, at 179.

154. *See, e.g.,* Trebilcock & Keshvani, *supra* note 106, at 556–557. I discuss the hypothetical bargain method at greater length *infra* notes 182–186 and accompanying text.

155. For a catalogue, see Lawson, *supra* note 124.

156. *See* Coleman, *The Normative Basis, supra* note 118, at 1105, 1107.

157. Coleman, *Markets, Morals, and the Law* (1988).

158. Posner, *Economics of Justice, supra* note 146, at 54–55.

159. *See* Jeffrie G. Murphy & Jules L. Coleman, *Philosophy of Law: An Introduction to Jurisprudence* 182 (1990); Posner, *Economics of Justice, supra* note 146, at 89.

160. *See* Richard Posner, *The Problems of Jurisprudence* 389 (1990).

161. Posner, *Economics of Justice, supra* note 146, at 89.

162. *See* Coleman, *Normative Basis, supra* note 119, at 1108 (Pareto efficiency blends utilitarian maximization and libertarian normative justifications); Posner, *Principles of Jurisprudence, supra* note 160, at 389 (Pareto criterion draws on ethical intuitions of utilitarianism and Kantian individualism). *See also* David Charny, "Hypothetical Bargains: The Normative Structure of Contract Interpretation," 89 *Mich. L. Rev.* 1815, 1848 (1991) (autonomy, fairness, and welfare maximization rationales all justify enforcement of actual agreement between parties); Trebilcock, *The Limits of Freedom of Contract, supra* note 144, at 21–22 (noting claim that private ordering "simultaneously promotes individual autonomy and advances social welfare").

163. *See* Lawson, *supra* note 124, at 86–87; Posner, *Economic Analysis of Law, supra* note 3, at 15.

164. Coleman, *Markets, Morals, and the Law, supra* note 157, at 98.

165. *See* Guido Calabresi & Philip Bobbit, *Tragic Choices* 85–86 (1978).

166. *See* Coleman, *Normative Basis, supra* note 119, at 1117–1131. One of the originators of the Kaldor-Hicks standard originally suggested that the prospect of theoretical compensation could serve to ground the test in consent. *See* Nicholas Kaldor, "Welfare Propositions of Economics and Interpersonal Comparisons of Utility," 49 *Econ. J.* 549, 551 n. 1 (1993). This claim, however, has been subject to searching criticism. *See, e.g.,* Coleman, *Normative Basis, supra* note 119, at 1117–1131.

167. There are difficulties, however, even with attempts to justify Kaldor-Hicks efficiency on utilitarian grounds. *See* Coleman, *Normative Basis, supra* note 119, at 1108–1113.

168. *See, e.g.* John Rawls, *A Theory of Justice* 22–27 (1970).

169. Posner, *Economic Analysis of Law, supra* note 3, at 15. Posner for awhile offered a principle of wealth maximization as a criterion that ostensibly incorporated greater emphasis on consent than the Kaldor-Hicks test while preserving some of its practical consequentialist benefits. *See* Posner, *Economics of Justice, supra* note 146, at 48–115. Criticisms of his suggestion, however, seem for the moment to have moved him close to a position

that equates wealth maximization and the Kaldor-Hicks criterion. *See, e.g.*, Posner, *Economic Analysis of Law, supra* note 3, at 16 ( referring to "[t]he Kaldor-Hicks or wealth maximization approach").

170. That is, the person holding the entitlement to marriage is the one who decides what level of compensation is sufficient to make her willing to surrender it. *See* Estin, *supra* note 106, at 531. On property rules and liability rules generally, see Guido Calabresi & Douglas Melamed, "Property Rules, Liability Rules, and Inalienability: One View of the Cathedral," 85 *Harv. L. Rev.* 1089 (1972).

171. June Carbone suggests another rationale for mutual consent divorce. When spouses divorce, both partners lose the expected benefits from continuation of the marriage. Under a fault-based divorce regime, fault offers the basis for determining which partner's expectation losses should be compensated. A mutual consent requirement serves the same function in the absence of a finding of fault, by leaving it to each party to determine whether he or she would be better off by staying in the marriage or by leaving and paying what the other party demands in compensation. Letter from June Carbone, May 14, 1996.

172. *See* On the harm principle, see John Stuart Mill, *On Liberty* 73–91 (Elizabeth Rapaport ed. 1978).

173. *See, e.g.*, Cohen, *supra* note 88, at 300–301.

174. *See* Posner, *Economic Analysis of Law, supra* note 3, at 62.

175. Put differently, mutual consent creates the possibility that there will be "excessive performance" of the marriage contract. *See* June Carbone, *Economics, Feminism, and the Reinvention of Alimony: A Reply to Ira Ellman*, 43 Vand. L. Rev. 1463, 1485–1490 (1990); Estin, *supra* note 106, at 568–569.

176. That is, the party with the entitlement to marriage would be required to relinquish it if paid a level of compensation determined by a third party such as a court. *See* Estin, *supra* note 106, at 532; Calabresi and Melamed, *supra* note 170.

177. Put differently, the concern of efficient damage theorists is with "excessive breach" of the marital contract. *See* Carbone, *supra* note 175, at 1485–1490; Estin, *supra* note 106, at 568–569.

178. *See* Lyn Baker & Robert Emery, "When Every Relationship is Above Average: Perceptions and Expectations of Divorce at the Time of Marriage," 17 *Law & Hum. Beh.* 439 (1993).

179. One might conceptualize this as compensation for the loss of the opportunity to marry a different person at the time of the marriage, a loss that tends to be more significant for women than men. *See* Carbone & Brinig, *supra* note 33; Cohen, *supra* note 88. Difficulties in calculating the value of forgone alternative opportunities available at the time of the contract, however, have led many courts and scholars in contract law to rely on the value of the expected benefits from contract performance as an indication of this figure. The assumption is that in a competitive market, the value of the contract will reflect expected benefits slightly greater at the margin than the next best contractual opportunity.

180. I say "theoretically" because of potential difficulties in calculating the emotional and psychological injury from divorce, as well as the search costs of finding another partner, which create the risk of undercompensation. This risk is what leads some theorists to recommend mutual consent divorce. *See* Parkman, *Reform of Divorce Provisions, supra* note 105.

181. *See* Parkman, *No-Fault Divorce, supra* note 90; Ellman, *supra* note 90.

182. Trebilcock & Keshvani, *supra* note 106, at 556.

183. *See* Coleman, *Normative Basis, supra* note 119, at 1123. *See also* Ronald Dworkin, "Why Efficiency?" 8 *Hofstra L. Rev.* 563, 576–577 (1980).

184. *See* Coleman, *supra* note 119, at 1123–1127; Dworkin, *supra* note 183, at 578–579.

185. The principle of autonomy conventionally understood emphasizes the importance of choice and consent to the assumption of obligation. The autonomy justification is not as strong for hypothetical as for actual agreements. Charny, *supra* note 162, at 1817 n. 11. Nonetheless, even though the parties may not have come to explicit agreement regarding the specific contingency in question, each has agreed to pursue a joint undertaking. Enforcement of a hypothetical bargain thus "purports to interpret the implications of the parties' own commitments to participate in fostering their own projects." *Id.* at 1825.

Hypothetical bargains may be justified on the ground of fairness in various ways. One may conclude that "the fact that the parties would have consented to a term seems to be strong evidence that the term is fair." *Id.* at 1836. Alternatively, one may vindicate fairness by constructing a hypothetical bargain that adjusts for differences in bargaining power, and seeks to change preferences so as to enhance parties' commitments to equity, or enforces social norms. *Id.* at 1836–1837.

186. As David Charny points out, analysts who would use a hypothetical bargain model must make decisions about two issues. First, at what level of generality should we describe the parties? Should we ask whether the particular individuals in question would have agreed to a term, or whether persons of the "type" represented by the parties would have done so? *Id.* at 1817. Because my concern here is not to construe an agreement between specific parties but to assess the consistency of a compensation rule in general with certain principles, I describe the parties to the hypothetical bargain as prospective husbands and wives.

Second, we must determine the characteristics that we will ascribe to the bargainers. *Id.* at 1817. With respect to prospective husbands and wives in general, should we conceptualize them as men and women constituted by our current cultural circumstances or as ideally rational bargainers? There are at least two reasons why I for the most part have chosen the latter. First, there appear to be systematic cognitive biases that lead parties contemplating marriage to underestimate the risk of divorce. *See* Baker & Emery, *supra* note 178. Structuring the hypothetical bargain so as to promote genuine autonomy in this setting thus seems to demand that we correct for this bias, so that neither party is left after divorce with resources insufficient to sustain a life of relative self-governance. Second, there tend to be systematic differences in bargaining power between men and women in intimate settings. *See* Charny, *supra* note 162, at 1877; Shelley Lundberg & Robert A. Pollak, "Separate Spheres Bargaining and the Marriage Market," 101 J. Pol. Econ. 988 (1993). To approximate a bargain that includes this feature "would be to perpetuate or reenact what many would condemn as the unjust distribution of power among men and women[.]" Charny, *supra* note 162, at 1877. Furthermore, structuring the hypothetical bargain so as to abstract from this difference in bargaining leverage "may help to change social attitudes about duties of men and women living in intimate relationships." *Id.* at 1876. Such a method seeks to vindicate not only autonomy but fairness as well. *See id.* at 1839 (decisionmaker who justifies enforcement of hypothetical agreements on ground of fairness "should idealize the construction of hypothetical bargains by conforming the terms of the contract to arrangements that ideally rational transactors would regard as fair") (footnote omitted). I do, however, take into account the contemporary influence of the external stance toward marriage when considering the parties' likely approach to bargaining. *See infra* note 188 and accompanying text.

Note that by declining to enforce a hypothetical bargain that men and women under current actual conditions might reach, we do not violate the principle of autonomy. By definition, we are not overriding an *actual agreement* between the parties, *id.* at 1833, and our construction of the bargain is animated in part by a desire to promote autonomy. *Id.* at 1834.

187. Trebilcock & Keshvani, *supra* note 106, at 557.

188. This assumes, notwithstanding my earlier defense of abstraction, see *supra* note 186, that the parties are constituted at least in part by their location in our cultural circumstances. Ascribing this orientation to the parties, however, does not threaten to undermine principles of autonomy and fairness in the way that would occur were we to ascribe to them the cognitive biases and differences in bargaining power that I have discussed earlier.

189. *See* Ellman, *supra* note 90, at 23–24. Nor does it seem likely that a couple would bargain for a marital contract that required the party at fault for ending the marriage to pay expectation damages. Any possibility of compensation in this instance would require the potential recipient to establish grounds for a fault-based divorce. This process could well be both expensive and acrimonious, and its difficulty would create a significant risk of no compensation. Furthermore, uncertainty about what conduct might be adjudicated to constitute fault arguably would constrain the freedom to seek more happiness elsewhere, which would not sit well with the strong contemporary emphasis on freedom of choice in intimate matters.

190. Such compensation most commonly would take the form of increases in the household standard of living.

191. *See* Amartya Sen, "Gender and Cooperative Conflicts," in *Persistent Inequalities: Women and World Development* 123 (Irene Tinker ed. 1990).

192. Carol Rose, "Women and Property: Gaining and Losing Ground," 78 *Va. L. Rev.* 421 (1992).

193. On the importance of attention to gender disparities in the allocation of resources within households, see Hanna Papanek, "To Each Less Than She Needs, From Each More Than She Can Do: Allocations, Entitlements, and Value," in Tinker, *supra* note 191, at 162.

194. *See* Wax, *supra* note 31.

195. Trebilcock & Keshvani, *supra* note 106, at 551–552.

196. On the need for such an account, see Frances Olsen, "The Family and the Market," 96 *Harv. L. Rev.* 1496 (1983).

## Four

1. Herbert Margolis, *Selfishness, Altruism, and Rationality* 15 (1982). *See also* Jane J. Mansbridge, "On the Relation of Altruism and Self-Interest," in *Beyond Self-Interest* 133, 135 (Jane J. Mansbridge ed. 1990) (unselfish or altruistic motives require one person to "make the other's good their own"); David A. Kennett, "Altruism and Economic Behavior: I," 39 *Am. J. Econ. & Sociol.* 183, 184 (1980) (altruism in the purest sense involves contributing to the well-being of another without obligation or expectation of some future benefit).

2. *See also* Collard, *supra* note 67, at 4–5.

3. *Id.* at 18.

4. *See, e.g.*, M.L. Hoffman, "Is Altruism Part of Human Nature?" 40 *J. Pers. & Soc. Psychol.* 761 (1981); D. L. Krebs, "Empathy and Altruism," 32 *J. Pers. & Soc. Psychol.* 1134 (1975). Representative of this motivation is Thomas Hobbes's answer to the question why he gave money to a beggar: "I was in pain to consider the miserable condition of the old man; and now my alms, giving him some relief, doth also ease me." John Aubrey, *Brief Lives* 159 (Richard Barber ed. 1982).

5. Patricia A. Schoenrade, C. Daniel Batson, J. Randall Brandt, and Robert E. Loud, Jr., "Attachment, Accountability, and Motivation to Benefit Another Not in Distress," 51 *J. Pers. & Soc. Psychol.* 557, 557 (1986).

6. *See, e.g.*, R. L. Archer, R. Diaz-Loving, P. M. Gollwitzer, M. H. Davis, & H. C. Foushee, "The Role of Dispositional Empathy and Social Evaluation in the Empathic Mediation of Helping," 40 *J. Pers. & Soc. Psychol.* 786 (1981); J. F. Dovidio, "Helping Behavior and Altruism: An Empirical and Conceptual Overview," in 17 *Advances in Experimental Social Psychology* 361

(L. Berkowitz ed. 1984); W. C. Thompson, C. L. Cowan, & D. L. Rosenhan, "Focus of Attention Mediates the Impact of Negative Affect on Altruism," 38 *J. Pers. & Soc. Psychol.* 291 (1980).

7. Cialdini, Schaller, et al., *supra* note 67; R. B. Cialdini, D. J. Bauman, & D. T. Kenrick, "Insights From Sadness: A Three-Step Model of the Development of Altruism as Hedonism," 1 *Devel. Rev.* 207 (1981).

8. Cialdini, Schaller, et al., *supra* note 67, at 750.

9. K. D. Smith, J. P. Keating, & E. Stotland, "Altruism Revisited: The Effect of Denying Feedback on a Victim's Status to Empathic Witnesses," 57 *J. Pers. & Soc. Psychol.* 641 (1989).

10. *Id.*

11. C. Daniel Batson, Judy G. Batson, Jacqueline K. Slingsby, Kevin L. Harrell, Heli M. Peekna, & R. Matthew Todd, "Empathic Joy and the Empathy-Altruism Hypothesis," 61 *J. Pers. & Soc. Psychol.* 413, 413 (1991).

12. For a description of this theory, see Schoenrade, et al., *supra* note 5.

13. These experiments are described in C. Daniel Batson, *The Altruism Question: Toward a Social Psychological Answer* (1991).

14. C. Daniel Batson, "Why Act for the Public Good? Four Answers," 20 *Pers. & Soc. Psychol. Bull.* 603 (1994). For studies refuting various egoistic theories, see Miho Toi & C. Daniel Batson, "More Evidence That Empathy is a Source of Altruistic Motivation," 43 *J. Pers. & Soc. Psychol.* 281 (1982) (desire to relieve distress of helper); Schoenrade, et al., *supra* note 5 (concern for accountability to person in distress); C. Daniel Batson, Janine L. Dyck, J. Randall Brandt, Judy G. Batson, Anne L. Powell, M. Rosalie McMaster, & Cari Griffitt, "Five Studies Testing Two New Egoistic Alternatives to the Empathy-Altruism Hypothesis," 55 *J. Pers. & Soc. Psychol.* 52 (1988) (gaining social or self-reward or avoiding social or self-punishment); C. Daniel Batson, Judy G. Batson, Cari A. Griffitt, Sergio Barrientos, J. Randall Brandt, Peter Sprengelmeyer, & Michael J. Bayly, "Negative-State Relief and the Empathy-Altruism Hypothesis," 56 *J. Pers. & Soc. Psychol.* 922 (1989) (relief of sadness or sorrow); John F. Dovidio, David A. Schroeder, & Judith L. Allen, "Specificity of Empathy-Induced Helping: Evidence for Altruistic Motivation," 59 *J. Pers. & Soc. Psychol.* 249 (1990) (relief of sadness or sorrow); C. Daniel Batson, et al., *Empathic Joy, supra* note 11 (desire to share vicariously in victim's joy at improvement).

15. Batson, "Why Act for the Public Good?," *supra* note 14, at 609.

16. Batson, et al., *Five Studies, supra* note 14, at 52 (citation omitted).

17. *See* Linnda R. Caporael, Robyn M. Dawes, John M. Orbell, & Alphons van de Kragt, "Selfishness Examined: Cooperation in the Absence of Egoistic Incentives," 12 *Beh. & Brain Sciences* 683 (1989); Robyn M. Dawes, Alphons J.C. van de Kragt, & John Orbell, "Cooperation for the Benefit of Us—Not Me, or My Conscience," in *Beyond Self-Interest* 97 (Jane J. Mansbridge ed. 1990); John Orbell, Alphons van de Kragt, & Robyn Dawes, "Explaining Discussion-Induced Cooperation," 54 *J. Pers. & Soc. Psychol.* 811 (1988).

18. This situation is of course classically expressed in the Prisoner's Dilemma. *See* Robert D. Luce & Howard Raiffa, *Games and Decisions* (1957).

19. Caporael, et al., *supra* note 17, at 684

20. *Id.* The outcome is deficient because the actors prefer some other outcome, but is an equilibrium because no group member receives a higher payoff for selecting some other course of action if others choose their dominating strategies. *Id.*

21. *Id.*

22. *Id.*

23. *Id.* at 686.

24. *Id.* at 688.

25. *Id.*

26. *See* Orbell, et al., *supra* note 17.

27. Caporael, et al., *supra* note 17, at 688–689. The intricacies of the research design of these experiments are laid out in the most detail in *id.* at 687–693.

28. Dawes, et al., in Mansbridge, *supra* note 17, at 103.

29. *Id.*

30. Alphons van de Kragt, John C. Orbell, & Robyn Dawes, with S. R. Braver & L. A. Wilson II, "Doing Well and Doing Good as Ways of Resolving Social Dilemmas," in *Experimental Social Dilemmas* 177 (Henk A. M. Wilke, Dave M. Messick, & Christel G. Rutte eds. 1986); Caporael, et al., *supra* note 17, at 690–691.

31. Dawes, et al in Mansbridge, *supra* note 17, at 99.

32. *Id.* at 109.

33. Caporael, et al., *supra* note 17, at 693–695, 696; Dawes, et al., in Mansbridge, *supra* note 17, at 109–110.

34. Caporael, et al., *supra* note 17, at 693.

35. *Id.* at 694. For assessments of this evolutionary argument, see "Open Peer Commentary," 12 *Beh. & Brain Sciences* 699–727 (1989). For a response to these assessments, see "Authors' Response," *id.* at 727–739.

36. Dawes, et al., *supra* note 17, at 109. The reference to verbal promises is based on findings that rates of contribution were significantly higher in groups in which all group members made verbal commitments to contribute than in groups in which not all members did so. Caporael, et al., *supra* note 17, at 728; Dawes, et al., *supra* note 17, at 107–108. Researchers suggest that two hypotheses are possible to explain this finding: (1) group identity is indicated by universal promising, but it is the solidarity rather than the promises that induce more cooperation in such groups; or (2) promises are effective, but only in a situation in which everyone has made them. *Id.* at 108. They argue that the influence of group discussion, even in the absence of promises, suggests that the first hypothesis is more powerful.

One recent study purports to distinguish between the effect of group identity and a norm of promise-keeping, and maintains that its findings are consistent with the latter but not the former. Norbert L. Kerr & Cynthia M. Kaufman-Gilliland, "Communication, Commitment, and Cooperation in Social Dilemmas," 66 *J. Pers. & Soc. Psychol.* 513 (1994). The study assumes that if group identification leads to a greater concern for group welfare, persons' rates of contribution will decrease if they believe that their contribution is unnecessary for the group to obtain the collective good, but will not decrease if they feel bound by an earlier promise to contribute. The study appears, however, to conflate what Herbert Margolis has termed "participation altruism" and "goods altruism." Margolis, *Selfishness, Altruism, and Rationality, supra* note 1, at 21. The former refers to my desire to participate in prosocial acts, so that it is important to me that *I* make a contribution to others' welfare. The latter refers to my desire that other people be better off. *Id.* It may be that group identity elicits both types of altruism, so that a person may be motivated to contribute to the acquisition of a public good, even if that contribution is superfluous, at least up to a certain point. Kerr and Kaufman-Gilliland do acknowledge this possibility: "Perhaps enhancing group identity can have a more direct, cooperation-contingent effect [than by producing a concern for group welfare] (e.g., making any progroup act, even an inefficacious one, more attractive)." Kerr & Kaufman-Gilliland, at 526–527. In any event, to reiterate, the studies of Dawes and his colleagues demonstrate the significance of group discussion even in the absence of promises.

37. Roderick M. Kramer & Marilynn B. Brewer, "Effects of Group Identity on Resource Use in a Simulated Commons Dilemma," 46 *J. Pers. & Soc. Psychol.* 1044 (1984).

38. *Id.* at 1055.

39. *Id.* at 1045.

40. *Id.*

41. Marilynn B. Brewer, "Experimental Research and Social Policy: Must It Be Rigor Versus Relevance?" 41 *J. Soc. Iss.* 159 (1985); Roderick M. Kramer & Marilynn B. Brewer, "Social Group Identity and the Emergence of Cooperation in Resource Conservation Dilemmas," in *Psychology of Decisions and Conflict*, Vol. 3 (H. Wilke, D. Messick, & C. Rutte eds. 1986).

42. *Id. See also* Marilynn B. Brewer & S. Schneider, "Social Identity and Social Dilemmas: A Double-Edged Sword," in *Social Identity Theory: Constructive and Critical Advances* (D. Abrams & M. Hogg eds. 1990) (individuals behave selfishly when a collective is large and amorphous, but are more likely to sacrifice self-interest for collective welfare when intermediate group identity is available).

43. Kramer & Brewer, *Effects of Group Identity, supra* note 37, at 1045.

44. *See also* Marilynn B. Brewer & Roderick M. Kramer, "Choice Behavior in Social Dilemmas: Effects of Social Identity, Group Size, and Decision Framing," 50 *J. Pers. & Soc. Psychol.* 543 (1986) (noting effect of collective identity on individual self-restraint when group is small or choice problem is framed as commons dilemma, or both; suggesting that effect is undermined by large group size in public goods dilemma).

45. Richard McAdams reviews some of these studies and concludes that the explanation for intergroup prosocial behavior is the subtle egoistic reward of "esteem or status" within the group. Richard McAdams, "Cooperation and Conflict: The Economics of Group Status Production and Race Discrimination," 108 *Harv. L. Rev.* 1005, 1007 (1995). He rejects the claim that the behavior in question is altruistic, on the ground that group members behave prosocially only toward each other and not toward members of other groups. *Id.* at 1017. The appeal in such instances, he argues, is "not to principle, but to solidarity." *Id.* McAdams neglects the point, however, that the expanded sense of self that typifies group identity can be motivated by the principle of altruism *toward group members.* Indeed, this seems a good definition of group solidarity. Because the self-concept in such instances is not defined by the boundary of the individual, an egoistic account misses phenomena that a theory that is sensitive to this expanded sense of self is able to capture. The section that follows discusses the psychological processes involved in the formation of such a group identity.

46. *See, e.g.*, Henri Tajfel, *Social Identity and Intergroup Relations* (1982); Henri Tajfel, *Human Groups and Social Categories* (1981); *The Social Dimension: European Developments in Social Psychology* (Henri Tajfel ed. 1984); John C. Turner, Michael A. Hogg, Penelope J. Oakes, Stephen D. Reicher, & Margaret Wetherell, *Rediscovering the Social Group: A Self-Categorization Theory* (1987); John C. Turner & H. Giles, *Intergroup Behavior* (1981).

47. Turner, et al., *Rediscovering the Social Group, supra* note 46, at 44.

48. John C. Turner, Penelope J. Oakes, S. Alexander Haslam, & Craig McGarty, "Self and Collective: Cognition and Social Context," 20 *Pers. & Soc. Psychol. Bull.* 454, 454 (1994)

49. Turner, et al., *Rediscovering the Social Group, supra* note 46, at 20.

50. *Id.*

51. *Id.* at 24.

52. Turner, et al., *Self and Collective, supra* note 48, at 455.

53. This point was emphasized by social interactionist theorists earlier in this century. *See, e.g.*, S. E. Asch, *Social Psychology* (1952); K. Lewin, *Field Theory in Social Science* (1952); K. Lewin, "Field Theory and Experiment in Social Psychology," 44 *Am. J. Soc.* 868 (1939); M. Sherif, *The Psychology of Social Norms* (1936); M. Sherif, *Group Conflict and Cooperation: Their Social Psychology.* For these scholars, "the notion that groups were composed of 'nothing but' individuals was . . . a platitude, which missed the point that people were changed psychologically in group settings." Turner, et al., *Rediscovering the Social Group, supra* note 46, at 12.

54. Turner, et al., *Rediscovering the Social Group*, supra note 46, at 15.

55. Marilynn B. Brewer, "The Social Self: On Being the Same and Different at the Same Time," 17 *Pers. & Soc. Psychol. Bull.* 475, 475 (1991).

56. Turner, et al., *Rediscovering the Social Group*, supra note 46, at 45.

57. Brewer, *The Social Self*, supra note 55, at 476.

58. Turner, et al., *Rediscovering the Social Group*, supra note 46, at 50–51; Turner, et al., *Self and Collective*, supra note 48, at 455.

59. Turner, et al., *Self and Collective*, supra note 48, at 455 (citation omitted).

60. Turner, et al., *Rediscovering the Social Group*, supra note 46, at 51. *See also* Turner, et al., *Self and Collective*, supra note 48, at 458 ("the variability of self-categorization is not a sign that the true identity of the person is being distorted by external circumstances").

61. Turner, et al, *Rediscovering the Social Group*, supra note 46, at 51.

62. Turner, et al., *Self and Collective*, supra note 48, at 458–459.

63. *Id.* at 460. On the importance of some sense of a relatively stable and unified self, see James M. Glass, *Shattered Selves: Multiple Personality in a Postmodern World* (1993); Eileen M. Donahue, Richard W. Robins, Brent W. Roberts, and Oliver P. John, "The Divided Self: Concurrent and Longitudinal Effects of Psychological Adjustment and Social Roles on Self-Concept Differentiation," 64 *J. Pers. & Soc. Psychol.* 834 (1993).

64. Turner, et al, *Rediscovering the Social Group*, supra note 46, at 52. *See also* Brewer, *The Social Self*, supra note 55, at 476. For experimental support, see D. A. Wilder & W. Cooper, "Categorization into Groups: Consequences for Social Perception and Attribution," in 3 *New Directions in Attribution Research* (J. H. Harvey, W. J. Ickes, & R. F. Kidd eds. 1981); D. Cartwright & A. Zander, *Group Dynamics* (1968).

65. Turner, et al., *Self and Collective*, supra note 48, at 456.

66. *Id.*

67. Brewer, *The Social Self*, supra note 55, at 477.

68. *Id.* at 478.

69. "In contrast to theories that emphasize the prepotency of the individuated self, this model holds that in most circumstances personal identity will *not* provide the optimal level of self-definition." *Id.*

70. Turner, et al., *Rediscovering the Social Group*, supra note 46, at 46. *See also* Dale T. Miller & Deborah Prentice, "The Self and the Collective," 20 *Pers. & Soc. Psychol. Bull.* 451, 452 (1994) ("the collective does not merely provide a context for making comparative judgments about the self; it is also part of the self"); Turner, et al., *Self and Collective*, supra note 48, at 460 ("the personal self is not more real, basic, or authentic than the collective self. They arise from the same general processes, and both are aspects of the normal variation of the self, a variation built into its function").

71. Brewer, *The Social Self*, supra note 55, at 476.

72. Turner, et al., *Self and Collective*, supra note 48, at 454–455 (emphasis in original).

73. *Id.*

74. *Id.* (emphasis in original).

75. Turner, et al., *Rediscovering the Social Group*, supra note 46, at 64.

76. Brewer, *The Social Self*, supra note 55, at 476. *See also* Turner, et al., *Rediscovering the Social Self*, supra note 46, at 65.

77. Turner, et al., *Rediscovering the Social Group*, supra note 46, at 40–41, 65.

78. *Id.* at 35. For experimental support, see W. Wilson, N. Chun, & M. Kayatani, "Protection, Attraction, and Strategy Choices in Intergroup Competition," 2 *J. Pers. & Soc. Psychol.* 432 (1965); W. Wilson & M. Kayatani, "Intergroup Attitudes and Strategies in Games Between Opponents of the Same or of a Different Race," 9 *J. Pers. & Soc. Psychol.* 24 (1968).

79. *See, e.g.*, Hazel Rose Markus & Shinobu Kitayama, "Culture and the Self: Implications for Cognition, Emotion, and Motivation," 98 *Psychol. Rev.* 224 (1991); Hazel Rose

Markus & Shinobu Kitayama, "A Collective Fear of the Collective: Implications for Selves and Theories of Selves," 20 *Pers. & Soc. Psychol. Bull.* 568 (1994); Theodore M. Singelis, "The Measurement of Independent and Interdependent Self-Construals," 20 *Pers. & Soc. Psychol Bull.* 580 (1994); H. C. Triandis, "The Self and Social Behavior in Differing Cultural Contexts," 96 *Psychol. Rev.* 506 (1989); K. Leung & M. Bond, "The Impact of Cultural Collectivism on Reward Allocation," 47 *J. Pers. & Soc. Psychol.* 793 (1984).

80. Markus & Kitayama, *Culture and the Self, supra* note 79, at 226.

81. Markus & Kitayama, *Fear of the Collective, supra* note 79, at 569.

82. Markus & Kitayama, *Culture and the Self, supra* note 79, at 227.

83. *See, e.g.,* S. Cousins, "Culture and Selfhood in Japan and the U.S.," 56 *J. Pers. & Soc. Psychol.* 124 (1989); A.K. Dalal, R. Sharma, & S. Bisht, "Causal Attributions of Ex Criminal Tribal and Urban Children in India," 119 *J. Soc. Psychol.* 163 (1983); J. G. Miller, "Culture and the Development of Everyday Social Explanation," 46 *J. Pers. & Soc. Psychol.* 961 (1984); Richard A. Shweder & Edmund J. Bourne, "Does the Concept of the Person Vary Cross-Culturally?" in *Culture Theory: Essays on Mind, Self, and Emotion* 158 (Richard A. Shweder & Robert A. LeVine eds. 1984).

84. *See, e.g.,* H. A. Kumagai & A. K. Kumagai, "The Hidden 'I' in Amae: 'Passive Love' and Japanese Social Perception," 14 *Ethos* 305 (1985); T. S. Lebra, *Japanese Patterns of Behavior* (1976); D. Matsumoto, "Cultural Influences on the Perception of Emotion," 20 *J. Cross-Cult. Psychol.* 92 (1989); D. Matsumoto, T. Kudoh, & H. Wallbot, "Antecedents of and Reactions to Emotions in the United States and Japan," 19 *J. Cross-Cult. Psychol.* 267 (1988); K. Miyake, J. Campos, J. Kagan, & D. L. Bradshaw, "Issues in Socioemotional Development," in *Child Development and Education in Japan* 239 (H. Stevenson, H. Azuma, & K. Hakuta eds. 1986); D. Stipek, B. Weiner, & K. Li, "Testing Some Attribution-Emotion Relations in the People's Republic of China," 56 *J. Pers. & Soc. Psychol* 109 (1989).

85. *See, e.g.,* T. Doi, *The Anatomy of Self: The Individual Versus Society* (1986); J. Misumi, *The Behavioral Science of Leadership: An Interdisciplinary Japanese Research Program* (1985); B. Mullen & C. A. Riordan, "Self-Serving Attributions in Naturalistic Settings: A Meta-Analytic Review," 18 *J. Appl. Soc. Psychol.* 3 (1988); S. H. Schwartz & W. Bilsky, "Toward a Theory of the Universal Content and Structure of Values: Extensions and Cross-Cultural Replications," 58 *J. Pers. & Soc. Psychol.* 878 (1990); J. R. Weisz, F. M. Rothbaum, & T. C. Blackburn, "Standing Out and Standing In: The Psychology of Control in America and Japan," 39 *Am. Psychol.* 955 (1984); T. Yoshida, K. Kojo, & H. Kaku, "A Study on the Development of Self-Presentation in Children," 30 *Jap. J. Educ. Psychol.* 30 (1982).

86. Markus & Kitayama, *Fear of the Collective, supra* note 79, at 575. *See also* Richard Shweder, *Thinking Through Cultures: Expeditions in Cultural Psychology* (1991).

87. Singelis, *supra* note 79, at 583. *See, e.g.,* D.P.S. Bhawuk & R.W. Brislin, "The Measurement of Intercultural Sensitivity Using the Concepts of Individualism and Collectivism," 16 *Intl. J Intercultural Rel.* 413 (1992); David Trafimow, Harry C. Triandis, & Sharon G. Goto, "Some Tests of the Distinction Between the Private Self and the Collective Self," 60 *J. Pers. & Soc. Psychol.* 649 (1991).

88. Trafimow, et al., *supra* note 87.

89. Markus & Kitayama, *Culture and the Self, supra* note 79, at 247.

90. Miller & Prentice, *supra* note 70, at 452.

91. Marilynn B. Brewer, "Ambivalent Sociality," 12 *Beh. & Brain Sci.* 699, 699 (1989) ("self-gratification and collective identity are independent, opposing processes that are reflected in ambivalence and variability of responding in the face of conflict between individual and collective welfare").

92. *See* Arthur Aron & Elaine N. Aron, *Love as the Expansion of Self* (1986); Arthur Aron, Elaine N. Aron, & Danny Smollan, "Inclusion of Other in the Self Scale and the Structure of Interpersonal Closeness," 63 *J. Pers. & Soc. Psychol.* 596 (1992); Arthur Aron, Elaine N.

Aron, Michael Tudor, & Greg Nelson, "Close Relationships as Including Other in the Self," 60 *J. Pers. & Soc. Psychol.* 241 (1991).

93. *See, e.g.*, Aron, et al., *Close Relationships, supra* note 92, at 251 ("the cognitive implications of being in a close relationship are that other is included in self").

94. *Id.* at 243.

95. *Id.* at 243–246.

96. *Id.* at 243.

97. *Id.* at 246–247.

98. *Id.* at 247–250.

99. Aron, et al., *Inclusion of Other, supra* note 92, at 608.

100. *Id.*

101. *Id.* at 606.

102. *Id.*

103. *Id.* at 601.

104. *Id.* at 610. *See also* D. M. Wegner, "The Self in Prosocial Action," in *The Self in Social Psychology* 131, 133 (D. M. Wegner & R. R. Vallacher eds. 1980) (suggesting that empathy may stem in part from blurred boundary between ourselves and others that may arise from initial lack of differentiation between self and caregiver in infancy).

105. Aron, et al., *Close Relationships, supra* note 92, at 243.

106. For a discussion of the efficacy of the methodology used to evoke these different kinds of settings, see Margaret S. Clark, "Evidence for the Effectiveness of Manipulations of Communal and Exchange Relationships," 12 *Pers. & Soc. Psychol. Bull.* 414 (1986).

107. Margaret S. Clark, Martha C. Powell & Judson Mills, "Keeping Track of Needs in Communal and Exchange Relationships," 51 *J. Pers. & Soc. Psychol.* 333, 333 (1986).

108. Margaret S. Clark & Judson Mills, "The Difference Between Communal and Exchange Relationships: What It Is and What It Is Not," 19 *Pers. & Soc. Psychol. Bull.* 684, 684 (1993).

109. *Id.* at 686.

110. *Id.* at 689.

111. Margaret S. Clark & Judson Mills, "Interpersonal Attraction in Exchange and Communal Relationships," 37 *J. Pers. & Soc. Psychol.* 12, 13 (1979).

112. Clark & Mills, *supra* note 108, at 690.

113. Clark, Powell, and Mills, *supra* note 107, at 338.

114. Margaret S. Clark, Judson R. Mills & David M. Corcoran, "Keeping Track of Needs and Inputs of Friends and Strangers," 15 *Pers. & Soc. Psychol Bull.* 533, 540 (1989).

115. *Id.* at 541; Margaret S. Clark, "Record Keeping in Two Types of Relationships," 47 *J. Pers. & Soc. Psychol.* 549 (1984).

116. Clark & Mills, *supra* note 111, at 16.

117. *Id.*

118. *Id.* at 18–23.

119. *Id.*

120. Margaret S. Clark & Barbara Waddell, "Perceptions of Exploitation in Communal and Exchange Relationships," 2 *J. Soc. & Pers. Relat.* 403 (1985).

121. Clark & Mills, *supra* note 108, at 686.

122. Lenahan O'Connell, "An Exploration of Exchange in Three Social Relationships: Kinship, Friendship and the Marketplace," 1 *J. Soc. & Pers. Relat.* 333 (1984).

123. *Id.* at 341.

124. *Id.* at 343

125. E. Walster, G. W. Walster, & E. Berscheid, *Equity: Theory and Research* 152–153 (1978).

126. *See* Martin at Michael W. Martin, "Satisfaction with Intimate Exchange: Gender-

Role Differences and the Impact of Equity, Equality, and Rewards," 13 *Sex Roles* 597, 598 (1985).

127. *See, e.g.*, Martin, *supra* note 126; Rodney M. Cate, Sally A. Lloyd, June M. Henton, & Jeffry H. Larson, "Fairness and Reward Level as Predictors of Relationship Satisfaction," 45 *Soc. Psychol. Q.* 177 (1982).

128. John Gottman, Cliff Notarius, Howard Markmen, Steve Bank, Bruce Yoppi, & Mary Ellen Rubin, "Behavior Exchange Theory and Marital Decision Making," 34 *J. Pers. & Soc. Psychol.* 14, 21 (1976). "Perhaps it is precisely this *lack* of reciprocity in a context of high positive exchange that characterizes stable positive interaction in nondistressed couples." *Id.* (emphasis in original).

129. John G. Holmes & Susan D. Boon, "Developments in the Field of Close Relationships: Creating Foundations for Intervention Strategies," 16 *Pers. & Soc. Psychol. Bull.* 23, 27 (1990).

130. *Id.. See also* Gottman, et al., *supra* note 128, at 21.

131. *See* Chapter 1, at 20–24.

132. *See* Donald Green & Ian Shapiro, *Pathologies of Rational Choice Theory* 14 (1994)(individuals in rational choice theory "are assumed to be uninterested in others' fortunes . . . except insofar as those fortunes impinge on their particular maximizing strategies").

133. *See* Holmes & Boon, *supra* note 129, at 27; O'Connell, *supra* note 122, at 337–38, 342–43. For a more extensive discussion of this phenomenon, see *infra* notes 235–249 and accompanying text, discussing attribution and overjustification theory.

134. Turner, et al., *Rediscovering the Social Group*, *supra* note 46, at 66.

135. *Id.*

136. *Id.* (emphasis in original).

137. *See* Margolis, *Selfishness*, *supra* note 1; Herbert Margolis, "Dual Utilities and Rational Choice," in *Beyond Self-Interest* 239 (Jane J. Mansbridge ed. 1990); Herbert Margolis, "A New Model of Rational Choice," 91 *Ethics* 265 (1981).

138. Margolis, *Selfishness*, *supra* note 1, at 12. There is an extensive literature, for instance, on why an individual votes in light of the time and bother involved compared to the miniscule chance that her vote will decide the election. For a summary, see Green & Shapiro, *supra* note 132, at 50–56.

139. Margolis, *New Model*, *supra* note 137, at 277.

140. *Id.* at 266 n. 4.

141. Margolis, *Selfishness supra* note 1, at 12.

142. Margolis, *New Model*, *supra* note 137, at 267.

143. *Id.* at 268.

144. *Id.* at 274.

145. *Id.* at 268.

146. Margolis, *Selfishness, supra* note 1, at 52.

147. Margolis, *Dual Utilities*, *supra* note 137, at 246.

148. *Id.* at 248.

149. Margolis, *Selfishness*, *supra* note 1, at 52.

150. Margolis, *Dual Utilities*, *supra* note 137, at 244 (emphasis in original); Margolis, *Selfishness*, *supra* note 1, at 41–42.

151. Margolis, *Selfishness*, *supra* note 1 at 15.

152. Margolis, *Dual Utilities*, *supra* note 137, at 240. Margolis suggests that this will be a function of two rules. First, the more social utility a person can gain with a marginal dollar relative to the private utility she could obtain, the more likely the actor will decide to allocate the dollar to social preferences. Second, even if the marginal ratio of the first rule is unchanged, the larger the overall ratio of social to private spending, the less likely

a person is to allocate another dollar to social preferences. Thus, the more that a person contributes to group interests, the greater must be the weight attached to social concerns in order to induce spending on those concerns. *Id.* at 240–241. Margolis argues that these allocation rules are explicable within the framework of evolutionary theory. Margolis, *Selfishness, supra* note 1, at 26–35.

153. *See, e.g.*, Kristin Monroe, "John Donne's People: Explaining Differences Between Rational Actors and Altruists Through Cognitive Frameworks," 53 *J. Pol.* 394, 398 (1991) (arguing that Margolis's dual utility model posits altruism as a subtle variation on self-interest). Obviously, I disagree with Monroe.

154. Margolis, *Dual Utilities, supra* note 137, at 243.

155. David Sciulli, "Weaknesses in Rational Choice Theory's Contribution to Comparative Research," in *Rational Choice Theory: Advocacy and Critique* 161, 166–167 (James S. Coleman & Thomas J. Fararo eds. 1992).

156. *See* Green & Shapiro, *supra* note 132, at 34.

157. Anatol Rapaport, "Egoistic Incentive: A Hypothesis or An Ideological Tenet?" 12 *Beh. & Brain Sci.* 719, 719 (1989). *See also* Susan Oyama, "Innate Selfishness, Innate Sociality," 12 *Beh. & Brain Sci.* 717, 717 (1989) (theory of egoistic incentives "becomes a universal explanation by redefining all alternatives in its own terms"); Amartya Sen, "Rational Fools," 6 *Philos. & Publ Aff.* 317, 322 (1977) ("It is possible to define a person's interests in such a way that no matter what he does can be seen to be furthering his own interests in every isolated act of choice").

158. Margolis, *Dual Utilities, supra* note 137, at 239.

159. James S. Coleman, "Individual Interests and Collective Action," in 1 *Papers on Non-Market Decision-Making* 49, 55 (1966). *See also* Green & Shapiro, *supra* note 132, at 36 (to the extent rational choice theorists transform disconfirming outcomes into data consistent with newly cast theory, dubious whether theory susceptible to any meaningful empirical evaluation); Edmund S. Sonuga-Barke, "The Fallacy of Selfish Unselfishness," 12 *Beh. & Brain Sci.* 721, 721 (1989) (given logical possibility of describing unselfish action in terms of egoistic incentives, concept of selfishness becomes "empty and redundant").

160. Rapaport, *supra* note 157, at 719. *See also* Collard, *supra* note 67, at 18 (once we drop the universal assumption of self-interest, we can distinguish between private and social preferences); Margolis, *Dual Utilities, supra* note 137, at 239 (a theory "with real analytical bite would specify when a person acts as if moved by social preferences and when by private preferences).

161. *See* Mansbridge, *Relation of Altruism and Self-Interest*, in Mansbridge, *supra* note 1, at 133, 142–43 (empathetic and moral considerations commonly regarded as independent of utility and as involving separate motivations to which we may assign greater or lesser virtue); Margaret Gilbert, "Folk Psychology Takes Sociality Seriously," 12 *Beh. & Brain Sci.* 707, 707 (1989) (in everyday talk and thought people often give and accept explanations of behavior in terms that are understood to rule out selfishness).

162. "Once a concept is defined so that it encompasses all the incidents that are members of a given category (in the case at hand, the motives for all human activities), it ceases to enhance one's ability to explain." Amitai Etzioni, *The Moral Dimension* 27 (1988).

163. Daniel M. Hausman, "Economic Methodology in a Nutshell," 3 *J. Econ. Persp.* 115, 119–122 (1989).

164. Milton Friedman, "The Methodology of Positive Economics," in *Essays in Positive Economics* 3 (1953).

165. *Id.* at 15, 31, 40.

166. *Id.* at 32. *See also* Posner, *Economic Analysis of Law, supra* note 3, at 17 ("A theory that sought faithfully to reproduce the complexity of the empirical world in its assumptions would not be a theory—an explanation—but a description").

167. Friedman, *supra* note 164, at 36. *See also* Posner, *Economic Analysis of Law*, *supra* note 3, at 17 ("abstraction is of the essence of scientific inquiry, and economics aspires to be scientific").

168. Friedman, *supra* note 164, at 41.

169. *Id.* at 40 (emphasis in original).

170. *Id.* at 14.

171. *Id.* at 19.

172. *Id.* at 20.

173. *Id.* at 21–22.

174. *Id.* at 22.

175. "[P]ositive economics is, or can be, an 'objective' science, in precisely the same sense as any of the physical sciences." *Id.* at 4. *See also* Donald McCloskey, *The Rhetoric of Economics* 5–11 (1985) (describing contemporary economics as based on a "modernism" that purports to mimic "objective" science).

176. *See, e.g.*, Hausman, *supra* note 163, at 121 (describing Friedman's position as "odd instrumentalism").

177. "In mechanics there can be no discrepancy between forces and their effects, because we have no source of information regarding the forces except the effects themselves." Frank H. Knight, "Economic Psychology and the Value Problem," in *The Ethics of Competition and Other Essays* 76, 84 (1935).

178. *See id.* at 80 (despite the claims of behaviorism, "we go right on thinking of conduct as in the main the effect of desire, and it seems impossible to talk sense about it from any other point of view").

179. Roger Trigg, *Understanding Social Science: A Philosophical Introduction* 44 (1985) (emphases in original). *See also* Alfred Schutz, "The Problem of Rationality in the Social World," in 2 *Collected Papers: Studies in Social Theory* 64, 85 (Arvid Brodersen ed. 1964) (we cannot understand social phenomena "apart from their placement within the scheme of human motives, human means and ends, human planning—in short—within the categories of human action"); Max Weber, "Objectivity and Understanding in Economics," in *The Philosophy of Economics* 99, 103 (Daniel M. Hausman ed. 1984) ("knowledge of *cultural* events is inconceivable except on a basis of the *significance* which the concrete constellations of reality have for us in certain *individual* concrete situations") (emphasis in original).

180. *See* Frank Knight, " 'What is Truth' in Economics?" in *On the History and Method of Economics* 151, 152 (1956) (for persons who sought to determine if the check system existed in a country, "it would be impossible to assert on the basis of any printed slip of paper or other object 'before them' whether the 'check system' existed or not"; one must be concerned with "purposes aimed at and results achieved").

181. Holmes & Boon, *supra* note 129, at 26.

182. *Id.*

183. *Id.*

184. *Id.* at 27.

185. *See, e.g.*, Steve Duck, *Meaningful Relationships* (1994); Timothy D. Stephen, "A Symbolic Exchange Framework for the Development of Intimate Relationships," 37 *Human Rel.* 393 (1984); Peter Singelmann, "Exchange as Symbolic Interaction: Convergences Between Two Theoretical Perspectives," 37 *Am. Sociol. Rev.* 414 (1972); David F. Haas & Forrest Deseran, "Trust and Symbolic Exchange," 44 *Soc. Psychol. Q.* 3 (1981). *See also* the discussion of entitlement schema in Chapter 1, at 5–6.

186. Holmes & Boon, at 27.

187. *See supra. See also* Etzioni, *supra* note 162, at 52 (those who have moral commitment to a course of action may persist in it longer than conventional self-interest theory would predict because they have more motivation to do so).

188. *See, e.g.*, Posner, *Sex and Reason*, *supra* note 14, at 442 (ultimate end of theorizing is "to enlarge our knowledge in order to improve our ability to predict and control").

189. Holmes & Boon, *supra* note 129, at 27–28.

190. Knight, *Economic Psychology*, *supra* note 177, at 90. *See generally id.* at 89–91.

191. *Id.* at 98.

192. *See, e.g.*, Clifford Geertz, *The Interpretation of Cultures* (1973); *Interpretive Social Science: A Reader* (Paul Rabinow & William Sullivan eds. 1979); Richard Shweder, *Thinking Through Cultures* (1991). For a historical antecedent, see Max Weber's concept of "Verstehen" in Max Weber, *Theory of Social and Economic Organization* 80 (1947).

193. Alfred Schutz, "The Problem of Rationality in the Social World," in Brodersen, *supra* note 179, at 64, 67.

194. Paul Rabinow & William M. Sullivan, "The Interpretive Turn: Emergence of an Approach," in Rabinow & Sullivan, *supra* note 192, at 1, 6.

195. For discussions of the problematic character for social science of an exclusive emphasis on individual mental states, see David Rubinstein, *Marx and Wittgenstein* 70 (1981); Trigg, *supra* note 179, at 47–58.

196. Debra Satz & John Ferejohn, "Rational Choice and Social Theory," 91 *J. Philos.* 71 (1994).

197. *Id.* at 77–81.

198. *Id.* at 78–79.

199. *Id.* at 76.

200. *Id.* at 73.

201. *Id.* at 74.

202. *Id.* at 75 (footnote omitted).

203. *Id.* at 76. *See also id.* (to be explanatory, rational choice theory must "bear some semantic relationship to individual decision making").

204. *Id.* at 74.

205. *Id.* at 85.

206. "[F]or many kinds of questions, the internalist interpretation of rational choice is inappropriate; it is often redundant or misleadingly concrete." *Id.* at 86.

207. *Id.* at 74.

208. *Id.* at 72.

209. *Id.* at 79.

210. *Id.* at 87.

211. Green & Shapiro, *supra* note 132, at 22.

212. Schutz, *Problem of Rationality*, *supra* note 193, at 85 (emphasis omitted). Shutz professes to borrow the term from Max Weber. *Id.*

213. *Id.* at 67.

214. *Id.* at 85.

215. For a suggestion that Schutz and Max Weber fit this description, see Trigg, *supra* note 179, at 44–49.

216. Similarly, Friedman's expert billiard player, see *supra* note 164 and accompanying text, may not perform the intricate computations that serve to model his behavior, but would have no difficulty in confirming that this process represents an idealized version of the enterprise in which he is engaged. Friedman's examples of the businessman and the billiard player thus indicate not that the realism of assumptions about these actors is irrelevant because the models work, but that the models work because they have at least some congruence with the actors' own understanding of what it is they are doing.

217. Knight, *"What is Truth" in Economics?*, *supra* note 180, at 172.

218. *Id.* at 173.

219. According to Max Weber, an ideal type "is formed by the one-sided *accentuation* of

one or more points of view and by the synthesis of a great many diffuse, discrete, more or less present and occasionally absent *concrete individual* phenomena, which are arranged according to those one-sidedly emphasized viewpoints into a unified *analytical* construct." Weber, *Objectivity and Understanding in Economics, supra* note 179, at 111 (emphasis in original).

220. Indeed, some question exists whether rational choice or economic theory offers much proven predictive power even with respect to behavior in domains conventionally regarded as relatively egoistic. *See, e.g.*, Green & Shapiro, *supra* note 132, at 5 (with respect to political analysis, "the stature of rational choice scholarship does not rest on a readily identifiable set of empirical successes"); Hausman, *supra* note 163, at 122 (raising question whether criterion of falsifiability for assessing neoclassical accounts of economic behavior is "a doctrine piously enunciated in the presence of philosophers or of their economist fellow travellers and conveniently forgotten when there is serious work to do").

221. James Boyd White, "Economics and Law: Two Cultures in Tension," 54 *Tenn. L. Rev.* 161, 166 (1986).

222. Charles Taylor, "Self-Interpreting Animals," in 1 *Philsophical Papers: Human Agency and Language* 45 (1985).

223. "[O]ur interpretation of ourselves and our experience is constitutive of what we are, and therefore cannot be considered as merely a view on reality, separable from reality, nor as an epiphenomenon, which can be by-passed in our understanding of reality." *Id.* at 47. *See also* William Sullivan, *Reconstructing Public Philosophy* 142 (1986) ("while molecules do not noticeably alter their behavior because a new theory has been published about them, conceptions of human behavior can and do change the way human beings act").

224. C. Wright Mills, "Situated Action and the Vocabulary Of Motives," 6 *Am. Sociol. Rev.* 904 (1940).

225. *See* Colin Campbell, *The Romantic Ethic and the Spirit of Modern Consumerism* 211– 212 (1987); Weber, *Theory of Social and Economic Organization, supra* note 192, at 98–99 (A.M. Henderson & Talcott Parsons eds. 1964). *See generally* Kenneth Burke, *A Rhetoric of Motives* (1950).

226. Quentin Skinner, *Foundations of Modern Political Thought, Vol. 1: The Renaissance* xii–xiii (1987). *See also* J.G.A. Pocock, "Virtue and Commerce in the Eighteenth Century," 3 *J. Interdisc. Hist.* 122 (1972) ("Men cannot do what they have no means of saying they have done; and what they do must in part be what they can say and conceive that it is").

227. Hilary Putnam, *Reason, Truth, and History* 139–141 (1981).

228. *Id.* at 140.

229. The first two examples are from *id.*

230. *Id.* at 140–141. *Cf.* Oliver Williamson, *Markets and Hierarchies, supra* note 45, at 38 (suggesting that the commercialization of blood can transform one's understanding of the meaning of voluntary noncommercial blood donation).

231. Robert H. Frank, Thomas Gilovich, & Dennis T. Regan, "Does Studying Economics Inhibit Cooperation?" 7 *J. Econ. Persp.* 159, 159 (1993).

232. *See, e.g., id.*; John Carter & Michael Irons, "Are Economists Different, and If So, Why?" 5 *J. Econ. Persp.* 171 (1991); Daniel Kahneman, Jack Knetsch, & Richard Thaler, "Fairness and the Assumptions of Economics," 59 *J. Bus.*, Part 1, S285 (1986); Gerald Marwell & Ruth Ames, "Economists Free Ride, Does Anyone Else?: Experiments on the Provision of Public Goods," IV, 15 *J. Publ. Econ.* 295 (1981).

233. *See* Frank, Gilovich, & Regan, *supra* note 231, at 167–168.

234. *Id.* at 168–170.

235. *See* Keith G. Allred, "Realizing the Advantages of Organizational Interdependencies: The Role of Attributionally Motivated Emotions," in *Attribution Theory: An Organizational Perspective* 253, 261 (Mark J. Martinko ed. 1995); John G. Holmes, "The Exchange Process in Close Relationships: Microbehavior and Macromotives," in *The Justice Motive in Social Behavior* 261, 271–275 (M.L. Lerner & S.C. Lerner eds. 1981); Clive Seligman, Russell H. Fazio, &

Mark P. Zanna, "Effects of Salience of Extrinsic Rewards on Liking and Loving," 38 *J. Pers. & Soc. Psychol.* 453 (1980). On the attribution process more generally, see H. H. Kelley, *Attribution in Social Interaction* (1971); *Attribution: Perceiving the Causes of Behavior* (E. E. Jones, D. E. Kanhouse, H. H. Kelley, R. E. Nisbett, S. Valins, & B. Weiner eds. 1972).

236. "Intrinsic and instrumental motives are psychologically distinct categories, with rather different implications." John K. Rempel, John G. Holmes & Mark P. Zanna, "Trust in Close Relationships," 49 *J. Pers. & Soc. Psychol.* 95, 110 (1985).

237. *See* Anderson, *Value in Ethics and Economics, supra* note 126, at 151 (delay in reciprocation between friends "expresses an intrinsic valuation of the recipient: gifts are given for the friend's sake, not merely for the sake of obtaining some good for oneself in return"); Holmes, *supra* note 235, at 271 (for inference to be drawn that one person is acting out of sense of responsiveness to another, "his behavior must in some way stand in contrast to that which would be expected if he were acting solely in accord with his egocentric concerns"). *See also* H. H. Kelley, *Interpersonal Relationships: Their Structures and Processes* (1979).

238. Holmes, *supra* note 235, at 274.

239. Seligman, et al., *supra* note 235, at 459.

240. *Id.*.

241. Seligman, et al., *supra* note 235, at 457. *See also* Garth J.O. Fletcher, Frank D. Fincham, Lori Cramer, & Nancy Heron, "The Role of Attributions in the Development of Dating Relationships," 53 *J. Pers. & Soc. Psychol.* 481, 485 (1987) (persons in dating relationships who emphasized external attributions for maintaining relationship reported significantly lower levels of love for partner than other subjects).

242. Fletcher, et al., *supra* note 241, at 485. One study does report that there was no difference for women in the correlation between love and the attribution of intrinsic and instrumental motives. Rempel, et al., *supra* note 236, at 108. The authors note, however, that the study did not manipulate the attribution of extrinsic motives to oneself, and conclude that the overall results of the study "underline the potential impact of intrinsic attributions on feelings of love for both men and women." *Id.* at 110.

243. Rempel, et al., *supra* note 236, at 109.

244. *See* Gary L. Hansen, "Moral Reasoning and the Marital Exchange Relationship," 131 *J. Soc. Psychol.* 71, 80 (1991); Bernard I. Murstein, Mary Cerreto, & Marcia MacDonald, "A Theory and Investigation of the Effect of Exchange Orientation on Marriage and Friendship," 39 *J. Marr. & Fam.* 543, 547–548 (1977).

245. O'Connell, *supra* note 122, at 341.

246. Holmes & Boon, *supra* note 129, at 27.

247. *Id.*

248. *See, e.g.,* Mark Barnett, Vera McMinimy, Gwyn Flover, & I. Masbad, "Adolescents' Evaluation of Peer's Motives for Helping," 16 *J. Youth & Adolesc.* 579 (1987); Daniel Bar-Tal, Amiram Raviv, & T. Zipora Leiser, "The Development of Altruistic Behavior: Empirical Evidence," 16 *Devel. Psychol.* 516 (1980); C. Daniel Batson, Jay S. Coke, M.L. Jasnoski, & Michael Hanson, "Buying Kindness: Effect of an Extrinsic Incentive for Helping on Perceived Altruism," 4 *Pers. & Soc. Psychol. Bull.* 86 (1978); Joan G. Miller & David M. Bersoff, "Cultural Influences on the Moral Status of Reciprocity and the Discounting of Endogenous Motivation," 20 *Pers. & Soc. Psychol. Bull.* 592 (1994); R. E. Nisbett & S. Valins, "Perceiving the Cause of One's Behavior," in E. E. Jones, et al., *Attribution, supra* note 235.

John Holmes explains the dynamics of this phenomenon:

If you have received a benefit from your partner, you may feel obligated to return a comparable benefit: a debt has been incurred. But if the contingent nature of your subsequent behavior is then made salient to your partner, its informational value is discounted in terms of any interpersonal disposition (affection, caring) that you might wish to express. And the value of your partner's initial act is somehow "cheapened" because you are acting as if he were anticipating such a benefit, that is, as if the action were predicated on such an expectation.

Holmes, *supra* note 235, at 272–273.

249. *See, e.g.*, Edward L. Deci, "Intrinsic Motivation, Extrinsic Reinforcement, and Inequity," 22 *J. Pers. & Soc. Psychol.* 113 (1972); David Greene & Mark R. Lepper, "Effects of Extrinsic Rewards on Children's Subsequent Intrinsic Interest," 45 *Child. Dev.* 1141 (1974); Mark R. Lepper & David Greene, "Turning Play into Work: Effects of Adult Surveillance and Extrinsic Rewards on Children's Intrinsic Motivation," 31 *J. Pers. & Soc. Psychol.* 479 (1975); Mark Lepper, David Greene, & R. E. Nisbett, "Undermining Children's Intrinsic Interest with Extrinsic Reward: A Test of the 'Overjustification' Hypothesis," 28 *J. Pers. & Soc. Psychol.* 129 (1973). One study suggests that negative emotional connotations regarding extrinsic reward may account for the decrease in motivation or willingness. Grace H. Petty & Clive Seligman, "Affect and the Overjustification Effect," 46 *J. Pers. & Soc. Psychol.* 1241 (1984).

250. *See, e.g.*, George Ainslie, *Picoeconomics: The Strategic Interaction of Successive Motivational States Within the Person* (1992); George Ainslie, "Self-Control," in *Choice Over Time* 177 (George Loewenstein & Jon Elster eds. 1992).

251. *See* Jon Elster, *Sour Grapes: Studies in the Subversion of Rationality* 43–108 (1983).

252. *Id.* at 43.

253. Elster discusses a similar example in *id.* at 45–46 and in Elster, "When Rationality Fails," *The Limits of Rationality*, *supra* note 11, at 32.

254. One may be aware, anticipate, and hope that placing intrinsic value on one's partner will produce such happiness, but this is different from cultivating a relationship directly for the purpose of bringing about one's own happiness. *See* Elster, *Sour Grapes*, *supra* note 251, at 55.


## Five

1. Testimony regarding "objective facts having no per se effect" on the other spouse generally is not privileged, United States v. Brown, 605 F.2d 389, 396 (8th Cir.), *cert.* denied, 444 U.S. 972 (1979), nor is testimony whose possible effect on the spouse defendant is merely "speculative," In re Snoonian, 502 F.2d 110, 113 (1st Cir. 1974). The privilege may not be invoked regarding "nontestimonial" evidence such as handwriting exemplars, see United States v. McKeon, 558 F. Supp. 1243, 1245- 47 (E.D.N.Y. 1983), or fingerprints, see United States v. Thomann, 609 F.2d 560, 564 (1st Cir. 1979).

2. Such proceedings have been held to include the grand jury, see In re Grand Jury Matter, 673 F.2d 688 (3d Cir.), *cert.* denied, 459 U.S. 1015 (1982), deportation hearings, see Garcia-Jaramillo v. INS, 604 F.2d 1236, 1238 (9th Cir. 1979), *cert.* denied, 449 U.S. 828 (1980), and probation revocation hearings, see Solis v. State, 673 S.W.2d 270, 275–76 (Tex. Ct. App. 1984), aff'd, 718 S.W.2d 282 (Tex. Crim. App. 1986).

3. *See, e.g.*, United States v. Burks, 470 F.2d 432 (D.C. Cir. 1972).

4. *See, e.g.*, United States v. Smith, 533 F.2d 1077 (8th Cir. 1976).

5. *See, e.g.*, United States v. Byrd, 750 F.2d 585 (7th Cir. 1984); United States v. Cameron, 556 F.2d 752 (5th Cir. 1977).

6. Wyatt v. United States, 362 U.S. 525 (1960); Stein v. Bowman, 38 U.S. (13 Pet.) 209 (1839); People v. McGregor, 635 P.2d 912 (Colo. Ct. App. 1981); see also Lord Audley's Case, 123 Eng. Rep. 1140, 1141 (1631).

7. *See* United States v. Allery, 526 F.2d 1362, 1367 (8th Cir. 1975); People v. Batres, 75 Cal. Rptr. 397, 399–400 (Ct. App. 1969). The exception also has been held applicable to

testimony relating to a crime against a third person committed during the same episode in which the spouse was injured. People v. Love, 339 N.W.2d 493, 496 (Mich. Ct. App. 1983), aff'd in part, rev'd in part, 391 N.W.2d 738 (Mich. 1986).

8. *See* United States v. Trammel, 583 F.2d 1166, 1169 (10th Cir. 1978), aff'd on other grounds, 445 U.S. 40 (1980); United States v. Van Drunen, 501 F.2d 1393, 1397 (7th Cir.), *cert.* denied, 419 U.S. 1091 (1974).

9. In re Grand Jury Subpoena United States, 755 F.2d 1022 (2d. Cir. 1985), vacated as moot sub nom. United States v. Koecher, 475 U.S. 133 (1986); In re Grand Jury Matter, 673 F.2d 688, 692-93 (3d Cir.), *cert.* denied, 459 U.S. 1015 (1982); In re Malfitano, 633 F.2d 276 (3d Cir. 1980).

10. *See* Trammel v. United States, 445 U.S. 40 (1980); Ala. Code. § 12-21-227 (1986); Cal. Evid. Code § 970 (West 1966); Conn. Gen. Stat. Ann. § 54-84a (West 1994); D.C. Code Ann. § 14-306(a) (1995); Ga. Code Ann. § 24-9-23 (1995); Ill. Ann. Stat. ch. 725, para. 125/6 (1993); Ky. Rev. Stat. Ann. § 421.210(1) (Michie 1992); La. Code Evid. Ann. art. 505 (West 1995); Me. Rev. Stat. Ann. tit. 15, § 1315 (West 1980); Md. Code Ann., Cts. & Jud. Proc. § 9-106 (1995); Mass. Gen. Laws Ann. ch. 233, § 20 (West 1986 & Supp. 1995); Mo. Ann. Stat. § 546.260 (Vernon 1987); Nev. Rev. Stat. Ann. § 49.295(1)(b) (Michie 1986); N.J. Stat. Ann. § 2A:84A-17(2) (West 1994); N.Y. Civ. Prac. L. & R. 4512(a) (McKinney 1992); N.C. Gen. Stat. §§ 8-56, 8- 57 (1994); Or. Rev. Stat. § 40.255(3) (1988); 42 Pa. Cons. Stat. Ann. § 5913 (Supp. 1995); R.I. Gen. Laws § 12-17-10 (1994); Vt. Stat. Ann. tit. 12, § 1605 (1973); Alaska R. Evid. 505; Haw. R. Evid. 505.

11. *See* Ariz. Rev. Stat. Ann. § 13-4062(1) (1989); Colo. Rev. Stat. § 13-90-107(1)(a)(I) (Supp. 1994); Idaho Code § 9-203 (1990); Mich. Comp. Laws Ann. § 600.2162 (West Supp. 1995); Minn. Stat. Ann. § 595.02.1(a) (West Supp. 1995); Miss. Code Ann. § 13-1-5 (Supp. 1993); Mont. Code Ann. § 26-1-802 (1993); Neb. Rev. Stat. § 27-505 (1989); Va. Code Ann. § 19.2-271.2 (Michie Supp. 1994); Wash. Rev. Code Ann. § 5.60.060 (West 1995); W. Va. Code § 57-3-3 (1966); Ark. R. Evid. 504; S.D. R. Evid. 504(b).

12. Bent v. Allot, 21 Eng. Rep. 50, 50 (Ch. 1579–1580).

13. *See* Lady Ivy's Trial, 10 How. St. Tr. 555, 644 (K.B. 1684); Cole v. Gray, 2 Vern. 79, 79, 23 Eng. Rep. 660, 661 (Ch. 1688); Anonymous, 1 Brownl. & Golds. 47, 123 Eng. Rep. 656 (C.P. 1613); Edward Coke, *A Commentary Upon Littleton* 6b (5th ed. 1656); William Hudson, *A Treatise of the Court of Star Chamber* (Francis Hargrave ed., The Legal Classics Library 1986) (c. 1635); cf. Lord Audley's Case, 123 Eng. Rep. 1140, 1141 (1631) (acknowledging privilege but finding exception for alleged crime by one spouse against another); Michael Dalton, *The Country Justice* ch. 164 § 2 (1727) (acknowledging privilege). But see Bankrupts Act, 21 Jam. I, ch. 19, § 6 (1623) (Eng.).

14. *See Trammel*, 445 U.S. at 44; Hawkins v. United States, 358 U.S. 74, 75 (1958); 5 Jeremy Bentham, *Rationale of Judicial Evidence* 344 (1827); Robert M. Hutchins & Donald Slesinger, "Some Observations on the Law of Evidence: Family Relations," 13 *Minn. L. Rev.* 675, 675 (1929).

15. The first mention of spousal disqualification appears to be in Coke, *supra* note 13, § 6b, some 48 years after Bent v. Allot, 21 Eng. Rep. 50 (Ch. 1579–1580). Scholars who regard the privilege as rooted in spousal disqualification point to Coke's statement that "a wife cannot be produced either against or for her husband, *quia sunt duae animae in carne una* [because they are two souls in one body], and it might be a cause of implacable discord and dissention between the husband & the wife. . . ." Coke, *supra* note 13, § 6b; see also Davis v. Dinwoody, 4 Term Rep. 678, 679, 100 Eng. Rep. 1241, 1241 (K.B. 1792). Professor Lempert, however, has suggested that Coke may have meant the rationale of unity to be applicable solely to the disqualification for interest, and the concern for marital harmony solely to the rule against adverse testimony. Richard O. Lempert, "A Right to Every Woman's Evidence," 66 *Iowa L. Rev.* 725, 728 n.10 (1981).

16. 8 John H. Wigmore, *Evidence in Trials at Common Law* § 2227, at 212 (John T. McNaugton ed., rev. ed. 1961).

17. United States v. Armstrong, 476 F.2d 313, 315 (5th Cir. 1973); accord *Hawkins*, 358 U.S. at 77–78.

18. *See* Hopkins v. Grimshaw, 165 U.S. 342 (1897); Fraser v. United States, 145 F.2d 139 (6th Cir. 1944), *cert.* denied, 324 U.S. 849 (1945).

19. *See* Margaret F. Brinig & Linda A. Schwartzstein, "Spousal Privileges," in *Testimonial Privileges* 332, 344 (Scott N. Stone & Ronald S. Liebman eds., 1983).

20. *See, e.g.*, United States v. Figueroa-Paz, 468 F.2d 1055, 1057 (9th Cir. 1972); United States v. Neal, 532 F. Supp. 942 (D. Colo. 1982); *see also* 8 Wigmore, *supra* note 16, § 2340, at 670 (asserting that the privilege is held by the communicating spouse). Several states, however, allow either spouse to hold the privilege. *See, e.g.*, Fla. Stat. Ann. § 90.504 (West 1979); Or. Rev. Stat. § 40.255(2) (1988); Alaska R. Evid 505(b); Haw. R. Evid. 505(b)(2). In Wolfle v. United States, 291 U.S. 7 (1934), the Supreme Court accepted without discussion the invocation of the privilege by the noncommunicating spouse.

21. *See* Pereira v. United States, 347 U.S. 1 (1954); United States v. Ferris, 719 F.2d 1405 (9th Cir. 1983); United States v. Lefkowitz, 618 F.2d 1313 (9th Cir.), *cert.* denied, 449 U.S. 824 (1980); *Brown*, 605 F.2d at 396 n.6; State v. Smith, 384 A.2d 687, 689–90 (Me. 1978).

22. *See* United States v. Kapnison, 743 F.2d 1450 (10th Cir. 1984), *cert.* denied, 471 U.S. 1015 (1985); United States v. Klayer, 707 F.2d 892, 894–95 (6th Cir.), *cert.* denied, 464 U.S. 858 (1983); State v. Newman, 680 P.2d 257, 266 (Kan. 1984).

23. *See* People v. Sanders, 443 N.E.2d 687, 695-96 (Ill. App. Ct. 1982), rev'd on other grounds, 457 N.E.2d 1241 (Ill. 1983); *Smith*, 384 A.2d at 689; State v. McMorrow, 314 N.W.2d 287, 289 (N.D. 1982).

24. *See Stein*, 38 U.S. (13 Pet.) at 223; *Byrd*, 750 F.2d at 591; United States v. Bolzer, 556 F.2d 948, 951 (9th Cir. 1977); United States v. Pensinger, 549 F.2d 1150, 1152 (8th Cir. 1977).

25. *Trammel*, 445 U.S. at 46 n. 7.

26. *See, e.g.*, United States v. Marashi, 913 F.2d 724, 730–31 (9th Cir. 1990); United States v. Sims, 755 F.2d 1239, 1243 (6th Cir.), *cert.* denied, 473 U.S. 907 (1985); United States v. Broome, 732 F.2d 363, 365 (4th Cir.), *cert.* denied, 469 U.S. 855 (1984).

27. *See, e.g.*, State v. Witchey, 388 N.W.2d 893, 895–96 (S.D. 1986); Wolf v. State, 674 S.W.2d 831, 841–42 (Tex. Ct. App. 1984). *But see* Johnson v. State, 451 So. 2d 1024, 1024 (Fla. Dist. Ct. App. 1984); State v. White, 480 A.2d 230, 232 (N.J. Super. Ct. Law Div. 1984).

28. *See* 1 *McCormick on Evidence* § 78 (John W. Strong ed., 4th ed. 1992); "Developments in the Law—Privileged Communications," 98 *Harv. L. Rev.* 1450, 1565 (1985) [hereinafter Developments in the Law].

29. *See* 1 *McCormick on Evidence*, *supra* note 28, § 78, at 295; Mark Reutlinger, "Policy, Privacy, and Prerogatives: A Critical Examination of the Proposed Federal Rules of Evidence as They Affect Marital Privilege," 61 *Cal. L. Rev.* 1353, 1381–82 (1973).

30. *See, e.g.*, Cal. Evid. Code §§ 1012, 1014 (West Supp. 1995); Mich. Comp. Laws Ann. § 330.1750 (West 1992); Ohio Rev. Code Ann. § 4732.19 (Anderson 1994).

31. *See, e.g.*, D.C. Code Ann. § 14-307 (1995); Ill. Ann. Stat. ch. 735, para. 5/8-802 (Smith-Hurd 1992); N.Y. Civ. Prac. L. & R. 4504 (McKinney 1992 & Supp. 1995); 42 Pa. Cons. Stat. Ann. § 5929 (1982).

32. *See, e.g.*, Ga. Code Ann. § 24-9-22 (1995); Ind. Code Ann. § 34-1-14-5(4) (Burns Supp. 1994); N.J. Stat. Ann. § 2A:84A-23 (West Supp. 1995).

33. *See, e.g.*, Ariz. Rev. Stat. Ann. § 32-3283 (1992); Minn. Stat. Ann. § 148B.39 (West 1989); N.H. Rev. Stat. Ann. § 328-C:9 (Supp. 1994).

34. *See, e.g.*, Nev. Rev. Stat. Ann. §§ 49.290 to .291 (Michie 1986 & Supp 1993); S.D. Codified Laws Ann. §§ 19-13-21.1 to-21.2 (1987); see also William P. Robinson, III, Testimonial Privilege and the School Guidance Counselor, 25 *Syracuse L. Rev.* 911, 918–24 (1974).

35. *See, e.g.*, Ark. Code Ann. §§ 17-39-107 to-108 (Michie 1992 & Supp. 1993); Del. Code Ann. tit. 24, § 3913 (1987); see also Richard Delgado, Comment, Underprivileged Communications: Extension of the Psychotherapist-Patient Privilege to Patients of Psychiatric Social Workers, 61 *Cal. L. Rev.* 1050 (1973).

36. Alaska Stat. §§ 12.45.049, 25.35.100 to .150 (Supp. 1994) (sexual assault and domestic violence); Cal. Evid. Code §§ 1035.4, 1035.8 (West Supp. 1995) (sexual assault); id. § 1037.2 (domestic violence); Conn. Gen. Stat. Ann. § 52-146(k) (West 1991 & Supp. 1995) (domestic violence and sexual assault); Fla. Stat. Ann. § 90.5035 (West Supp. 1995) (sexual assault); Ill. Ann. Stat. ch. 735, para. 5/8-802.1 (Smith-Hurd 1992 & Supp. 1995) (sexual assault); id. at para. 5/8-802.2 (domestic violence).

37. Richards of Rockford, Inc. v. Pacific Gas & Elec. Co., 71 F.R.D. 388, 390-91 (N.D. Cal. 1976).

38. One severe early critic of the privilege was Jeremy Bentham. See 5 Bentham, *supra* note 14, at 339–344.

39. 8 Wigmore, *supra* note 16, § 2228, at 221.

40. 8 *Id.* §2228, at 216 (emphasis in original).

41. 8 *Id.* § 2228, at 217.

42. *Id.*

43. 8 *Id.* § 2228, at 220–21.

44. Model Code of Evidence Rule 215 cmt. a (1942).

45. Committee on Rules of Practice and Procedure, Judicial Conference of the United States, Proposed Rules of Evidence for the United States District Courts and Magistrates, in 46 F.R.D. 161, 263–66 (1969) (preliminary draft); Committee on Rules of Practice and Procedure, Judicial Conference of the United States, Proposed Rules of Evidence for the United States Courts and Magistrates, in 51 F.R.D. 315, 369–71 (1971) (revised draft) [hereinafter Revised Proposed Rules].

46. Revised Proposed Rules, *supra* note 45, at 369.

47. Barbara G. Glenn, "Comment, The Deconstruction of the Marital Privilege," 12 *Pepp. L. Rev.* 723, 740 (1985); see, e.g., Charles L. Black, Jr., "The Marital and Physician Privileges—A Reprint of a Letter to a Congressman," 1975 *Duke L.J.* 45, 48– 49; Thomas G. Krattenmaker, Testimonial Privileges in Federal Courts: An Alternative to the Proposed Federal Rules of Evidence, 62 *Geo. L.J.* 61, 85, 94 (1973); Reutlinger, *supra* note 29, at 1368– 93; Paul F. Rothstein, The Proposed Amendments to the Federal Rules of Evidence, 62 *Geo. L.J.* 125, 131 (1973).

48. Fed. R. Evid. 501.

49. Unif. R. Evid. 23(2) cmt. (1953).

50. Unif. R. Evid. 504(b) (1986).

51. Unif. R. Evid. 504(c) (1986).

52. 445 U.S. 40, 53 (1980).

53. 358 U.S. 74 (1958).

54. *Trammel*, 445 U.S. at 53. This rule had been suggested earlier in Paul F. Rothstein, "A Re-Evaluation of the Privilege Against Adverse Spousal Testimony in the Light of Its Purpose," 12 *Int'l & Comp. L.Q.* 1189, 1191–1202 (1963).

55. *Trammel*, 445 U.S. at 51.

56. *Id.* at 52.

57. *Id.*

58. *See, e.g.*, Homer H. Clark, Jr., *The Law of Domestic Relations in the United States* 544 (2d ed. 1988); David Medine, "The Adverse Testimony Privilege: Time to Dispose of a 'Sentimental Relic'," 67 *Or. L. Rev.* 519 (1988). One exception is Richard Lempert, who not only has defended the privilege but has argued that *Trammel* was wrongly decided. See Lempert, *supra* note 15, at 733, 735–39.

59. *See, e.g.,* Act of April 28, 1983 Iowa Acts ch. 37, § 6 (amending Iowa Code § 726.4 (1983); N.M. R. Evid. 11-505.

60. *See Trammel,* 445 U.S. at 48.

61. *See supra* note 11.

62. *See* In re Martenson, 779 F.2d 461, 464 (8th Cir. 1985).

63. *See, e.g., Byrd,* 750 F.2d at 585, 590.

64. As Berger and Luckmann note, "no other form of social relating can reproduce the plenitude of symptoms of subjectivity present in the face-to-face situation." Peter L. Berger & Thomas Luckmann, *The Social Construction of Reality* 28 (1966); *see also* Peter Berger & Hansfried Kellner, *Marriage and the Construction of Reality,* 46 *Diogenes* 1 (1964).

65. Appreciation of this may be the implicit reason that some courts have held that the communications privilege prevents disclosure of any act done in the presence of one's spouse. *See, e.g.,* Smith v. State, 344 So. 2d 915, 919 (Fla. Dist. Ct. App.), *cert.* denied, 353 So. 2d 679 (Fla. 1977); Shepherd v. State, 277 N.E.2d 165, 166 (Ind. 1971), or any information gained as a result of the marriage, *see,* e.g., Prudential Ins. Co. v. Pierce's Adm'x, 109 S.W.2d 616 (Ky. 1937).

One might argue that such unavoidable revelation is analogous to physical characteristics or exemplars, as to which a person has been deemed to have no reasonable expectation of protection from disclosure. *See* Holt v. United States, 218 U.S. 245, 252–53 (1910). Such attributes, however, are obvious not only to one's spouse but to the world at large. The kind of involuntary revelation that characterizes much of marriage, however, involves information not readily accessible to the public but revealed in a setting in which individuals largely are encouraged to be free of inhibition.

66. *See* Fed. R. Evid. 505 advisory comm. note (Rev. Draft 1971); 1 *McCormick on Evidence, supra* note 28, at 309–10; Black, *supra* note 47, at 49; Hutchins & Slesinger, *supra* note 14, at 682. *But see* Reutlinger, *supra* note 29, at 1371–76.

67. Professor Black's defense of the privilege may represent a common view:

> Is it so obvious that the effect of *prior* knowledge on conduct is the one and only reason for respecting the privacies of human life? Is it not the intrinsically private character of the relation, and the reciprocal indecency of invading that privacy, rather than the parties' knowledge of the law of evidence, that chiefly justifies confidentiality?

Black, *supra* note 47, at 49; see also Krattenmaker, *supra* note 47, at 92.

68. *See, e.g.,* In re Baby M, 537 A.2d 1227 (N.J. 1988) (enforceability of "surrogate" motherhood contract); In re Petition of Doe, 638 N.E.2d 181 (Ill.), *cert.* denied, 115 S. Ct. 499 (1994), and *cert.* denied, 115 S. Ct. 2600 (1995) (right of biological father belatedly informed of paternity vs. right of adoptive parents); Lucinda Franks, "The War for Baby Clausen," *The New Yorker,* 22 March 1993, at 56.

69. As Joseph Raz suggests, "A symbolic action . . . illuminates, for those who understand it, the nature of the choices they have in matters far beyond that action itself. . . ." Joseph Raz, *The Morality of Freedom* 350 (1986).

70. Clifford Geertz, *Local Knowledge: Further Essays in Interpretive Anthropology* 175 (1983).

71. Joseph R. Gusfield & Jerzy Michalowicz, "Secular Symbolism: Studies of Ritual, Ceremony, and the Symbolic Order in Modern Life," 10 *Ann. Rev. Soc.* 417, 426 (Ralph H. Turner & James F. Short, Jr. eds., 1984); see also Lawrence Rosen, *The Anthropology of Justice: Law as Culture in Islamic Society* 36 (1989) (viewing legal proceedings as expressive acts in which community draws on "store of symbols" to depict a meaningful vision of the world).

72. Consider, for instance, that many people support or oppose the death penalty regardless of the extent to which it actually serves to deter crime, on the ground that its presence or absence is an important statement about social values. For studies of the symbolic dimension of the death penalty, see David B. Chandler, *Capital Punishment in Canada:*

*A Sociological Study of Repressive Law* (1976); John Lofland, "The Dramaturgy of State Executions," in *State Executions* 275 (1977); Tom R. Tyler & Renee Weber, "Support for the Death Penalty: Instrumental Response to Crime, or Symbolic Attitude?" 17 *Law & Soc'y Rev.* 21 (1982). Discussions of the symbolic significance of other areas of the law include Joseph R. Gusfield, *Symbolic Crusade: Status Politics and the American Temperance Movement* (1963); Rozann Rothman, "The First Amendment: Symbolic Import—Ambiguous Prescription," 1 *Res. Law & Soc.* 59 (Rita J. Simon ed., 1978). On the symbolic dimension of law more generally, see Model Penal Code § 2.09(2) explanatory note (1985); Thurman W. Arnold, *The Symbols of Government* 34 (1935); see also Milner S. Ball, *Lying Down Together: Law, Metaphor, and Theology* (1985); James B. White, *Heracles' Bow: Essays on the Rhetoric and Poetics of the Law* (1985). For analyses of public policy measures as symbolic statements, see Murray Edelman, *Political Language: Words That Succeed and Policies That Fail* (1977); Murray Edelman, *Politics as Symbolic Action* (1971); Murray Edelman, *The Symbolic Uses of Politics* (1964); Peter K. Manning, *Police Work: The Social Organization of Policing* (1977).

73. As one scholar suggests, family law serves "both as a mechanism for meeting the needs of family members and as a vehicle for expressing our values and aspirations about family life to ourselves and to our children." Barbara B. Woodhouse, "Sex, Lies, and Dissipation: The Discourse of Fault in a No-Fault Era," 82 *Geo. L.J.* 2525, 2526 (1994). For further discussion of the law's effects on our perceptions of society and our relationships with others, see Mary A. Glendon, *Abortion and Divorce in Western Law* (1987); Milton C. Regan, Jr., *Family Law and the Pursuit of Intimacy* 176–83 (1993); Katharine T. Bartlett, "Re-Expressing Parenthood," 98 *Yale L.J.* 293 (1988); Katharine T. Bartlett & Carol B. Stack, "Joint Custody, Feminism and the Dependency Dilemma," 2 *Berkeley Women's L.J.* 9 (1986); Barbara B. Woodhouse, "Hatching the Egg: A Child-Centered Perspective on Parents' Rights," 14 Cardozo L. Rev. 1747 (1993).

74. Robert M. Cover, "The Supreme Court 1982 Term, Foreword: *Nomos* and Narrative," 97 *Harv. L. Rev.* 4, 4–5 (1983).

75. For an example of this strain in moral theory, see David Gauthier, *Morals by Agreement* (1986). For examples in political theory, see John Rawls, *A Theory of Justice* (1971); John A. Simmons, *Moral Principles and Political Obligation* (1979). For discussions of the tradition of reconstructing obligations in consensual terms, see Nancy Hirschmann, *Rethinking Obligation: Feminist Method for Political Theory* 77–125 (1992); Carole Pateman, *The Problem of Political Obligation: A Critical Analysis of Liberal Theory* (1979).

76. *See* People v. Delph, 156 Cal. Rptr. 422 (Ct. App. 1979) (holding that marital communication privilege is inapplicable to nonmarried cohabitants).

77. *See* Anthony Giddens, *Modernity and Self Identity* (1991).

78. 125 U.S. 190 (1888).

79. *Id.* at 211. Historically, commentators have recognized that the terms of marriage are regulated by law and not by the will of the participants. *See* 1 Joel P. Bishop, *New Commentaries on Marriage, Divorce, and Separation* 7 (Chicago, T.H. Flood 1891); James Schouler, *A Treatise on the Law of the Domestic Relations* 22 (Boston, Little Brown 1870); Joseph Story, *Commentaries on the Conflict of Laws* 184–86 (Melville M. Bigelow ed., 8th ed., Boston, Little Brown 1883).

80. Anthony Giddens, *The Transformation of Intimacy*, 58 (1992).

81. For an overview of the basic elements of hypothetical bargain theory, see Jody S. Kraus, *The Limits of Hobbesian Contractarianism* 1–27 (1993). *See also* the discussion of hypothetical bargains in Chapter 3 at 57–58.

82. Men comprised 81 percent of those arrested in 1992. Federal Bureau of Investigation, U.S. Dep't of Justice, *Uniform Crime Reports for the United States 1992*, at 234 (1993). In 1991, they constituted almost 91 percent of jail inmates, and 94.5 percent of state prison inmates. Bureau of the Census, U.S. Dep't of Com., *Statistical Abstract of the United States 1993*, at 210

(113th ed. 1993). As a result, "the party benefiting from the exclusion of evidence is usually a man, and the witness prevented from testifying or choosing to testify is usually a woman." Developments in the Law, *supra* note 28, at 1587 (footnote omitted).

83. *See, e.g.*, Neb. Rev. Stat. § 27–505(a)(b) (1994). In federal and most state courts, this can include acts or gestures meant to communicate. See, e.g., United States v. Ferris, 719 F.2d 1405, 1408 (9th Cir. 1983); Arnold v. State, 353 So. 2d 524, 527 (Ala. 1977); State v. Newman, 680 P.2d 257, 266 (Kan. 1984).

84. *See, e.g.*, State v. Smith, 384 A.2d 687, 690–91 (Me. 1978); State v. Teel, 712 P.2d 792, 794–95 (N.M. Ct. App. 1985).

85. *See, e.g.*, Resnover v. State, 372 N.E.2d 457, 459 (Ind. 1978).

86. *See* Blau v. United States, 340 U.S. 332, 333 (1951); State v. Levi, 686 P.2d 9, 11 (Haw. 1984).

87. Thus, an objection to the elicitation of testimony about one communication will not serve as an objection to testimony about others. Rather, the privilege must be asserted with respect to each instance of communication, on pain of waiver of the privilege. *See* United States v. Figueroa-Paz, 468 F.2d 1055, 1057 (9th Cir. 1972).

88. Annette C. Baier, "Trust and Antitrust" in *Moral Prejudices* 127 (1994).

89. This assumption is reflected, for instance, in decisions holding that one spouse may be liable to the other under federal wiretapping law for recording his or her telephone conversations without consent, even when the parties are living together in an ongoing marriage. *See, e.g.*, Heggy v. Heggy, 944 F.2d 1537 (10th Cir. 1991), *cert.* denied, 503 U.S. 951 (1992); Kempf v. Kempf, 868 F.2d 970 (8th Cir. 1989); see also Dorian L. Rowe, "Comment, Wiretapping and the Modern Marriage: Does Title III Provide a Federal Remedy for Victims of Interspousal Electronic Surveillance?" 91 *Dick. L. Rev.* 855, 881 (1987). Other courts, however, have construed the federal wiretapping statute to include an implicit exception for such conduct. *See, e.g.*, Anonymous v. Anonymous, 558 F.2d 677 (2d Cir. 1977); Simpson v. Simpson, 490 F.2d 803 (5th Cir.), *cert.* denied, 419 U.S. 897 (1974); Perfit v. Perfit, 693 F. Supp. 851 (C.D. Cal. 1988).

Two scholars have argued that individuals engage in adjustments of boundaries between themselves and others by regulating the amount of self-disclosure they provide through verbal transmission of information. See generally Valerian J. Derlega & Alan L. Chaiken, "Privacy and Self-Disclosure in Social Relationships," 33 *J. Soc. Issues* 102 (1977).

90. 445 U.S. 40 (1980).

91. *Id.* at 52.

92. For a discussion of this general view, see Milton C. Regan, Jr., "Reason, Tradition, and Family Law: A Comment on Social Constructionism," 79 *Va. L. Rev.* 1515 (1993).

## Six

1. "To love is to surrender oneself to another and to make oneself vulnerable. It is a lowering of defenses which lays one open to the risk of terrible hurt and unhappiness." John R.S. Wilson, In One Another's Power, 88 *Ethics* 299, 302 (1978).

2. Annette C. Baier, "Trust and Its Vulnerabilities," in *Moral Prejudices* 130, 133 (1994).

3. R. E. Ewin, "Loyalty and Virtues," 42 *Phil. Q.* 403, 411 (1992).

4. Katharine T. Bartlett, "Re-Expressing Parenthood," 98 Yale L. J. 293, 301 (1988).

5. *See* Annette C. Baier, "Trusting People," in *Moral Prejudices, supra* note 2, at 183, 196; Diego Gambetta, "Can We Trust Trust?" in *Trust: Making and Breaking Cooperative Relationships* 213, 218–19 (Diego Gambetta ed., 1988); John K. Rempel, John G. Holmes, & Mark P. Zanna, "Trust in Close Relationships," 49 *J. Pers. & Soc. Psychol.* 95, 97 (1985); Laurence Thomas, "Trust, Affirmation, and Moral Character," in *Identity, Character, and Morality* 235, 252 (Owen Flanagan & Amelie O. Rorty eds. 1990).

6. *See* Bernard Barber, *The Logic and Limits of Trust* 167 (1983) (law may serve as device that is alternative to trust).

7. As Robin West suggests, "[T]he content of our moral beliefs themselves—the ordinary beliefs of most citizens regarding what is right and wrong, just and unjust, or good and evil—may be heavily influenced by the particular legal system under which we live." Robin West, *Narrative, Authority, and Law* 1–2 (1993). *See also* June L. Tapp & Felice J. Levine, "Legal Socialization: Strategies for an Ethical Legality," 27 *Stan. L. Rev.* 1, 5 (1974–1975).

8. Mary A. Glendon, *Rights Talk* (1991); Alexis De Tocqueville, *Democracy in America* 261 (Legal Classics Library 1988) (1838). On the traditional influence of law in American culture, see Robert A. Ferguson, *Law and Letters in American Culture* (1984).

9. Bartlett, *supra* note 4, at 301. She elaborates: "A hands-off approach by the law to questions of parenthood would abdicate any societal responsibility for norms of parenthood; yet a tight, comprehensive set of controls would remove from parents the discretion to act, upon which the capacity of moral decisionmaking actually depends." *Id.*

10. Thurman Arnold, *The Symbols of Government* 129 (1935). See generally *id.* at 128–48.

11. *See* Richard O. Lempert, "A Right to Every Woman's Evidence," 66 *Iowa L. Rev.* 725, 736–38 (1981).

12. Bartlett, *supra* note 4, at 301.

13. *Id.* at 304.

14. Jon Elster, "When Rationality Fails," in *The Limits of Rationality* 19, 45 (Karen S. Cook & Margaret Levi eds., 1990).

15. Jon Elster, *The Cement of Society* 110 (1989).

16. *Id.* at 111 (emphasis in original).

17. *Id.* at 142.

18. *Id.* at 98–99.

19. George Fletcher, *Loyalty* 3 (1993).

20. Lynne McFall, "Integrity," 98 *Ethics* 5, 16 (1987).

21. *See* John Hardwig, "Should Women Think in Terms of Rights?" in *Feminism and Political Theory* 53, 74 (Cass R. Sunstein ed. 1990); Michael Stocker, "The Schizophrenia of Modern Ethical Theories," 73 *J. Phil.* 453 (1976).

22. Lawrence A. Blum, "Vocation, Friendship, and Community: Limitations of the Personal-Impersonal Framework," in *Identity, Character, and Morality*, *supra* note 5, at 173, 178.

23. For a discussion of what I have called "role identification," see Milton C. Regan, Jr., *Family Law and the Pursuit of Intimacy* 25–26 (1993).

24. *See* Charles Taylor, The Ethics of Authenticity 40 (1991); Blum, *supra* note 22, at 194.

25. *See* David B. Annis, "The Meaning, Value, and Duties of Friendship," 24 *Am. Phil. Q.* 349, 351–52 (1987).

26. Bruce C. Hafen, "The Constitutional Status of Marriage, Kinship, and Sexual Privacy—Balancing the Individual and Social Interests," 81 *Mich. L. Rev.* 463, 476 (1983).

27. Jeremy Waldron, "When Justice Replaces Affection: The Need for Rights," 11 *Harv. J. L. & Pub Pol'y* 625, 647 (1988).

28. We might distinguish, for instance, between trust as confidence in the predictability of a person's behavior, which need not rely on inferences of motive, and trust based on attributions of disposition or intention. *See* Rempel et al., *supra* note 5, at 96–97.

29. *See, e.g.*, Robert Axelrod, *The Evolution of Cooperation* (1984); Gambetta, *supra* note 5, at 225.

30. We can conceptualize this as the process of manipulating the payoff matrices of the parties by reducing the risk and thus the expected cost of cooperation. *See* Robert Axelrod & Robert O. Keohane, "Achieving Cooperation Under Anarchy: Strategies and Institutions," in *Cooperation Under Anarchy* 225, 228 (Kenneth A. Oye ed., 1986).

31. *See* Gambetta, *supra* note 5, at 225–29.

32. Axelrod, *supra* note 29, at 85 (describing cooperative exchanges between Allied and German soldiers during World War I).

33. *See* Annette C. Baier, "Sustaining Trust," in *Moral Prejudices, supra* note 103, at 152, 176; Gambetta, *supra* note 5, at 234. Similarly, Albert Hirschman suggests that "morality and civic spirit" represent resources "whose supply may well increase rather than decrease through use. . . ." Albert O. Hirschman, "Against Parsimony: Three Easy Ways of Complicating Some Categories of Economic Discourse," 74 *Am. Econ. Rev.* 89, 93 (1984).

34. Gambetta, *supra* note 5, at 234 (citation omitted).

35. *See* id. at 235.

36. "Neither *Hawkins*, nor any other privilege, prevents the Government from enlisting one spouse to give information concerning the other or to aid in the other's apprehension. It is only the spouse's testimony in the courtroom that is prohibited." Trammel v. United States, 445 U.S. 40, 52 n.12 (1980). For examples of such aid see, e.g., United States v. Lefkowitz, 618 F.2d 1313, 1318 (9th Cir.) (informing IRS about fraudulent records), *cert.* denied, 449 U.S. 824 (1980); State v. Newman, 680 P.2d 257, 266-67 (Kan. 1984) (giving sworn statement to investigator and prosecutor before magistrate); State v. Welch, 448 So. 2d 705, 711-12 (La. Ct. App.) (taping telephone conversation for police), *cert.* denied, 450 So. 2d 952 (La. 1984); Bishop v. State, 582 S.W.2d 86, 90 (Tenn. Crim. App. 1979) (giving statement to investigators).

37. Joseph R. Gusfield, "Introduction," in Kenneth Burke, *On Symbols and Society* 1, 39 (Joseph R. Gusfield ed., 1989); see also Joseph R. Gusfield & Jerzy Michalowicz, "Secular Symbolism: Studies of Ritual, Ceremony, and the Symbolic Order in Modern Life," 10 *Ann. Rev. Soc.* 417 (Ralph H. Turner & James F. Short, Jr., eds. 1984).

38. As Lawrence Rosen has suggested, a legal proceeding can be seen as a ritual that "gains its meaning—its connectedness to and summation of its people's culture—not from one 'rational' or 'irrational' element alone, but from the way it structures the entire process into an expressive form, a total performance, that accords with a people's felt sense of things." Lawrence Rosen, *The Anthropology of Justice: Law as Culture in Islamic Society* 36 (1989).

39. Meir Dan-Cohen, "Decision Rules and Conduct Rules: On Acoustic Separation in Criminal Law," 97 *Harv. L. Rev.* 625, 630 (1984).

40. *See, e.g., Lefkowitz,* 618 F.2d at 1319 n.8; United States v. Harper, 450 F.2d 1032, 1045–46 (5th Cir. 1971).

41. Meir Dan-Cohen, "Responsibility and the Boundaries of the Self," 105 *Harv. L. Rev.* 959 (1992).

42. *Id.*; see also Marion Smiley, *Moral Responsibility and the Boundaries of Community* (1992).

43. Dan-Cohen, *supra* note 41, at 961 (emphasis omitted).

44. *Id.* at 963–64.

45. *Id.* at 962.

46. *Id.* at 964.

47. *Id.* at 972.

48. *Id.* at 969.

49. *Id.* at 970.

50. *Id.*

51. *Id.* at 1001.

52. *Id.* at 975; cf. *id.* at 1003.

53. As I have argued, the act of marriage itself is not particularly persuasive as the basis for an attribution of consensual obligation in this circumstance.

54. Similarly, Marion Smiley suggests that attribution of causal responsibility is influenced by "our configuration of social roles and our conception of communal boundaries." Smiley, *supra* note 42, at 12. She argues:

If, for instance, we view those suffering as members of the individual's community . . . we are more likely to see a direct connection between the suffering and the individual's own actions. If, on the other hand, we do not include them in the individual's community, we are more likely to consider the causal connection indirect and to refrain from holding the individual herself responsible for the harm in question.

*Id.*

55. Dan-Cohen, *supra* note 41, at 987. Thus, for instance, Dan-Cohen suggests a citizen of the United States might have felt some degree of responsibility for the Vietnam War, a reaction that in turn may have motivated efforts to end that conflict. *Id.* at 987–88.

56. Conspiracy liability does encourage a sense of collective responsibility, but, unlike the privilege, it is participation in the conspiracy, rather than marriage per se, that is the responsibility base in that instance. The coconspirator exception thus means that the law promotes an expansive sense of self with respect to one's associates in crime, but not with respect to one's spouse.

57. To reiterate, I defer until later in this chapter the question whether we should use the adverse testimony privilege to promote an internal stance toward marriage in the setting of a criminal trial.

58. *See* generally Wesley N. Hohfeld, "Some Fundamental Legal Conceptions as Applied in Judicial Reasoning," 23 *Yale L.J.* 16 (1913); Joseph W. Singer, "The Legal Rights Debate in Analytical Jurisprudence from Bentham to Hohfeld," 1982 *Wis. L. Rev.* 975.

59. *See* Ohio Rev. Code Ann. § 2945.42 (Anderson 1993) (criminal only, with some exceptions). For an explanation of the privilege, see State v. Goodin, 21 N.E.2d 482 (Ohio Ct. App. 1938); Pa. Cons. Stat. Ann. § 5924 (1982) (civil, with some exceptions); Wyo. Stat. § 1-12-104 (1988) (civil and criminal, with some exceptions).

60. Gloria M. Sodaro & Paul A.J. Wilson, "Spousal Privileges," in 2 *Testimonial Privileges* § 5.02, at 5-3 (Scott N. Stone & Robert K. Taylor eds., 2d ed. 1993).

61. Approximately 83 percent of divorcing men and 78 percent of divorcing women in the United States eventually remarry. J. Thomas Oldham, "Putting Asunder in the 1990s," 80 *Cal. L. Rev.* 1091, 1100 n.45 (1992) (book review).

62. Even if only 1 percent of married persons were aware of the privilege, that would represent over one million people. See U.S. Bureau of the Census, *Statistical Abstract of the United States 1994*, at 55 (114th ed. 1994) (114.5 million married persons in the United States in 1993).

63. *See* Katherine Barrett & Richard Green, "Know Your Children's Rights," *Ladies' Home J.*, Sept. 1994, at 156; Elizabeth Kolbert, "Our New Participatory Tabloid Videocracy," *N.Y. Times*, 17 July 1994, § 4, at 3; Mary Nemeth, "Hot Off the Presses: Sensational Stories Fuel America's Tabloid-Inspired Media Machine," *Maclean's*, 24 Jan. 1994, at 66; Betsy Streisand, "A Courtroom Classic," *U.S. News & World Rep.*, 11 July 1994, at 26.

64. Christopher S. Stern, "Cameras Banned from Federal Courts," *Broadcasting & Cable*, 26 Sept. 1994, at 7.

65. Walter Goodman, "The Summer's Top Crime Drama, Continued," *N.Y. Times*, 4 July 1994, at A40.

66. David Firestone, "New Police Policy Opens Doors to TV," *N.Y. Times*, 16 July 1994, at A24.

67. Melanie Warner, "Time Inc. Ventures' Crime Prototype," *Inside Media*, 30 Mar. 1994, at 4.

68. *See* Nemeth, *supra* note 63, at 66–67. On the complex phenomenon of popular legal culture, see Anne Norton, *Republic of Signs: Liberal Theory and American Popular Culture* 139–54 (1993); Anthony Chase, "Toward a Legal Theory of Popular Culture," 1986 *Wis. L. Rev.* 527; "Symposium: Popular Legal Culture," 98 *Yale L.J.* 1545 (1989).

69. Kolbert, *supra* note 63; see also Rennard Strickland, "Beyond the Law School Classroom," *The Newsletter (Ass'n of Amer. Law Schools)*, Nov. 1994, at 1–2.

70. *See* Kolbert, *supra* note 63.

71. Joseph F. Sullivan, "Woman Pleads Guilty to Lesser Counts in Kidnapping," *N.Y. Times*, July 1, 1992, at B4.

72. Diane Rehm Show (National Public Radio broadcast, July 29, 1992).

73. *See* Mark Reutlinger, Policy, Privacy, and Prerogatives: A Critical Examination of the Proposed Federal Rules of Evidence as They Affect Marital Privilege," 61 *Cal. L. Rev.* 1353, 1377–78 (1973); "Developments in the Law: Legal Responses to Domestic Violence," 106 *Harv. L. Rev.* 1475 (footnotes omitted); *cf.* "Comment, Marital Privileges and the Right to Testify," 34 *U. Chi. L. Rev.* 196, 200 n.25 (1966–1967).

74. Elster, *The Cement of Society*, *supra* note 15, at 111.

75. *See* 8 John H. Wigmore, *Evidence in Trials at Common Law* § 2228, at 217–21 (John T. McNaughton ed., rev. ed. 1961).

76. *See, e.g.,* Colo. Rev. Stat. § 19 5-213 (Supp. 1995).

77. *See* Edmund Leach, "Anthropological Aspects of Language: Animal Categories and Verbal Abuse," in *New Directions in the Study of Language* 23 (Eric H. Lenneberg ed., 1964).

78. *See* Jane M. Cohen, "Posnerism, Pluralism, Pessimism," 67 *B.U. L. Rev.* 105, 154-55 (1987). For concerns about commodification more generally, see Margaret J. Radin, Compensation and Commensurability, 43 *Duke L.J.* 56 (1993); Margaret J. Radin, "Market-Inalienability," 100 *Harv. L. Rev.* 1849 (1987).

79. *See* Margaret F. Brinig, "A Maternalistic Approach to Surrogacy: Comment on Richard Epstein's "Surrogacy: The Case for Full Contractual Enforcement," 81 *Va. L. Rev.* 2377, 2384 & n.27 (1995).

80. *See* Reutlinger, *supra* note 73, at 1375.

81. *See, e.g.,* Fed. R. Evid. 407.

82. *See, e.g.,* Fed. R. Evid. 409.

83. *See, e.g.,* Fed. R. Evid. 408.

84. *See, e.g.,* Guido Calabresi, *The Costs of Accidents* (1970); A. Mitchell Polinsky, *An Introduction to Law and Economics* 37–49, 65–71, 95–104 (1983). For an assessment of criticisms that tort law does not influence behavior, which concludes that this body of law may have some moderate degree of influence, see Gary T. Schwartz, "Reality in the Economic Analysis of Tort Law, Does Tort Law Really Deter?" 42 *UCLA L. Rev.* 377 (1994).

85. Carl E. Schneider, "State-Interest Analysis in Fourteenth Amendment 'Privacy' Law: An Essay on the Constitutionalization of Social Issues," 51 *Law & Contemp. Probs.* 79, 97–100 (1988).

86. *Id.* at 97.

87. 440 U.S. 268 (1979).

88. *See* Lenore J. Weitzman & Ruth B. Dixon, "The Alimony Myth: Does No-Fault Divorce Make a Difference?" 14 *Fam. L.Q.* 141, 143 (1980).

89. *Orr*, 440 U.S. at 283.

90. *See* Michael M. v. Superior Court, 450 U.S. 464, 493 n.8 (1981) (Brennan, J., dissenting).

91. *See* Frances Olsen, "Statutory Rape: A Feminist Critique of Rights Analysis," 63 *Tex. L. Rev.* 387, 404–06 (1984); Wendy W. Williams, "The Equality Crisis: Some Reflections on Culture, Courts, and Feminism," 7 *Women's Rts. L. Rep.* 175, 185–88 (1981). The Supreme Court upheld a state statutory rape statute in *Michael M.*, 450 U.S. at 464 (plurality opinion).

92. The literature is vast, but one useful compilation of some of it is *Cultural Models in Language and Thought* (Dorothy Holland & Naomi Quinn eds., 1987).

93. Brief for the United States at 21, Trammel v. United States, 445 U.S. 40 (1980) (No. 78–5705); see also *Trammel*, 445 U.S. at 52–53.

94. Lempert, *supra* note 11, at 735.

95. The government asserted in its *Trammel* brief that this often is the case. Brief for the United States at 21, *Trammel* (No. 78-5705).

96. *See* Blum, *supra* note 22; Lawrence A. Blum, *Moral Perception and Particularity* (1994); Carol Gilligan, *In A Different Voice* (1982); Virginia Held, *Feminist Morality* 66 (1993; Nel Noddings, *Caring: A Feminine Approach to Ethics and Moral Education* (1984).

97. *See* Fletcher, *supra* note 19.

98. Ewin, *supra* note 3, at 418–19.

99. *Id.* at 419.

100. *See* Josiah Royce, "The Philosophy of Loyalty," in *2 The Basic Writings of Josiah Royce* 855, 860 (John J. McDermott ed., 1969). Royce focused on loyalty to causes, but his discussion makes clear that this concept is meant to encompass loyalty to particular persons.

101. *See supra* notes 1–6 and accompanying text.

102. *See* Marilyn Friedman, *What Are Friends For?* 40 (1993). For a general discussion of the value of loyalty, see Ewin, *supra* note 3.

103. *See* Marcia Baron, *The Moral Status of Loyalty* 21 (1984); Fletcher, *supra* note 19, at 171.

104. *See* Baron, *supra* note 103, at 19.

105. On this dilemma, see Robert Weisberg, "Deregulating Death," 1983 *Sup. Ct. Rev.* 305 (Philip B. Kurland, Gerhard Casper & Dennis J. Hutchinson eds.).

106. *See, e.g.*, David Medine, "The Adverse Testimony Privilege: Time to Dispose of A 'Sentimental Relic,' " 67 Or. L. Rev. 519, 547 (1988). Professor Medine does argue that the evidence that would be obtained in such cases would be "potentially critical," *id.*, but the small number of cases in which the privilege excludes important evidence suggests that the aggregate effect of the privilege on law enforcement probably is not significant.

107. Stephen Macedo, *Liberal Virtues: Citizenship, Virtue, and Community in Liberal Constitutionalism* 244 (1990).

108. Sophocles, *Antigone* (Richard E. Braun trans., Oxford University Press 1973) (n.d.).

109. On reflective equilibrium, see John Rawls, *A Theory of Justice* 20–21, 48–51.

110. *Id.* at 462–72.

111. Owen Flanagan & Kathryn Jackson, "Justice, Care, and Gender: The Kohlberg-Gilligan Debate Revisited," in *Feminism and Political Theory* 37, 50 (Cass R. Sunstein ed. 1990).

112. *See* Lempert, *supra* note 11, at 734.

113. *Trammel*, 445 U.S. at 53.

114. On the philosophical debate, see Michael Philips, "The Question of Voluntariness in the Plea Bargaining Controversy," 16 *Law & Soc'y Rev.* 207 (1981– 1982).

115. We might see this as asking "the woman question." See Katharine T. Bartlett, "Feminist Legal Methods," 103 *Harv. L. Rev.* 829, 837 (1990).

116. For useful compilations of the intrafeminist debate on this ethic, see *An Ethic of Care: Feminist and Interdisciplinary Perspectives* (Mary J. Larrabee ed., 1993); *Science, Morality & Feminist Theory*, *supra* note 32; *Women and Moral Theory* (Eva F. Kittay & Diana T. Meyers eds., 1987).

117. *See e.g.*, Amy Wax, *Bargaining in the Shadow of the Law: Is There A Future for Egalitarian Marriage?* (unpublished manuscript).

118. *See* Model Penal Code § 2.09(3) & comment 5 (1962).

119. *See, e.g.*, Model Penal Code § 2.09(1), which provides: "It is an affirmative defense that the actor engaged in the conduct charged to constitute an offense because he was coerced to do so by the use of, or a threat to use, unlawful force against his person or the person of another, that a person of reasonable firmness in his situation would have been unable to resist."

120. For feminist insights into some of the potential limitations of legal standards based on the reasonable person, see Kathleen A. Lahey, "Reasonable Women and the Law," in *At the Boundaries of Law* 3 (Martha A. Fineman & Nancy S. Thomadsen eds., 1991); Kim L. Scheppele, "The Reasonable Woman," *Responsive Community*, Fall 1991, at 36. For a case that

dramatically illustrates different perspectives on women's consent and coercion in the context of rape, see Rusk v. State, 406 A.2d 624 (Md. Ct. Spec. App. 1979), rev'd, 424 A.2d 720 (Md. 1981).

121. Model Penal Code § 2.09(1) (1962).

122. Id. comment 3 (1985).

123. See, e.g., State v. Kelly, 478 A.2d 364, 375–78 (N.J. 1984). One alternative suggestion with respect to the syndrome is that self-defense doctrine incorporate more subjective elements, to which evidence of battering would be deemed relevant without reference to battered-woman syndrome. See David L. Faigman, Note, "The Battered Woman Syndrome and Self-Defense," 72 Va. L. Rev. 619, 643–47 (1986).

124. See, e.g., Wright v. State, 402 So. 2d 493, 497–98 (Fla. Dist. Ct. App. 1981); Jackson v. State, 558 S.W.2d 816, 819–20 (Mo. Ct. App. 1977); State v. Toscano, 378 A.2d 755 (N.J. 1977) (dicta).

125. For a discussion of the factors which influence women to stay in abusive relationships, see Christine A. Littleton, "Women's Experience and the Problem of Transition: Perspectives on Male Battering of Women," 1989 U. Chi. Legal F. 23, 31– 47; Martha R. Mahoney, "Legal Images of Battered Women: Redefining the Issue of Separation," 90 Mich. L. Rev. 1, 10–24 (1991).

126. For a survey of legal measures dealing with domestic violence, see Developments in the Law, supra note 73, at 1498.

127. See Thompson v. Thompson, 218 U.S. 611, 617–18 (1910) (interspousal tort immunity); Michael G. Hilf, "Marital Privacy and Spousal Rape," 16 New Eng. L. Rev. 31 (1980) (marital rape).

128. 428 U.S. 52 (1976).

129. Id. at 58. The statute provided an exception for cases in which a physician certified that an abortion was necessary to save the life of the mother. Id.

130. Id. at 70.

131. Id. at 71.

132. Id.

133. Pamela S. Karlan & Daniel R. Ortiz, "In A Different Voice: Relational Feminism, Abortion Rights, and the Feminist Legal Agenda," 87 Nw. U. L. Rew. 858, 877 (1993).

134. A title-based system distributed property at divorce in accordance with who held title to it. For a description of the operation of this system, see Herbert Jacob, The Silent Revolution 113 (1988).

135. For a discussion of the difficulty of conceptualizing an ethic of care detached from gender considerations, see Carrie Menkel-Meadow, "What's Gender Got to Do With It? The Politics and Morality of an Ethic of Care," 22 N.Y.U. Rev. Law & Soc. Change 265 (1996) (review essay in response to Joan C. Tronto, Moral Boundaries: A Political Argument for an Ethic of Care (1993)).

136. See Tronto, supra note 135, at 117–22.

137. It might also lead us to give particular attention to measures promoting an internal stance toward marriage that may have more impact on men than women. The requirement of greater financial responsibility to a former spouse may be such an instance. See, e.g., Milton C. Regan, Jr., "The Boundaries of Care: Constructing Community After Divorce," 31 Hous. L. Rev. 425 (1994); Milton C. Regan, Jr., "Spouses and Strangers: Divorce Obligations and Property Rhetoric," 82 Geo. L.J. 2303 (1994).

138. See, e.g., Regan, Family Law and the Pursuit of Intimacy, supra note 23; Allen M. Parkman, No-Fault Divorce: What Went Wrong? (1992); Martha A. Fineman, The Illusion of Equality: The Rhetoric and Reality of Divorce Reform (1991); Lenore J. Weitzman, The Divorce Revolution (1985); Deborah L. Rhode & Martha Minow, "Reforming the Questions, Questioning the Reforms: Feminist Perspectives on Divorce Law," in Divorce Reform at the Crossroads 191 (Stephen D. Sugarman

& Herma H. Kay eds., 1990); Schneider, *supra* note 85, at 107; Elizabeth S. Scott, "Rational Decisionmaking About Marriage and Divorce," 76 Va. L. Rev. 9 (1990).

### Seven

1. The average woman working full time for a wage earns only 71 percent of the amount earned by her male counterpart. Bureau of Labor Statistics, U.S. Dept. Of Labor, Empl. & Earnings 71 (July 1987). The average college-educated woman earns less than an average man with a high-school diploma. Cynthia M. Taeuber & Victor Valdisera, Bureau of the Census, U.S. Dept. Of Commerce, Current Population Reports, Special Studies, Series P-23, No. 146, *Women in the American Economy* 31 (1986). Only 1 percent of white men and women are employed in occupations in which women earn as much as 90 percent of men; almost 75 percent are in jobs in which women earn less than 70 percent of what men earn. Victor Fuchs, *Women's Quest for Economic Equality* 51 (1986). One study concludes that in general the difference in economic well-being between men and women was as large in 1986 as it had been in 1960. *Id.* at 3. For various ideas on the source of this phenomenon, see Fuchs, *supra* note 1, at 4; Kathleen Gerson, *Hard Choices* (1985); Carol Rose, "Women and Property," 78 *Va. L. Rev.* 421 (1992).

2. This is not to say that disparities in access to resources, and consequently in power, do not exist in ongoing marriages.

3. Wright v. Wright, 469 A.2d 803 (Del. Fam. Ct. 1983).

4. *Id.* at 805.

5. Postema v. Postema, 471 N.W.2d 912 (Mich. Ct. App. 1991).

6. *Id.* at 915.

7. O'Brien v. O'Brien, 489 N.E.2d 712 (N.Y. 1985).

8. *See, e.g.,* Elkus v. Elkus, 572 N.Y.S.2d 901 (N.Y. App. Div. 1991).

9. The right may be protected by other legal doctrines, such as contract. Furthermore, persons may acquire property rights through other means, such as gift or inheritance. Labor and exchange are paradigmatic, however, because they can occur in a world of independent strangers who lack any personal feeling toward one other.

10. Elaine Tyler May, *Great Expectations: Marriage and Divorce in Post-Victorian America* 27 (1980).

11. *See generally* Marylynn Salmon, *Women and the Law of Property in Early America* (1986).

12. While the term "contract" was used, it was clear that the parties generally were not free to vary the rights and obligations of spouses established by law. *See, e.g.,* Joel Bishop, 1 *New Commentaries on Marriage, Divorce, and Separation* 7 (1981); Maynard v. Hill, 125 U.S. 190, 211.

13. These typically included behavior such as cruelty, desertion, and adultery.

14. As one scholar suggested, labeling alimony in such a system as a substitute for a wife's right to support during marriage seemed unsatisfactory. "Why should there be such a substitute? Would it not be more logical to say that when the marriage is dissolved all rights and duties based upon it end?" Homer Clark, *The Law of Domestic Relations in the United States* § 16.1 (2d ed. 1988).

15. *See id.* at 421. Furthermore, segregation of women within the home continued to create an economically dependent class of persons who would be dramatically disadvantaged if a right to support after divorce were abolished. *See* Mary E. O'Connell, "Alimony After No-Fault: A Practice in Search of a Theory," 23 *New Eng. L. Rev.* 437, 458 (1988).

16. *See, e.g.,* Webber v. Webber, 199 P.2d 934, 937 (Cal. 1948).

17. *See, e.g.,* Bishop, *supra* note 12, Vol. 2, at 220; Rice v. Rice, 239 N.E.2d 256 (Mich. 1931).

18. *See, e.g.,* Kelly v. Kelly, 209 S.W.2d 335, 338 (Ky. 1919). *See generally* O'Connell, *supra*

note 15, at 467–469 (discussing use of both tort and contract theories in conceptualizing fault-based divorce).

19. O'Connell, *supra* note 18, at 180. *See* Margaret F. Brinig & June Carbone, "The Reliance Interest in Marriage and Divorce," 62 *Tul. L. Rev.* 855, 862 (1988).

20. O'Connell, *supra* note 15, at 471 (footnote omitted).

21. *See, e.g.*, Lenore Weitzman, *The Divorce Revolution* 143–145 (1985).

22. *See, e.g.*, Everett v. Everett, 52 Cal. 383 (1877).

23. *See* Linda D. Elrod and Robert G. Spector, "A Review of the Year in Family Law," 25 *Fam. L. Q.* 417, 807 (1997).

24. Mary Ann Glendon, *Abortion and Divorce in Western Law* 68 (1987).

25. Brinig & Carbone, *Reliance Interest, supra* note 19, at 867.

26. The Uniform Marriage and Divorce Act (UMDA), for instance, states that "the distribution of property upon the termination of a marriage should be treated, as nearly as possible, like the distribution of assets incident to the dissolution of a partnership." UMDA, Prefatory Note, 9A U.L.A. 149 (West 1987). *See also* Price v. Price, 503 N. E. 2d 684, 687 (N.Y. 1986); White v. White, 324 S.E.2d 829 (N.C. 1985); Steinke v. Steinke, 376 N.W.2d 839 (Wis. 1985).

27. *See* Carol Bruch, "Of Work, Family Wealth, and Equality," 17 *Fam. L.Q.* 99, 100 (1983); Herma Hill Kay, "An Appraisal of California's No-Fault Divorce Law," 75 *Calif. L. Rev.* 291, 313 (1987); Joan M. Krauskopf, "Theories of Property Division/Spousal Support: Searching for Solutions to the Mystery," 23 *Fam. L.Q.* 253, 272 (1989).

28. *See, e.g.*, R.I. Gen. Laws 15–5–16.1(a).

29. *See* Sally Goldfarb, "Marital Partnership and the Case for Permanent Alimony," in *Alimony: New Strategies for Pursuit and Defense* 45, 46 (American Bar Association Family Law Section 1988); Herma Hill Kay, "Commentary: Toward a Theory of Fair Distribution," 57 *Brooklyn L. Rev.* 755, 766 (1991); Bea Ann Smith, "The Partnership Theory of Marriage: A Borrowed Solution Fails," 68 *Tex. L. Rev.* 689, 697 (1990).

30. *See* Mary Ann Glendon, *The Transformation of Family Law* 227–228 (1989).

31. In this regard, they follow the approach of the UMDA. *See* UMDA, *supra* note 26, at 307, 308(a).

32. Martha Fineman, *The Illusion of Equality: The Rhetoric and Reality of Divorce Reform* 40–43 (1991).

33. *See* Patricia A. Cain, "In Search of a Normative Principle for Property Division at Divorce," 1 *Tex. J. Women & Law* 249, 266 (1992 (Book Review); Smith, *supra* note 29, at 734. *See also* Suzanne Reynolds, "The Relationship of Property Division and Alimony: The Division of Property to Address Need," 56 *Fordham L. Rev.* 827 (1988).

34. Fineman, *supra* note 32, at 40.

35. The fact that the spouses may not have expressly come to such an agreement is irrelevant, as long as it is possible to reconstruct their relationship and its obligation in consensual terms. As Nancy Hirschmann points out, liberal consent theory typically rests not on the occurrence of explicit acts of consent, but on implied consent, hypothetical consent, or voluntary acceptance of benefits as the basis for postulating legitimate obligation. Nancy Hirschmann, *Rethinking Obligation: Feminist Method for Political Theory* 8 (1992).

36. It is conceivable that one ex-spouse may have to fulfill her obligation by making periodic payments to the other after divorce because of insufficient liquid assets at the time of divorce. Such payments, however, do not represent honoring a claim to ongoing financial support, but are merely a practical means of fulfilling an obligation that ideally would be met by a lump-sum payment at divorce.

37. *See, e.g.*, Shilkett v. Shilkett, 285 S.W.2d 67, 70 (Mo. Ct. App. 1955); Doyle v. Doyle, 158 N.Y.S.2d 909, 912 (N.Y. Sup. Ct.1957).

38. *See* Reva Siegel, "Home as Work: The First Women's Rights Claims Concerning Wives Household Labor," 103 Yale L.J. 1073 (1994).

39. *Id.* at 1127–1132.

40. *Id.* at 1127–1131.

41. *Id.* at 1155–1156.

42. *Id.* at 1125.

43. *Id.* at 1193.

44. *See* Isabel Marcus, "Locked In and Locked Out: Reflections on the History of Divorce Law Reform in New York State," 37 *Buff. L. Rev.* 375, 464, 467 n. 342 (1988/89).

45. *See* Reynolds, *supra* note 33.

46. *See, e.g.*, Barbara Baker, *Family Equity at Issue* (1987); Weitzman, *supra* note 21; Rosalyn B. Bell, "Alimony and the Financially Dependent Spouse in Montgomery County, Maryland," 22 *Fam. L.Q.* 225 (1988); Greg J. Duncan & Saul Hoffman, "A Reconsideration of the Economic Consequences of Marital Dissolution," 22 *Demography* 485 (1985); Thomas J. Espenshade, "The Economic Consequences of Divorce," 41 *J. Marr. & Fam.* 615 (1979); Marsha Garrison, "Good Intentions Gone Awry: How New York's Equitable Distribution Law Affected Divorce Outcomes," 57 *Brooklyn L. Rev.* 619 (1991); James B. McLindon, "Separate but Unequal: The Economic Disaster of Divorce for Women and Children," 21 *Fam. L.Q.* 351 (1987); Heather R. Wishik, "Economics of Divorce: An Exploratory Study," 20 *Fam. L.Q.* (1986).

47. *See, e.g.*, Eleanor Maccoby & Robert Mnookin, *Dividing the Child* (1993).

48. Allen Parkman, *No-Fault Divorce: What Went Wrong?* 1–2, 75–78, 112 (1992); Weitzman, *supra* note 21, at 26–28; Marsha Garrison, "The Economics of Divorce: Changing Rules, Changing Results," in *Divorce Reform at the Crossroads* 75 (Stephen D. Sugarman & Herma Hill Kay eds. 1990); Stephen D. Sugarman, "Dividing Financial Interests on Divorce," in *Divorce Reform*, at 130,135.

49. *See* Weitzman, *supra* note 21, at 70–109; Garrison, *Good Intentions*, *supra* note 46, at 662–666. Garrison's study of negotiated divorce settlements in New York state revealed that the median net worth of couples in contested divorce cases was a little over $23,000, representing only about seven months' income for the typical divorcing family. *Id.* at 662–664. Furthermore, only 19 percent of these assets were in liquid form. *Id.* at 666.

50. *See, e.g.*, In re Marriage of Grubb, 745 P.2d 661 (Colo. 1987).

51. Garrison, *supra* note 46, at 730.

52. Sugarman, *supra* note 48, at 149.

53. *See* Parkman, *supra* note 48, at 130. The seminal work on human capital is Gary Becker, *Human Capital* (1964).

54. Parkman, *supra* note 48, at 130.

55. Joan M. Krauskopf, "Recompense for Financing Spouse's Education: Legal Protection for the Marital Investor in Human Capital," 28 *Kan. L. Rev.* 379 (1980).

56. *Id.* at 380.

57. *Id.*

58. *Id.*

59. *Id. See also* Lester Thurow, *Investment in Human Capital* 25–26 (1970).

60. Krauskopf argues, for instance, that one may be able "to determine the average earnings of, for example, a white urban male with four years of college education and postgraduate study leading to a Master's degree in business administration. From actuarial data one may also determine that individual's life expectancy." *Id.* at 383. An economist could then use that data in conjunction with predictions of economic trends to "make a reasonably probable calculation of a particular individual's future earnings." *Id.*

61. *Id.*

62. Krauskopf observes that studies indicate that these opportunity costs typically constitute a large percentage of the total investment cost in obtaining an education—in some cases as much as three-fourths of the cost. *Id.* at 384.

63. *Id.* at 384 (footnote omitted).

64. *Id.* at 401. She suggests that, absent contrary evidence, a court also should presume that the parties intended to share equally the costs of the investment, which include both direct expenses and forgone income. *Id.*

65. *Id.* at 401.

66. *Id.* at 416.

67. *Id.* at 409–413.

68. *Id.* at 411.

69. *Id.* at 415–416.

70. Cynthia Starnes, "Divorce and the Displaced Homemaker: A Discourse on Playing with Dolls, Partnership Buyouts and Dissociation Under No-Fault," 60 *U. Chi. L. Rev.* 67 (1993).

71. *Id.* at 125.

72. *Id.* at 120.

73. *Id.*

74. *Id.*

75. *Id.* at 122.

76. *Id.* at 121.

77. *Id.* at 122.

78. *Id.* at 123.

79. *Id.* at 72.

80. *Id.* at 124.

81. *Id.* at 126.

82. *Id.*

83. *Id.* at 126–127.

84. *Id.* at 133.

85. *Id.* at 143.

86. *Id.* at 134–135.

87. *Id.* at 135.

88. *See id.* at 136 n. 309.

89. *Id.* at 138.

90. *See, e.g.,* Anonymous v. Anonymous, 19 Fam. L. Rep. 1564 (BNA) (N.Y. Sup. Ct., Sept. 24, 1993) (partnership interest in law firm); Elkus v. Elkus, 572 N.Y.S.2d 901 (N.Y. Sup. Ct. App. Div. 1991) ("career and/or celebrity status" of opera singer); O'Brien v. O'Brien, 489 N.E.2d 712 (N.Y. 1985) (medical license).

91. *See* Woodworth v. Woodworth, 337 N.W.2d 332 (Mich. Ct. App. 1983). For a contrary view from a different panel of the same court, see Postema v. Postema, 471 N.W.2d 912 (Mich. Ct. App. 1991) (law degree constitutes marital property, but supporting spouse entitled only to reimbursement of contributions). Other states that have considered the issue have overwhelmingly rejected the view that degrees or license should be classified as marital property. *See* cases cited in chapter 8, notes 108–109.

92. *See, e.g.,* Hollander v. Hollander, 18 Fam. L. Rep. 1029 (BNA) (Md. Ct. Spec. App. 1991) (dental practice); Piscopo v. Piscopo, 557 A.2d 1040 (N.J. Super. Ct. App. Div. 1989) (celebrity status of entertainer); Hurley v. Hurley, 615 P.2d 256 (N.M. 1980) (medical practice). While not all courts use the term consistently, "goodwill" generally is regarded as the returns to a business attributable to the reputation of the business, distinct from the value that reflects the efforts of the individuals within it. *See generally* Allen Parkman,

"The Treatment of Professional Goodwill in Divorce Proceedings," 28 *Fam. L.Q.* 213 (1984). Most states that have considered the issue have held that goodwill must be marketable in order to be classified as marital property.

93. *See, e.g.*, Lowery v. Lowery, 413 S.E.2d 731 (Ga. 1992); In re Marriage of Francis, 442 N.W.2d 59 (Iowa 1989).

94. *See* Parkman, *supra* note 48; Allen Parkman, "Recognition of Human Capital as Property in Divorce Settlements," 40 *Ark. L. Rev.* 439 (1987).

95. Parkman, *supra* note 48, at 132; Parkman, *supra* note 94, at 448. Parkman's proposed model property distribution statute reflects this assumption by providing that human capital acquired during marriage is the difference between anticipated earnings at divorce and at marriage, and that for a spouse who remains active in the paid labor force during marriage, the presumption is that the career pursued is the one anticipated at the time of marriage. *Id.* at 152.

96. "In the exceptional cases in which when the investment after the marriage is substantial, it is appropriate to treat the human capital as marital property." Parkman, *supra* note 94, at 448. *See also* Parkman, *supra* note 48, at 152.

97. Parkman, *supra* note 94, at 447.

98. Parkman, *supra* note 48, at 132.

99. *Id.*

100. *Id.* at 152.

101. *Id.* at 445.

102. Parkman, *supra* note 48, at 134–135.

103. "The level of reimbursement should be reduced as the duration of the marriage increases, since the non-student spouse would have received benefits over the years from the investment." Parkman, *supra* note 94, at 455. *See also* Parkman, *supra* note 48, at 134.

104. Parkman, *supra* note 48, at 134.

105. *Id.* at 456.

106. *Id.* at 457.

107. Ira Mark Ellman, "The Theory of Alimony," 77 *Calif. L. Rev.* 1 (1989). For commentary on Ellman, see June Carbone, "Economics, Feminism, and the Reinvention of Alimony: A Reply to Ira Ellman," 43 *Vand. L. Rev.* 1463 (1990); Carl E. Schneider, "Rethinking Alimony: Marital Decisions and Moral Discourse," 1991 *B.Y.U. L. Rev.* 197.

108. Ellman, *supra* note 107, at 46. *See also* Gary Becker, *A Treatise on the Family* 14–37 (1991 rev. ed.).

109. Ellman, *supra* note 107, at 44.

110. *Id.* at 42.

111. *Id.* at 65.

112. *Id.* at 47.

113. *Id.* at 51.

114. *Id.* at 54.

115. *Id.* at 58.

116. *Id.* at 60.

117. *Id.* at 60–61. He would make an exception when the decision to remain at home was made so that a wife could make significant contributions to her husband's business success. *Id.* at 63.

118. *Id.* at 67.

119. *Id.*

120. *Id.* at 60.

121. *Id.* at 72.

122. *Id.*

123. *See, e.g.*, Alaska (alimony and property division); California (alimony); Florida (alimony and property); Indiana (alimony); Minnesota (alimony); In re Marriage of Williams, 714 P.2d 548 (Mont. 1986) (alimony); New Jersey (alimony).

124. *See* Arizona (alimony); California (alimony); Florida (alimony and property division); Georgia (alimony); Illinois (alimony)(education); Minnesota (alimony); New York (alimony and property division); Ohio (alimony); Pennsylvania (alimony and property division); Vermont (property); Wisconsin (alimony and property division).

125. The American Law Institute, *Principles of the Law of Family Dissolution: Analysis and Recommendations, Proposed Final Draft* (February 14, 1997) 257–406. Compensatory spousal payments are intended to take the place of alimony or spousal maintenance. *Id.* at §5.02 comment a, p. 262.

126. The draft states: "Previous versions of the material contained in the Draft were tentatively approved by members of the American Law Institute at the 1995 and 1996 annual meetings. As of the date of publication, however, this Draft does not represent the final position of the Institute on any of the issues with which it deals." *Id.* at i. The chief reporter for the project is Ira Mark Ellman; the other reporters are Katharine T. Bartlett and Grace Ganz Blumberg.

127. *Id.* § 5.02(1).

128. *See* §§5.03(2)(a), 5.05.

129. §5.05, Comment a.

130. §§5.03(3)(d), 5.15. The award in this instance is calculated by adding the obligor's direct educational costs and share of living expenses during the period of education or training; subtracting from this sum: (1) the income of the obligor during that period, (2) the amount of any outstanding debt incurred during that period that is assigned to the obligor, and (3) expenditures made during that period from the obligor's separate property; and adjusting for inflation between the time the education was obtained and the divorce. *Id.* §5.15(4).

131. *Id.* §§5.03(2)(b), 5.06. A loss in earning capacity is presumed in such cases. *See* §5.06(2).

132. *Id.* §§5.03(2)(c), 5.12. A claimant in these cases "has the burden of persuading the fact finder that an earning capacity loss has been incurred, that it arose from such care, and that it has not been substantially restored by the time of dissolution." §5.12(2).

133. *Id.* §§5.03(3)(b), 5.16. A person seeking compensation under this provision must be ineligible for an award under sections providing compensation for a primary caretaker of children or a spouse in a long-term marriage. §5.16(1). "In the ordinary case an award under this section serves as transitional assistance to an obligee who can be expected to recover his or her former income." §5.16, comment c. The value of the award in most cases "should be for half the amount necessary to allow the obligee to recover his or her premarital living standard." §5.16(3).

134. The husband in *O'Brien*, *supra* note 7, for instance, was required to compensate his ex-wife for her share of the earnings made possible by the acquisition of his medical license by making 11 payments ultimately totaling $188,000, and to take out a life insurance policy on himself protecting his former wife from being deprived of the payments in case of his untimely death.

135. Krauskopf, *supra* note 55, at 386.

136. *See, e.g.*, UMDA, *supra* note 26, at §307, comment; Starnes, *supra* note 70.

137. This implicit conceptualization owes much to the application of social exchange theory to marriage. This approach characterizes spouses as engaged in a continuous, although not necessarily conscious, exchange of a variety of tangible and intangible resources. When an unfavorable balance of exchange occurs, spouses either renegotiate the terms of

their relationship or leave it for an alternative that offers a more favorable cost-benefit ratio. *See generally Family Relationships: Rewards and Costs* (Ivan Nye ed. 1982); *Social Exchange in Developing Relationships* (Robert L. Burgess & Ted L. Huston eds. 1979).

138. *See* Ellman, *supra* note 107, at 75; ALI Proposed Final Draft, *supra* note 125, at §5.15 and comment a.

139. This is not to say that *all* inequalities of exchange during marriage are compensable. Difficulties in determining how to allocate the costs and benefits of many marital expenditures, for instance, lead the ALI Draft to clarify that compensatory spousal payments "are not meant to provide compensation for inequities in the spousal give and take during marriage." ALI Proposed Final Draft, *supra* note 125, at 5.02, comment c. The point rather is that the requirement for making *any* financial claim at divorce based on human capital theory is that the claimant must identify some instance in which there has been an unequal exchange during marriage.

140. Ellman, *supra* note 107, at 52.

141. ALI Proposed Final Draft, *supra* note 125, at §5.02, comment a.

142. *Id.* at 262.


## Eight

1. *See* Thomas C. Grey, *The Disintegration of Property*, in 23 *Nomos: Property* 69 (J. Roland Pennock & John W. Chapman eds. 1980).

2. Alexis de Tocqueville, *Democracy in American* 638–639 (George Lawrence tr. & J.P. Mayer ed. 1969).

3. Herbert McCloskey & John Zaller, *The American Ethos: Public Attitudes Toward Capitalism and Democracy* 143 (1984). *See generally* William B. Scott, *In Pursuit of Happiness: American Conceptions of Property from the Seventeenth to the Twentieth Century* 1–49 (1977).

4. Jennifer Nedelsky, *Private Property and the Limits of Constitutionalism* 248 (1990). As Mary Ann Glendon suggests, "In America, when we want to protect something, we try to get it characterized as a right. To a great extent, it is still the case that, when we *specially* want to hold on to something (welfare benefits, a job) we try to get the object of our concern characterized as a property right." Mary Ann Glendon, *Rights Talk: The Impoverishment of Political Discourse* 31 (1991) (emphasis in original).

5. *Id.* at 224.

6. *See* David Schultz, "Political Theory and Legal History: Conflicting Depictions of Property in the American Founding," 37 *Am. J. Legal Hist.* 464 (1993).

7. William Blackstone, II *Commentaries On The Laws Of England* *2 (1979).

8. *See* Grey, *supra* note 1, at 69. *See also* Glendon, *supra* note 4, at 22–25.

9. Joseph William Singer, *The Reliance Interest in Property*, 40 *Stan. L. Rev.* 611, 634 (1988). *See also* "The Dead Hand and the Law of Trusts in the Nineteenth Century," 37 *Stan. L. Rev.* 1189 (1985); Charles Donahue, Jr., "The Future of the Concept of Property Predicted from Its Past," in 22 *Nomos: Property* 28 (1980).

10. Singer, *supra* note 9, at 634–635. *See also* Duncan Kennedy, "Form and Substance in Private Law Adjudication," 89 *Harv. L. Rev.* 1685, 1728–1731 (1976); William Simon, "Rights and Redistribution in the Welfare State," 38 *Stan. L. Rev.* 1433 (1986).

11. Singer, *supra* note 9, at 636. As the Supreme Court recently declared: "Individual freedom finds tangible expression in property rights." United States v. Good, 510 U.S. 43, 61 (1993).

Singer, *supra* note 9, at 637.

13. *See also* Mary Ann Glendon, *Rights Talk, supra* note 4, at 24.

14. *See* Nedelsky, *supra* note 4.

15. *Id.* at 6.

16. *Id.* at 2. *See also* Frank Michelman, "Possession vs. Distribution in the Constitutional Idea of Property" 72 *Iowa L. Rev.* 1319, 1321 (1987).

17. Nedelsky, *supra* note 4, at 229.

18. *Id.* at 3. For one such critique of the notion of natural entitlements, see Cass Sunstein, "Neutrality in Constitutional Law (With Special Reference to Pornography, Abortion, and Surrogacy)," 92 *Colum. L. Rev.* 1 (1992).

19. Nedelsky, *supra* note 4, at 259.

20. *Id.*

21. Jennifer Nedelsky, "Law, Boundaries, and the Bounded Self," in *Law and the Order of Culture* 162, 181 (Robert Post ed. 1991). *See also* Laura Underkuffler, "On Property: An Essay," 100 Yale L.J. 127, 147 (1990).

22. Nedelsky, *supra* note 21, at 171–172.

23. Dorothy Corkville Briggs, *Your Child's Self-Esteem* 129 (1974).

24. Nedelsky, *Law, Boundaries, and the Bounded Self, supra* note 21, at 171.

25. Underkuffler, *supra* note 21, at 147.

26. Nancy Hirschmann, *Rethinking Obligation: A Feminist Method for Political Theory* (1992).

27. *Id.* at 237.

28. *Id.* at 5.

29. *Id.* at 233–234.

30. John Locke, *Two Treatises of Government* 347–348 (Peter Laslett ed. 1965).

31. Hirschmann, *supra* note 26, at 48.

32. Thus, hypothetical consent, implied consent, and the acceptance of benefits have all been advanced as refinements on the model of voluntarily assumed obligation. *Id.* at 8.

33. *Id.* at 235. *See also* Robert Goodin, *Protecting the Vulnerable* (1987).

34. Hirschmann, *supra* note 26, at 23.

35. *Id.* at 124.

36. *Id.* at 59.

37. *Id.*

38. On the centrality of the public-private dichotomy to liberal theory, see also Carole Pateman, "Feminist Critiques of the Public/Private Dichotomy," in *Feminism and Equality* 102 (Anne Phillips ed. 1987).

39. Jennifer Nedelsky, "Reconceiving Autonomy: Sources, Thoughts, and Possibilities," 1 *Yale J. Law & Fem.* 7 (1989).

40. *See also* Hirschmann, *supra* note 26, at 8.

41. Nedelsky, *supra* note 39, at 11.

42. *Id.*

43. *Id.* at 12.

44. *Id.* at 21.

45. *Id.* at 30.

46. Hirschmann, *supra* note 26, at 237.

47. *Id.* at 241.

48. *Id.* at 22.

49. *Id.* at 9.

50. *See* Martha Fineman, *The Illusion of Equality: The Rhetoric and Reality of Divorce Reform* 39–52.

51. David Ellerman, "On the Labor Theory of Property," 16 *Phil. Forum* 293, 293 (1985).

52. Melville B. Nimmer, "The Right of Publicity," 19 *Law & Contemp. Prob.* 203 (1954). *See also* McFarland v. E & K Corp., 18 USPQ 2d (BNA) 1246, 1247 (D. Minn. 1981), Palmer v. Schonhorn Enterprises, Inc., 232 A.2d 458, 462 (N.J. Super. 1967).

53. McCloskey & Zaller, *supra* note 3, at 226.

54. Among "liberals," the respective percentages were 68 percent and 4 percent; among

"conservatives," 82 percent and 2 percent; and among "strong conservatives," 88 percent and 0 percent. *Id.*

55. Locke, *supra* note 30, at Chapter V, section 27 (emphasis in original).

56. *Id.* (emphasis in original).

57. *Id.* at section 40 (emphasis in original).

58. *See supra* notes 30–38 and accompanying text. *See also* Jean Bethke Elshtain, *Public Man, Private Woman: Women in Social and Political Thought* 116–127 (1993 2d ed.).

59. *See* Locke, *supra* note 30, at 209–210.

60. "Government has no other end but the preservation of Property." *Id.* at 347.

61. Catherine Valcke, "Locke on Property: A Deontological Interpretation," 12 *Harv. J. Law & Pub. Pol.* 941, 949 (1989).

62. *See* Walton H. Hamilton, "Property—According to Locke," 41 *Yale L.J.* 864 (1932).

63. *See, e.g.,* "Restatement of Restitution" section 58 (1937); In re Estate of Talty, 5 N.W.2d 584 (Iowa 1942); Harold C. Havinghurst, "Services in the Home—A Study of Contractual Concepts in Domestic Relations," 41 *Yale L.J.* 386, 402 (1932).

*See generally* Ann Laquer Estin, "Maintenance, Alimony, and the Rehabilitation of Family Care," 71 *N.C. L. Rev.* 721, 762–767 (1993).

64. *See* Simon, *Rights and Redistribution, supra* note 10, at 1431.

65. *See id.* at 1466. Thus, for instance, the drafter of the Social Security Act distinguished between benefits payable on the basis of earnings and on the basis of need, and explicitly referred in the statute to the former but not the latter as entitlements. *Id.* at 1451.

66. *Id.* at 1458 (footnote omitted).

67. Simon notes that benefits for women based on the earnings of their spouses are inadequate for women with children who do not marry, who are not married for the ten years necessary to qualify for divorced spouse benefits, or who become disabled before the age when they can qualify for disabled spouse benefits, which is age 50. *Id.* at 1482–1483.

68. *Id.* at 1483.

69. In 1987, more than half of child care workers earned less than $5.00 per hour. *Who Cares for America's Children: Child Care Policy for the 1990's* 158 (Cheryl D. Hayes, John L. Palmer, & Martha J. Zaslow eds. 1990). "Low pay, lack of benefits, and stressful working conditions are the major reasons child care providers leave their jobs in such high numbers." *Id.* at 159. *See also* Alfred J. Kahn & Sheila B. Kammerman, *Child Care: Facing the Hard Choices* 222 (1987). Some 96 percent of child care workers are women. U.S. Dept. of Labor, *Labor Force, Employment, and Earnings* 394 (1993).

70. Bureau of Labor Statistics, Table 3: "Median Usual Weekly Earnings of Full-Time Wage and Salary Workers by Occupation and Sex, Quarterly Averages, Not Seasonally Adjusted," July 22, 1997.

71. *See, e.g.,* Paula England, *Comparable Worth: Theories and Evidence* 164 (1992); Jerry A. Steinberg & Ronnie J. Steinberg, "Compensating Differentials and the Male-Female Wage Gap: Evidence from the New York State Comparable Worth Study," 69 *Soc. Forces* 439 (1990); Ronnie Steinberg, "Social Construction of Skill: Gender, Power, and Comparable Worth," 17 *Work & Occupations* 449 (1990). Jobs requiring "nurturant" skills are described as those in which an employee provides a service to an individual or a small group with whom the worker has a face-to-face relationship. England, at 136. Some of the occupations in which nurturant skills are required to some degree include nurses, various types of therapists, teachers, counselors, social workers, librarians, cashiers, sales clerks, waiters and waitresses, dental assistants, and health aides. *Id.* at 138.

72. "It is important to realize that this penalty does not result from nurturant jobs requiring less cognitive skill, being concentrated in lower-paying industries, or having other nonpecuniary amenities, since these variables are included in the models and thus are held

constant in assessing this effect. Nor does it result from a wage penalty for female jobs since the sex composition of jobs is also controlled as this effect is assessed." England, *supra* note 71, at 164.

73. *Id.*

74. *Id.* at 40.

75. *Id.* at 117.

76. Simon, *supra* note 10, at 1434.

77. *Id.* at 1466.

78. *See id.* at 1477. On the general limitations of reliance on private law analogies, see *id.* at 1504–1516.

79. Jennifer Hochschild, *What's Fair? American Beliefs about Distributive Justice* (1981).

80. "[T]hese domains are organizing devices for groups of issues, not conceptually distinct units of analysis." *Id.* at 82.

81. *Id.* at 81.

82. *Id.*

83. *Id.*

84. *Id.*

85. *Id.* at 106.

86. *Id.* at 107.

87. *Id.*

88. *Id.* at 52.

89. *Id.*

90. *Id.*

91. *Id.*

92. *Id.* at 111.

93. *Id.* at 52.

94. *Id.* at 141.

95. *Id.* at 52, 142.

96. *Id.* at 65.

97. *Id.* at 65 (footnote omitted).

98. *Id.* at 148.

99. *Id.* at 186.

100. *Id.*

101. *Id.* at 183.

102. Nedelsky, *supra* note 4, at 205.

103. *Id.* at 208.

104. *Id.* at 209. Nedelsky distinguishes her argument from the claim of historians such as Charles Beard that the Constitution was designed to protect propertied interests. "That claim is crudely true," she says, "but it misses what is most important about property in the formation of the Constitution. the distortion of the problems and potential of republican government. My emphasis is not on economic interest, but on the structure of ideas and institutions." *Id.* at 2 (footnote omitted). The distortion, she maintains, occurred because the framers' conception of the dilemma of democracy had inequality built into it: "The problem of protecting the rights of the propertied few against the demands of the many is not the same as protecting individuals from the ever-present possibility of collective oppression." *Id.* at 208.

105. *Id.* at 245.

106. Need is still in most statutes as one of several factors to consider in property and maintenance decisions. There is now a strong presumption against maintenance, however, the award traditionally most closely associated with need. Furthermore, as Martha Fineman

has suggested and Suzanne Reynolds has documented, factors relating to contribution now are given far more prominence than need in financial determinations. *See* Fineman, *supra* note 50, at 40–43, 49–51; Suzanne Reynolds, "Relationship of Property Division and Alimony: The Division of Property to Address Need," 56 *Fordham L. Rev.* 827 (1988).

107. *See* Elkus v. Elkus, 572 N.Y.S.2d 901 (N.Y. Sup. Ct. App. Div. 1991); Hodge v. Hodge, 486 A.2d 951, 951 (Pa. Super. 1984).

108. *See, e.g.* In re Marriage of Olar, 747 P.2d 676 (Colo. 1987) (en banc); In re Marriage of Sullivan, 184 Cal. Rptr. 796 (1982); Lowery v. Lowery, 413 S.E.2d 731 (Ga. 1992); Goldstein v. Goldstein, 423 N.E.2d 1201 (Ill. App. 1981); Drapek v. Drapek, 503 N.E.2d 946 (Mass. 1987).

The only state high court that has accepted the argument that enhanced earning capacity is marital property is New York. *See* Elkus V. Elkus, *supra* note 107.

109. *See, e.g.,* In re Marriage of Wisner, 631 P.2d 115 (Ariz. App. 1981); Nelson v. Nelson, 736 P.2d 1145 (Alk. 1987); In re Marriage of Olar, 747 P.2d 676 (Colo. 1987); Lowery v. Lowery, 413 S.E.2d 731 (Ga. 1992); Drapek v. Drapek, 503 N.E.2d 946 (Mass. 1987).

110. Graham v. Graham, 574 P.2d at 77.

111. *Id.*

112. In re Marriage of Olar, 747 P.2d at 679–80. *See also* Hughes v. Hughes, 438 So.2d 146 (Fla. Dist. Ct. pp. 1983); Lowery v. Lowery, 413 S.E.2d 731 (Ga. 1992); Hoak v. Hoak, 370 S.E.2d 473 (W.Va. 1988).

113. Hoak v. Hoak, 370 S.E.2d at 476.

114. Archer v. Archer, 493 A.2d 1074, 1080 (Md. App. 1985).

115. Nedelsky, *supra* note 4, at 254.

116. *Id.* at 253.

117. *Id.* at 253 and note 148.

118. *Id.* at 253. *See also* Margaret Jane Radin, "Property and Personhood," 34 *Stan. L. Rev.* 957, 960–961 (1982).

119. *See, e.g.,* UMDA, *supra* note 26, at 316.

120. *See, e.g.,* Drapek v. Drapek, 503 N.E.2d 946 (Mass. 1987); Wehrkamp v. Wehrkamp, 357 N.W.2d 264 (S.D. 1984); Hoak v. Hoak, 370 S.E.2d 473 (W.VA. 1988).

121. Moffit v. Moffit, 749 P.2d 343, 347 (Alk. 1988); Hoak v. Hoak, 370 S.E.2d at 477 n. 4; Wehrkamp v. Wehrkamp, 357 N.W.2d at 266. *See also* George Norton, "The Future of Alimony: A Proposal for Guidelines," in *Alimony: New Strategies for Pursuit and Defense* 176, 182 (A.B.A. Sec. Fam. L. 1988).

122. In re Marriage of Sullivan, 184 Cal. Rptr. At 802 (Kaufman, Acting P.J., concurring).

123. *See, e.g.,* discussions of such statutes in St. Pierre v. St. Pierre, 357 N.W.2d 250 (S.D. 1984); Holbrook v. Holbrook, 309 N.W.2d 343 (Wis. 1981).

124. J. Thomas Oldham, *Divorce, Separation, and the Distribution of Property* §9–13 (1987).

125. *Id.*

126. *See* Harriet N. Cohen & Patrician Hennessey, "Valuation of Property in Marital Dissolutions," 23 *Fam. L.Q.* 339, 344 (1989); Nelson v. Nelson, 736 P.2d 1145 (Alk. 1987).

127. Hanson v. Hanson, 738 S.W.2d 429, 434 (Mo. 1984) (en banc).

128. *See, e.g.,* Wilson v. Wilson, 741 S.W.2d 640 (Ark. 1987); Prahinski v. Prahinski, 540 A.2d 833 (Md. App. 1988); Taylor v. Taylor, 386 N.W.2d 851 (Neb. 1986).

129. *See, e.g.,* Taylor v. Taylor, *supra* note 128; Prahinski v. Prahinski, *supra* note 128; Thompson v. Thompson, 576 So.2d 267 (Fla. 1991).

130. *See, e.g.,* Mocnik v. Mocnik, 838 P.2d 500 (Okl. 1992).

131. Moffitt v. Moffitt, 749 P.2d 343, 347 n. 3 (Alk. 1988).

132. *See* In re Marriage of Bookout, 833 P.2d 800 (Colo. App. 1991).

133. *Id.* at 804–805.

134. *See, e.g.,* In re Marriage of Graham, 574 P.2d 75 (Colo. 1978); Lowery v. Lowery, 413 S.E.2d 731 (Ga. 1992); Archer v. Archer, 493 A.2d 1074 (Md. App. 1985).

135. *See* UMDA, *supra* note 26, at §316 and comment.

136. *See, e.g.,* Commonwealth ex rel. Kaplan v. Kaplan, 344 A.2d 578 (Pa. Super. 1975).

137. *See* Allen Parkman, "Recognition of Human Capital as Property in Divorce Settlements," 40 Ark. L. Rev. 439 443–53 (1987).

138. *Id.* at 448.

139. *Id.* at 444.

140. *Id.* at 445.

141. *Id.* at 448.

142. *Id.*

143. *Id.* at 445.

144. Allen Parkman, *No-Fault Divorce: What Went Wrong?* (1992).

145. *Id.* at 444.

146. *Id.*

147. Parkman would include in those expenses any diminution in human capital suffered by the supporting spouse as a result of her support.

148. This may be because a man sees his role as primary breadwinner or because he sees his personal autonomy as linked to career advancement. *See* Kathleen Gerson, *No Man's Land: Men's Changing Commitments to Family and Work,* Table 14, at 327 (1993).

149. *See, e.g.,* Arlie Hochschild with Anne Machung, *Second Shift: Working Parents and the Revolution at Home* (1989); Julie A. Heath & David H. Ciscel, "Patriarchy, Family Structure, and the Exploitation of Women's Labor," 22 *J. Econ. Iss.* 781 (1988).

150. *See, e.g.,* Rosanna Hertz, *More Equal than Others: Women and Men in Dual-Career Marriages* 131–146 (1986); Steven L. Nock & Paul W. Kingston, "Time with Children: The Impact of Couples' Work-Time Commitments," 67 *Soc. Forces* 59 (1988).

151. For a review of research that concludes that there is no evidence that being married is a source of career enhancement for men, see Cohen & Haberfeld, "Why Do Married Men Earn More than Unmarried Men?" 20 *Soc. Sci. Res.* 29 (1991).

152. *See, e.g.,* Drapek v. Drapek, 503 N.E.2d 946 (Mass. 1987); DeLaRosa v. DeLaRosa, 309 N.W.2d 755 (Minn. 1981); Mahoney v. Mahoney, 453 A.2d 527 (N.J. 1982). As one court stated, financial and emotional support, as well as homemaking services are important, but they "bear no logical relation to the value of the resulting degree." Hoak v. Hoak, 370 S.E.2d 473 (W.Va. 1988).

153. Postema v. Postema, 471 N.W.2d 912 (Mich. App. 1991).

154. *See* J. Crane & Alan Bromberg, *Law of Partnership* 489 (1968).

155. Uniform Partnership Act 18(a), 18(f), 6 U.L.A. 213.

156. *See* Crane & Bromberg, *supra* note 154, at 375–376. *See, e.g.,* Conna v. Conna, 468 N.Y.S.2d 482, 489–90 (App. Div. 1983).

157. "Partnership law does not look forward to the effects of the commercial partnership on the business partners' relative earning capacities." Krauskopf, *Theories, supra* note 27, at 263.

158. Ira Mark Ellman, "The Theory of Alimony," 77 *Calif L. Rev.* 1 (1989).

159. *Id.* at 36–40.

160. Crane & Bromberg, *supra* note 154, at 422.

161. Ellman, *supra* note 158, at 39.

162. Starnes, *supra* note 70, at 124.

163. *Id.* at 125.

164. *Id.* at 124.

165. Ellman, *supra* note 158, at 78. *See also* John Eekelaar & Mavis Maclean, *Maintenance after Divorce* 146 (1986); Starnes, *supra* note 70, at 130 n. 290.

166. 469 A.2d 803 (Del. Fam. Ct. 1983).

167. In addition to the home, whose net value was about $28,000, the wife received some $57,000 in other property as part of an equal division of assets. *Id.* at 810.

168. *Id.* at 805.

169. 441 N.W.2d 66 (Mich. Ct. App. 1989).

170. *Id.* at 70.

171. *Id.*

172. *Id.* at 73.

173. *Id.* at 68.

174. *Id.* at 72.

175. *See also* Wehrkamp v. Wehrkamp, *supra* note 120; Taylor v. Taylor, 386 N.W.2d at 851, 869.

176. Parkman, *supra* note 144, at 141.

177. *Id.*

178. *Id.* at 142.

179. 452 A.2d 951 (Del. 1982).

180. *Id.* at 953.

181. Mary E. O'Connell, "Alimony After No-Fault: A Practice in Search of a Theory," 23 New Eng. L. Rev. 437, 506 (1988).

182. *Id.* at 499.

183. *See id.* at 501–503. Furthermore, suggests O'Connell, the theory typically is incapable of "capturing the subtler effects of the adoption of a feminine lifestyle," such as choosing a career with an eye to the possibility of interrupted or reduced employment during her childrearing years. *Id.* at 503.

184. Cal. Civ. Code §4800.3 (West Supp. 1987).

185. Nelson v. Nelson, 736 P.2d 1145 (Alk. 1987). *See also* In re Marriage of Wisner, 631 P.2d 115 (Ariz. Ct. App. 1981); Wilson v. Wilson, 741 S.W.2d 640 (Ark. 1987); Wright v. Wright, 469 A.2d 803 (Del. Fam. Ct. 1983). *See also* Oldham, *supra* note 124, at §9–26.

186. Parkman, *supra* note 137, at 455.

187. *Id.* at 457.

188. Parkman, *supra* note 144, at 132.

189. 453 A.2d 527 (N.J. 1982).

190. *Id.* at 533.

191. 631 P.2d 115 (Ariz. Ct. App. 1981).

192. *Id.* at 123. *See also* In re Marriage of Sullivan, 184 Cal. Rptr. 796, 802 (Cal. Ct. App. 1982) (Kaufman, J., concurring); Bold v. Bold, 574 A.2d 552, 558 (Pa. 1990) (J., dissenting).

193. *See, e.g.,* In re Marriage of Pyeatte, 661 P.2d 196, 203 (Ariz. Ct. App. 1982); Bold v. Bold, 574 A.2d 552, 556 (Pa. 1990).

194. While a majority of both men and women in one survey, for instance, indicated that a wife should be compensated for financial support of her husband's professional education, only 19 percent of women and 25 percent of men believed that a woman should receive alimony for her years of work as a homemaker or mother. Weitzman, *supra* note 21, at 151–153. The ALI Proposed Final Draft, for instance, provides for reimbursement only of "financial contributions" to a spouse's education or training in Section 5.15.

195. For articulations of this point, see Mary Ann Glendon, *The New Family and the New Property* 65–66 (1981); Martha Fineman, "Societal Factors Affecting the Creation of Legal Rules for Distribution of Property at Divorce," 23 Fam. L.Q. 279, 299 (1989).

196. *See* Fineman, *supra* note 50, at 52.

197. Ira Ellman does purport formally to reject a partnership model as the appropriate analogy for divorce law, for the sake of an approach that characterizes marriage as a distinctive relationship in which we should encourage sharing. *See* Ellman, *supra* note 158,

at 33–40, 50–51. As Carl Schneider has pointed out, however, Ellman's theory "rewards only investments of a 'self-interested' bargainer, explicitly excluding other forms of sharing." Carl Schneider, "Rethinking Alimony: Marital Decisions and Marital Discourse," *1991 B.Y.U. L. Rev.* 197, 242. Ellman thus does the opposite of what most reformers do: he professes to adopt a model based on the uniqueness of marriage while implicitly advancing one that is premised on economic partnership principles.

198. *See, e.g.,* Francesca Cancian, *Love in America* (1987), Theodore Caplow, H. Bahr, B. Chadwick, R. Hill & M. Williamson, *Middletown Families* 128 (1983); Joseph Veroff, Elizabeth Douvan, & Ronald Kulka, *The Inner American* 168 (1981).

199. Peter Berger & Hansfried Kellner, "Marriage and the Construction of Reality," 46 *Diogenes* 1, 1 (1964).

200. *See generally* Susan Krauss Whitbourne & Joyce B. Ebmyer, *Identity and Intimacy in Marriage* (1990).

201. *See* Marjorie E. Kornhauser, *Love, Money, and the IRS: Family, Income Sharing, and the Joint Income Tax Return* 45 Hastings L.J. 63 (1993), Beatrice Rogers, "The Internal Dynamics of Households: A Critical Factor in Development Policy," in *Intra-Household Resource Allocation: Issues and Methods for Development Policy and Planning* 1 (Beatrice Rogers & Nina Schlossman eds. 1990).

202. *See* Philip Blumstein & Pepper Schwartz, *American Couples* 53–56 (1983); Susan Moller Okin, *Justice, Gender, and the Family* 158 (1989).

203. Blumstein & Schwartz, *supra* note 202, at 96.

204. *Id.*

205. *Id.* at 95.

206. Deborah L. Rhode & Martha Minow, "Reforming the Questions, Questioning the Reforms: Feminist Perspectives on Divorce Law," in *Divorce Reform at the Crossroads*, 191, 193 (Stephen D. Sugarman & Herma Hill Kay eds. 1990), *See also* Glendon, *supra* note 195, at 65; Susan W. Prager, "Sharing Principles and the Future of Marital Property Law," 25 *UCLA L. Rev.* 1, 6 (1977).

207. *See* Elizabeth Scott, "Rational Decisionmaking About Marriage and Divorce," 76 *Va. L. Rev.* 9, 22–25 (1990).

208. Lynn A. Baker & Robert E. Emery, "When Every Relationship is Above Average: Perceptions and Expectations of Divorce at the Time of Marriage," 17 *Law & Human Beh.* 439, 443 (1993).

209. *Id.*

210. *Id.* at 446.

211. *See* O'Connell, *supra* note 181, at 501, 503; Schneider, *supra* note 197.

212. Emily Hancock, "The Dimensions of Meaning and Belonging in the Process of Divorce," 50 *Amer. J. Orthopsychiat.* 18, 19 (1980). *See also* Carole Riessman, *Divorce Talk* (1990).

213. On the frequent neglect of such issues with regard to the family, see Okin, *supra* note 202.

214. In this respect, my proposal differs from the income sharing model of Jane Rutheford. *See* Jane Rutheford, "Duty in Divorce: Shared Income as a Path to Equality," 58 *Ford. L. Rev.* 539, 577–592 (1990).

215. The Uniform Probate Code, for instance, uses the duration of marriage as a factor in determining a surviving spouse's share of the decedent's estate. *See* John Langbein & Lawrence W. Waggoner, "Redesigning the Spouse's Forced Share," 22 *Real Prop. Probate & Tr. J.* 303 (1987).

216. *See* Jana B. Singer, *Divorce Reform and Gender Justice*, 67 N.C. L. Rev. 1103, 1117–1118 (1989).

217. *See* Singer, *Divorce Reform, supra* note 216, at 1119. This predictability would provide clearer guidance for spouses negotiating over the consequences of divorce. *See* Robert

Mnookin & Lewis Kornhauser, "Bargaining in the Shadow of the Law: The Case of Divorce," 88 *Yale L.J.* 950 (1979).

218. *See* Garrison, *Good Intentions, supra* note 46, at 738.

219. A spouse in a brief marriage, for example, might have made sacrifices that would be significantly undercompensated by an equalization approach based on the length of the marriage. This provision would bear some resemblance to Section 5.16 of the ALI Proposed Final Draft. That section permits an award in childless marriages of brief duration in which one spouse's contributions or sacrifice of educational or occupational opportunities for the sake of the marriage creates a disparity in the spouses' ability after divorce to regain a premarital standard of living.

220. *See, e.g.,* Garrison, *Good Intentions, supra* note 46, at 738; Sally Goldfarb, "Marital Partnership and the Case for Permanent Alimony," in *Alimony, supra* note 121, at 51; Norton, *supra* note 121, at 183–184; Singer, *Divorce Reform, supra* note 216, at 1117–1118; Smith, *supra* note 29, at 742. Stephen Sugarman has described as a "fair notice" theory the approach that most resembles the one that I describe here. *See* Stephen D. Sugarman, "Dividing Financial Interests on Divorce," in *Divorce Reform, supra* note 206, at 160–163.

221. *See, e.g.,* Woodworth v. Woodworth, 337 N.W.2d 332 (Mich. App. 1983); Grove v. Grove, 571 P.2d 477 (Ore. 1977); Weir v. Weir, 374 N.W.2d 858 (N.D. 1985).

222. ALI Proposed Final Draft No. 2, §5.05.

223. *Id.* §5.05(3). The draft does not itself establish the length of a marriage, the disparity in income that would qualify for such treatment, or the percentages that would be applied to the difference in income. Its illustration of one possibility in comment a to §5.05 uses five years or more as the length of a marriage that would be eligible for compensation under this section, a disparity of 25 percent, and a percentage of .01 for each year of marriage, not to exceed .4. Thus, the maximum that a spouse would receive in this example would be 40 percent of the difference in income after a 40-year marriage.

224. *Id.* at 321.

225. *Id.* at 320.

226. *Id.* at 325.

227. *Id.* at 327.

228. *Id.* at 328.

229. *Id.* at 325.

230. *Id.* at 358.

231. *Id.* at 364.

232. *Id.*

233. *Id.* at 365.

234. *Id.* at 367.

235. *Id.* §5.05, comment c.

236. C.B. Macpherson, "Human Rights and Property Rights," 24 *Dissent* 72, 77 (1977). *See also* Margaret Jane Radin, "Lacking a Transformative Social Theory: A Response," 45 *Stan. L. Rev.* 409, 417 (1993).

237. On the latter point, see June Carbone, "Economics, Feminism, and the Reinvention of Alimony: A Reply to Ira Ellman," 43 *Vand. L. Rev.* 1463 (1990).

238. On the striking variations in valuation, see Oldham, *supra* note 124, at 9–9; Louise B. Raggio, "Don't Men Have Rights Too?—Or, Lifetime Alimony, an Idea Whose Time Has Come and Gone," in *Alimony, supra* note 121, at 33, 39. In one New York case, for instance, the wife's expert valued her law degree at $194,200, while her husband's expert valued it at $583,700. Holihan v. Holihan, *N.Y. Law J.,* January 1, 1987.

239. Milton C. Regan, Jr., *Family Law and the Pursuit of Intimacy* 140–143 (1993).

240. See Okin, *supra* note 202, at 137 (emphasis omitted); Amy Wax, *Bargaining in the Shadow of the Market, supra* note 31.

241. Okin, *supra* note 202, at 147; *see* also Joshua Cohen, "Okin on Justice, Gender and Family," 22 *Can. J. Phil.* 263, 282–285 (1992).

242. *See* Vicki Schultz, "Telling Stories About Women and Work: Judicial Interpretations of Sex Segregation in the Workplace in Title VII Cases Raising the Lack of Interest Argument," 103 *Harv. L. Rev.* 1749 (1990).

243. This was of course a major point of controversy in Equal Employment Opportunities Commission (EEOC) v. Sears, Roebuck & Co., 628 F. Supp. 1264 (N.D. Ill.), *aff'd*, 839 F. 2d 302 (7th Cir. 1988), in which Sears successfully defended underrepresentation of women in its commission sales force by contending that women preferred noncommission jobs because they are less competitive, more flexible, and afford more opportunities for social contact and friendships. *Id.* at 1308.

244. See Robin L. West, *Caring for Justice* (1997); Marilyn Friedman, *What Are Friends For? Feminist Perspectives on Personal Relationships and Moral Theory* 126–134 (1993).

245. On the dangers of rejecting rights discourse for more informal approaches, particularly for those who historically have been disadvantaged, see Patricia J. Williams, *The Alchemy of Race and Rights* 146–165 (1991).

246. Martha Minow, *Making All the Difference: Inclusion, Exclusion, and American Law* 307–308 (1990).


## Conclusion

1. On practical reasoning, see Steven Salkever, *Finding the Mean* (1990).

2. The controversial nature of such measures is reflected, for instance, in the debate over policies regarding consensual sexual activity by members of the armed forces.

3. See, e.g., Jersey Shore Medical Center v. Estate of Baum, 417 A.2d 1003 (N.J. 1980).

4. This is an approach that formerly was taken by Connecticut, see Conn. Gen. Stat. § 46.10 (1977), but since has been repealed, see Conn. Gen. Stat. § 466–37 (1977).

5. See, e.g., John F. Kennedy Hospital v. Bludworth, 452 So. 2d 921 (Fla. 1984).

6. See, e.g., the statute upheld in Cruzan v. Director, Missouri Dept. of Health, 497 U.S. 261 (1990).

7. The Act is at U.S.C. §§ 1901–1963 (West 1983 & 1997 supp.). For an excellent analysis of the Act's efforts to mediate between individual and communal concepts of identity, see Mary L. Shanley, "Unencumbered Individuals and Embedded Selves: Dichotomous Thinking in Family Law," in *Debating Democracy's Discontent: Essays on American Politics, Law, and Public Philosophy* (Anita L. Allen & Milton C. Regan, Jr., eds. 1998).

8. Mississippi Band of Choctaw Indians v. Holyfield, 490 U.S. 30 (1989).

9. 25 U.S.C. § 1915. The Act does provide that a court may consider as one factor parental preference. *Id.* § 1915(c).

10. Michael J. Sandel, *Democracy's Discontent* 350 (1996).

11. One good example of an analysis that is sensitive to such questions is Jeff Spinner, *The Boundaries of Citizenship* (1994).

# Index

Cover, Robert, 95
coverture, doctrine of, 8
Crafton, Steven, 45
criminal trial. *See also* adverse testimony
    privilege; narratives of marriage
    potential witness and, 122–26
    as setting for narrative of marriage, 106,
      117–22
    state concerns and, 126–128
culture. *See also* American culture
    self-concept and, 69–70
    symbolic significance of privilege law
      and, 90, 93–95, 113
current legal outcomes
    compensation for expected gain and,
      176–81
    enhanced earning power as property
      and, 176–78
    reflection of property rhetoric in, 175–
      87
    reimbursement of contributions and,
      181–87
    return on investment and, 178–81

Dan-Cohen, Meir, 114, 115, 116
Dawes, Robyn M., 64–66, 230
death penalty, 126
Denny, Reginald, 118
Descartes, René, 16
de Tocqueville, A., 162
"disclosure reciprocity," 100–101
distance motif, 20, 28–29, 49–50
divorce. *See also* fault-based divorce; no-
    fault divorce
    asymmetry of risk from, 60
    evolution in models of obligation and,
      142–48
    experience of, 189–91
    mutual consent divorce and, 42, 46, 54–
      55, 226
    Pareto efficiency criterion and, 54–57
    probability of, and economic approach,
      43, 44
    promotion of external stance and, 144–
      48
    promotion of internal stance and, 142–
      44
    rational choice theory and, 39–40, 42
divorce awards. *See also* alimony; post-
    divorce income; property rhetoric

compensation for expected gain and,
    149–53, 176–81
compensation for losses and, 153–57,
    172, 183–84, 192, 193–94
economic approach to, 42, 46–47, 144–
    48
economic inequality as norm and, 174–
    75
efficiency and, 55–56
enhanced earning power as property
    and, 176–78
equalization requirement and, 190–92
evolution from internal to external
    stances toward, 13–14, 141–48
expectation damages and, 56–58, 228
gender implications of, 13, 201
human capital theory and, 148–60
length of marriage and, 185–86, 191–92,
    196–97
reimbursement of contributions and,
    181–87
return on investment and, 178–81
traditional law of, 143–44
domestic labor. *See also* human capital
    theory
    divorce compensation for, 46, 146
    economic partnership model and, 146
    labor desert theory and, 169–72

economic approach. *See also* rational choice
    theory
    communicative exchange and, 21
    concept of efficiency and, 47–48, 52–59
    egoistic reward thesis and, 63–67, 73
    external stance toward marriage and, 47–
      48, 59, 85
    as framework in family law, 12–13, 33–
      34, 61
    individual as unit of analysis and, 48–50
    influence of, 34
    mental states and, 42–43
    no fault divorce reforms and, 13–14
    phenomenology of internal stance and,
      33–34
    prosocial behavior and, 62–77
    prosocial preference thesis and, 74–77
    risks in adoption of, 83
    role of theory and, 77–85
    theory of the family based on, 43–44
    tort liability and, 120–21

economic approach (*continued*)
    as unitary account, 33
    usefulness of, 33–34
economic domain, 173–74
educational support, and divorce
        compensation, 149–51, 154, 177–78
efficiency, concept of, 47–48, 52–59. *See also*
        Pareto efficiency criterion; rational
        choice theory
"efficient damage" theory, 55–56
egoistic reward thesis, 63–67, 73
Ellman, Ira, 155–56, 159, 181, 183, 266
Elster, Jon, 35, 84, 109–10, 119
"empathy-altruism" hypothesis, 64
England, Paula, 262
*Equal Employment Opportunities Commission
        (EEOC) v. Sears, Roebuck & Co.,* 269
equality, principle of, and property
        rhetoric, 172–75
equitable distribution statutes, 145–47
ethic of care
    ethic of justice and, 27–29, 141–42
    gender stereotypes and, 128–29
evidentiary rules, assumptions behind, 120–
        22. *See also* Uniform Rules of
        Evidence
Ewin, R. E., 107, 124
exchange relationships, 71–73
exchange theory, 21, 103
expectation damages, 56–58
external stance toward marriage, 5, 15–22.
        *See also* property rhetoric
    adverse testimony privilege and, 102–5,
        122–33, 134–35
    communications privilege and, 90, 96–
        102
    concept of efficiency and, 47–48, 52–59
    divorce awards and, 13–14, 144–60
    economic approach and, 20, 47–59, 59,
        85
    as incomplete, 22, 23–24
    moral concepts and, 11–12, 17
    private ordering and, 51–52
    process of rational choice and, 48–50
    spousal privilege law and, 96–105

fairness
    adverse testimony privilege and, 122–23,
        201
    hypothetical bargain model and, 227
    property rhetoric and, 173–74

"families of choice," 6
family law
    focus on marriage in, 6–11
    weighting of internal and external
        stances and, 30
fault-based divorce, 142–44, 195–96
federal law on spousal privilege, 4, 13, 89,
        90–91
feminist criticism
    association of marriage with patriarchy
        and, 7–8
    communications privilege and, 97
    complex emotions of women in
        relationship and, 130
    external stance toward marriage and,
        11
    relational approach to autonomy and,
        166–68
    spousal labor and, 146
    statutory rape law and, 121
Ferejohn, John, 80
Fineman, Martha, 145
Fisher, Amy, 118
Flanagan, Owen, 127
"free-market model," 163
"free-will" paradigm, 114, 115
Freud, S., 79
Friedman, Lawrence, 20
Friedman, Marilyn, 18, 25
Friedman, Milton, 77–78, 81, 238

Gambetta, Diego, 112
Garrison, Marsha, 256
Gauthier, David, 20, 41
Geertz, Clifford, 95
gender effects. *See also* women
    adverse testimony privilege and, 102–3,
        128–33, 201
    attributable to wage labor market, 196–
        97
    communications privilege and, 99
    as consideration in legal assessment, 200–
        201
    traditional divorce awards and, 143–44
Giddens, Anthony, 20–21
Gilligan, Carol, 18, 28
goodwill, 177–78
*Graham v. Graham,* 176
Gregory K., 118
group identity, 25. *See also* social identity
        theory; spousal identity

New Jersey, 3–4, 134
New York, 153
Nimmer, Melville, 169
no-fault divorce
  concept of marriage and, 144–48
  economic approach and, 54–57, 144–48
  economic partnership model and, 181–83
  external stance and, 13–14, 144–48
  fault in alimony determinations and, 45
  marriage contract and, 45–46, 58
"nomos," 188–90
"nonunit" schema, 6
normative considerations
  adverse testimony privilege and, 109–11, 119
  ascription of responsibility and, 115
  cost-benefit approach to relationships and, 72–73, 109-11
  economic sharing and, 189
  efficiency and, 47–48
  principle of equality and, 173–74
  private ordering and, 51
  property rights and, 169
Nussbaum, Martha, 29

O'Brien, Loretta, 140
O'Connell, Mary, 185
Okin, Susan Moller, 24, 196
opportunistic behavior
  expectation damages and, 56 57
  legal incentives for, 202
  rational choice theory, 39, 52
Orr v. Orr, 121
overcompensation problem, 55

Pareto efficiency criterion
  defined, 52–53
  divorce compensation and, 54–58
  drawbacks to use of, 53
  justification for use of, 53
  marriage and, 54
Parkman, Allen, 148, 153–55, 179–80, 185, 186
partnership model
  divorce and, 151–53
  economic vs. marital partnership models and, 190, 192
  marriage as economic partnership and, 144–48

reimbursement of contributions and, 181–83
patriarchy, and marriage, 7–8
Peters, H. Elizabeth, 46
Planned Parenthood of Central Missouri v. Danforth, 131
political domain, 173
Posner, Richard, 41, 42, 54, 225
post-divorce income
  arguments for spousal entitlement to, 147–48, 149–53, 171–72
  income equalization approach and, 190–93, 195–97
  property rhetoric and, 171, 176–78
Postema, Kathryn, 139–40
"postulate of adequacy," concept of, 80–81
"predictionism," 77–79
"principle of gradually merging responsibility," 192-93
private ordering, 51–52
property rhetoric. See also human capital theory
  alternative to, 188–95
  autonomy as independence model and, 162, 163–69
  as basis for divorce awards, 54, 141–42, 144–48
  concerns about deemphasis of, 194–97
  current legal outcomes and, 175–87
  economic inequality and, 162, 172–75
  human capital theory and, 157–60, 179–80, 181–87
  market labor desert theory and, 162, 169–72
  mythology of property, 162, 163–75
  need for more expansive discouse and, 187–88
  risks in reliance on, 142
prosocial behavior
  economic approaches to, 62–63
  egoistic reward thesis and, 63–67, 73
  prosocial preference thesis, 74–77
public broadcasting support, 64
public-private distinction
  labor desert theory and, 169–70
  social contract theory and, 17–18, 166
  state intrusion in marriage and, 201–2
"pure relationship"
  communications privilege and, 97, 98, 100–102
  economic approach and, 51–52

"pure relationship" (*continued*)
    reflexivity and, 20–22, 97, 100–102, 107–8
    trust and loyalty and, 107–8
Putnam, Hilary, 82–83

"radical externalism," 80
Radin, Margaret, 47
Rapaport, Anatol, 76
rational choice theory, 34–35. *See also*
        economic approach
    altruistic behavior and, 40–43
    divorce compensation and, 155–56
    external stance and, 20, 47–59
    marriage as long-term contract and, 36–39
    marriage as relationship of exchange
        and, 35–36
    process of rational choice and, 48–50
Rawls, J., 127
realism, 77–79
"reciprocal altruism," 40
reflexivity, and "pure relationship," 20–22,
        97, 100-102, 107–8
relational sense of self, 27–29
Rempel, John K., 240
Reso, Sidney, 3–4, 113
responsibility
    adverse testimony privilege as narrative
        and, 114–17
    communal boundaries and, 249
    consent as criterion for, 51–52, 167
    equalization approach and, 191
    internal stance and, 26–27
    paradigms for ascription of, 114–17
    recognition vs. assumption of, 26–27,
        166–68, 191
return on investment approach, 178–81
Riessman, Catherine, 7
Rose, Carol, 60
Rosen, Lawrence, 249
"Rotten Kid Theorem," 40
Royce, Josiah, 124

Sandel, Michael, 204
Sartre, Jean-Paul, 23–24
Satz, Debra, 80
Schneider, Carl, 267
Schutz, Alfred, 79

Seale, Arthur, 3–4, 89, 113, 119
Seale, Irene, 3–4, 89, 112–13, 119, 134
"self-authorship," 11, 17. *See also* external
        stance toward marriage
self-concept
    close personal relationships and, 70–73
    interdependent utility function and, 74–77
    social identity and, 67–70
self-disclosure, 21, 112. *See also*
        communications privilege
"sexually based primary relationship," 6
Shutz, Alfred, 80–81
Siegel, Reva, 146
Simon, William, 170–72
Simpson, O.J., 118
Singer, Joseph, 163
Skinner, Quentin, 82
Smiley, Marion, 249
Smith, Susan, 118
Smith, William Kennedy, 118
social contract theory
    external stance and, 16–18
    family relationships as excluded from,
        165–66
    property rhetoric and, 164–65
    women and, 17–18, 164–68
social exchange theory, 20, 259
social identity theory, 67–70
socializing domain, 173, 174
social life
    domains of, 173–74
    internal and external stances framework
        and, 12, 204–205
    relevance of marital norms for, 10–11
social psychology research, 5–6, 63–67
social roles. *See* group identity; spousal
        identity
social welfare programs, 170, 172, 196–97
speculative calculation, and property
        rhetoric, 177, 179, 183
spousal identity
    communications privilege and, 96–97
    experience of divorce and, 189–90
    individual vs. communal view of, 3–12
    post-divorce autonomy and, 191
    "role morality" and, 111
spousal labor. *See also* domestic labor
    market model and, 35–36
    specialization of tasks and, 36–39, 218